THE CRIME BOOK

THE CRIME BOOK

FOREWORD BY
CATHY SCOTT

DK LONDON

SENIOR EDITOR
Helen Fewster

US SENIOR EDITOR
Karyn Gerhard

MANAGING ART EDITOR
Michael Duffy

MANAGING EDITOR
Angeles Gavira Guerrero

ART DIRECTOR
Karen Self

ASSOCIATE PUBLISHING DIRECTOR
Liz Wheeler

PUBLISHING DIRECTOR
Jonathan Metcalf

SENIOR JACKET DESIGNER
Mark Cavanagh

JACKET EDITOR
Claire Gell

JACKET DESIGN
DEVELOPMENT MANAGER
Sophia MTT

PRE-PRODUCTION PRODUCERS
Andy Hilliard, Gillian Reid

SENIOR PRODUCER
Anna Vallarino

ILLUSTRATIONS
James Graham

DK DELHI

JACKET DESIGNER
Dhirendra Singh

EDITORIAL COORDINATOR
Priyanka Sharma

SENIOR DTP DESIGNER
Harish Aggarwal

MANAGING JACKETS EDITOR
Saloni Singh

TOUCAN BOOKS

EDITORIAL DIRECTOR
Ellen Dupont

SENIOR DESIGNER
Nick Avery

SENIOR EDITOR
Nathan Joyce

DESIGNER
Thomas Keenes

EDITORS
Abigail Mitchell, Dorothy Stannard,
Guy Croton, Debra Wolter

EDITORIAL ASSISTANTS
Autumn Green, Joseph Persad

ARTWORK COMMISSIONING
Simon Webb

ADDITIONAL GRAPHICS
Dave Jones

INDEXER
Marie Lorimer

PICTURE RESEARCH
Susannah Jayes

PROOFREADER
Marion Dent

original styling by

STUDIO 8

First American Edition, 2017
Published in the United States by
DK Publishing
1745 Broadway, 20th Floor,
New York, NY 10019

Copyright © 2017
Dorling Kindersley Limited
DK, a Division of Penguin Random House LLC
23 24 25 10 9 8 7 6 5 4 3
048—322082—Feb/2021

Published in Great Britain by
Dorling Kindersley Limited.

A catalog record for this book is available
from the Library of Congress.
ISBN 978-0-7440-2850-8

DK books are available at special
discounts when purchased in bulk
for sales promotions, premiums,
fund-raising, or educational use.
For details, contact: DK Publishing Special
Markets, 1745 Broadway, 20th Floor,
New York, NY 10019
SpecialSales@dk.com

Printed and bound in China

For the curious
www.dk.com

CONTRIBUTORS

SHANNA HOGAN

Shanna Hogan is an award-winning journalist and *The New York Times* best-selling author of three true-crime books including *Picture Perfect: The Jodi Arias Story*. An Arizona State University journalism graduate, Shanna has written for numerous publications, received more than 20 awards for her feature writing and investigative reporting, and has appeared on numerous shows, including *The View, Dateline, 20/20, CNN, Oxygen*, and *Investigation Discovery*. Shanna lives in Phoenix, Arizona, with her husband and two dogs.

MICHAEL KERRIGAN

Michael Kerrigan was educated at University College, Oxford. His many books include *A History of Punishment, The War on Drugs, The American Presidency: A Dark History, The Catholic Church: A Dark History*, and *A Handbook of Scotland's History*. He writes regular reviews for *The Times Literary Supplement* and lives with his family in Edinburgh.

LEE MELLOR

Lee Mellor, Ph.D. (abd) is a criminologist, lecturer, musician, and the author of six books on crime. He is currently finishing his doctorate at Montreal's Concordia University specializing in abnormal homicide and sex crimes. As the chair of the American Investigative Society of Cold Cases' academic committee, he has consulted with police on cold cases in Pennsylvania, Missouri, Ohio, and London, Ontario. He resides in Toronto, Canada.

REBECCA MORRIS

Rebecca Morris is *The New York Times* best-selling author of *A Killing in Amish Country*, and *If I Can't Have You*, with Gregg Olsen. An experienced journalist, she is also the author of the best-selling *Ted and Ann—The Mystery of a Missing Child and Her Neighbor Ted Bundy*. She lives in Seattle, Washington.

CATHY SCOTT

Cathy Scott, a *Los Angeles Times* best-selling author, is an established crime writer and investigative journalist for *The New York Times* and Reuters. Best known for writing *The Killing of Tupac Shakur* and *The Murder of Biggie Smalls*, she has written extensively about street gangs and organized crime, including mob daughter Susan Berman in *Murder of a Mafia Daughter*, and drug kingpin "Freeway" Rick Ross. She is the author of several other true crime works, including *The Rough Guide to True Crime, The Millionaire's Wife*, and *Death in the Desert*, which was adapted into a full-length movie starring Michael Madsen in 2016.

CONTENTS

WHITE COLLAR CRIMES

ORGANIZED CRIME

KIDNAPPING AND EXTORTION

MURDER CASES

SERIAL KILLERS

ASSASSINATIONS AND POLITICAL PLOTS

FOREWORD

From the Mafia-ridden streets of Sicily, Italy, to backcountry roadways of southern California traveled by Hells Angels' bikers, *The Crime Book* features every facet of lawlessness. These high crimes and misdemeanors range from petty to deadly—all of which are spellbinding accounts within this compelling genre.

While crime is one of the greatest problems across the ages and spanning the globe, people are increasingly fascinated with the criminal mind, as evidenced by popular true-crime TV shows featuring desperados and the misdeeds they commit. *Time* magazine called the phenomenon a euphoric effect on human emotions that is comparable to a roller-coaster ride. With the advent of modern technology, the details of these crimes are now brought to people's living rooms across the globe, with gavel-to-gavel televised criminal trials and news reports aired internationally in real-time.

The telling of these tragedies is so popular that the *Investigation Discovery* network devotes hours of air time to addictive true-crime programming, including grisly murders, such as that of the Black Dahlia—a story also told in this book. It is one of the oldest unsolved murder cases in Los Angeles, California, and has been depicted in several feature films and true-crime books. The appeal is comparable to people not being able to look away from traffic accidents.

The hundred or so crimes and perpetrators featured in these pages are told by four seasoned, best-selling true-crime authors—Lee Mellor, Shanna Hogan, Rebecca Morris, and Michael Kerrigan—along with my own telling of tales. These stories not only give readers a look into the lives and psyche of the criminals but also examines the in-depth and often lengthy police work needed to bring the perpetrators to justice. With a rare perspective by writers with expert vantage points, these chapters thoroughly examine across continents and decades, all genres of crime, including the first known homicide committed against a Neanderthal man 430,000 years ago.

In telling some of these tales, these accomplished writers followed the footsteps of street-weary detectives and sometimes cagey, tough-to-catch crooks. They include the modern-day impersonator Frank Abagnale, Jr., of *Catch Me if You Can* movie fame, and the glamorous life of elusive international jewel thief Doris Payne, who escaped authorities not once, but three times.

As a fact-based crime journalist and author for more than two decades, I am fascinated by these stories. I followed newspapers articles as a teenager and dreamt of one day being able to follow a case from beginning to end by writing about it. That goal was realized when I became a newspaper reporter in 1987 and an author a decade later.

During my journalism career, I have been particularly attracted to domestic violence cases, having been a victim myself for six years. I understand first-hand what women—and sometimes men—go through, and why they find it difficult to leave.

My first brush with crime, however, occurred during my second year of college, and it stayed with me. I grew up in a crime-free, middle-class suburb of San Diego, California, with near-perfect weather and safe neighborhoods. So, it was shocking when, on a spring night, I became a target, along with my twin sister and two neighborhood girlfriends. We took a weeknight jog just as we had dozens of times before. We never felt at risk—that is, until a man stepped out of the darkness, naked from the waist down. We screamed and ran to a neighboring house, from where we called police. Because of our descriptions of his nearby car, police quickly located him. Officers did not witness the indecent exposure, so I was designated as the one to make a citizen's arrest, right there on the street. Weeks later, as we gathered at the courthouse to testify against him, the suspect pleaded guilty minutes before the trial was to begin.

Criminal law has fascinated me ever since. My hope is that you too will be just as fascinated by the variety of offences included in the following true accounts in this book.

Cathy Scott,
Author, *Murder of a Mafia Daughter* and *The Killing of Tupac Shakur*

INTRODU

CTION

Crimes—the illegal actions that can be prosecuted and are punishable by law—are all around us, from comparatively petty misdemeanors to truly heinous acts of unspeakable evil.

The perpetrators of these varied transgressions have long fascinated academics and the wider public, who have sought answers to questions about whether some people are more likely to commit crimes than others, and whether there are certain characteristics unique to criminals.

Indeed, the Ancient Greeks were fascinated by the "science" of physiognomy—the study of how certain facial features can reveal something about a person's character or nature. While such a thought now sounds somewhat ridiculous, physiognomy was widely accepted by the Ancient Greeks and underwent periodic revivals over the centuries, the most notable spearheaded by Swiss writer Johann Kaspar Lavater in the 1770s.

What unites the crimes covered in this book is their status as "notorious" in one way or another. Whether it is because of their breathtaking ingenuity, brazen opportunism, machiavellian scheming, or abominable malevolence, these crimes stand out over the centuries. While many of the perpetrators are viewed with distaste and disgust, some have been highly romanticized over the years for their rebelliousness and contempt for obeying the rules. This is often in spite of the extremely serious nature of their crimes, such as with Bonnie and Clyde, the Great Train Robbers, and Phoolan Devi.

Some cases have broken new ground, and in some instances have led to the swift passage of new laws to protect the public and deter others from committing similar crimes. Public outrage during the investigation into the highly publicized Lindbergh Baby

Laws are like cobwebs, which may catch small flies, but let wasps and hornets break through.
Jonathan Swift

kidnapping in 1932 prompted Congress to enact the Federal Kidnapping Act just one month later. Also known as the Lindbergh Law, the Act made kidnapping a federal crime punishable by death.

Other cases have involved pioneering legal defense strategies, such as with the 1843 case of Daniel M'Naghten, the first of its kind in UK legal history. M'Naghten was acquitted of a high-profile murder based on a criminal-insanity defense, and remanded to a State Criminal Lunatic Asylum for the remainder of his life.

Crime through the years
Throughout history, pivotal moments have brought new crimes to the fore. In the late 19th century, for example, lawlessness increased with the growth of towns and cities, in part because of a lack of official police forces to rein in outlaws and bring them to justice. One of those was the Wild West's Jesse James and his infamous James–Younger Gang, who became the first gang in the US to rob trains and banks during daylight hours.

During the Prohibition period in the US, from 1920 to 1933, organized crime proliferated when outfits such as Chicago's

Sheldon Gang vied to become the major liquor suppliers in the city's southwest Irish belt.

The number of offenses in the US increased so much during that time span that the International Association of Chiefs of Police began to compile crime statistics. This culminated in the release of the Uniform Crime Reports—the first published in January 1930—which were pulled together via a voluntary cooperative effort from local, county, and state law enforcement agencies. This became a vital tool to monitor the number and types of offenses committed across the US. It caught on and inspired law enforcement agencies in other countries around the world to follow suit.

The ultimate transgression

When it comes to murder, it is invariably savage and disturbing. Whether an organized hit-for-hire, a crime of passion, or a wanton act of violence against a stranger, the act is final and tragic.

History's first homicide is believed to have taken place some 430,000 years ago. However, it was only discovered in 2015, when archaeologists working in Atapuerca, Spain, pieced together the skull of a Neanderthal and found evidence that he or she had been bludgeoned to death and thrown down a cave shaft.

There is an undeniable public fascination with serial killers—especially those where the culprit has never been caught. The cases of Jack the Ripper in London and the Zodiac killer in California are both enduring sources of contemporary analysis and speculation. Some crimes are so horrifying that the name of the perpetrator becomes indelibly linked with indescribable evil. Ted Bundy, who committed the gruesome murders of dozens of young women in the 1970s in the Pacific Northwest, is a case in point. The fact that Bundy seemed a charming, respectable man

He who commits injustice is ever made more wretched than he who suffers it.
Plato

heightened the shock factor: he did not conform to a stereotypical vision of a monstrous serial killer.

Villains and technology

The 1962 escape from Alcatraz Federal Penitentiary caused an international sensation. Investigators concluded that the fugitives died trying to make their way across San Francisco Bay—but evidence unearthed in 2015 calls this into question. If such an escape were to happen today, a massive manhunt would be streamed live across the internet, making it more difficult for the criminals to get away.

The technological improvements in the detection and solving of crimes, such as DNA fingerprinting, is accompanied by an increasing sophistication in the techniques criminals use to commit them and to evade capture. In 2011, Russian hacker Aleksandr Panin accessed confidential information from more than 50 million computers. In February 2016, hackers stole $81 million from the central Bank of Bangladesh without even setting foot in the country. While criminal methods may have evolved over time, though, our fascination with crime and its perpetrators remains as strong as it ever has been. ■

BANDITS, ROBBERS, ARSONIS

AND
TS

Irishman Thomas Blood attempts to steal the English **Crown Jewels** from the Tower of London.

Pirate Edward "Blackbeard" Teach **plunders ships** in the Caribbean and along the East Coast of America.

Jesse James leads the James–Younger Gang in **train and bank robberies** across the American Midwest.

1671

1716–18

1866–82

1676

1827–28

1930–34

In England, **highwayman** John Nevison rides 200 miles (320 km) in a single day in order to construct an alibi.

Scottish graverobbers William Burke and William Hare turn to murder to make money **selling corpses** for dissection.

Bonnie and Clyde go on a **crime spree** across several US states, kidnapping and murdering when cornered.

The general public has long romanticized bandits, admiring their courage, audacity, and unwillingness to live by the rules of others. Many have been regarded as daredevils rather than simply common criminals. Such was the public's perception of Bonnie Parker and Clyde Barrow, outlaws operating in 1930s America, who traveled in a Buick sedan and hid out in boarding houses and empty barns between robberies and murders. Bonnie and Clyde's crimes were heinous, but they captured the public imagination and attracted throngs of supporters who relished reports of their latest exploits.

It was no different for the Great Train Robbers, a 15-member gang who targeted the Glasgow to London mail train in 1963. Wearing helmets, ski masks, and gloves, they stole 120 mailbags containing more than £2.6 million (about $68 million today) in cash and seriously injured train engineer Jack Mills. Yet sections of the British public glorified the Great Train Robbers, pleased that some of them evaded justice, and ignored their violent and illegal exploits.

Like other famous robberies and criminal partnerships, the stories of the Great Train Robbery and Bonnie and Clyde have been made into movies that appealed to the public's age-old love of villains.

The notion of the loveable rogue is not entirely fanciful. John Nevison, a British highwayman of the 1670s, was renowned for his gentlemanly manner. Holding up stagecoaches on horseback, he apologized to his victims before taking their money. Bizarrely, it almost became an honor to be robbed by Nevison. His legendary status was cemented through his impulsive 200-mile (320-km) journey from the county of Kent to York to establish an alibi for a robbery that he committed earlier in the day—a feat that earned him the nickname "Swift Nick."

Ingenious crimes

Sometimes we cannot help but admire the breathtaking audacity of certain crimes and their perpetrators. One of the boldest robberies in modern times occurred in midair over the northwestern US in November 1971. The hijacker of a Boeing 727, who became known as D. B. Cooper, fled by parachute, taking with him a ransom of $200,000 in $20 bills.

The **Great Train Robbers** steal more than £2.6 million (about $68 million today) from the Glasgow to London mail train.

1963

In Washington state, a man going by the name of D. B. Cooper **hijacks a plane**, extracts a $200,000 ransom, and escapes by parachute

1971

In Uttar Pradesh, India, Phoolan Devi, known as the **Bandit Queen**, carries out dozens of highway robberies.

1979–83

Professional fire investigator and secret arsonist John Leonard Orr **sets a series of deadly fires** in southern California.

1984–91

In Belgium, thieves break into the vault of the Antwerp Diamond Center, **stealing diamonds** worth $100 million.

2003

Veteran thieves loot the Hatton Garden Safe Deposit Company in central London, in the **largest burglary in UK history**.

2015

In the French town of Nice a few years later, thieves committed what was then the biggest heist in history when they drilled their way into the Société Générale bank from the city's sewer system.

In 2003, a gang of thieves showed similar ambition when they broke into a seemingly impregnable underground vault two floors beneath the Antwerp Diamond Center, to commit what was dubbed the "perfect crime." The gang made off with a haul worth around $100 million. The ringleader made one fatal mistake, though, leaving traces of his DNA close to the crime scene.

Art heists also tend to capture the public's imagination, because they often demonstrate brazen opportunism with little thought for the consequences. Take, for example, the 2003 case of amateur art thief Robert Mang, who climbed up the scaffolding outside a museum and squeezed through a broken window to steal a multimillion dollar work by the Italian artist Benvenuto Cellini. There was, however, no market for the miniature masterpiece and he was forced to bury it in the woods.

Darker acts

Not all bandits and robbers inspire a grudging respect for the remarkable nerve of the offender. The case of bodysnatchers William Burke and William Hare—who in early 19th-century Edinburgh turned to murder to supply cadavers for Dr. Robert Knox's anatomy classes at the city's university—is a grisly tale. The spate of arson attacks committed by fire investigator John Leonard Orr in California were especially dark and disturbing. This case was fiendishly difficult to crack, because much of the evidence was destroyed by the fire. A partial fingerprint left on an unburned part of his incendiary device led to his arrest.

Unlike Bonnie and Clyde and the Great Train Robbers, who became legendary figures courtesy of the media, Orr created his own legend and earned a reputation for being the first investigator at the scene of the crimes that he secretly committed. But Orr's fearlessness and skill as a master manipulator are what he shares with the bandits and robbers featured in this chapter. They have all entered criminal history on account of their notoriety, which in some cases extends to mythic status. ∎

FATHER OF ALL TREASONS
THOMAS BLOOD, 1671

IN CONTEXT

LOCATION
Tower of London, UK

THEME
Jewel theft

BEFORE
1303 Richard of Pudlicott, an impoverished English wool merchant, steals much of Edward I's priceless treasury of gems, gold, and coins at Westminster Abbey.

AFTER
September 11, 1792 Thieves break into the Royal Storehouse, the Hôtel du Garde-Meuble de la Couronne, in Paris, and steal most of the French Crown Jewels; many, but not all, are later recovered.

August 11, 1994 Three men make off with jewelry and precious stones worth $60 million ($96 million today) at an exhibition at the Carlton Hotel, Cannes, France.

Irish-born Thomas Blood (1618–80) fought for the Parliamentarians against Charles I's Royalists in the English Civil War (1642–51), and the victorious Oliver Cromwell rewarded him with estates in his home country. These lands were confiscated during the Restoration of the Monarchy under Charles II, which Blood deemed a wrong that needed to be put right. He hatched a plan to steal the Crown Jewels, not only for financial gain but also to symbolically decapitate the king, echoing the fate of King Charles I, in 1649.

Early in 1671, disguised as the fictitious clergyman Reverend "Ayloffe," and with a female accomplice posing as his wife, Blood paid the Master of the Jewel Office, the elderly Talbot Edwards, for a tour. "Mrs. Ayloffe" feigned illness during the tour, and Edwards and his wife came to her aid. A grateful Reverend Ayloffe made further visits, gaining Edwards's trust. On May 5, Ayloffe persuaded Edwards to bring out the jewels, and immediately let in his waiting friends. Overpowering and beating Edwards, the gang flattened the crown and sawed the scepter in half to make it easier to carry. They attempted to escape on horseback but were quickly caught.

The king confounded his subjects by offering Blood a royal pardon. Some suggested that the king had been amused by Blood's boldness; others that the king had recruited him as spy. Either way, Blood subsequently became a favorite around the royal court. ∎

> It was a gallant attempt, however unsuccessful! It was for a crown!
> **Thomas Blood**

See also: The Société Générale Bank Heist 44–45 ▪ The Antwerp Diamond Heist 54–55 ▪ The Affair of the Diamond Necklace 64–65

A CIVIL, OBLIGING ROBBER

JOHN NEVISON, 1676

IN CONTEXT

LOCATION
Gad's Hill, near Rochester, Kent, UK

THEME
Highway robbery

BEFORE
1491–1518 Humphrey Kynaston, a high-born English highwayman, robs travelers in Shropshire, allegedly giving his takings to the poor.

AFTER
1710s Louis Dominique Garthausen, known as "Cartouche," commits highway robberies in and around Paris.

1735–37 Highwayman Dick Turpin carries out a series of robberies in the Greater London area. He is captured in York in 1739 and is executed for horse theft.

Highwayman John Nevison (1639–94) was supposedly nicknamed "Swift Nick" by King Charles II after the truth was finally revealed about his most famous exploit. After robbing a traveler near Rochester, Kent, Nevison was in desperate need of an alibi, so he devised a cunning plan. He crossed the Thames River and galloped 200 miles (320 km) to York in a single day, then engaged the Lord Mayor of York in conversation and made a bet over a game of bowls. Nevison made sure that the Lord Mayor knew the time (8 p.m.). The ruse paid off, and the Lord Mayor later acted as Nevison's alibi during his trial. The jury could not conceive that a man was physically able to ride the distance Nevison covered in a single day, and so he was found not guilty.

Nevison was a veteran of the 1658 Battle of Dunkirk and was skillful with horses and weapons. He was also courteous and elegant, which he believed put him above the rank of a common thief. *The Newgate Calendar*, a

Nevison's flamboyant style and courtly manners are evident in this 1680 depiction of his alleged meeting with King Charles II.

publication that details the exploits of fabled criminals, said he was "very favourable to the female sex" on account of his courtesy and style. This elevated his standing and had the bizarre effect of making it something of an honor to have been robbed by him. ∎

See also: The Great Train Robbery 30 35

DAMNATION SEIZE MY SOUL IF I GIVE YOU QUARTERS
EDWARD "BLACKBEARD" TEACH, 1716–18

IN CONTEXT

LOCATION
The Caribbean and East Coast of North America

THEME
Piracy

BEFORE
1667–83 Welsh privateer and later Royal Navy Admiral Sir Henry Morgan becomes famous for attacks on Spanish settlements in the Caribbean.

1689–96 Captain William Kidd, a renowned Scottish privateer and pirate hunter, plunders ships and islands in the Caribbean.

AFTER
1717–18 Barbadian pirate "Gentleman" Stede Bonnet, nicknamed for his past as a wealthy landowner, pillages vessels in the Caribbean.

1719–22 Bartholomew "Black Bart" Roberts, a Welsh pirate, raids hundreds of ships in the Americas and West Africa.

Although far from the most successful pirate, Edward "Blackbeard" Teach is undoubtedly the most notorious. Originally an English privateer during Queen Anne's War (1702–13), he turned to piracy when the hostilities ceased.

In 1716, Blackbeard traveled to the "pirate's republic" of Nassau in the Bahamas. There, he met Captain Benjamin Hornigold who placed him in charge of a sloop. Together the pair plundered ships in the waters around Cuba, Bermuda, and along the East Coast of America.

Hornigold and Teach soon encountered the Barbadian pirate "Gentleman" Stede Bonnet, who had been seriously wounded battling a Spanish man-of-war. Half of Bonnet's crew had perished and the remaining 70 were losing faith in his leadership. The three men joined forces, with Bonnet temporarily ceding command of his sloop, the *Revenge*, to Blackbeard.

Taking charge

During a raid near Martinique in November 1717, Hornigold acquired the 200-ton frigate *La Concord de Nantes*. Hornigold placed

Blackbeard's fearsome appearance matched his reputation, but evidence suggests he only used force as a last resort. His swashbuckling was greatly romanticized after his death.

Blackbeard in charge of this prized vessel. Blackbeard renamed it *Queen Anne's Revenge*.

In December, King George I passed the Indemnity Act, which pardoned any pirate who officially renounced his lifestyle. Hornigold—who had been replaced as captain by his and Blackbeard's combined

See also: The Hawkhurst Gang 136–37

pirate crews after he voted against a decision to attack any ship they wanted, including British ships—took the King's pardon and parted ways with Blackbeard.

Eventually, Bonnet's men deserted him, choosing to serve under Blackbeard's command. Blackbeard put a surrogate in charge of the *Revenge*, and kept Bonnet as a "guest" on his ship. Soon after, Blackbeard sailed to North Carolina, where he blockaded the port of Charleston, capturing nine ships and ransoming a wealthy merchant and politician.

Upon sailing away from Charleston, the *Queen Anne's Revenge* ran aground. Anchoring their fleet at Topsail Inlet, Bonnet and Blackbeard traveled by land to Bath, North Carolina, in June 1718 where they were granted pardons by Governor Charles Eden. However, while Bonnet remained there, Blackbeard crept back to the fleet, plundered the *Revenge* and two other ships in the fleet, and transferred the goods to his sloop, the *Adventure*.

> Let's jump on board, and cut them to pieces.
> **Edward "Blackbeard" Teach**

Having violated the terms of his pardon, Blackbeard now had a sizable bounty on his head. On November 22, 1718, two Royal Navy sloops commanded by Lieutenant Robert Maynard caught up with the *Adventure* at Ocracoke Harbor.

Last stand

Outmaneuvering the Royal Navy's ships, Blackbeard lured them onto a sandbar. Rather than escaping, he fired two broadside attacks at Maynard's ship. When the smoke cleared, only the lieutenant and a few crew members remained on deck. Blackbeard ordered his band of 23 pirates to board the vessel.

As his men clambered onto the ship, 30 armed sailors emerged from below decks. A bloody battle ensued. Maynard and Blackbeard both aimed their flintlock pistols at each other and fired. Blackbeard's shot missed but Maynard's struck Blackbeard in the abdomen. Blackbeard recovered, however, and broke Maynard's sword in two with a mighty blow of his cutlass. Before he could capitalize on his brief advantage, though, one of Maynard's men drove a pike into Blackbeard's shoulder. Outnumbered and outgunned, Blackbeard's crew surrendered, but he continued to fight. He finally fell dead after five gunshot wounds and 20 sword wounds.

Maynard ordered his men to hang Blackbeard's head from the bowsprit. Later, it was mounted on a stake near the Hampton River as a warning to pirates. ∎

Privateer Sir Henry Morgan attacks and captures the town of Puerto del Principe in Cuba in this engraving from 1754.

"Legal" piracy

Sociologists have long recognized that crime and deviance are situational—crimes change over time and from one location to the next. Piracy is a good example of this phenomenon.

In the mid-13th century, Henry III of England started to issue licenses, called "privateering commissions," which allowed sailors to attack and plunder foreign vessels. After 1295, these licenses were known as *letters of marque*. Privateers became much more numerous in the 16th–18th centuries, with some working without royal consent, including Francis Drake, who carried out raids on Spanish shipping. During Queen Anne's War, British privateers regularly plundered French and Spanish ships. However, when hostilities between the nations ended, these same professional plunderers suddenly found themselves on the other side of the law. Clearly, what is considered criminal depends on shifting social structures, which are in turn dictated by larger political and economic realities.

BURKE'S THE BUTCHER, HARE'S THE THIEF, KNOX THE BOY THAT BUYS THE BEEF

BURKE AND HARE, 1827–28

IN CONTEXT

LOCATION
Edinburgh, Scotland, UK

THEME
Bodysnatching and multiple murder

BEFORE
November 1825 Thomas Tuite, a bodysnatcher, is captured by a sentry in Dublin, Ireland, in possession of five bodies and with his pockets full of sets of teeth.

AFTER
November 7, 1876 A gang of counterfeiters breaks into Oak Ridge Cemetery in Springfield, Illinois, to steal Abraham Lincoln's body and hold it for a $200,000 (about $4.6 million today) ransom. The plot is foiled by a Secret Service agent posing as a member of the gang.

A pair of Irish immigrants became unlikely grave robbers—and ultimately killers—in 19th-century Scotland when greed got the better of them.

William Burke and William Hare worked as laborers in Edinburgh, where they met in 1827 after Burke and his companion, Helen McDougal, moved into a lodging house in Edinburgh run by Hare and his wife Margaret.

When an elderly lodger died of natural causes and still owed rent, Burke and Hare sneaked into the cemetery, dug up his coffin, snatched his body, and carried it in a tea chest to Edinburgh University's medical school.

Dr. Robert Knox, a popular anatomy lecturer who urgently needed corpses for dissection lessons, paid them £7 and 10 shillings (about $820 today) for the body.

A unique business idea

Inspired by their success, the pair repeated it again and again, robbing newly-buried coffins and selling the cadavers to Knox. They soon tired of digging up graves in the middle of the night. So, in November 1827 when a lodger became ill, Burke expedited the man's demise by covering his mouth and nose while forcibly restraining him—a smothering technique that became known as "burking."

That first murder was the start of the duo's killing spree, targeting strays and prostitutes on the streets of Edinburgh. Their *modus operandi* involved plying a victim with drink until they fell asleep. Then, Burke smothered them using his unique technique. They loaded

Hare (left) and Burke (right) financially exploited a shortage in the legal supply of cadavers at a time when Edinburgh was the leading European center of anatomical research.

See also: Jack the Ripper 266–73

Robert Knox was a preeminent Scottish anatomist whose career was overshadowed by his involvement in the Burke and Hare case.

the body into a tea chest and transported it at night to Dr. Knox's surgery. They received £7–10 (about $950) for each body.

Burke and Hare got away with murder for 11 months until the body of Irishwoman Margaret Docherty was discovered by two guests at

Hare's boarding house, Ann and James Gray. The Grays notified the police, and an inquiry led them to Dr. Knox. Docherty's body had since been moved to the university lecture hall, which had become Knox's dissecting theater.

After a newspaper report pointed the finger at Burke and Hare, there was a public outcry for their prosecution. William Burke, William Hare, Helen McDougal, and Margaret Hare were all arrested by police shortly afterward and charged with murder. Dr. Knox was questioned by police, but was not arrested as he had not technically broken the law.

Every man for himself

Requiring more evidence for a conviction, the court's Lord Advocate attempted to extract a confession from one of the four, and he chose Hare. He was offered immunity from prosecution and testified that Burke had committed the murders. Burke was subsequently convicted of three murders and, on January 28, 1829,

I am sure… that in the whole history of the country— nothing has ever been exhibited that is in any respect parallel to this case.
Lord Meadowbank

hanged in front of a cheering crowd numbering up to 25,000. People were said to have paid up to £1 ($110 today) for a good view overlooking the scaffold.

Burke's body was publicly dissected by Dr. Knox's rival, Dr. Monro, at the anatomy theater of Edinburgh University's Old College, attracting so many spectators that a minor riot occurred. His skeleton was later donated to Edinburgh Medical School. Hare, although he confessed to being an accomplice, was freed, and fled to England. With his reputation in tatters, Knox moved to London to try to revive his medical career.

In all, Burke and Hare killed 16 victims in what became known as the West Port Murders. The murders led to the passing of the Anatomy Act 1832, which increased the supply of legal cadavers by authorizing the dissection of unclaimed bodies from workhouses after 48 hours. This proved effective in reducing cases of bodysnatching. ∎

Diagnosing psychopathy

The Hare Psychopathy Checklist (named after Canadian psychologist Robert Hare) is a diagnostic tool used to identify a person's psychopathic tendencies. Originally designed to assess people accused of crimes, it is a 20-item inventory of personality traits assessed primarily via an interview. The subject receives a score for each trait depending on how well each one applies to them. The traits include lack of remorse; lack of empathy; inability to accept responsibility for actions; impulsivity; and pathological tendency toward lying.

When psychopaths commit crimes, it is likely that their acts are purposeful. The motives of psychopathic killers often involve power or sadistic gratification. Not all violent offenders are psychopaths, but FBI investigations found that psychopathic offenders have more serious criminal histories and tend to be more chronically violent.

THEY WERE BRAVE FELLOWS. THEY WERE TRUE MEN
THE JAMES-YOUNGER GANG, 1866–82

IN CONTEXT

LOCATION
Missouri, Kansas, Kentucky, Arkansas, Iowa, Texas, and West Virginia, US

THEME
Armed robbery

BEFORE
1790–1802 Samuel "Wolfman" Mason and his band of followers prey on riverboat travelers on the Ohio and Mississippi rivers, US.

1863–64 William "Bloody Bill" Anderson, a pro-Confederate guerrilla leader during the American Civil War, leads a band of outlaws against Federal soldiers in Missouri and Kansas, US.

AFTER
1897 Al Jennings, a prosecuting attorney-turned-outlaw, forms the Jennings Gang, and robs trains in Oklahoma, US.

From February 1866 to September 1876, the outlaw James-Younger Gang robbed 12 banks, five trains, five stagecoaches, and an exposition ticket booth. Their crime spree began in the wake of the American Civil War (1861–65) when the James brothers—Jesse and Frank—joined forces with the Younger brothers—Cole, Jim, John, and Bob. They all fought as Confederate bushwhackers attacking civilian Unionists during the Civil War. After the hostilities ended, Jesse James turned the group into a bank-robbing posse.

Some historians credit the gang with the first daylight armed robbery in the US when they targeted the Clay County Savings Association in Liberty, Missouri, in 1866. In all their train robberies, the gang only robbed passengers twice, when their takings were especially low. They committed robberies every couple of months, hiding out in between jobs to avoid the law. They were aided by sympathizers who offered their homes as hideouts. The gang used maps and compasses, and avoided well-traveled roads, making it difficult to pursue them.

Jesse James (left) posing with two of the Younger brothers. Despite Jesse's romanticized image and comparisons to Robin Hood, there is no evidence that he gave their loot to the poor.

The gang grew, and they drifted between Midwest states, pulling off robberies of banks, trains, and stagecoaches, in Missouri, Kansas, Kentucky, Arkansas, Iowa, Texas, and West Virginia. On June 3, 1871, they robbed a bank in Corydon, Iowa, but were identified as suspects. From then on, they became known as the James-Younger Gang.

See also: Bonnie and Clyde 26–29 ▪ Butch Cassidy's Wild Bunch 150–51

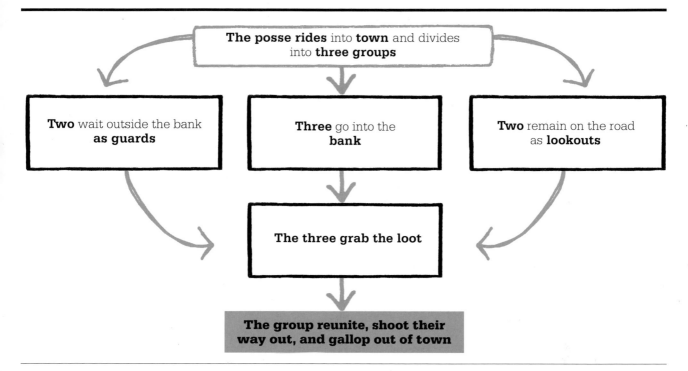

The posse rides into **town** and divides into **three groups**

Two wait outside the bank **as guards**

Three go into the **bank**

Two remain on the road as **lookouts**

The three grab the loot

The group reunite, shoot their way out, and gallop out of town

Tracking them down

In 1874, following a train robbery in Missouri, the Adams Express Company, who suffered the biggest loss during the robbery, enlisted the services of the Pinkerton National Detective Agency to catch the gang.

In March 1874, Allan Pinkerton, the agency's founder, sent detective Joseph Whicher to pursue James, but Whicher was found dead the day after he arrived. An outraged Pinkerton sent a group of detectives to track the gang down in January 1875, but they succeeded only in killing Jesse's eight-year-old half brother and wounding Jesse's mother with an incendiary device during a botched raid. Condemned for this act, Pinkerton withdrew and the gang continued unabated.

The James-Younger Gang dissolved in 1876 when the Younger brothers were arrested during an ambush while attempting to rob the Northfield First National Bank in Minnesota. The James brothers were both wounded in the legs, but escaped on horseback and kept low profiles until three years later, when Jesse formed another gang. The James Gang's reign ended in 1882 when fellow member Robert Ford betrayed and shot Jesse James in the back inside James's home in St. Joseph, Missouri, in order to collect the $10,000 ($239,000 today) bounty on his head. ▪

The romanticization of outlaws

The exploits of Old West outlaws have been exaggerated and romanticized, despite the fact that many were killers. The captivating allure of criminals seems to be based on conflicted feelings of both attraction and repulsion, of love and hatred.

Outlaws embody freedom in their refusal to obey laws, representing the boundary-crossing children that we used to be. They are also eulogized for unexpected benevolence: the courteous highwayman and figures, including Robin Hood, were popularized for their supposed altruistic motives and for "serving" the people.

The public reaction to Robert Ford's murder of Jesse James in 1882 is a case in point, as it caused a national sensation. Newspaper articles were published across the US, including in *The New York Times*. Such was James's allure that people traveled from far and wide to see the body of the legendary robber.

IT'S FOR THE LOVE OF A MAN THAT I'M GONNA HAVE TO DIE

BONNIE AND CLYDE, 1930–34

IN CONTEXT

LOCATION
Central US

THEME
Outlaws

BEFORE
July 14, 1881 The outlaw known as "Billy the Kid" is shot dead by Sheriff Pat Garrett in Fort Sumner, New Mexico.

February 3, 1889 The outlaw Myra Maybelle Starr, better known as Belle Starr, is gunned down near King Creek, Oklahoma.

AFTER
July 22, 1934 Depression-era gangster and bank robber John Dillinger is killed by federal agents while fleeing arrest.

November 27, 1934 FBI agents kill George "Baby Face" Nelson, a bank robber and gangster then labeled "Public Enemy Number One."

In the late night hours of April 13, 1933, two police cars pulled up to an apartment on Oak Ridge Drive in the windswept city of Joplin, Missouri. Living inside the rented apartment were five infamous outlaws known as the Barrow Gang, including Bonnie Parker and Clyde Barrow. The gang had spent the past 12 days in hiding, after carrying out a series of armed robberies and kidnappings in Missouri and neighboring states.

As lawmen hollered for the occupants to get out, Barrow grabbed his favorite weapon—a M1918 Browning Automatic Rifle—and opened fire through a broken

See also: The James-Younger Gang 24–25 ▪ The Wild Bunch 150–51

> No man but the undertaker will ever get me… I'll take my own life.
> **Clyde Barrow**

cigar between her teeth and holds a pistol in her hand. Soon the story of the outlaw lovers dominated the front pages of newspapers across the country.

Criminal superstars

Their four-year crime spree, during which they robbed banks and killed lawmen, titillated the American public. Far from their glamorized image, however, the Barrow Gang's crimes were punctuated by narrow escapes, bungled robberies, and fatal injuries.

With the FBI still a fledgling agency without the power to combat interstate bank robberies and kidnappings, the period between 1931 and 1935 become known as the "Public Enemy Era"—a time when high-profile criminals wrought significant damage amid the background of the Great Depression.

From their first meeting in 1930, Parker and Barrow shared an instant connection and she became his loyal companion. Shortly after their romance sparked, Barrow was arrested for burglary and sent to the Eastham prison facility in Texas. There he committed his »

window. His paramour Parker laid down cover fire with her own gun, the bullets splintering the surrounding trees. Amid the hail of gunfire, the gang killed two Missouri law officers, Detective Harry McGinnis and Constable J.W. Harryman.

Bonnie and Clyde escaped, leaving behind possessions including an arsenal of weapons, Parker's handwritten poems, and rolls of undeveloped film, which

Wearing her iconic high heels, Bonnie playfully points a shotgun at Clyde in 1932. Parker later sustained serious burns to her leg in a car crash, leaving her barely able to walk.

would turn the young lovers into folk legends and eventually lead to their downfall.

In the photos, the pair playfully posed with automatic weapons, standing in front of a stolen vehicle. In one picture, Parker is clenching a first murder, using a lead pipe to beat an inmate who had assaulted him. After Parker smuggled a gun inside the prison, Barrow escaped, but was later recaptured.

The spree begins

In February 1932, Barrow was paroled, emerging from jail a hardened and bitter criminal seeking revenge against the prison system for the abuses he suffered behind bars. Reuniting with Parker, Barrow assembled a rotating core of associates, robbing rural gas stations and kidnapping and killing when cornered.

Between 1932 and 1934, the gang is believed to have killed several civilians and at least nine lawmen. Barrow was officially accused of murder for the first time in April 1932, when he shot and killed a storeowner after a robbery. A few months later, Barrow and another gang member killed a deputy and wounded a sheriff who approached them at a country dance in Oklahoma. It was the first time a Barrow Gang member had killed an officer of the law.

In April 1933, Clyde's brother Buck was released from prison. He and his new bride, Blanche, joined the gang at the apartment in Joplin, Missouri, eventually attracting the attention of the police after 12 days of loud, alcohol-fueled parties. The gang's newfound notoriety after the shootout made it increasingly difficult to evade capture, hunted by the police, pursued by the press, and followed by an eager public.

For the next three months, the gang moved from Texas to Minnesota and Indiana, sleeping at campgrounds. They robbed banks, kidnapped people, and stole cars, committing the crimes near the borders of states to exploit the pre-

The Dallas Morning News issue announcing the death of Bonnie and Clyde sold 500,000 copies. A group of Dallas newsboys later sent the largest floral tribute to Parker's funeral.

FBI "state line rule" that prevented officers from crossing state lines while in pursuit of a fugitive.

Public opinion changes

Eventually the killings became so cold-blooded that the public's fascination with the duo soured. The Texas Department of Corrections commissioned former Texas Ranger Captain Frank A. Hamer, with the specific task of taking down the Barrow Gang. Hamer formed a posse, comprising a unique collaboration of Texas and Louisiana police officers. It was one of the most highly publicized and intense manhunts in US history.

By the summer of 1933, the gang began to fall apart. On June 10, while driving fast on a new road near Wellington, Texas, Barrow accidentally flipped their car into a ravine. Parker sustained third-degree burns to her right leg. Without proper medical care, her

injuries seriously impeded her ability to walk on her own. She was often carried by Barrow.

A month later, during a July 19 shootout with police in Missouri, a bullet struck Buck in the head. Blanche was also wounded and blinded in one eye. Despite his terrible injuries, Buck remained conscious and he and the rest of the gang escaped.

The trail ends

Days later, on July 24, Buck was shot in the back during another shootout, and he and Blanche were captured. Buck was taken to a

It is much better that they were both killed, rather than to have been taken alive.
Blanche Barrow

hospital where he died on July 29, from pneumonia after surgery, but not before doctors injected him with stimulants so that he could answer law officers' questions.

Barrow and Parker's trail ended on a road that cut through Louisiana's Piney Forest on State Highway 154, south of Sailes. Led by Hamer, the posse of law officers had tracked and studied the pair's movements and discovered that the gang camped on the edges of state borders.

Using a tip that the couple would be in the area, Hamer predicted their pattern and set up an ambush point along the rural Louisiana highway. At around 9:15 a.m. on May 23, 1934, six officers concealed in the bushes saw Barrow's stolen Ford V8 approaching at high speed and sprayed the car with a total of 130 rounds. Barrow and Parker were shot dozens of times, each sustaining multiple fatal wounds.

The death car became the subject of so much interest that fakes began to appear. The local sheriff tried to keep the car but was sued by the owner. It is now on display at a casino in Nevada.

When the bullet-ridden Ford was towed to town, with the bodies still inside, a crowd of curious onlookers surrounded the car. Spectators collected souvenirs, including pieces of Parker's bloody clothes and hair. One man even tried to cut off Barrow's trigger finger. Items belonging to the pair, including stolen guns and a saxophone, were also kept by members of the posse and sold as souvenirs.

The ambush remains highly controversial, given that there were no attempts to take the pair alive.

Prentiss Oakley, the Louisiana deputy who fired the first shot, later expressed his regret that the outlaws had not been offered a chance to surrender to them.

The bloody end of Bonnie and Clyde heralded the end of the "Public Enemy Era" of the 1930s. By the summer of 1934, the US government had enacted statutes that made kidnapping and bank robbery federal offenses—a legal breakthrough that finally allowed FBI agents to chase and apprehend bandits across state lines. ∎

The 1967 adaptation of the pair's crime spree starred Warren Beatty and Faye Dunaway and presented them as attractive and even chic.

Celebrity criminals

Bonnie and Clyde emerged as the first celebrity criminals of the Depression era, partly due to the intense newspaper and radio coverage of their crimes.

Outlaws like George "Baby Face" Nelson and "Pretty Boy" Floyd also became legends with their deadly stories appearing on front pages of newspapers across the country. During this time, a disillusioned, angry public, faced with unemployment and extreme poverty, held the gangsters in high esteem, with newspapers, magazines, and radio programs broadcasting their daily exploits. Bonnie and Clyde's legend intensified with the successful Academy Award-winning 1967 biographical film *Bonnie and Clyde*, which exposed the couple's exploits to a new generation. It was considered groundbreaking for its relaxed presentation of sex and violence. However, such a glamorized portrayal elicited troubling ethical questions, as several couples have attempted similar sprees, claiming to have been inspired by the famous outlaws.

YOU'LL NEVER BELIEVE IT THEY'VE STOLEN THE TRAIN

**THE GREAT TRAIN ROBBERY,
AUGUST 8, 1963**

IN CONTEXT

LOCATION
**Ledburn,
Buckinghamshire, UK**

THEME
Train robbery

BEFORE
15 May, 1855 Approximately 200 lb (91 kg) of gold is stolen from safes on board a South Eastern Railway train running between London Bridge and Folkestone, UK.

June 12, 1924 Notorious outlaws the Newton Gang carry out a postal train robbery near Rondout, Illinois, and steal around $3 milllion, making it the biggest train robbery in history at that time.

AFTER
March 31, 1976 A train traveling from Cork to Dublin, Ireland, is robbed near the village of Sallins by members of the Irish Republican Socialist Party.

At the beginning of the 1960s, life for many Londoners was poverty-stricken and drab. The austerity of postwar rationing was a recent memory, ending only six years before.

Having acquired the taste for easy money by taking advantage of his work in a sausage factory to sell black-market meat, Ronald Christopher "Buster" Edwards, was graduating to robberies with his friend Gordon Goody. Their brushes with the law brought them into contact with Brian Field, a lawyer's clerk. His services did not stop at preparing their defenses. For a cut of the proceeds Field would pass the duo details of his firm's clients as potential targets.

Early in 1963, Field introduced them to a stranger known only as "the Ulsterman." Believed to be Belfast-born Patrick McKenna, this corrupt Manchester postal worker brought intriguing news: large cash sums were being carried on the overnight mail trains from Glasgow to London. A tempting target—if above Goody's and Edwards' pay-grade. They took the information to an experienced South London

Am I one of a minority in feeling admiration for the skill and courage behind the Great Train Robbery?
Graham Greene

criminal called Bruce Richard Reynolds. In the months that followed, Reynolds started to put together an ad-hoc gang.

Best-laid plans
The plan was elegantly simple. The gang would stop the train in open countryside in Buckinghamshire at Sears Crossing, close to the village of Ledburn, where a signal could be interfered with. While this was the perfect place to stop the train, high embankments made it unsuitable for unloading the loot. For that, the train would be moved to nearby

Ronnie Biggs

He objected to being dismissed as the gang's "teaboy," but Ronnie Biggs's role could hardly be considered crucial in the Great Train Robbery. Born in Stockwell, south London, in 1929, he was a somewhat hapless burglar and armed robber when he met Bruce Reynolds in Wandsworth Prison. The Great Train Robbery was to be his first and only major heist. His main responsibility was the recruitment of "Stan Agate," the gang's replacement driver, who was not actually able to move the train because he was not familiar with the type of locomotive used.

Biggs's fingerprints were found on a ketchup bottle at the gang's hideout and he was arrested three weeks later. He escaped Wandsworth Prison using a rope ladder on July 8, 1965. He traveled to Brussels, then on to Australia before settling in Brazil in 1970, which did not then have an extradition treaty with the UK. Eventually, Biggs returned to the UK on a jet paid for by *The Sun* newspaper in exchange for exclusive rights to his story. Biggs was arrested minutes after landing at RAF Northolt on May 7, 2001.

See also: The James–Younger Gang 24–25 ▪ The Wild Bunch 150–51

The train was halted just before Bridego Bridge where the gang formed a human chain down the embankment. They loaded the loot onto a waiting van where the black car is in the image.

Bridego Bridge. The mail train was typically long, its cars manned by up to 80 postal workers who spent the journey sorting letters and packages. The gang discovered that High-Value Packages (HVPs) were stored in the second car from the front, so the gang planned to uncouple just the first two cars. Once they reached Bridego Bridge, they could unload sacks of registered mail using a human chain from the high embankment to a dropside truck waiting on the road below.

Reynolds refused to leave anything to chance, so in case the hijacked driver refused to carry out their demands, one of the gang would spend months studying locomotive manuals. Posing as a schoolteacher, he persuaded a driver on a suburban line to take him along for a ride: watching closely, he picked up certain basics. Reynolds also recruited a fully experienced driver to make sure. Field, meanwhile, negotiated the purchase of the abandoned Leatherslade Farm, roughly 30 miles (50 km) from Sears Crossing, which would be their hideout after the robbery.

Signal victory

Just before 7.00 p.m. on Wednesday, August 7, the train left Glasgow, with veteran driver Jack Mills at the controls and his co-driver David Whitby beside him. The HVP coach was carrying over £2.6 million (about $68 million today) in cash rather than the £300,000 ($8 million today) or so the gang had been expecting because of the UK public holiday on the previous Monday during which time the banks close.

By the time the train reached Sears Crossing, gang members had tampered with the signal lights; they slipped a glove over the green light to blot it out and wired up the red "stop" sign to a separate

It is the British press that made the "legend" that you see before you, so perhaps I should ask you who I am.
Ronnie Biggs

battery. A surprised Mills brought the train to a halt and Whitby went to investigate. When he tried to report in from the trackside telephone, he found that the wires had been cut.

As Whitby made his way back toward the train, he was hurled down the steep embankment by men in motorcycle helmets and ski masks. Meanwhile, gang members wearing masks and gloves climbed into Mills' cab and knocked him unconscious with an iron bar; others uncoupled the cars from the rear of the HVP coach, and overpowered and handcuffed the postal workers.

It soon became clear that the replacement driver—a retiree known as "Stan Agate" to the gang—was unable to operate the state-of-the-art Class 40 diesel-electric locomotive. So, having knocked out Mills, the robbers had to revive him so he could take them up the line to Bridego Bridge. **»**

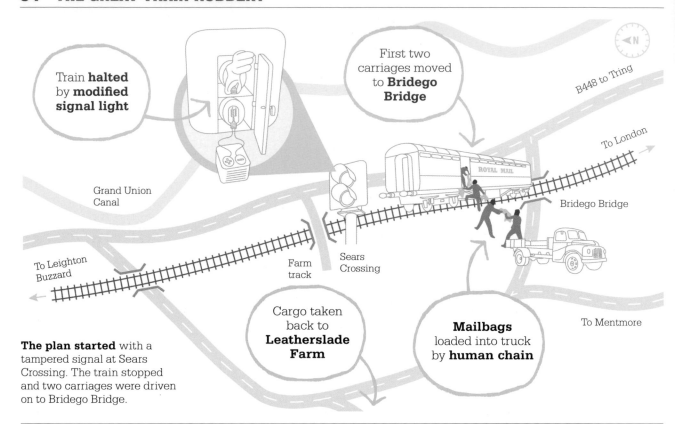

Train **halted** by **modified signal light**

First two carriages moved to **Bridego Bridge**

B448 to Tring

To London

Grand Union Canal

ROYAL MAIL

Bridego Bridge

To Leighton Buzzard

Farm track

Sears Crossing

To Mentmore

Cargo taken back to **Leatherslade Farm**

Mailbags loaded into truck by **human chain**

The plan started with a tampered signal at Sears Crossing. The train stopped and two carriages were driven on to Bridego Bridge.

Passing the mailbags along a human chain down the embankment, the gang quickly loaded the truck. Warning the handcuffed postal workers in the HVP carriage not to call the police for 30 minutes, the gang made their triumphant way back to the hideout at Leatherslade Farm.

An inevitable slip-up

It was indeed a "great train robbery," and if it all sounds like something from a movie, that is because in recent decades, such elaborately organized heists have been much more popular with movie makers than with criminals.

Not only are crimes like this risky, but they are enormously labor-intensive. Up to 17 men appear to have been involved in the robbery, although to this day, a few participants remain unidentified.

The gang members split the loot evenly, so as not to cause division, which would have added a potential source of danger.

However, the high number of people involved carried risks, such as a gang member being indiscrete with his loot or talking about the

Obviously you are a thief because you like money, but the second thing is the excitement of it.
"Buster" Edwards

robbery. In the end, an acquaintance of the ringleaders— in prison himself and hopeful of a deal—passed on some gossip that he had heard through the grapevine, providing a vital lead for the investigators to pursue.

The plan unravels

Meanwhile, in the robbers' farmhouse, confidence had given way to tension. The plan had been to lie low for a week, but it was soon apparent that the police— systematically sweeping the surrounding countryside—were closing in. Detectives had noted the robbers' 30-minute warning to the HVP-carriage staff, which suggested a hideout within half-an-hour's drive. Police searched Leatherslade Farm after a neighbor reported unusual activity at the farm. The robbers had gone,

Leatherslade Farm, later dubbed "Robber's Roost" by the press, was searched by police after farmworker John Maris tipped them off, convinced that the robbers were hiding there.

but fingerprints were found on a Monopoly game they had played—using real cash—as well as on a ketchup bottle. The conspiracy's collapse was as abrupt and chaotic as its planning had been patient. Eleven of the robbers were quickly caught together in south London.

The majority of the 11 were jailed for 30 years, a severe sentence for a crime in which nobody had been killed. However, it helped generate sympathy for the robbers. Two of them escaped prison—in August 1964, friends of gang member Charlie Wilson broke into Birmingham's Winson Green Prison to snatch him; the next July, Ronnie Biggs climbed over the wall at Wandsworth Prison, London.

Mythical status

The robbery's audacity could not be denied, but the long-term trauma inflicted upon the train crew was easier to ignore. Mills suffered from post-traumatic headaches for the rest of his life and never fully recovered from his injuries. Whitby died a few years later, at the age of 34, from a heart attack. However, these tragedies were overshadowed by an increasing romanticization of the crime, intensified by the fact that only a fraction of the £2.6 million ($68 million) haul was recovered. The robbery occurred at a time when brazen irreverence toward old-fashioned authority was in vogue—and at a time in which artist Andy Warhol claimed that everyone would be famous for 15 minutes. Biggs recorded music with the Sex Pistols and Edwards became the subject of the film *Buster* (1988)—his part played by rock star Phil Collins. Just three years after the crime, *The Great St. Trinian's Train Robbery* was released, playing on the idea that serious crime could be comic entertainment. ∎

Compassionate release

On August 6, 2009, after falling gravely ill with pneumonia, 80-year-old Ronnie Biggs was released on "compassionate" grounds—a rarity in the UK. Under the Prison Service Order 6000, a prisoner can only apply in the event of "tragic family circumstances" or if he or she is suffering from a terminal illness with death likely to result within a few months. Biggs survived until December 2013, but this courted little controversy. By contrast, two weeks after Biggs was released, Abdelbaset Al-Megrahi, convicted of the 1988 bombing of Pan Am Flight 103, was freed on compassionate grounds by the Scottish Justice Secretary, a decision condemned by the British and US press.

Megrahi had been diagnosed with terminal prostate cancer, but his release from the hospital caused an outcry, as did the arrival of Colonel Gaddafi's personal aircraft to repatriate him, and the hero's welcome he received back home in Libya.

Three men arrested in connection with the robbery are led away by police, holding blankets over their heads. The intense media interest is evident at the top left of the image.

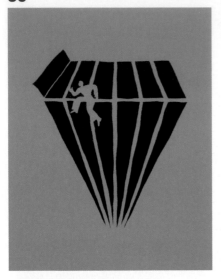

ADDICTED TO THE THRILL
BILL MASON, 1960s–1980s

IN CONTEXT

LOCATION
Dr. Armand Hammer's apartment, southern Florida, US

THEME
Jewel theft

BEFORE
1950–1998 Peter Scott, a Northern Irish cat burglar, commits some 150 burglaries before he is caught in 1952; in 1960, he steals a $260,000 necklace belonging to actress Sophia Loren.

AFTER
2004–06 Accomplished Spanish thief Ignacio del Rio confesses to more than 1,000 burglaries committed in Los Angeles over just a two-year period, taking $2 million in jewelry and a painting by Degas worth $10 million.

Bill Mason was an unexceptional property manager by day, but by night he was a notorious cat burglar. While unsuspecting owners slept he scaled walls, tiptoed across parapets, clambered onto balconies, and shimmied through barely open windows.

On a wet and windy night, Mason executed a plan weeks in the making. Straining every sinew, he climbed a full 15 floors up the outside of the apartment building of oil tycoon Dr. Armand Hammer, where he found the balcony door unlocked. He tossed the contents of Mrs. Hammer's jewelry box, worth several million dollars, into one of her pillowcases.

Ironically, on his way out, Mason found the front door secured by an easily pickable single lock. He made his escape through an open window on the third floor and used a grappling hook to help lower himself to the ground. Mason diligently concealed his tracks at every turn; the police did not identify a single suspect.

To the astonished occupants, it would seem as if the jewels had simply evaporated.
Bill Mason

Over a 20-year period of targeting the rich and famous—including swimmer and actor Johnny "Tarzan" Weissmuller, who lost an Olympic gold medal—Mason stole approximately $100 million in jewelry. The adrenalin surge he felt during the robbery and the glamour of these furtive brushes with the stars was addictive.

Mason was eventually caught in a sting operation, and later wrote the memoir *Confessions of a Master Jewel Thief*, published in 2003. ∎

See also: John MacLean 45 ▪ The Antwerp Diamond Heist 54–55 ▪ Doris Payne 78–79

TO ME IT IS ONLY SO MUCH SCRAP GOLD

THE THEFT OF THE WORLD CUP, MARCH 1966

IN CONTEXT

LOCATION
Central Hall, Westminster, London, UK

THEME
Priceless trophy theft

BEFORE
October 9, 1964 Jack Roland Murphy, a surfing champion, breaks into the Gems and Minerals Hall at the American Museum of Natural History and steals the J.P. Morgan jewel collection.

AFTER
December 19, 1983 The Jules Rimet Trophy is stolen again, this time from the Brazilian Football Confederation in Rio de Janeiro. It has never been recovered.

December 4, 2014 Sixty Formula 1 trophies are stolen by a group of seven men who drive a van through the doors of the Red Bull Racing headquarters in England.

For England's football fans, 1966 lives in the memory as the only year in which their team ever won the World Cup. The theft of the famous Jules Rimet Trophy four months before the tournament started, however, meant that England captain Bobby Moore nearly had to hold an imitation trophy in celebration.

On display in Westminster's Central Hall, London, the cup was guarded, but thieves sneaked in between patrols and forced open its glass case. Despite a full-scale investigation, the Metropolitan Police were no nearer a solution when a note arrived demanding £15,000 (about $350,000 today) for the trophy's safe return.

An attempt to entrap the sender did catch a petty criminal named Edward Betchley but failed to produce the trophy. Not until Pickles, a collie dog being taken for a walk by his owner David Corbett, unearthed a parcel beneath the hedge outside his owner's home in Upper Norwood, south London, did the missing cup come to light.

The story is still striking in terms of calculating "value" when it comes to crime—and whether some items are too well-known to be worth stealing. The original trophy, melted down—the only way a gang could have disposed of it—would have been worth little in monetary terms. Its symbolic significance, however, was priceless. A replica was produced in the original's place and fetched £254,000 ($638,000) at auction in 1997. ∎

Pickles the dog netted his owner a £5,000 ($115,000) reward, which he used to buy a house in Surrey. Pickles was later awarded a silver medal by the National Canine Defense League.

See also: Thomas Blood 18 ▪ The Theft of the Cellini Salt Cellar 56

MISS, YOU'D BETTER LOOK AT THAT NOTE

D.B. COOPER, NOVEMBER 24, 1971

The Northwest Orient Boeing 727 that D.B. Cooper hijacked is shown here at Portland International Airport, Oregon, in 1968. Its rear stairway is situated directly underneath the tail.

O n the afternoon of November 24, 1971, an unidentified man in his mid 40s, wearing a dark suit and black clip-on tie and carrying a black attaché case, jumped into criminal folklore. The man, who later would be dubbed D.B. Cooper by the press, boarded Northwest Orient's Flight 305 from Portland, Oregon, to Seattle, Washington.

During the flight, he passed flight attendant Florence Schaffner a note telling her he had a bomb in his case. After showing her the device, he stated his demands: he wanted four parachutes, a fuel truck waiting for the plane when it landed at Seattle-Tacoma Airport, and $200,000 in $20 bills. If his demands were not met, he would blow up the plane. What happened later that evening, however, remains one of the most perplexing mysteries in US criminal history.

Parachute escape

When the plane landed in Seattle, Cooper allowed the passengers and two of the three flight attendants to leave. Officials handed over the money and the parachutes. Cooper ordered the pilots to fly toward Mexico City at a maximum altitude of 10,000 feet (3,000 m) and at the minimum airspeed possible without stalling. About 45 minutes into the flight south, he sent the flight attendant to the cockpit and put on his parachute. Somewhere north of Portland he lowered the rear stairs and jumped out of the Boeing 727 and into the dark, rainy night. He left behind two of the parachutes and his tie.

The FBI launched a massive manhunt and the military was called in. Helicopters and a thousand troops on foot searched the area where they guessed Cooper might have landed, conducting door-to-door searches. A military spy plane even

Back in the early '70s, late '60s, hijackings weren't uncommon. The philosophy of the day was 'Cooperate, comply with his demands, and we'll deal with it when the plane lands.'
Larry Carr

photographed the Boeing 727's entire flight path. None of them found anything.

All the authorities had to go on was that the unidentified man had apparently bought a ticket in the name of either Dan or Dale Cooper. When police interviewed the man who sold the plane tickets that day, they asked if any of the passengers looked suspicious. Without hesitating, the airline employee replied, "Yes, Dale Cooper." The police subsequently told a reporter the suspect's name was "D. Cooper". However, the reporter, who didn't quite catch the name, asked "D or a B?" The police officer responded, "Yes." And thus the legend of D.B. Cooper was born.

Profiling Cooper

Schaffner gave police a physical description of the hijacker—in his mid 40s, between 5 feet 10 inches and 6 feet tall, 170–180 lbs, and with close-set brown eyes. She told police that the hijacker was well-spoken, polite, and calm. He was a bourbon drinker, and paid his drinks tab, even attempting to give her the change. Schaffner also disclosed that the hijacker asked if the flight crew wanted any food during the stop at Seattle. He had said that McChord Air Force Base was a 20-minute drive away from Seattle-Tacoma Airport—a detail that most civilians would not have known. His choice of plane—a 727-100—was also ideal for a bail-out escape. These factors indicated that he may well have been an Air Force veteran.

However, his lack of safety equipment, thermal clothing, or helmet, which would have afforded him little protection from the -70°F (-57°C) wind chill, seems to throw doubt on the claim he was a military man. FBI investigators at the time of the incident argued from the outset that he simply would not have survived the jump.

Money discovered

More than eight years later, in February 1980, eight-year-old Brian Ingram and his family were picnicking by the Columbia River close to the city of Vancouver, Washington. As the family cleared a spot for a campfire, Brian unearthed a packet of money in the sand near the river. His remarkable find, totaling $5,800 in $20 bills—of

I'm not so convinced that the investigation is dead or this story is over by any stretch.
Geoff Gray

which he was allowed to keep $2,850— matched the serial numbers of the ransom money handed over to Cooper on the tarmac at Seattle-Tacoma airport.

The FBI searched the beach and dredged the river but found nothing else. Nevertheless, the search reignited the public's interest in the legend of D.B. Cooper, and the missing $144,200.

The D.B. Cooper hijacking had all the ingredients of a legend—he got away with it, no one was hurt, and his fate remains a mystery. Public interest was periodically reinvigorated by news that the FBI was still looking for D.B. Cooper. **»**

The FBI produced a composite drawing of D.B. Cooper in 1972 based on recollections of the crew and his fellow passengers.

Criminal profiling

Criminal profiling is the process of identifying the most likely type of person to have committed a particular crime. Investigators look at behavior, personality traits, and demographic variables, including age, race, and location to build up a psychological picture of a suspect.

In the case of D.B. Cooper, his knowledge of the aviation industry and of the Boeing 727 suggest that he may have spent time in the Air Force, but his lack of skydiving skills suggest that he worked as an ancillary aviation worker, such as a cargo loader. It is possible that he lost his job during the economic downturn in the aviation industry in 1970–71 and this provided the financial motivation to commit the crime.

The fact that the FBI could not find anyone local who disappeared from the area shortly after the crime opens up the tantalizing possibility that D.B. Cooper may have been a local man who simply returned home and did his normal job as usual on the Monday morning.

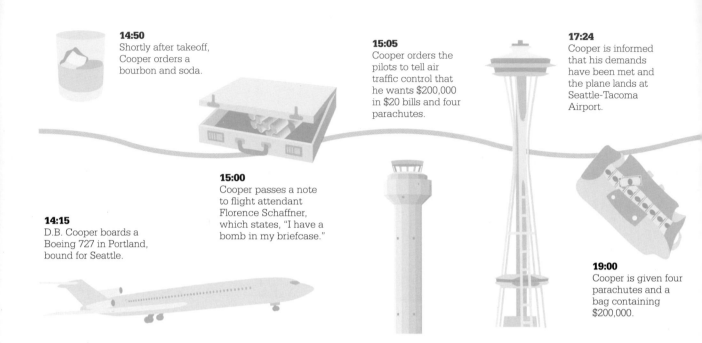

14:50
Shortly after takeoff, Cooper orders a bourbon and soda.

15:05
Cooper orders the pilots to tell air traffic control that he wants $200,000 in $20 bills and four parachutes.

17:24
Cooper is informed that his demands have been met and the plane lands at Seattle-Tacoma Airport.

15:00
Cooper passes a note to flight attendant Florence Schaffner, which states, "I have a bomb in my briefcase."

14:15
D.B. Cooper boards a Boeing 727 in Portland, bound for Seattle.

19:00
Cooper is given four parachutes and a bag containing $200,000.

At one point they decided to treat the case as if it were a bank robbery and appealed to the public in a bid to extract any relevant information. They released previously unknown facts about the case, including that he was wearing a clip-on tie, and the D.B. Cooper frenzy started up again.

Comic theory

When Seattle Special Agent Larry Carr took over the FBI's investigation in 2008, he disclosed that most of the messages he received were from people asking him not to solve the case. It seemed that D.B. Cooper had become a folk hero to some.

Nevertheless, Carr went diligently about his business. He thought it was possible the hijacker took his name from a French-Canadian comic book. In the fictional series, never translated into English, Royal Canadian Air Force test pilot Dan Cooper takes part in adventures in outer space and historical events of that era. One episode, published around the date of the hijacking, features an illustration of Dan Cooper parachuting on the cover. This led Carr to suspect that the hijacker had been a member of the Air Force, but also that he had spent time overseas where he could have read the comic book.

With the development of DNA profiling, FBI agents took another look at the clip-on tie Cooper left behind on the plane. They found a partial DNA sample on the tie but it did not match up with any suspects they had looked at over the years.

Promising leads

One intriguing suspect was Vietnam veteran L.D. (Lynn) Cooper. His niece, Marla Cooper, contacted the FBI in 2011, claiming she had been keeping a 40-year-old family secret—that her uncle Lynn Doyle Cooper was D.B. Cooper. She said she was eight years old when her uncle came home badly injured, a day or two after Thanksgiving in 1971. He claimed that he had been hurt in a car crash. She said she heard him tell the family "our money troubles are over." Cooper, who had died by the time his niece went to the FBI, worked as an engineering surveyor, which may have given him some of the training he needed to make the successful jump, and knowledge of the safest places to land in the area.

Marla Cooper loaned the FBI a guitar strap she thought would contain his DNA but no DNA was found on it. She put investigators in touch with her uncle's daughter, but the woman's DNA did not match the sample on the clip-on tie—which may or may not have D.B. Cooper's DNA. Still, the FBI

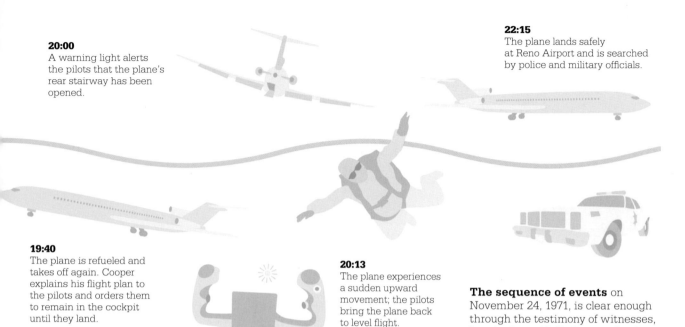

20:00
A warning light alerts the pilots that the plane's rear stairway has been opened.

22:15
The plane lands safely at Reno Airport and is searched by police and military officials.

19:40
The plane is refueled and takes off again. Cooper explains his flight plan to the pilots and orders them to remain in the cockpit until they land.

20:13
The plane experiences a sudden upward movement; the pilots bring the plane back to level flight.

The sequence of events on November 24, 1971, is clear enough through the testimony of witnesses, but the fate of D.B. Cooper after he exited the plane remains a mystery.

called it "a promising lead," but investigators were never able to definitely connect L.D. Cooper to the hijacking. At the end of the investigation, the FBI was still attempting to match a fingerprint to prints the hijacker left on the Boeing 727.

Lasting legacy
The D.B Cooper case prompted a spate of copycat crimes, particularly in the two years immediately after the hijacking. In 1972 alone, 15 similar skyjackings were attempted, but all of the perpetrators were captured. In total, approximately 160 planes were hijacked in American airspace between 1961 and 1973, after

which security was improved markedly and both passengers and their luggage began to be screened.

Whether D.B. Cooper survived the jump or not, his legacy lives on through an aircraft component that was named for him. In 1972, The Federal Aviation Authority (FAA) ordered all Boeing 727s to add what was later named a "Cooper vane," a mechanical aerodynamic wedge that prevents the rear stairway from being lowered in flight.

The enigmatic D.B. Cooper case is the world's only unsolved skyjacking. After investigating thousands of leads over 45 years, the FBI announced in July 2016 that it was ending active investigation of the case, but insisted that the file remains open. Meanwhile, the legend of D.B. Cooper lives on in music, movies, documentaries, scores of books, and in the lives of thousands of armchair sleuths. ∎

Dan Cooper was the name that the unidentifed man gave to the airport cashier. Along with the clip-on tie and the money recovered in 1980, this ticket is the only proof of his existence.

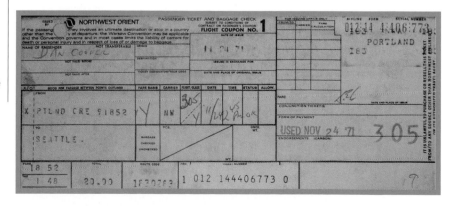

WITHOUT WEAPONS, NOR HATRED, NOR VIOLENCE
THE SOCIÉTÉ GÉNÉRALE BANK HEIST, JULY 16–20, 1976

IN CONTEXT

LOCATION
Nice, France

THEME
Bank vault heist

BEFORE
January 1976 The British Bank of the Middle East in Beirut, Lebanon, is robbed by guerrillas, who make off with safe deposit boxes containing £22 million (about $206 million today).

AFTER
December 19–20, 2004 An armed gang steals £26.5 million ($58.7 million) in cash from the vaults of the Donegall Square branch of the Northern Bank in Belfast, Northern Ireland.

August 6, 2005 A gang of thieves tunnel into the vault of a branch of Brazil's central bank in the city of Fortaleza and steal more than $65 million in cash.

During the 1976 Bastille Day weekend in Nice, France, a team of 20 men, led by French photographer and former paratrooper Albert Spaggiari, broke into the Société Générale bank. They had spent two months drilling a 25-foot (7.5-m) tunnel from the city's sewers into the vault.

Once they made it to the vault, the gang spent four days prying open over 400 safe deposit boxes, while cooking meals, drinking wine, and using antique silver tureens as toilets. The "sewer gang," escaped with $8–10 million in gold, cash, jewelry, and gems. Before fleeing, Spaggiari scrawled on the vault's wall in French, "sans armes, ni haine, ni violence" ("without weapons, nor hatred, nor violence"), identifying himself as a higher class of criminal.

Dubbed the "heist of the century" by the press, it was then the largest bank theft in history. However, by the end of October 1976, Spaggiari had been arrested and confessed to the crime. During a trial hearing, he made a daring escape by distracting the judge, jumping through a window and onto a parked car, before driving off on a waiting motorcycle.

He was later convicted in absentia and sentenced to life in prison but remained hidden until his death in 1989. Six other men were arrested; three were acquitted and the others sentenced to between five and seven years in prison. The loot from the heist has never been recovered. ∎

All the pleasures that come with the life of a crook do not make up for the heavy sacrifices.
"Amigo," a member of Spaggiari's team

See also: The Antwerp Diamond Heist 54–55 ∎ The Hatton Garden Heist 58–59

I STOLE FROM THE WEALTHY SO I COULD LIVE THEIR LIFESTYLE
JOHN MACLEAN, 1970s

IN CONTEXT

LOCATION
Florida, US

THEME
Cat burglary

BEFORE
1850s–1878 English burglar Charles Peace carries out multiple burglaries in Manchester, Hull, Doncaster, and around Blackheath, in southeast London.

AFTER
2006–09 A gang of thieves dubbed the Hillside Burglary Gang burgle 150 houses of wealthy residents in the area overlooking Sunset Boulevard in Los Angeles.

1983–2011 Accomplished Indian thief Madhukar Mohandas Prabhakar commits at least 50 burglaries in wealthy areas of Mumbai, India, amassing a fortune.

Dubbed the "Superthief," John (Jack) MacLean was estimated to have committed some 2,000 burglaries during the 1970s. He targeted wealthy victims and made off with more than $100 million in loot. His most renowned raid was a $1 million jewelry theft at the Fort Lauderdale mansion of a Johnson & Johnson company heiress in 1979. Although he stole only from the rich, he was far from a Robin Hood figure. He used his millions to fund a lifestyle like that of his victims, buying a helicopter, a speed boat, a sea plane, and a summer home.

MacLean was finally caught in 1979 after a crystal-studded walkie-talkie linked him to the Fort Lauderdale robbery. He used the time in prison to write a memoir entitled *Secrets of a Superthief*, which was published in 1983.

While MacLean was incarcerated, investigators noticed that a series of rapes and sexual battery cases, which detectives had attributed to a man with a talent for slipping past locks and

The mugshot of John MacLean in 1979 after he was arrested for the Fort Lauderdale robbery. He later boasted about this crime in his memoir.

alarms, had completely stopped. In 1981, MacLean was charged with two offenses, but the cases were subsequently dismissed. However, after scientific advancements in DNA testing, MacLean was arrested in October 2012 for two of hundreds of rapes he is believed to have committed decades ago. ∎

See also: Bill Mason 36 ▪ Doris Payne 78–79

SING OF MY DEEDS, TELL OF MY COMBATS... FORGIVE MY FAILINGS
PHOOLAN DEVI, 1979–FEBRUARY 1983

IN CONTEXT

LOCATION
Uttar Pradesh, India

THEME
Banditry

BEFORE
1890s The Big Swords Society, a peasant self-defense group, is formed in northern China to protect against bandits.

1868 Vigilantes break into a jail in New Albany, Indiana, killing three members of the train-robbing Reno Gang.

AFTER
1980s The Sombra Negra (Black Shadow) group forms in El Salvador, murdering criminals and gang members.

2013 Self-styled "Diana, Huntress of Bus Drivers" kills two in Ciudad Juárez, Mexico, as vengeance for alleged murders and rapes perpetrated by the city's bus drivers.

As the villagers of Behmai in Uttar Pradesh, India, prepared for a wedding on Valentine's Day 1981, 18-year-old Phoolan Devi plotted her revenge.

Seven months earlier, the low-caste teenage gang member had been kidnapped by a rival, largely high-caste gang in Behmai. For three weeks, Devi was locked up and repeatedly raped. She escaped with the help of two members of her gang and a low-caste villager, before rallying the rest of her gang and returning to the village.

Phoolan Devi's weapon of choice was a rifle, which gang leader and partner Vikram Mallah taught her to use. She eventually laid down the rifle in front of cheering supporters.

Her gang rounded up 22 of Behmai's male villagers, including two of her rapists, and on Devi's orders, shot dead each one. Known as the Behmai massacre, it was then India's largest mass execution and prompted a huge manhunt. The legend of the "Bandit Queen" was born.

See also: The James–Younger Gang 24–25 ▪ The Wild Bunch 150–51

> I alone knew what I had suffered. I alone knew what it felt like to be alive but dead.
> **Phoolan Devi**

Robin Hood figure

Devi became a heroine to India's lower caste, her crimes glorified as retribution for the oppression of women in rural India.

Born on August 10, 1963, to a low-caste family in rural Uttar Pradesh, Devi grew up very poor. At 11, her parents forced her to marry a man three times her age in exchange for a cow. In 1979, after fleeing her abusive husband, she was shunned by her parents, who considered her a disgrace.

At 16, with limited options for survival, she became the sole female dacoit (armed bandit) in a local gang. Devi soon rose to lead the gang, carrying out dozens of raids and highway robberies, attacking and looting upper-caste villages, and kidnapping rich people for ransom. In one of her most famous crimes, her gang captured and looted a town, then distributed the goods to the poor, further cementing her status as a Robin Hood figure.

Catch and release

Devi spent two years evading capture, concealed by the villagers she spent her life protecting. But in February 1983, she negotiated both her own surrender and the surrender of her gang members for considerably reduced sentences.

Devi was arrested in front of thousands of cheering onlookers and later charged with 48 crimes, including 30 charges of robbery and kidnapping. She spent the next 11 years in prison awaiting trial, but remained a beacon of hope for

Bandit Queen, a film about Devi's life, was released in 1994. It was initially banned by the Indian censor for being subversive and for its frank depiction of the brutality of rape.

the poor and downtrodden. Devi was released on parole in 1994, and all charges were dropped.

She took up politics and was elected as a Member of Parliament (MP). However, on the afternoon of July 25, 2001, three masked men ambushed and fatally shot her. One of her killers claimed that Phoolan Devi's assassination was carried out as revenge for the upper-caste men murdered during the Behmai massacre. ▪

Crime and candidacy

In some countries, criminals guilty of committing certain crimes are not permitted to run for public office. The rationale is that serious criminal conduct is inconsistent with the obligations of citizenship, and if someone is incapable of being a citizen, they should not be entitled to hold office. However, there is also evidence to suggest that voters perceive citizens who break the law for their own ends much less favorably than people who break the law for what they believe to be the public good. Nothing prevented Phoolan Devi, charged with multiple serious crimes including kidnapping and banditry, from running for office. A champion of the lower castes and a heroine to oppressed women, she had a sizeable following. However, she was far from universally adored, particularly among higher castes, many of whom were outraged that she was allowed to stand as a candidate. She was elected as an MP in the 1996 Indian General Election, winning with a majority of 37,000 votes. Devi lost her seat the following year but regained it in 1999.

THE FIRE

BECOMES A MISTRESS,

A LOVER

JOHN LEONARD ORR, 1984–91

IN CONTEXT

LOCATION
Southern California, US

THEME
Serial arson

BEFORE
1979–80 Bruce Lee (born Peter Dinsdale) committed 11 acts of arson in and around his hometown of Hull, Yorkshire, UK.

AFTER
1985–2005 Thomas Sweatt, a prolific American arsonist, set close to 400 fires, the majority of which were in the Washington, D.C. area.

1992–93 Paul Kenneth Keller, a serial arsonist from Washington state, set 76 fires in and around Seattle during a six-month spree.

With its arid climate and expanses of wilderness, California is a magnet for firestarters. But none of them have come close to the level of fiery devastation wrought upon people and property by John Leonard Orr. In the early 1980s, a series of blazes began in the Los Angeles area, sometimes as many as three a day. In one incident, 65 homes were reduced to smoldering ash. But it was not until October 10, 1984, that human lives were extinguished by the flames. At 7 p.m., the public address system at Ole's Home Center in South Pasadena blared an emergency warning. Noticing smoke pouring out of the hardware department, cashier Jim Obdan rushed to help customers flee the store, and was badly burned in the process. Fortunately, though, he lived to tell the tale. Co-workers Jimmy Cetina and Carolyn Kraus were not so lucky. Nor were customers Ada Deal and Matthew Troidl, a loving grandmother and her two-year-old grandson.

The following morning, arson investigators searched the blackened ruins for the point of

> John Orr wanted to be a Los Angeles police officer for a long time. He applied in 1981. He passed all of the tests except one. It was the psychological test.
> **Joseph Wambaugh**

origin—where a fire first begins—to determine its cause. Unable to locate it, they concluded that it was an electrical accident. But one seasoned arson investigator—Captain Marvin Casey of the Bakersfield Fire Department—was certain the fire had been intentionally set in a stack of flammable patio cushions.

In January 1987, a number of suspicious fires broke out north of Pasadena in the city of Bakersfield. At a craft store, Marvin Casey discovered an incendiary device in a trash can of dried flowers. It was crude but effective—three matches bound to the middle of a cigarette by a rubber band and concealed within a sleeve of yellow lined paper. After lighting the cigarette, the offender would have ample time to distance themself before the cigarette burned down far enough to ignite the matches and start the fire.

Later that same day, a second conflagration erupted in a trash can of pillows and foam rubber at Hancock Fabric store in Bakersfield. The trail of arson continued in rapid succession with one fire in Tulare

Pyrophilia

While the vast majority of arsonists are insurance fraudsters or attention seekers, the pyromaniac is a unique breed, fascinated by fire to the point of compulsively setting them. Even rarer than the pyromaniac is the pyrophile—Greek for "fire-lover"—a person who is sexually aroused by the flames, the smell of smoke, the intense heat, and (sometimes) the whirr of sirens racing to combat the inferno. Numerous entries in Orr's mostly

autobiographical *Points of Origin* indicate that the lead character, Aaron Stiles (i.e. Orr himself), possessed this dangerous paraphilic disorder.

Joseph Wambaugh, who worked as a detective sergeant in the Los Angeles Police Department for 20 years before he became a bestselling author, chronicled Orr's life in his book *Fire Lover*. Wambaugh reported that the linking of fire and sex in Orr's manuscript is continuous, and a key facet of Orr's motivation, a theory shared by investigator Marvin Casey.

followed by another two in Fresno. With the exception of the Bakersfield craft store, Casey determined that every fire had begun in a pile of pillows.

An audacious theory

This *modus operandi* (MO) did not escape Casey, who noted that the arson attacks had progressed sequentially from Los Angeles north along Highway 99 to Fresno. Nor did the troubling realization that the fires had occurred immediately before and after an annual arson investigator's conference in Fresno.

Casey began to develop a controversial theory: the fires were set by one of the 300 arson investigators who had attended the Fresno symposium. He obtained a list of the attendees, reducing the list of suspects to the 55 who had traveled alone through Bakersfield on Highway 99.

Unsurprisingly, when Casey shared his suspicions with his fellow arson investigators he was either ignored or ostracized. Yet he persevered, convincing the Bureau of Alcohol, Tobacco, and Firearms (ATF) to conduct scientific testing on the yellow paper recovered from the craft store. The ATF lab applied ninhydrin (a chemical used to detect ammonia) to the paper on the off chance that it would react to amino acids from fingerprint

The "Pillow Pyro" started a fire that swiftly became a firestorm in Glendale, California, in June 1990. A total of 67 properties were damaged or destroyed in the blaze, including this house.

residue. To the technician's and Casey's surprise, a partial fingerprint appeared. Using a special photographic filter to deepen the contrast and reveal the ridge detail, the technician was able to render a usable print. It was entered into the Automated Fingerprint Identification System (AFIS) where it was compared to the fingerprints of criminals across the country. When the AFIS failed to produce a match, Casey asked the ATF to compare the print to »

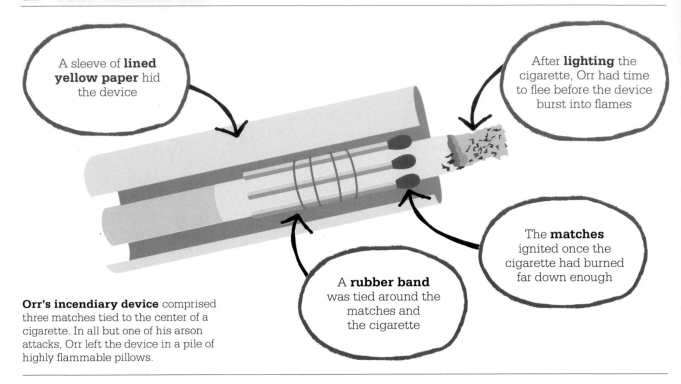

A sleeve of **lined yellow paper** hid the device

After **lighting** the cigarette, Orr had time to flee before the device burst into flames

The **matches** ignited once the cigarette had burned far down enough

A **rubber band** was tied around the matches and the cigarette

Orr's incendiary device comprised three matches tied to the center of a cigarette. In all but one of his arson attacks, Orr left the device in a pile of highly flammable pillows.

the fingerprints of the 55 conference attendees on his list. His request was denied.

For two years, the case sat in limbo. Then, in March 1989, a series of fires flared up again, this time along Highway 101, the road that led directly to Pacific Grove, the venue for the annual arson investigators' symposium. Reinvigorated, Casey compared the list of Pacific Grove conference attendees to the previous one, narrowing the number of his suspects down to ten. Certain that the arsonist was among them, he convinced Fresno ATF agents to steathily obtain the fingerprints of his ten suspects and compare them to the partial print. To Casey's shock and disappointment, the results came back negative.

Catching a break

Beginning in late 1990, a series of fires in Los Angeles prompted the development of the "Pillow Pyro Task Force," deriving its name from the offender's MO. Like the earlier blazes, the fires had been set in retail outlets during business hours.

In March 1991, the head of the task force, Tom Campuzano, distributed a leaflet containing information about this MO to the Fire Investigators Reaction Strike Team (FIRST), an association of fire departments without an arson investigator as a permanent staff

It's my opinion that he set in excess of 2,000 fires over a period of about 30 years.
Michael J. Cabral

member. After reading the pamphlet, Scott Baker of the California State Fire Marshal's Office told Campuzano about Marvin Casey and his much-maligned theory.

At long last, Casey had found an influential arson investigator who was sympathetic to his cause. Campuzano and Casey met to discuss the case, and Casey handed over a copy of the partial fingerprint to the taskforce. They ran the print through a database of every person who had ever applied for a job with the LAPD, and this time they struck gold. The partial print matched the left ring fingerprint of John Leonard Orr: one of the ten names on Marvin Casey's list. Whether by sheer luck or professional incompetence, Orr had avoided being matched in 1989.

Orr was a 41-year-old fire captain with many years of experience investigating arson. He was well liked, charming, and had

Orr's day of reckoning arrived at the conclusion of his murder trial in June 1998. His defense lawyers argued that faulty wiring was to blame for the Ole fire, but the jury found Orr guilty.

developed a legendary reputation for always being the first to arrive on the scene. As a result of Casey's findings, however, Orr was placed under surveillance, with a monitoring device secretly attached to the bumper of his car. Orr found and removed it, only to have police fix another under his dashboard when he brought in his vehicle for maintenance.

When the set of the popular television drama *The Waltons* was engulfed in flames on the afternoon of November 22, 1991, in Burbank, Teletrac showed Orr driving home from the scene of the fire at 3:30 a.m. to receive the dispatcher's report. Tellingly, although the dispatcher incorrectly reported the address of the fire, Orr still managed to arrive at the correct location.

Although they lacked the necessary evidence to make an arrest, the taskforce realized that as long as Orr remained at large, human lives were at risk. They quickly applied for a warrant to search his home. In a briefcase, investigators found a cache of cigarettes, matches, and rubber bands, while his car yielded sheets of lined yellow paper. Even more damning was a video Orr had shot on March 14, 1990, of a hillside residence in Pasadena, followed by footage of the same house ablaze on October 2, 1992. Crucially, Orr had penned a manuscript for a novel entitled *Points of Origin* in which the protagonist Aaron Stiles (an anagram of "I Set LA Arson"), lived the double-life of an arson investigator and firestarter.

Not only did Stiles employ the same incendiary device as the "Pillow Pyro," he also set fires on his way to arson conferences and had burned down a hardware store, killing a little boy named Matthew.

Frightening revelations

John Leonard Orr was arrested on December 4, 1991, and charged with five counts of arson. But his true day of judgment arrived on June 25, 1998, when the California State Court convicted him on four counts of first-degree murder related to the 1984 Ole inferno, for which he received a sentence of life in prison without parole.

Orr's personal charm was later attributed to psychopathy, because it was accompanied by other notably psychopathic traits, including manipulativeness, vanity, and lack of remorse. Alhough Orr still maintains his innocence, after his arrest, the number of major fires

in the area dropped from an annual average of 67 to 1. Given that Orr had been a secret serial arsonist, it is likely that he had a sixth sense for fires because he set them. This suspicion prompted Deputy District Attorney Michael J. Cabral to estimate that Orr set more than 2,000 fires over a 30-year period, making him one of the most prolific arsonists in US history.

In a final gruesome twist, *Points of Origin* features a scene in which Aaron Stiles sexually assaults and murders a young girl in a vehicle, which is then burned. Investigators claim to have identified the case, but lack conclusive evidence of Orr's involvement. Two additional fire-related deaths described in *Points of Origin* remain unaccounted for. If these horrific passages turn out to be true, Orr is not only an arsonist and mass murderer, but also a sexually motivated serial killer. ∎

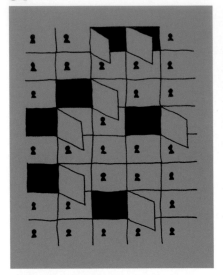

IT WAS THE PERFECT CRIME

THE ANTWERP DIAMOND HEIST, FEBRUARY 15–16, 2003

IN CONTEXT

LOCATION
Antwerp Diamond Center, Belgium

THEME
Vault heist

BEFORE
March 18, 1990 Two thieves disguised as police officers enter the Isabella Stewart Gardner Museum in Boston, Massachusetts, trick security officers, and steal 13 priceless works of art.

AFTER
February 18, 2013 Eight masked gunmen posing as police officers steal $50 million in diamonds from an armored van on the tarmac of Brussels Airport, Belgium.

For hundreds of years, most of the world's rough diamonds—worth many billions of dollars—have passed through Antwerp, Belgium, making it the largest diamond district in the world and a coveted target for audacious burglars.

Great heists depend on great planning. The 2003 break-in at the Antwerp Diamond Center was years in the making and was not dubbed "the perfect crime" without good reason.

A life-long thief from Palermo, Sicily, who specialized in charming his victims, Leonardo Notarbartolo posed as a diamond merchant and rented an office in the Antwerp Diamond Center two years before the robbery. This enabled him to gain 24-hour access to the building, with his own safe deposit box located within the vault.

Without a trace

On the night of February 16, 2003, Notarbartolo and a group of five thieves known as "The School of Turin" broke into the diamond center's vault.

Despite nine different layers of security, including cameras and infrared heat and motion sensors,

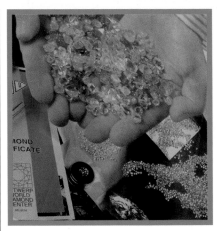

Antwerp's reputation as a world diamond center is well founded, with 85 percent of all rough diamonds passing through the city and over $16 billion in cut diamonds sold each year.

the gang looted 123 of the vault's 160 individual safe deposit boxes without setting off any alarms or leaving behind any signs of forced entry. The staff at the diamond center did not even notice that a robbery had been committed until February 17. They also discovered that the security camera tapes were missing. After combing the vault, investigators estimated that the haul amounted to $100 million in diamonds, other precious gems, gold, and jewelry.

See also: The Société Générale Bank Heist 44 ▪ The Hatton Garden Heist 58–59

The nine security layers at the Antwerp vault

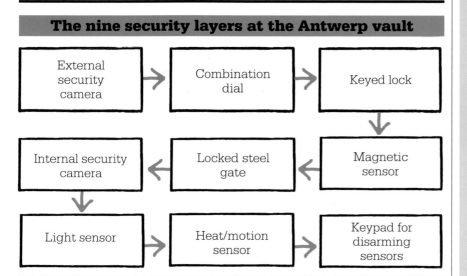

External security camera → Combination dial → Keyed lock

Keyed lock → Magnetic sensor → Locked steel gate → Internal security camera

Internal security camera → Light sensor → Heat/motion sensor → Keypad for disarming sensors

The unfinished sandwich

Everything had gone like clockwork for the gang, but they became sloppy during their escape. One gang member, known as "Speedy" (later identified by police as Pietro Tavano), hastily discarded a bag of trash in a forest alongside the E19 freeway north of Brussels.

A local farmer found the bag and called the police after noticing envelopes from the Antwerp Diamond Center, a videotape, and a half-eaten salami sandwich, which was later discovered to contain traces of Notarbartolo's DNA. Notarbartolo was subsequently arrested, along with three accomplices including Speedy, for committing what the press had labeled "the heist of the century." Police searched Notarbartolo's apartment and discovered 17 diamonds in his home safe, which they traced back to the vault. More diamonds were found hidden in a rolled-up carpet. In 2005, Notarbartolo was sentenced to 10 years; his fellow conspirators were jailed for five years each.

I may be a thief and a liar but I am going to tell you a true story.
Leonardo Notarbartolo

Missing puzzle pieces

Notarbartolo claimed in a 2009 interview with *Wired* magazine that a diamond merchant hired The School of Turin for the heist, and that the robbery was part of a complex insurance fraud. Authorities doubted this claim, however, and did not pursue it. What is beyond doubt, though, is that except for a few stones, the loot has never been found. The fifth member of the gang, nicknamed the "King of Keys," has also not yet been identified. ∎

The Diamond Squad

In 2000, the Belgian Ministry of Justice established a special police force to guard and investigate crimes taking place in Antwerp's diamond district. This unique six-member police force is led by inspectors who are uniquely well connected with the diamond business. The head of the "Diamond Squad," Agim De Bruycker, was in charge of the investigation into the Antwerp Diamond Heist that secured Notarbartolo's arrest.

However, in March 2015, De Bruycker was arrested on suspicion of money laundering. Diamonds worth $550,000 were later discovered in his home. Members of his team had allegedly become suspicious after he purchased an expensive villa and a new Range Rover shortly after his divorce was finalized. De Bruycker was consequently suspended pending an investigation.

De Bruycker's arrest is not the only scandal to befall the diamond squad. In 2004, €1.6 million ($1.75 million) worth of diamonds, seized as part of a fraud investigation, vanished from police custody. They have not been recovered.

HE WAS AN EXPERT IN ALARM SYSTEMS
THE THEFT OF THE CELLINI SALT CELLAR, MAY 11, 2003

IN CONTEXT

LOCATION
Kunsthistorisches Museum, Vienna, Austria

THEME
Art theft

BEFORE
August 21, 1911 Leonardo da Vinci's famed Mona Lisa is stolen from Paris's Louvre Museum, but recovered two years later when the thieves attempt to sell it.

AFTER
October 16, 2012 A Romanian gang breaks into the Kunsthal Museum in the Netherlands and steals seven paintings worth $24 million.

S tealthily dodging high-tech motion sensors and round-the-clock security guards, an amateur art thief climbed up the scaffolding outside Vienna's Kunsthistorisches Museum, crawled through a broken second-floor window, shattered a display case, and fled with one of the world's great Renaissance artifacts.

The early morning theft of the gold-plated salt cellar, worth an estimated $65 million, on May 11, 2003, caused a scandal across Austria. The intricate, 10-inch (25-cm) sculpture depicting a trident-wielding Neptune was the masterpiece of Benvenuto Cellini, the famed 15th-century Italian sculptor.

Despite its multimillion-dollar value, the statue was essentially unsellable because no legitimate art dealer would touch it. Following

two failed ransom attempts by the thief, in January 2006, police arrested 50-year-old Robert Mang, a security alarm specialist and avid sculpture collector. He soon confessed, admitting that the theft was "rather spontaneous."

Mang led police to the Renaissance treasure, buried in a wooded area 55 miles (90 km) northeast of Vienna. Mang had wrapped the sculpture in linen and plastic and placed it in a lead box to protect it from damage. In September 2006, Mang was sentenced to four years in prison but was released early, in 2009. ∎

The salt cellar was finished by Cellini in 1543 and presented to King Francis I of France. It is the only remaining item of precious metal work attributed to the Italian sculptor.

See also: Bill Mason 36 ▪ The Theft of the World Cup 37 ▪ John MacLean 45

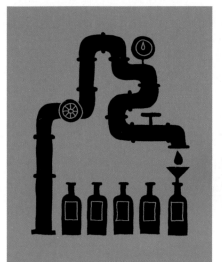

WEIRD AND UNBELIEVABLE, BUT IT'S A VERY REAL CRIMINAL CASE
THE RUSSIA-ESTONIA VODKA PIPELINE, 2004

IN CONTEXT

LOCATION
Narva, Estonia

THEME
Smuggling

BEFORE
1916 After the state of Michigan bans alcohol sales, rum-runners smuggle liquor by boat over the border from Windsor, Ontario, in Canada to Detroit, Michigan.

August 12, 1998 Lithuanian police uncover a pipeline used to smuggle alcohol from Latvia across the border into Lithuania.

AFTER
January 6, 2014 Philadelphia police arrest a local attorney for illegally selling bottles of fine wine out of the basement of his home; in all, they confiscate 2,500 bottles valued between $150,000 and $200,000.

From August to November 2004, a team of enterprising smugglers operated a remarkable 1¼-mile (2-km) pipeline under the Kyrgyzstan River to transport huge quantities of vodka from Russia to the ex-Soviet country of Estonia in order to avoid paying duty.

Estonia had only just joined the European Union on May 1, 2004, where vodka fetched a much higher price than it did in Russia. Unfortunately for the smugglers, however, they could not find a single buyer for the illegal vodka in the country's capital, Tallinn. They finally offloaded it in Tartu, Estonia's second-largest city.

The operation was uncovered by chance when workers digging planting holes for trees found the pipeline along the bottom of a reservoir near the border town of Narva. Customs officials seized 306 gallons (1,400 liters) of the alcohol and shut down the pipeline. They also later discovered a large quantity of untaxed alcohol hidden in a truck in Tallinn.

> The investigation also revealed that the men had tried to sell some of the alcohol in Tallinn ... but the quality of the spirit was too bad.
> **Mari Luuk**

Officials estimated that by the time the gang of 11 Russian and Estonian smugglers were caught, they had already pumped 1,638 gallons (7,450 liters) of vodka from Russia to Estonia.

Two years later, Estonian police discovered another smuggling pipeline under the same river, but it was shut down before any alcohol was illegally transported into the European Union. ■

See also: The Hawkhurst Gang 136–37 ■ The Beer Wars 152–53

OLD-SCHOOL LONDON CRIMINAL GENTS

THE HATTON GARDEN HEIST, APRIL 2015

IN CONTEXT

LOCATION
London, UK

THEME
Vault heist

BEFORE
September 11, 1971
Burglars, including Brian Reader, break into the safe deposit boxes at the Baker Street branch of Lloyds Bank in London, stealing an estimated £3 million (about $45 million today).

July 12, 1987 Thieves pose as potential customers at the Knightsbridge Safe Deposit Center in London to gain access before holding up staff and making off with about £60 million ($228 million) in cash and jewelry.

AFTER
February 4–5, 2016
Computer hackers attempt to steal $951 million from the central bank of Bangladesh.

B y the early spring of 2015, veteran career criminal Brian Reader, age 76, had spent three years planning "one last job." Reader had the pedigree, having participated in the Baker Street Robbery of 1971. This time, he recruited friends John "Kenny" Collins, 74, Terry Perkins, 67, and Danny Jones, 60, among others.

On the first weekend of April 2015, with the Easter holiday and Passover due to coincide, the Hatton Garden Safe Deposit Company was to close its doors on Thursday night and would not open again until the following Tuesday. The entire district, renowned as London's jewelry quarter, was to be deserted for the long weekend.

They were analogue criminals operating in a digital world.
Scotland Yard

A diamond-core drill, stolen from a nearby demolition site four months before the heist, was used to bore three overlapping holes through the reinforced concrete wall.

Without a hitch

The last of the Hatton Garden Safe Deposit Company staff left the building at around 8:20 p.m. Five minutes later, security cameras captured footage of a gang of men heading down into the vault via an elevator shaft.

They were led by a man nicknamed "Mr. Ginger" by the press for the red hair visible beneath his cap, but he was referred to among the gang as "Basil." Three others were visible, each pushing a large commercial garbage can on wheels: the robbers clearly expected a major haul. For the moment, however, no one saw

See also: The Great Train Robbery 30–35 ▪ The Société Générale Bank Heist 44 ▪ The Antwerp Diamond Heist 54–55

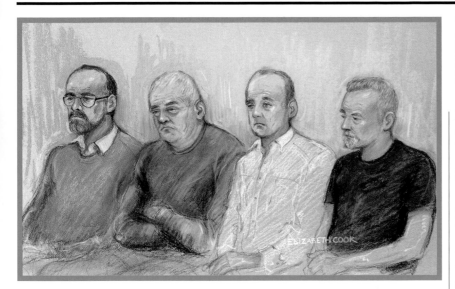

The **"Diamond Wheezers"** as the press dubbed them were jailed for a lenient combined total of 34 years. Perkins and Jones even thanked the judge as they were led away.

this footage—nor did the Metropolitan Police react to an alert from the vault's alarm.

The alarm also alerted the vault's security monitoring company. They called Alok Bavishi, the son of the safe deposit center's joint director, who was temporarily in charge. Although Bavishi was incorrectly informed that the police were already at the scene, he phoned a security guard to check out the building. The guard found nothing wrong when he looked through the main door—a lucky break for the gang, particularly as lookout Collins had fallen asleep while he was on duty.

Meanwhile, Basil and his associates made two trips to the vault. By the time they fled the area, at 6:45 a.m. on Sunday morning, they had ransacked 72 boxes and taken £14 million ($21 million) worth of loot.

Tracking them down
However, the gang unwittingly left an electronic trail. They had tried to disable the security cameras and the vault's alarms, but only with partial success. The gang's careless use of their cell phones also provided the police with clues. Access to phone records and vehicle-tracking data established that gang members Perkins, Collins, and Jones had regularly met at the Castle pub in Islington, north London, while planning the raid. A police surveillance operation later recorded Reader, Collins, and Perkins in the Castle pub boasting about how they had accessed the vault.

Mystery mastermind
Seven men were eventually arrested and convicted for the Hatton Garden robbery, but Basil eluded capture. According to the testimony of Danny Jones, Basil was an ex-policeman and the mastermind behind the raid. Basil clearly was the most professional member of the gang and had been careful to conceal his face with a bag when making his way into the waiting van. He is believed to have been the inside man, letting himself into the building with a set of keys and bypassing several layers of security. Both Basil and more than £10 million ($12 million) worth of jewelry, gold, and gems are unaccounted for. ▪

One last job

The British press and the public were tickled by the venerable age of the men accused of the Hatton Garden heist. There was a certain charm to the revelation that Reader used a senior citizen's bus pass to get to Hatton Garden; that lookout Kenny Collins had napped on duty; and that Terry Perkins had remembered to pack his diabetes medication.

Superficially, the gang members seemed like they could have been anyone's grandfathers. However, many of them were dangerous career criminals bonded by friendship, a shared skillset, and nostalgia for past adventures.

For years, Reader had cultivated a "safety-first" approach to keep him ahead of the law. He had aborted risky robberies and taken long sabbaticals when things turned "hot." Finally, though, it seems that he could not resist the allure and prestige of this opportunity, abandoning his tried-and-tested approach for one last job.

CON ART

STS

In France, Jeanne de la Motte **deceives a wealthy cardinal** with the aim of obtaining a diamond necklace.

Czech-born Victor Lustig pretends to be a member of the French government wishing **to sell the Eiffel Tower** as scrap metal.

Using fake identities and her natural charm, Doris Payne embarks on a career as a **jewel thief**.

1785

1925

1952

1879

1946

Wealthy French socialite Thérèse Humbert **borrows vast sums of money** against the promise of a bogus inheritance.

In Paris, artist Elmyr de Hory begins to **forge works by famous painters** to sell to wealthy individuals and galleries.

Confidence tricks, so-called because they exploit people's trust, are among the oldest crimes in the world. Human nature is on the side of the perpetrators—without a good reason, most people tend to trust others. Victims often learn the hard way that if an offer seems too good to be true, it probably is.

A con artist is a manipulator who cheats or tricks others by persuading them to believe something that is not true. Through deception, by lying, cheating, and fooling their targets into believing they can make easy gains, con artists exploit their victims, usually to obtain money themselves but also for other advantage. The legal consequences of such trickery depend on the circumstances and the laws of the land.

Con artists are also known as "hustlers," "grifters," and "tricksters." They derisively call their victims "marks," "suckers," or "gulls." Just how their victims get duped is not as puzzling as it may seem. Some tricksters deliberately target the elderly, lonely, or vulnerable, but almost anyone can be susceptible to their scams, especially when they fall prey to a convincing get-rich-quick scheme that appears genuine. The impact of the crime can be substantial. In 18th-century France, for example, the scandalous machinations of social climber and trickster Jeanne de la Motte, in a case that became known as the Affair of the Diamond Necklace, helped to reinforce the monarchy's unpopularity—which led to the French Revolution and the destruction of the *ancien régime*.

Champion swindlers

Some cases involve extraordinary levels of self-confidence on the part of the con artist. In the 1960s, master impostor Frank Abagnale evaded law enforcement for years, impersonating six different professionals, including a pilot, a doctor, a lawyer, and an FBI agent. Victor Lustig succeeded in selling the Eiffel Tower for scrap metal to a gullible businessman.

In other cases, it is the simplicity and brazen nature of the attempted deception that is astounding, such as the champion race horse disguised as a novice with a slap of white paint in Australia's Fine Cotton scandal, although that ruse was swiftly exposed. The escape from Alcatraz was much more intricately planned, with the escapees placing paper-

Master impostor Frank Abagnale **impersonates a pilot** to travel the world and enjoy a lavish lifestyle.

In Germany, forger Konrad Kujau fools the world into believing documents penned by him are actually **Hitler's diaries**.

1964

1978

1962

1972

1984

In the US, three prisoners trick guards and pull off one of the most famous jailbreaks in history—**the escape from Alcatraz**.

Clifford Irving falsely claims that Howard Hughes has asked him to write his biography **and tricks publishing executives** into giving him a large advance.

In the Fine Cotton horse racing scandal in Australia, a crime syndicate **substitutes a champion horse** for a novice.

---

mache heads in their beds to convince the guards that they were sleeping instead of digging their way out of the island prison.

In most cases, it is an individual or an organization that is fooled, but hundreds were taken in by art forger Elmyr de Hory's remarkable paintings—he sold more than a thousand works by "Picasso," "Matisse," and "Modigliani" to collectors and galleries worldwide.

Master forger Konrad Kujau also managed to fool most of the world with the Hitler diaries. Historians proclaimed their authenticity, newspapers ran extracts, and publishing companies vied for the rights. Often, those who fall for such hoaxes are reluctant to believe they have been duped. The publishers of the extracts from the Hitler diaries and the Howard Hughes biography continued to stand by their scoops long after everyone else realized they had been scammed. And many individuals, after realizing that they have been deceived, are reluctant to contact the authorities, for fear of being ridiculed. Victor Lustig banked on this in his audacious sale of the Eiffel Tower; it worked because he successfully predicted his victim's embarrassment at being duped.

Underlying psychology
What con artists have in common is the power of persuasion. The most successful perpetrators share three personality traits—psychopathy, narcissism, and Machiavellianism—which allow them to carry out their crimes without feeling remorse or guilt.

However, making a profit is not always their goal. According to psychologists, con artists simply gain great satisfaction from pulling off their scams, regardless of the amount of money they make.

Many con artists use disguises as part of their *modus operandi*, which makes it difficult for law enforcement agencies to catch them, especially before the aid of digital technology. Police may also hesitate to go after culprits, because in some jurisdictions, stealing property is considered a civil issue rather than a crime. In addition, police are generally more concerned with catching violent criminals and terrorists than apprehending grifters. The crimes of the grifter can be difficult to prove, and the perpetrators are less likely to be prosecuted. ■

UNDER THE INFLUENCE OF BAD COUNSELS... I FELL A MARTYR

THE AFFAIR OF THE DIAMOND NECKLACE, 1785

IN CONTEXT

LOCATION
Paris, France

THEME
Jewelry scam

BEFORE
1690s William Chaloner leads a highly successful coin counterfeiting gang in Birmingham and London, England; he is hanged in 1699 for high treason after targeting the Royal Mint.

AFTER
1923 Lou Blonger, the kingpin of an extensive ring of con men who operated in Denver, Colorado, for more than 25 years, is finally convicted after a famous trial dogged by allegations that Blonger's associates attempted to bribe members of the jury.

In 1785, Queen Marie Antoinette was embroiled in a notorious scandal at the French court over a diamond necklace. Confidence trickster Jeanne de la Motte orchestrated a ruse, impersonating the queen to deceive a wealthy cardinal. The implications of this swindle had unintentionally far-reaching consequences and helped to bring about the French Revolution.

Royal commission

In 1772, King Louis XV enlisted the jewelers Boehmer and Bassenge to create an elaborate necklace for Madame du Barry, his mistress. The jewelers created a diamond necklace that weighed 2,800 carats and featured 647 stones. It took several years to make and cost 2 million livres (about $10 million today). By the time it was finished, Louis had died from smallpox and du Barry was banished by his heir, Louis XVI. The jewelers tried to sell the necklace to Marie Antoinette, but she declined it.

A cunning plan

Jeanne de Valois-Saint-Rémy was a descendant of an illegitimate son of King Henri II (1547–59). In 1780, she

The necklace was a work of art, featuring festoons, pendants, and tassels. In creating it without a firm commission, the jewelers took a huge risk, which nearly bankrupted them.

married Nicolas de la Motte, an officer of the gendarmes, and they styled themselves as Count and Countess de la Motte. They were granted a modest pension from the king, but it was not enough to provide Jeanne either with the lifestyle she desired or reflect the social status she felt entitled to.

Learning that the jewelers were trying to find a buyer for the necklace, Jeanne hatched a plan

See also: The Crawford Inheritance 66–67 ▪ Frank Abagnale 86–87 ▪ Clifford Irving 88–89

I can see I have been cruelly deceived.
Cardinal Louis de Rohan

to acquire it, sensing the ideal opportunity for her financial and social advancement. Among her acquaintances was Cardinal Louis de Rohan, who had fallen out of favor with the queen and was eager to reconcile. In 1784, Jeanne convinced the cardinal that she enjoyed Marie-Antoinette's favor and tricked him into writing to the queen. De la Motte's accomplice Rétaux de Villette forged replies from "the queen" on gilt-edged stationery. The exchanges became so amorous that de Rohan believed

A schemer through and through, Jeanne de la Motte escaped prison dressed as a boy. She fled to London where she wrote a memoir of the diamond necklace scandal in which she defended her actions.

he and the queen were in love. After requests from de Rohan for the pair to meet, Jeanne hired a prostitute to impersonate Marie-Antoinette and organized a rendezvous in the gardens of the Palace of Versailles. Having gained his trust, Jeanne informed de Rohan that the queen wanted to buy the diamond necklace, but could not be seen to do so at a time when many people in Paris were starving. De Rohan agreed to cover the cost in instalments and the jewelers handed over the necklace.

Fraud exposed

When de Rohan's first payment was insufficient, the jewelers protested to Marie-Antoinette, but she denied requesting the necklace. De Rohan was brought before the king and queen to explain himself and the

swindle was finally exposed. The prostitute and the de la Mottes were convicted and Villette was banished, but de Rohan was acquitted. De la Motte was publicly flogged and branded with a "V" for *voleuse* (robber) and imprisoned but escaped ten months later. Already scapegoated for the country's financial plight, the trial destroyed the queen's fragile reputation. Eight years later, she was executed during the French Revolution. The necklace was never found. ▪

This satirical engraving mocks Cardinal de Rohan's gullibility and crookedness, seen here offering up the necklace to de la Motte.

Preying on vulnerability

Jeanne de la Motte executed a near-perfect confidence trick to dupe Cardinal de Rohan, first seducing him, then preying on his desperation, vulnerability, and vanity. She also waited until she had earned his trust before asking anything of him in return.

However, she did make one potentially fatal error, signing the notes from the queen with "Marie Antoinette de France." It is possible that the cardinal was not aware of the custom that French queens signed with their

given names only, but it is unlikely, given that he had previously worked as the French ambassador to the court of Vienna and would have been skilled in diplomatic protocol. It is more likely that the cardinal was blinded by de la Motte's power of persuasion. He was brought back down to earth by the king, furious that a high-ranking noble could be duped by such an obvious error. Although he was lampooned as a fool, he received popular support; his acquittal was deemed a victory over the unpopular royals.

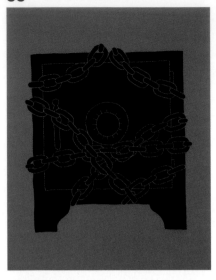

PEOPLE TOOK THEIR HATS OFF TO SUCH A SUM

THE CRAWFORD INHERITANCE, 1879–1902

IN CONTEXT

LOCATION
Paris, France

THEME
Fake inheritance scam

BEFORE
1821–37 Scottish soldier and con man General Gregor MacGregor extorts money from British and French investors looking to settle in a fictional Central American territory.

AFTER
1880s American con woman Bertha Heyman, also known as "Big Bertha," persuades dozens of rich men to lend her money with the promise that she will pay them back from a fictional inheritance.

1897–1904 Canadian forger and con artist Cassie L. Chadwick claims to be the illegitimate daughter and heiress of steel tycoon Andrew Carnegie, and swindles banks out of millions of dollars.

I n 1898, on the verge of bankruptcy, a French banker named Girard contacted the woman with whom he had invested his fortune, begging for some of the money he was owed. When wealthy socialite Thérèse Humbert refused, Girard put a gun to his head and pulled the trigger in despair. Girard's suicide was the beginning of the end of Humbert's 20-year career swindling the French elite of nearly 100 million francs (about $534 million today).

Fake inheritance

Born Thérèse Daurignac in France, she grew up an impoverished peasant. Although she was neither wealthy nor well educated, Thérèse was charming and adept at lying and manipulation. She claimed she was of noble blood and convinced her first cousin, Frédéric Humbert, the son of a prominent French mayor, to marry her. The two then moved to Paris, where her father-in-law's connections helped Thérèse to gain fame and influence among French society.

In 1879, Thérèse told a tale of an unusual inheritance, claiming that she saved the life of American millionaire Robert Crawford while

The scandal attracted the interest of the press across Europe. This image of the arrest in Madrid was published in the Italian newspaper *La Domenica del Corriere*.

on a train journey. As a reward, Crawford supposedly made Thérèse the beneficiary of his will, with a provision that the fortune be kept in a safe until her younger sister was old enough to marry one of Crawford's nephews. However, Robert Crawford did not exist and nor did the inheritance.

Using the fictional inheritance as collateral, Thérèse began to borrow money from rich friends.

See also: The Affair of the Diamond Necklace 64–65 ▪ Charles Ponzi 102–07 ▪ Bernie Madoff 116–21

She persuaded me to lend her my money, first a little, and then more, until all I have in the world has gone into her pockets.
Victim of Thérèse Humbert

While her husband may have been a dupe at first, he became her accomplice and the pair lived lavishly on the borrowed funds. The Humberts went on spending sprees, buying country mansions, a steam yacht, and fine clothing. In total, they borrowed 50 million francs ($265 million) on the promise of their mysterious fortune.

Dissatisfied with the sizable sums she appropriated, in 1893, Thérèse launched a fraudulent insurance company, Rent Viagere. The company targeted small businessmen with the promise of large returns on small investments. Thérèse and Frédéric went on to squander more than 40 million francs ($215 million), with old investors paid using the funds of new victims.

Borrowed time
Following Girard's suicide, French investigators began to look into the Humberts' financial affairs. But it was her creditors rather than the police who ultimately exposed the fraud. By the late 1890s, many of the people she had borrowed from joined forces and concluded that even her significant "inheritance" would not be sufficient to repay all of her extensive loans.

Her schemes finally unraveled in 1901, when one of her creditors sued her. A Parisian court judge ordered the safe opened, to reveal nothing but a brick and an English halfpenny. By then, Thérèse and her husband had fled the country. In December 1902, the couple were arrested in Madrid and extradited to Paris.

Both Thérèse and Frédéric were sentenced to five years' hard labor. Thérèse emigrated to the US and she died penniless in Chicago, Illinois, in 1918. ▪

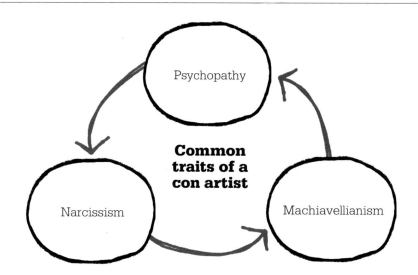

Common traits of a con artist

Psychopathy

Narcissism

Machiavellianism

The power of persuasion
Con artists use the power of persuasion to swindle their victims. After identifying a target, a fraudster will study them, researching their behavior and talking with them to determine weaknesses. The con artist will then guide them toward their scam, using flattery, fear, or the promise of wealth to gain the subject's trust and confidence. Typically, the lies are laced with enough truth to distract the victim and make the patter more believable. If the victim objects, the swindler may play on their emotions to gain sympathy. The goal is to lie, cheat, and fool people with empty promises.

Many successful con artists exhibit the same three traits—psychopathy, narcissism, and machiavellianism—known collectively as the "Dark Triad." These characteristics allow con artists to swindle people out of their money without the perpetrators feeling a sense of either remorse or guilt.

THE SMOOTHEST CON MAN THAT EVER LIVED
THE SALE OF THE EIFFEL TOWER, 1925

IN CONTEXT

LOCATION
Paris, France

THEME
Landmark scam

BEFORE
1901 William McCloundy, a con man from New Jersey, sells the Brooklyn Bridge to a foreign tourist and is jailed for grand larceny.

AFTER
1947 American con man George C. Parker "sells" New York public landmarks, including the Brooklyn Bridge, to wealthy foreign tourists multiple times.

2010 Penniless Yorkshire truck driver Anthony Lee attempts to sell the Ritz Hotel in London for £250 million (about $445 million today) and succeeds in obtaining a deposit of £1 million ($1.78 million) before he is caught by the police.

Victor Lustig was a specialist in tall tales, and none of them were taller than his plan to sell the Eiffel Tower for scrap metal.

Born in 1890 in the town of Hostinné, in what is now the Czech Republic, Lustig became fluent in several European languages and moved to France. He started his criminal career as a swindler preying on wealthy travelers on transatlantic ocean liners.

One of his lucrative scams involved a money-printing "invention," which he claimed printed perfect $100 bills. He convinced gullible victims that the device took several hours of "chemical processing" to print two $100 bills that he presented to the targets. In fact, they were simply real $100 bills that he had loaded into the machine without their knowledge.

Hugely impressed by the results, amazed victims bought his machines for as much as $30,000. It would take at least a few hours for victims to realize that they had been scammed—and when they did, Lustig was long gone.

Conning Capone

Although he was a talented and slick con man, Lustig would occasionally take significant risks, such as revisting the scene of his famous crime to try and sell the Eiffel Tower for a second time.

The audacity required for this remarkable scam pales in comparison to the nerve needed to swindle Al Capone in the late 1920s, but that is exactly what Lustig did. He convinced the Chicago crime boss to invest $50,000 to finance a stock deal, with the promise that he would double Capone's money. Unknown to Capone, Lustig placed the money in a safe deposit box and returned it two months later, apologizing that the deal he was banking on had fallen through. Full of admiration for Lustig's integrity, Capone rewarded him with $5,000. Lustig had shrewdly hoped for this outcome from the beginning, but had taken a huge risk when he tangled with Capone. This caper secured Lustig's reputation as one of the bravest con men in history.

See also: The Crawford Inheritance 66–67 ▪ Frank Abagnale 86–87

Victor Lustig was not only an extraordinary "salesman" and a charming, sophisticated operator; he also had a talent for evading capture.

Official business

Based in Paris in 1925, Lustig read a newspaper story about how the Eiffel Tower was rusting and required repairs. It was built for the 1889 Paris Exposition and was intended to be dismantled and moved to another location in 1909.

Sensing an opportunity, Lustig sent out letters on fake government stationery to five businessmen in which he claimed to be the Deputy Director General of the Ministry of Posts and Telegraphs. In the letters, he asked for a meeting at the Hotel de Crillon to discuss a business contract. Believing the opportunity to be genuine, the five men all met with a smartly dressed, courteous Lustig. He revealed that the government intended to sell the Eiffel Tower for scrap metal and would take bids for the right to demolish the tower. He flattered their egos by claiming that the five of them had been recommended based on their honest reputations.

Lustig had rented a limousine and invited the men for a tour of the tower. Lustig identified the most socially and financially insecure target, Andre Poisson, who desperately wanted to join the ranks of the Parisian business elite, and who felt that this was the right opportunity for him to do so.

The plan pays off

Poisson's wife became suspicious about the secret and hasty nature of their dealings, sowing seeds of doubt in her husband's mind. Lustig met with Poisson again and "came clean," confessing that he wanted to discreetly solicit a bribe for the contract, hence the clandestine behavior. Reassured, Poisson not only paid for the 7,000 tons of scrap iron but also gave the con man a bribe of $70,000.

Lustig correctly predicted that Poisson would be too humiliated to report the fraud. Six months later, Lustig attempted to repeat the scam but failed, narrowly avoiding arrest. Lustig later moved to the US to continue his criminal career. ▪

I cannot understand honest men. They lead desperate lives full of boredom.
Victor Lustig

Lustig's Ten Commandments for con men

> Be a patient listener

> Never look bored

> Wait for the other person to reveal their political opinions, then agree with them

> Wait for the other person to reveal their religious views, then agree with them

> Hint at intimate details but don't follow up unless the other person shows interest

> Never discuss illness unless a special concern is shown

> Never pry (they will tell you all eventually)

> Never boast, just let your importance be quietly obvious

> Never be untidy

> Never get drunk

DOMELA'S STORY RINGS WITH THE HIGH LUNACY OF GREAT FARCE

HARRY DOMELA, 1926

IN CONTEXT

LOCATION
Central Germany

THEME
Serial imposture

BEFORE
1817 Cobbler's daughter Mary Baker exposes upper-class vanities by passing herself off as Princess Caraboo from the fictitious island of Javasu.

1830 German swindler Karl Wilhelm Naundorff goes to his grave insisting that he is the rightful king of France, Prince Louis-Charles.

AFTER
2004 French-born impostor Christophe Rocancourt is jailed for five years following a long career spent conning investors out of their money. He used many aliases, even claiming to be a Gallic relative of the Rockefeller family.

One of the most notorious figures of the Roaring Twenties, trickster Harry Domela spent a lifetime pretending to be someone else. In 1918, the Freikorps—a private paramilitary group in which 15-year-old Domela was serving in his native Latvia—was called to Berlin to help stage a putsch. After the putsch failed, his unit was demobilized and Domela was left alone, adrift, and penniless. As a foreigner, he was denied a German passport and forbidden to work.

Domela decided to enter high society in a bid to improve his desperate circumstances. He assumed false identities, using

See also: Frank Abagnale 86–67 ▪ The Tichborne Claimant 177

Despite a humble background and an impoverished present, Harry Domela (far left) managed to convince Heidelberg's pro-monarchy elite that he was the kaiser's grandson (left).

aristocratic names and titles. In 1926, his life changed irrevocably when one of these acts of deception went awry. The story highlights Germany's obsession with royalty in that era, and the gullibility of the country's wealthy, privileged elite.

Charismatic chancer

When he was 20, Domela moved to Hamburg, where he made some money playing cards. He used it to visit the historic university city of Heidelberg where, adopting a confident air, he masqueraded for some weeks as Prince Lieven, lieutenant of the Fourth Reichswehr cavalry regiment, Potsdam. He became friendly with members of one of the exclusive, and snobbish, student societies, who immediately accepted him. He was entertained lavishly, wined and dined, and thoroughly enjoyed the experience.

However, Domela knew his deception might be uncovered at any time. Before that could happen, he moved on to the city of Erfurt. There, he selected one of the nicest

hotels, checked in as Baron Korff, and demanded one of their top suites. The hotel manager noticed that the new guest with the grand manners bore a striking resemblance to young Wilhelm of Hohenzollern, grandson of Kaiser Wilhelm, the last German emperor. The two men were around the same age and of a similar build and appearance. The hotel manager

speculated that the prince might be traveling incognito, using the pseudonym Baron Korff. The rumor started circulating around Erfurt. Although the monarchy had been abolished in 1918, many aristocratic Germans were still devoted to the deposed royal family, the Hohenzollerns. Domela insisted that he was not the prince, but he was happy to subtly sustain the illusion, especially as it meant he did not have to pay his hotel bill.

Domela made a trip to Berlin, but returned quickly to Erfurt when all the staff at his hotel addressed him as Your Majesty—word had spread. Then one day, during a visit by the mayor, he was asked to sign a book; he caved in and wrote "Wilhelm, Prince of Prussia." For the next few weeks, Domela fully embraced his new royal persona as the "son" of Crown Prince »

The Real Harry Domela

Harry Domela was born in 1904 or 1905 into a humble but respectable family in Kurland, a duchy ceded to the Russians in 1795 (now part of Latvia). His parents were part of the minority Baltic German population. Domela's father died soon after his birth; he later became estranged from his mother and lost his brother in World War I. At the age of 15, he joined the German volunteer corps that fought against the Latvians. He later lost his

citizenship, and joined thousands of other destitute people trying to survive in a shattered postwar Germany.

Despite having no papers, Domela managed to eke out a meager living, but soon became an unemployed wanderer. When a street contemporary drew his attention to the huge number of dispossessed aristocrats around—Germany's nobility had recently been stripped of their titles and status—Domela developed the skills and attributes necessary to pose as one himself.

A crowd gathers around Harry Domela at the Berlin cinema he opened in 1929 to show the film version of his memoirs. He later unsuccessfully sued the filmmakers of a rival adaptation.

Domela found legitimate success with his book: it sold about 120,000 copies. Two plays were made about his life, and Domela even played himself in one. He also sold the film rights, and starred in the resulting movie, *The False Prince* (1927).

In 1929, Domela set up a small cinema in Berlin. It opened with a showing of *The False Prince*. Ultimately, the cinema was not a success. As it lost Domela increasing amounts of money, the first act of his life came to an end. His economic situation, as well as the growing fascist mood in Berlin, led Domela to look for new opportunities. In 1933, he left Germany for the Netherlands, where he hid behind a new identity: Victor Szakja.

New beginnings
In Amsterdam, Domela often attended communist rallies in support of the Soviet Union. At one of these, he connected with Jef Last, a left-wing Dutch writer. Last introduced Domela to the French

Wilhelm and Crown Princess Cecilie. He was invited to other towns in the region, where the rich and titled vied to host dinners and hunting outings in his honor. When he walked the streets, ladies stopped to curtsy and gentlemen bowed, while members of the military saluted him in public. Although he accepted many gifts during his "tours," among them tickets to the opera in the royal box, Domela never asked for money. He relished the benefits of his grand deception, especially the full board and lodging, but soon felt disgusted by the fawning adulation that greeted him, particularly because the country was now a republic. He was aware, too, that he could not keep up the pretense indefinitely.

Changing fortunes
Early in 1927, the local press caught on to the story of the prince's visit to Heidelberg. Some commentators were critical of the attention being lavished on a former royal. Worried

that the reports would soon spread and expose him, Domela decided to travel to France and join the Foreign Legion. As he boarded the train, he was arrested by police.

For the next seven months, Domela was held in a prison in Cologne, Germany, awaiting trial for fraud. During his incarceration he wrote about his experiences in a book he titled *A Sham Prince: The Life and Adventures of Harry Domela as Written by Himself in Prison at Cologne, January to June 1927*. After he received his first advance from his publisher, he sent his "mother," Crown Princess Cecilie, a bouquet of flowers from prison with a touching note.

At his trial, the court ruled that while he had taken advantage of prominent members of society, his scheme had been mostly harmless and he was acquitted. Shortly after his release, he was even invited for tea by Crown Princess Cecilie after he appeared unannounced at her royal palace.

To Her Imperial Highness the Crown Princess Cecilie. I was honored to be taken for your son.
Harry Domela

author André Gide. The pair became close, staying up late to discuss Nietzsche and Hölderlin.

By 1936, the Nazi regime was taking control of Germany and, as a homosexual, returning to his adopted homeland was not an option for Domela. Instead, at the onset of the Spanish Civil War, he and Last, both committed antifascists, were accepted into a Spanish Republican regiment. In 1939, the Civil War ended, and Domela traveled to France. His life

Always fearful of being discovered and arrested—he had no passport or papers and was therefore considered stateless—Domela was an outsider who was constantly on the move.

followed a rootless cycle of left-wing agitation and imprisonment common to thousands of dispossessed antifascists across Europe at that time.

He was briefly detained in a prison camp by the Vichy France regime, until his friend André Gide used his influence to get him released. Domela then made his way to Belgium where, as an illegal alien, he depended on material support from friends, including Last and Gide. He returned to the south of France, where he was once again interned, and spent 18 months in prison. In 1942, he obtained a Mexican visa and left Europe.

Into obscurity

En route to South America, Domela was detained by the British in Jamaica as an illegal alien. He was imprisoned for a further two and a half years. On his release he made his way to Cuba, where he was involved in a car accident that left

When the Crown Prince and I heard about his exploits, we were convulsed with laughter. So I invited him to tea. A charming young man with excellent manners.
Crown Princess Cecilie

him with severe injuries. Soon afterward, beaten down by his run of bad luck, he attempted, unsuccessfully, to take his own life.

By the end of World War II, Domela had relocated to Venezuela, where he found work at a Coca-Cola factory. He disappeared into anonymity and resumed his solitary existence. In the 1960s, he finally found his calling as a teacher of art history in Maracaibo, while living under an assumed identity.

In 1966, after decades crisscrossing the globe under a series of aliases to avoid awkward questions about his status, Domela's identity was once again called into question. A Spanish colleague suspected Domela was one of the thousands of former Nazi party members who had escaped from Germany at the end of World War II and sought refuge in South America. Domela's old friend Jef Last was able to provide Domela's accuser with an affidavit about his true identity. This restored Domela's good name, but he still lost his position at the school.

It is believed Domela spent the rest of his days in hiding. He died, penniless, on October 4, 1979. ∎

Impersonating royalty

Throughout history, ambitious fraudsters have assumed the identities of kings, queens, princes, princesses, and other royals. Some of these charlatans impersonated real monarchs, living or dead, while others invented fraudulent titles and even fake countries. Their motivations vary from case to case. For some, the charade offered a chance to gain political power, make money, or simply realize a fantasy of living as a member of royalty.

One royal who has been impersonated numerous times is Russian princess Anastasia Romanov. In 1918, she and her family were killed by Bolshevik revolutionaries. As her body was buried in an unknown location, rumors persisted that she was still alive. Dozens of women have claimed to be Anastasia, while others have claimed to be her elder sisters Maria, Tatiana, and Olga. However, in 1991, DNA tests on bones found in woods near Yekaterinburg proved that the entire Romanov family was killed together.

IF MY WORK HANGS IN A MUSEUM LONG ENOUGH, IT BECOMES REAL

ELMYR DE HORY, 1946–68

IN CONTEXT

LOCATION
Europe and North and South America

THEME
Art forgery

BEFORE
1932–45 Dutch portraitist Han van Meegeren forges hundreds of paintings by famous artists, duping buyers out of more than $30 million.

AFTER
1978–88 British art forger Eric Hebborn sells hundreds of paintings, drawings, and sculptures; he later writes *The Art Forger's Handbook*, published shortly before his death in 1996.

1981–94 Dutch painter and art forger Geert Jan Jansen produces more than 1,600 forged artworks.

Elmyr de Hory's legendary 23-year career as an art forger began one afternoon in April 1946, when his wealthy friend Lady Malcolm Campbell, the widow of racing driver Sir Malcolm Campbell, visited his small art studio in Paris. Among de Hory's own Postimpressionist paintings, Campbell noticed an unsigned, unframed, abstract drawing of a young girl. Incorrectly identifying it as a work by Pablo Picasso, she asked if de Hory would sell it, and for $100 ($1,210 today), he agreed.

At the time of the sale of this fake "Picasso," de Hory was a 40-year-old classically trained artist who had found limited success

See also: Clifford Irving 88–89 ▪ Konrad Kujau 90–93

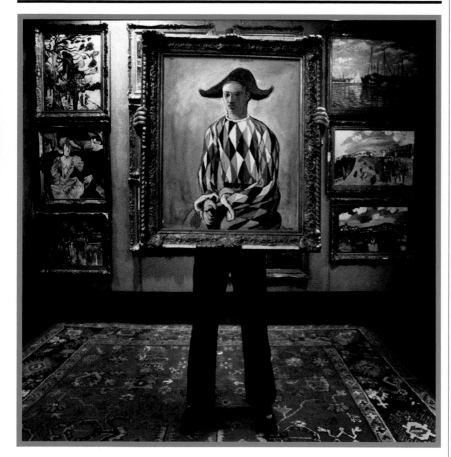

Identifying forgeries

The most common method of verifying art is through the documented history of the artwork's ownership. This can be forged, however, so art experts also deploy a range of other techniques.

An art historian may be called upon to assess the overall style and brushwork to see if they match the artist and time period. The colors in the painting are also analyzed, since not all paint colors have been available throughout history. This technique was famously used to expose a supposed 17th-century painting by Frans Hals as a fake, because it revealed that a collar was painted with zinc oxide, which was not available until 1728.

Scientists examine the surface the work is painted on to check if it has been artificially aged. Ultraviolet light and optical microscopes are used to determine if the fine cracks that naturally appear over time are genuine.

A technique called "X-ray diffraction" can detect whether a canvas has been used multiple times, which is often a hallmark of a genuine master artist.

selling nondescript paintings and portraits. He had traveled to Paris hoping to gain fame and fortune. There, however, he found that his Postimpressionist style was regarded as passé compared to the fashionable abstract expressionistic paintings then in vogue.

Following the unexpected sale of the bogus "Picasso" drawing, de Hory produced other "Picassos" and began to target art galleries. He claimed to be a Hungarian aristocrat displaced in the postwar diaspora, offering what remained from his family's art collection. De Hory's next victim—a gallery owner—bought three "Picasso" drawings for $400 ($3,940 today).

Even after de Hory was exposed as a forger, his paintings were still highly sought after, because of the quality of his work. This imitation Picasso was sold at Phillips auction house in 2000.

Partner in crime

Soon, de Hory joined forces with a man named Jacques Chamberlin, who became his art dealer, accomplice, and close friend. Together, the pair traveled all over Europe selling the forgeries. Although they were supposed to share the profits equally, Chamberlin actually kept most of the money. When de Hory discovered the deception, he ended the partnership. **»**

Elmyr de Hory's life was a series of ups and downs, with brief periods of fame and fortune punctuated by investigations by galleries and law enforcement agencies.

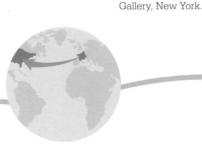

1949
Forges his first Modigliani and sells it to the Niveau Gallery, New York.

1952
Sells a "Matisse" to Harvard University's Fogg Art Museum with several "Modiglianis" and a "Renoir." The assistant director is suspicious and returns them.

1938
Arrested in Hungary as a political "undesirable" after its regime allies with Nazi Germany and imprisons artists and intellectuals.

1946
Sells a drawing to Lady Malcolm Campbell, which she mistakes for a Picasso.

1951
Sells a "Matisse" to Kansas City's Atkins Museum of Fine Arts and a "Picasso" to the William Rockhill Nelson Gallery of Art, also in Kansas City.

Briefly relocating to Rio de Janeiro, Brazil, de Hory lived off the sales of his fakes and also began painting his own works again. However, the paintings he created in his own style did not bring in the kind of money that he had become used to from selling forgeries.

In August 1947, de Hory moved to the US and used his charm to ingratiate himself with members of the American art world. Suddenly,

> Who would prefer a bad original to a good fake?
> **Elmyr de Hory**

he had the opportunity to sell his forgeries to hundreds of galleries. He also expanded his repertoire to include "works" by Matisse, Modigliani, and Renoir.

Safety first

De Hory took precautions to avoid the attention of the police. He remained discreet about his real profession and provided plausible reasons why he was selling art at discounted prices to art collectors and dealers. He was also careful never to sell his fakes to the general public—only to art insiders.

However, in 1955, one of de Hory's forgeries was exposed by art dealer Joseph Faulkner, who reported him to the FBI. Fearful of arrest, de Hory fled to Mexico. He was soon arrested—not for fraud, however, but as a murder suspect after an Englishman was found dead. De Hory spent the majority of his money paying off the police.

Dark days

De Hory returned to the US later that year, lying low in Los Angeles and trying to sell his own work, but he soon moved to New York. When no one was interested in his art, he sank into depression, and in 1959, at age 52, he attempted suicide.

A new friend, Fernand Legros, who had attended de Hory's housewarming party in New York, drove de Hory to Florida to recuperate. The pair soon ran out of money, so de Hory produced three lithographs and sent Legros out in one of de Hory's old suits to try and sell them. This proved to be a successful arrangement, and Legros soon persuaded de Hory to hire him as his art dealer for a 40 percent commission on each sale. And so began a partnership that would last for eight years.

De Hory and Legros moved to Ibiza, an autonomous territory of Spain, where they settled down in

1955
Investigated by the FBI and flees to Mexico with a falsified birth certificate; he is later arrested as a suspect in a murder investigation.

1959
Attempts suicide and travels to Florida with Fernand Legros to convalesce.

1969
Capitalizes on his celebrity status and tells his story to novelist Clifford Irving, who writes the biography *Fake!*

1957
Visits the Detroit Institute of Art and finds one of his "Matisse" paintings in the French collection.

1968
Arrested and imprisoned for two months in an Ibizan jail; he is banished and leaves for Portugal.

---

a beautiful house overlooking the Mediterranean. From Ibiza, they sold forged art to dealers around the world.

Doubts resurface

In 1964, the quality of de Hory's forgeries began to deteriorate. Art dealers and experts became suspicious and several gallery owners who had purchased de Hory's paintings alerted Interpol and the FBI.

By 1967, as more of de Hory's paintings were exposed as fakes, his forgery career came to an abrupt end. Legros sold 46 of de Hory's bogus masterpieces to Texas oil tycoon Algur Meadows between 1964 and 1966, but after discovering that the paintings were forgeries, Meadows contacted the police.

An international warrant was issued for Legros's arrest and he was detained in Switzerland.

De Hory went on the run, but returned to Ibiza in November 1967, in the belief that he was safe there.

Lasting legacy

However, the Spanish authorities began to investigate de Hory and charged him with a number of crimes, including homosexuality. He was imprisoned in Ibiza between August and October 1968, although he was treated well, and was permitted to have books, a deck chair, and wear his own clothes, among various other comforts. On his release from prison, de Hory was expelled from the island for a period of one year. De Hory moved to Portugal but eventually returned to Ibiza.

Meanwhile, the French police built a case against him and intended to extradite him for dealing in fake art. Aware that extradition was imminent, on December 11, 1976, de Hory took

his own life with an overdose of sleeping pills. The same year, Legros was extradited to France from Brazil, where he was hiding after failing to honor the conditions of a suspended sentence in Switzerland. In France, Legros was charged with forgery and fraud for defrauding Meadows. He was imprisoned for two years and died a pauper in 1983.

De Hory is renowned as history's greatest art forger, creating more than 1,000 works during his career. His remarkable story caught both the attention of author Clifford Irving, who wrote the successful biography *Fake* (1969), and Orson Welles, who made the documentary *F for Fake* (1973) about his life and work.

There are some art experts who believe that many of de Hory's forgeries have not yet been discovered and still hang in galleries around the world. ∎

IT'S NOT STEALING BECAUSE I'M ONLY TAKING WHAT THEY GIVE ME

DORIS PAYNE, 1952–2015

IN CONTEXT

LOCATION
US, France, UK, Greece, Switzerland

THEME
Jewel theft

BEFORE
1883–85 Sofia Ivanovna Blyuvshtein, a legendary Russian con artist, perpetrates numerous thefts from hotel rooms; she is eventually caught and sentenced to imprisonment with hard labor.

AFTER
1991 Yip Kai Foon commits five armed robberies of Hong Kong goldsmiths, making off with $2 million worth of jewels; he is arrested after a gun fight, during which he was shot in the back, in May 1996.

1993 A gang of international jewel thieves known as the Pink Panthers commit the first in a series of jewelry store robberies, stealing more than $500 million in gold and gems.

Doris Payne, an octogenarian with a criminal record dating back to 1952, did not plan a career as an international jewel thief. She wanted to be a ballerina. But at the age of 13, when she felt slighted by a white store owner after being allowed to try on a wristwatch, she went to leave the store, only realizing at the door that she was still wearing the watch. She gave it back, but this event showed her that she could get away with theft.

Doris Marie Payne was born on October 10, 1930, in a coal miner's camp in Slab Fork in southern West Virginia to an African American father and a Sioux mother. The youngest of six children, she was raised in segregated America, and quit high school to work at an assisted-living facility for the elderly. This was to be her only real job.

An accomplished thief

A single mother of two in her early twenties, in 1952 Doris Payne realized that she could support herself through stealing from high-end jewelry stores. She devised a clever *modus operandi* utilizing her natural charm and sleight of hand

Age 85, Doris Payne was arrested again in October 2015. She was caught on CCTV stealing a pair of $690 Christian Dior earrings from a Saks department store in Atlanta, Georgia.

in order to distract store clerks while she tried on a wide variety of expensive rings.

She put them on one finger, then another, and moved them about so much that the clerks eventually lost track of what she had tried on. All the while she kept asking questions about the cut, the clarity, or the number of carats to provide a further distraction.

Payne perfected her routine, presenting herself in a stately, refined manner, wearing elegant dresses, designer shoes, hoop earrings, and perfectly coiffed short

See also: Bill Mason 36 ▪ The Antwerp Diamond Heist 54–55 ▪ The Affair of the Diamond Necklace 64–65

hair. Her greatest gift was her ability to captivate an audience with her stories, which would encourage the victim to relax, and divert their attention away from the jewels they were selling.

A quick getaway

Payne read *Town & Country* magazine, perusing the jewelry advertisements for ideas of pieces to steal. She then traveled from Cleveland, Ohio, to a specific store to acquire the item she wanted. After performing her routine, she simply walked out of the store, telling the clerk that she would ponder the purchase over lunch, and leave wearing the jewelry.

The clerks invariably did not notice the thefts until some time later, allowing Payne enough time to get away, usually in a taxi. Payne then returned to Ohio to sell her takings to a fence—a person who knowingly buys stolen goods and sells them—based in Cleveland.

Prison time

Payne used 20 aliases and nine different passports to travel the world robbing jewelry stores. Her most famous heist was the 1974 theft of a 10.5-carat emerald-cut diamond worth $500,000 from Cartier in Monte Carlo, Monaco.

She extended her skillset to perfect the art of escaping custody. She performed this feat three times; from a guarded hotel room in Monte Carlo, from a Texas hospital after faking an illness, and lastly from a Paris jail. The longest time Payne served in prison was in Colorado, where she was detained for five years for stealing a $57,000 diamond ring in 1998 from a Neiman Marcus store. She fled Denver while still on parole. Payne was not always successful at escaping capture, however, and served a string of short jail terms.

Elderly offender

Payne was arrested in 2013, at age 83. She convinced store staff at a Palm Springs jeweler that she had received a $25,000 insurance payout and wanted to treat herself. She left wearing a diamond ring worth more than $22,000. A judge ordered her to serve several months in jail and, upon her release, to stay away from jewelry stores. She did not honor this order, however, and was rearrested in October 2015.

Payne was the subject of a 2014 documentary *The Life and Crimes of Doris Payne*, which portrayed her as a rebel who defied society's prejudices to find her own version of the American Dream. ▪

Enters store dressed as an elegant, **wealthy woman**

↓

Starts browsing for **diamond rings**

↓

Engages **clerk** in conversation and asks to see an assortment of items

↓

Uses **charm** to cause the clerk to forget how many items were **outside the case**

↓

Leaves the store wearing the jewelry

Career criminal

Few criminals are still going strong in their eighties, especially after a lucrative 60-year career during which they have become a celebrity.

Doris Payne recalls telling her father as a little girl that she wanted to travel the world, making little piles of salt and flour on areas of world maps she someday wanted to visit. Her chosen "career" certainly enabled that, taking her to France, the United Kingdom, Switzerland, and Greece.

At 75, Payne vowed to abandon her life of crime, but came out of retirement to steal a coat in 2010 and a diamond ring the following year.

Part of Payne's motivation is undoubtedly that theft has afforded her an extravagant lifestyle. However, Payne also appears to be motivated by the thrill of fooling store owners and the adrenalin rush associated with getting away with theft. The only regrets Payne has admitted to are the times she got caught. She does not appear to have any plans to retire.

THEY INFLATED THE RAFT AND LEFT THE ISLAND. AFTER THAT NOBODY SEEMS TO KNOW WHAT HAPPENED

ESCAPE FROM ALCATRAZ, JUNE 11, 1962

IN CONTEXT

LOCATION
San Francisco, California, US

THEME
Jailbreak

BEFORE
March 2, 1935 Six inmates escape the penal colony of French Guiana by boat; all but Parisian native René Belbenoît are later apprehended.

AFTER
June 10, 1977 James Earl Ray, imprisoned for the murder of civil rights leader Martin Luther King Jr., escapes the Brushy Mountain State Prison in Tennessee, along with six other inmates; they are all recaptured three days later.

September 25, 1983 Two Irish republican prisoners at Maze Prison in County Antrim, Northern Ireland, use smuggled guns to hold guards hostage and escape along with 36 other members of the IRA in the biggest prison break in British history.

May 31, 1984 Six inmates on death row at Mecklenburg Correctional Center in Virginia overpower guards, change into their uniforms, and bluff their way out of the prison in a van.

I n the late hours of June 11, 1962, three inmates at Alcatraz Federal Penitentiary entered criminal folklore by performing the seemingly impossible feat of breaking out of the maximum-security prison and making for the shore on an improvised inflatable raft. What became of the escapees is one of the most perplexing mysteries in American history.

The escape plan was years in the making and should have involved four inmates—brothers Clarence and John Anglin, Frank Morris, and Allen West—but only

I got back into the cell house and all the cons were hollering, 'They got away! They got away! They got away!'
**Darwin Coon,
Alcatraz inmate**

"The Rock" is a 47-acre (19 ha) island situated a daunting 1¼ miles (2 km) offshore. Its strategic position has made it ideal as a military base, and as a maximum-security prison.

three made it out of their cells. The trio scaled a 30-foot (9-m) wall and crossed a rooftop, before maneuvering down a 50-foot (15-m) pipe to the ground below. They also climbed two 12-foot (3½-m) barbed-wire perimeter fences. All of this they achieved while hauling a makeshift raft, which they inflated and launched into the icy waters.

Daunting task
Alcatraz was regarded as an escape-proof prison, with its unmatched security and isolated, inhospitable location surrounded by the cold waters and strong currents of San Francisco Bay. In its history as a federal prison, from 1934–63, only one inmate—John Paul Scott—is known to have made it off the island alive. In December 1962, six months after the fabled "Escape from Alcatraz", Scott scrambled through a storage room window under the kitchen and

See also: The Great Train Robbery 30–35 ▪ D.B. Cooper 38–43

The mugshots taken of Clarence Anglin (right), his brother John Anglin (center), and Frank Lee Morris (far right) upon their separate arrivals to Alcatraz in 1960 and 1961.

swam ashore. He was found by the Golden Gate Bridge—unconscious due to hypothermia—and was immediately recaptured.

In total, 36 inmates tried to break out of Alcatraz in 14 separate attempts. Of those, 23 were caught, six were shot dead, and two drowned. Five are listed as "presumed drowned:" the Anglin brothers, Morris, Theodore Cole, and Ralph Roe. Cole and Roe made it to the water on December 16, 1937, after filing through flat iron window bars, but they did so on a stormy night when the currents were particularly treacherous, reducing the likelihood that they reached the shore alive.

Exploiting a weakness
In December 1961, the Anglins, Morris, and West found themselves in adjacent cells and became friends. According to West, that same month he began to devise an escape plan after finding discarded saw blades in a corridor. Searching for a weak point in the rear wall of their cells, they discovered that the ventilation duct openings under the sinks could be loosened.

The quartet painstakingly chiseled away, taking turns to act as a lookout by using a periscope they had fashioned to spy on the guards. They used a variety of crude tools, including sharpened spoons and an improvised drill constructed from the motor of a broken vacuum cleaner to remove an entire section of each of their cell walls. They also made the most of the daily "music hour," the time prisoners were allowed to play instruments, which conveniently concealed the noise the four men made digging their tunnels.

The tunnels opened up into an unguarded utility corridor behind the cell tier. There they climbed up a shaft of steam pipes and ducts to the building's roof, where they cut away the ventilation fan. Hidden on the roof, the four men built a makeshift workshop for the next phase of the plot—escaping from the island.

Collecting for the cause
To conceal their nocturnal activities and continue unhindered, they sculpted dummy heads, using a cement powder mixture. These were decorated with flesh-colored paint from art kits and human hair collected from the prison barbershop floor.

The four men positioned the dummies on their pillows and stuffed clothing and towels under the bed covers to give the appearance of a body to avoid discovery during bed checks. »

The escapees

John and Clarence Anglin began robbing banks together in the 1950s. In 1956, they were arrested and sentenced to 15–20 years in federal prison. After failed escape attempts at different penitentiaries, they were transferred to Alcatraz: John arrived in late 1960, and Clarence in early 1961.

The brothers were housed on the same cellblock as convicted bank robber Frank Lee Morris. An orphan who was raised in foster homes, Morris began his life of crime at 13 and by his late teens had a long criminal record that included convictions for armed robbery.

While serving 10 years in the Louisiana State Penitentiary for bank robbery, Morris escaped. He was recaptured a year later in the act of committing a burglary, and was sent to Alcatraz in 1960. He possessed an exceptionally high IQ, and is often credited as the mastermind behind the escape—despite Allen West's claim to be the instigator of the audacious plan.

The five key components of the plan

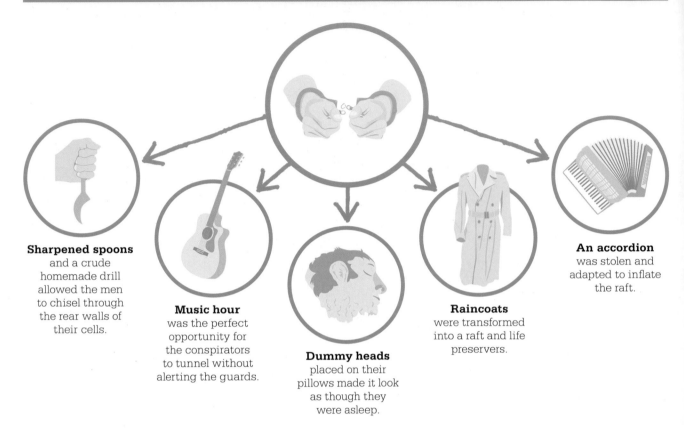

Sharpened spoons and a crude homemade drill allowed the men to chisel through the rear walls of their cells.

Music hour was the perfect opportunity for the conspirators to tunnel without alerting the guards.

Dummy heads placed on their pillows made it look as though they were asleep.

Raincoats were transformed into a raft and life preservers.

An accordion was stolen and adapted to inflate the raft.

In the darkness of the prison, it appeared they were sleeping. In their workshop, they assembled a variety of stolen objects, including more than 50 rubber raincoats, which the quartet used to create both a raft and life preservers. They stitched together the seams and sealed them with the heat from a steam pipe to make the devices watertight. They stole an accordion from a fellow inmate and repurposed it as a bellows to inflate the life raft, and they made crude wooden paddles.

Man down
Once their preparations were complete, the men chose to escape on the night of June 11, 1962.

However, there was a problem. The opening to West's tunnel had started to become visible, so he had patched it up with a makeshift cement mix. When it dried, the hole narrowed and West was unable to climb through. By the time he was able to widen the hole sufficiently, the others had left without him.

Meanwhile, the three men climbed out of the ventilation shaft onto the roof, inadvertently making a loud crash that alerted the guards—but as there were no further noises, the guards did not investigate. The trio scaled the barbed-wire fences and inflated their raft. Investigators later estimated that they left the island

at 10 p.m., and departed toward Angel Island, 2 miles (3 km) to the north. The following morning the ruse was uncovered when guards found the dummy heads. As word of the remarkable prison break spread around the jail, inmates began to chant "They got away! They got away!"

The manhunt begins
For the next 10 days, law enforcement agencies conducted an extensive air, sea, and land search. On June 14, the Coast Guard discovered a paddle, about 200 yards (180 m) off the southern shore of Angel Island. A boater also found a wallet wrapped in plastic containing photographs of the

An Alcatraz prison guard in the utility corridor holds a small section of the wall that one of the inmates chiseled free. From this corridor, the inmates could make it up to the roof of the cellblock.

Anglin family. On June 21, shreds of raincoat material, believed to be remnants of the raft, were recovered on the beach. The following day, a prison boat picked up a makeshift life preserver.

Neither human remains, nor any other physical evidence of the men's fate has ever been found. FBI investigators concluded that while it was theoretically possible for one or more of the inmates to have reached Angel Island, the water temperature and strong currents within the bay made it highly unlikely.

Once the escape was discovered, West cooperated with investigators on the proviso that he would be spared punishment for his part in the plot. He provided a detailed description of their intended escape, and told investigators that once they reached land the plan was to steal clothes and a car. The FBI investigated but determined that there were no vehicle thefts or

> I really do believe the boys made it out of here. I do believe the boys are alive today.
> **Marie Widner**

clothing-store burglaries in the days following the escape. This strengthened their belief that the three escapees had perished in the icy waters.

New leads

On December 31, 1979, after an investigation lasting 17 years, the FBI closed its file. Their official finding was that the prisoners most likely drowned in the cold waters of the bay while attempting to reach Angel Island. They turned the case over to the U.S. Marshal Service, who continued to investigate.

In October 2015, the Anglin family breathed new life into the case. They produced Christmas cards, which they claimed the Anglin brothers had sent to their mother in the three years following their escape. The handwriting was found to be a match but the date they were written could not be determined. The Anglin family also revealed a photograph purporting to show the brothers on a Brazilian farm in 1975. A forensic expert working on a subsequent *History Channel* investigation deemed it highly likely that the photograph shows the Anglins alive in 1975.

Declassified FBI documents also released in October 2015 revealed that FBI Director Edgar Hoover was told in 1965 that the Anglins could be hiding in Brazil, contrary to the agency's public line on the case. Secretly, Hoover ordered investigators to Brazil to search for them in 1965 but found no trace of the Anglin brothers. Whatever the truth may be of the escapees' fate, it seems this incredible case is far from over. ∎

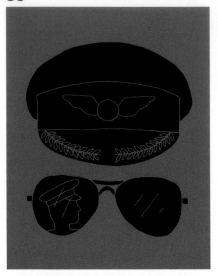

AT THE TIME, VIRTUE WAS NOT ONE OF MY VIRTUES
FRANK ABAGNALE, 1964–69

IN CONTEXT

LOCATION
New York, Utah, Louisiana, and Georgia, US

THEME
Imposter and check forger

BEFORE
1874 James Reavis, a master forger, uses false documents to claim land in central Arizona and western New Mexico, then sells the property deeds for over $5 million ($107 million today).

AFTER
1992 Michael Sabo, a master imposter and check forger from Pennsylvania, is convicted of bank fraud, forgery, grand larceny, and identity theft.

1998 John Ruffo, a former US bank executive, swindles multiple banking institutions out of $350 million; he is caught and sentenced to 17 years in prison, but disappears on the day he is due to start his jail term.

Just after learning that his parents were divorcing, 16-year-old Frank William Abagnale Jr. left home with a small bag of belongings, including a check book, and headed to New York's Grand Central Station. In the six years that followed, Abagnale became a legendary imposter, performing feats of con artistry that confounded FBI detectives.

Standing 6 feet (1.8 m) tall and passing as a twenty-something, Abagnale changed one digit on his driver's license to increase his age to 26 and took a job as a delivery boy. Frustrated with his income, he started writing checks that bounced. Police were already searching for him as a runaway, so Abagnale fled to Miami.

The "skywayman"
Passing a hotel in the city, Abagnale noticed a flight crew and was struck by an idea: he could pose as a pilot, travel the world, and never have a problem cashing checks. The next day, he called the Pan American World Airways office and asked for the purchasing department, claiming that the hotel

Redemption

Frank Abagnale demonstrates a pronounced and enduring need to atone for his crimes. He is still associated with the FBI 42 years after he was first assigned there as part of his conditional release, and he has refused to accept payment for government work he has performed. Abagnale has also turned down the offer of pardons from three different Presidents, insisting that "a paper won't excuse my actions, only my actions will."

Using his unique skillset for good, Abagnale has become a renowned expert on personal and corporate identity theft, fraud protection, and security. In 1976, Abagnale founded his own security company and his fraud prevention programs have been implemented by 14,000 corporations, law enforcement agencies, and financial institutions worldwide.

Abagnale became friends with Joseph Shea—the agent who led the investigation into him—and they remained close until Shea's death in 2005.

See also: The Sale of the Eiffel Tower 68–69 ▪ Clifford Irving 88–89

Since his release, Frank Abagnale has transformed from master con artist into one of the world's most respected authorities on fraud, forgery, and embezzlement.

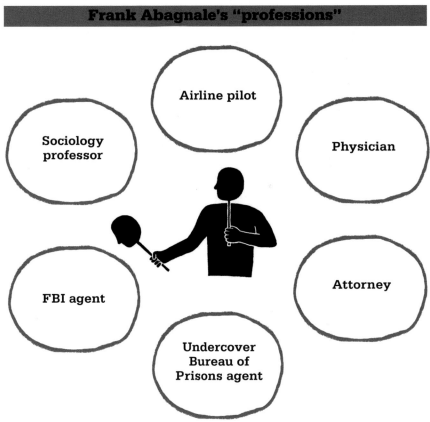

Frank Abagnale's "professions"

- Airline pilot
- Physician
- Sociology professor
- Attorney
- FBI agent
- Undercover Bureau of Prisons agent

he was staying at had lost his uniform. They directed him to their New York supplier, who fitted him for a new uniform.

Abagnale used adhesive stickers from a model Pan Am airplane to make a Pan Am pilot's license, and found that he could use it to travel the world for free, courtesy of an airline policy offering free rides to each other's pilots.

Career changes

After two years as a "pilot," he moved to Utah, changed his name to Frank Adams, forged a diploma, and was hired as a sociology professor at Brigham Young University for a semester. Next, despite never attending law school, Abagnale passed the Louisiana state bar exam on his third try. He was recruited as a legal assistant by the corporate law division of the Louisiana Attorney General's office. Abagnale left the job after a year when a lawyer started to question his credentials. He then passed himself off as a pediatrician in a Georgia hospital, working under the alias of Dr. Frank Williams. All the while, he passed fake checks and dummy bank deposit slips, effectively leaving a trail for the FBI to follow.

Flight risk

Abagnale was finally apprehended in 1969 in France. He was deported to the US, but escaped the aircraft and fled to Canada, where he was rearrested in Montreal. He then escaped again, posing as an undercover prison agent, and fled to Washington, D.C., where he narrowly evaded capture by impersonating an FBI agent. He was captured by chance when he walked past two NYPD detectives in an unmarked police car. Abagnale was sentenced to 12 years in prison, but four years into his term he was released on the condition he work for the FBI for the remainder of his sentence.

Abagnale later founded a security company advising banks on how to avoid and combat fraud. His 1980 biography, *Catch Me If You Can*, was filmed by Steven Spielberg and released in 2002. ■

I WAS ON A TRAIN OF LIES. I COULDN'T JUMP OFF
CLIFFORD IRVING, 1972

IN CONTEXT

LOCATION
New York City, US

THEME
Literary hoax

BEFORE
1844 *The New York Sun* reports that Irish balloonist Thomas Monck Mason has flown across the Atlantic Ocean, but it is revealed as a hoax perpetrated by Edgar Allan Poe.

AFTER
1998 Author William Boyd releases a biography of fictional American artist Nat Tate to jokingly hoax the New York art world, aided by David Bowie, who reads out passages of the book at the "launch party."

2015 Author Laura Harner's book *Coming Home Texas* is withdrawn from sale when it is revealed she has plagiarized a novel by *New York Times* bestselling author Becky McGraw.

A literary forgery made headlines in 1972 after author Clifford Irving convinced American publishing house McGraw-Hill that Howard Hughes, America's wealthiest and most elusive man, had invited Irving to write his biography.

Irving produced a letter he claimed was from Hughes, telling the publisher that he had contacted Irving to praise one of his books. He added that Hughes had sent him audiotapes and a manuscript. The author banked on the fact that Hughes, a recluse since 1958, would not want to draw the attention of the media or police and would do nothing to prevent the book's publication.

Sealing the deal
Editors at McGraw-Hill invited Clifford Irving to their New York offices and presented contracts for both Irving and Hughes to sign. The publishers offered a $100,000 ($566,000 today) advance for Irving and $400,000 ($2.3 million today) for Hughes. Before he turned in the manuscript, however, Irving renegotiated the total advance for the sum of $765,000 ($3.4 million today). Irving's friend and

Howard Hughes became hugely successful in his 1930s but was plagued by psychological problems in later life.

collaborator, children's author Richard Suskind, forged Hughes's signature on the contract, and McGraw-Hill did not question it.

The publishers sent Irving the checks for Irving and Hughes's respective advances. Irving's then-wife Edith deposited the checks made out to H.R. Hughes in a Swiss bank account that she had recently opened under the name "Helga R. Hughes."

See also: The Affair of the Diamond Necklace 64–65 ▪ The Sale of the Eiffel Tower 68–69 ▪ Elmyr de Hory 74–77

Irving's hoax worked because the base on which he built was largely genuine.
***Time* magazine**

Two lucky breaks

In the course of their research, Irving and Suskind were shown an unfinished manuscript about Hughes's former business manager, written by author James Phelan. Phelan was not aware that Irving had been given the manuscript, large parts of which Irving plundered and claimed as his own.

In late 1971, Irving delivered a completed manuscript to his editors at McGraw-Hill, and they made plans to publish the following year. Learning this, Hughes's attorneys intervened, expressing doubts to Irving's publisher as to the autobiography's authenticity. McGraw-Hill continued to back Irving after a handwriting firm inspected writing samples, and declared them to be authentic.

The gamble backfires

Hughes finally came out of seclusion two months before the book's planned release in March 1972 to hold a telephone press conference with reporters. He denounced the book as a fake and McGraw-Hill rescinded its contract. *Time* magazine, in a February 1972 issue, named Irving "Con Man of the Year."

The police investigated Irving, and a grand jury convened to consider charges of mail fraud, perjury, and forgery. He was indicted with "conspiracy to defraud through use of the mails" but instead of going to trial, he pleaded guilty, was fined $10,000, ordered to refund his publisher $765,000, and sentenced to 30 months in a federal penitentiary. Irving filed for bankruptcy the same year. Edith was sentenced to two months' imprisonment and Suskind was given six months in jail for larceny and conspiracy.

Irving's remarkable story was published in 1977, and a major film adaptation followed in 2006. ▪

Irving with the typewriter used to write the Hughes manuscript. His story was adapted into the film *Hoax* (1981); Irving was hired as an adviser but disliked the end product, and asked for his name to be cut from the credits.

Edith Irving played a crucial role in the hoax, and effected a disguise to conceal her identity when depositing Hughes's checks into the new bank account she opened.

The art of the hoax

Hoaxers often go to great lengths to make a scam appear plausible. Clifford Irving did not simply make up the interviews with Hughes in the book, he acted them out with Suskind, with Irving playing Hughes and Suskind playing Irving.

The material that Irving had lifted from author James Phelan appeared plausible because it was genuine, based on real experiences with someone who knew Hughes well. This combined with Irving's undeniable literary skill—he had enjoyed success in 1969 with his biography of art forger Elmyr de Hory (see pp. 74–77)—to make the book a compelling read. The timing of the book was also perfect, because there was an international appetite to learn the truth about the eccentric, reclusive billionaire.

Irving later admitted his secret: he was taken in by his own lies. The only thing he misjudged was Hughes himself, who, contrary to Irving's prediction, finally broke his silence to decry Irving.

ORIGINALLY I COPIED HITLER'S LIFE OUT OF BOOKS, BUT LATER I BEGAN TO FEEL I WAS HITLER

KONRAD KUJAU, 1978–84

IN CONTEXT

LOCATION
Stuttgart, Germany

THEME
Document forgery

BEFORE
April 2, 1796 A forger named William Henry Ireland sells a play he claims to be a lost work of William Shakespeare.

AFTER
January 23, 1987 American forger Mark Hofmann is sentenced to life in prison after he pleads guilty to forging Mormon historical documents and murdering two witnesses.

February 2007 Italian senator Marcello Dell'Urti claims to have located fascist leader Benito Mussolini's diaries from 1935–39; they are later exposed as forgeries by Italian historians.

Working surreptitiously out of the backroom of his shop in Stuttgart, Germany, Konrad Kujau handwrote lengthy journal entries in old German Gothic script, filling the pages of plain black notebooks.

On completing each book, he poured tea over it and bashed the pages together to give them a worn, tattered appearance. Finally, he adorned the notebook with a red wax seal in the form of an Imperial eagle, a black ribbon from a genuine Nazi document, and gold lettering using Gothic script. After toiling away nearly every day for three years, Kujau had crafted 61 volumes of journals purportedly

See also: Elmyr de Hory 74–77 ▪ Clifford Irving 88–89

written by Nazi dictator Adolf Hitler. One of history's most infamous forgeries, they became known as the Hitler Diaries.

Forging a career
Raised in a poor family in Germany, Kujau had long been fascinated with the Nazi regime. He began his career in forgery as a teenager, selling fake autographs of East German politicians.

In 1967, he opened a shop in Stuttgart, forging and selling Nazi paraphernalia. Kujau's creations included an introduction to a sequel to Hitler's autobiography *Mein Kampf*, as well as the beginnings of an opera and poems supposedly written by him.

Kujau might have remained a petty criminal and amateur forger had it not been for a reporter from the German investigative news magazine *Stern*. Just as Gerd Heidemann's career reached an impasse after more than 20 years on the magazine, his interest in

Konrad Kujau brandishes one of the Hitler Diaries at the start of his trial in Hamburg in 1984.

Hitler and the Third Reich, which included a collection of Nazi memorabilia, led him to Kujau.

Putting pen to paper
In 1978, after weeks spent practicing Hitler's handwriting, Kujau penned the first diary entry, drawing on historical documents, newspapers, medical records, and books. He used cheap notebooks purchased in Berlin and a mixture of blue and black ink diluted with water, so that it flowed easily from his modern pen. Another major error that no one noticed at the time was made when Kujau attached Hitler's initials to the front of the book. He accidentally used an "F" instead of an "A" because both letters looked very similar in Gothic script.

That same year, Kujau sold the first Hitler Diary entitled *Political and Private Notes from January to June 1935* to a collector. He »

> I regret that the normal method of historical verification has been sacrificed to the perhaps necessary requirements of a journalistic scoop.
> **Hugh Trevor-Roper**

Authenticating historic documents
Every historical manuscript is unique, whether a letter, diary, or handwritten item. To determine authenticity and authorship of undated historical documents, forensic investigators conduct historical, scientific, and stylistic analysis. These experts can examine the method of printing, the address, and the mail stamp to determine the era in which it was created.

Many forgeries are uncovered by identifying the presence of material that did not exist at the time. Scientific analysis of the paper used can be especially revealing, and investigators use a number of tools at their disposal, from magnification to molecular spectroscopy, which highlights how much of the ink has decayed over time and provides clues as to when a document was written.

Examining the ink used to write a historic document can also determine what kind of tool—typically a pen, a quill, or a pencil—was used, which may reveal more information about the time period in which it was written.

made up a fantastic yet plausible tale about how the diaries had been recovered from a Nazi plane crash in 1945 and hidden away for decades in a barn.

Making a deal

At the end of 1979, news of the diary began to filter through to collectors of Hitler memorabilia. Desperate for a journalistic scoop, Heidemann tracked down Kujau, who told him there were more volumes hidden in East Germany. Heidemann took the news to *Stern*, whose publishers provided him with the money to purchase them.

Heidemann promised Kujau 2.5 million deutsche marks (about $2 million today) for the "rest" of the diaries. The forger set to work, producing 60 more volumes. By the end of February 1981, *Stern* had spent nearly 1 million marks ($775,000) on the diaries. Less than half had gone to Kujau: Heidemann kept the rest, duping both the newspaper and the forger. After the delivery of 12 diaries, Heidemann claimed the price had risen, telling *Stern* that it had become harder to smuggle them out of East Germany.

The last volume of the Hitler Diaries, complete with Kujau's authentication, was sold at Berlin auction house Jeschke, Greve, and Hauff for €6,500 ($8,250) in 2004.

Heidemann continued to purchase the diaries throughout 1981, periodically telling *Stern* of price increases. Ultimately, Heidemann would collect 9.3 million marks ($7.2 million) from *Stern*, of which Kujau received less than a third. The journalist lived lavishly off the proceeds, buying an apartment, expensive cars, and more Nazi memorabilia from Kujau.

In April 1982, *Stern*'s management asked handwriting experts to verify the diaries, providing them with samples of Hitler's writing. Unbeknownst to the experts, the samples were from Heidemann's collection of Nazi memorabilia and had also been forged by Kujau. The experts declared the journals to be genuine. The first historian to examine the diaries, Professor Hugh Trevor-Roper, proclaimed them authentic, bolstering the confidence of *Stern*'s management, but later tarnishing the historian's reputation.

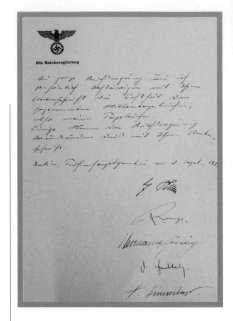

In late April 1983, *Stern* broke the story of the existence of the diaries, triggering a flurry of headlines around the world. The diaries, it said, revealed that Hitler's Final Solution was to deport the Jewish people, not annihilate them, which led some commentators to say the history of the Third Reich would have to be rewritten.

Suspicions surface

However, the banality of some of the entries caused more skeptical historians to denounce the documents as forgeries. When suspicions about their authenticity grew, *Stern* commissioned forensic experts from Germany's Bundesarchiv (Federal Archive) to analyze the diaries.

Meanwhile, *Stern*'s April 28 issue gave the public its first glimpse of the diaries. The following day, Heidemann met with Kujau and bought the last four volumes. Within a week, *Stern* management learned that the forensic experts had determined conclusively that the diaries were

Konrad Kujau

Born in poor circumstances in 1938 in Löbau, Germany, Konrad Kujau was one of five children. In 1933, his parents joined the Nazi Party and Kujau grew up idolizing Adolf Hitler, a fixation that continued after Hitler's suicide and the defeat of Nazi Germany in World War II.

By the 1960s, Kujau was a petty criminal with a record for forgery, theft, and fighting in bars. In 1970, while visiting family in East Germany, he found that many people there owned Nazi memorabilia, in spite of laws prohibiting this. Seeing an opportunity, Kujau bought Nazi items on the black market and took them back to West Germany to sell.

By 1974, Kujau had amassed such a collection of Nazi memorabilia at his home that his wife Edith asked him to move it, so he rented a shop in Stuttgart to store and sell it. It was then that he started to increase the value of his items by adding details. He gradually became more ambitious and began to forge Hitler's manuscripts.

fakes. The journals were made with postwar ink, paper, glue, and binding. Ultraviolet light showed a fluorescent element in the paper that did not exist in 1945. The bindings of one of the diaries included polyester, a fiber that was not created until 1953.

Before *Stern* could make their own announcement on the findings, the German government stepped in and declared that the diaries were clear forgeries. *Stern*'s management demanded Heidemann reveal the name of his source, which he did.

The downfall

By then, Kujau and his wife had fled to Austria. Upon learning that Heidemann had double-crossed him, the forger turned himself in to the police. Bitter that Heidemann had kept so much of the money, he claimed the journalist had known the diaries were fake.

On August 21, 1984, Heidemann and Kujau stood trial for defrauding *Stern* out of 9.3 million marks ($7.2 million). Both men blamed each other during the trial. In July 1985, Heidemann was sentenced to four years and eight months and Kujau to four years and six months.

When Kujau was released from jail in 1987, he embraced infamy. He found a market painting and selling copies of famous artworks and became a minor celebrity on TV, until he died of cancer in 2000 at age 62. Heidemann was also released from prison in 1987 but never worked as a journalist again. The scandal was hugely detrimental for *Stern*. The once-lauded magazine was disgraced for irresponsible journalism. ∎

A talented painter, after his release, Kujau began creating works in the style of other artists, selling them as "genuine Kujau fakes."

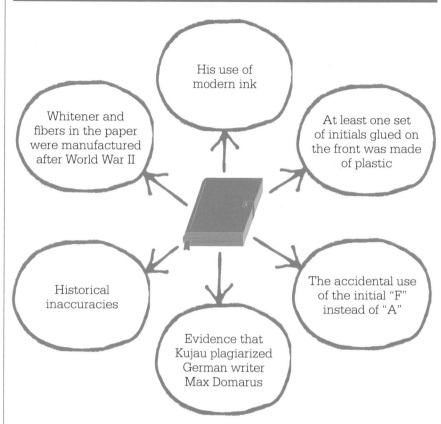

Six clues that the diaries were forged

- His use of modern ink
- Whitener and fibers in the paper were manufactured after World War II
- At least one set of initials glued on the front was made of plastic
- Historical inaccuracies
- Evidence that Kujau plagiarized German writer Max Domarus
- The accidental use of the initial "F" instead of "A"

IF THIS IS NOT A RING-IN I'M NOT HERE

THE FINE COTTON SCANDAL, AUGUST 18, 1984

IN CONTEXT

LOCATION
Brisbane, Queensland, Australia

THEME
Betting scam

BEFORE
1844 The Epsom Derby, reserved for three-year-old horses, is won by four-year-old Maccabeus, disguised as Running Rein; the culprit, Levi Goldman, escapes to France.

July 16, 1953 Two French horses with identical markings are swapped at Spa Spelling Stakes in Bath, England. The four men involved are given sentences varying from nine months to three years.

AFTER
March 1, 2007 Australian racing jockey Chris Munce is convicted of taking bribes in exchange for racing tips and sentenced to 20 months in jail.

The evening before the Commerce Novice Handicap race, held at Brisbane's Eagle Farm racetrack on August 18, 1984, horse trainer Hayden Haitana and businessman John Gillespie applied white paint and brown hair dye to a champion seven-year-old horse. Not being a novice, the champion horse was ineligible for entry into the race, but Haitana, Gillespie, and other members of a syndicate including businessman Robert North planned to substitute their champion horse for an eligible runner, an illegal practice called a "ring-in."

Racing under the name Fine Cotton, the substitute horse started the race slowly but quickly picked up pace, galloping swiftly around the corner, and edging out early favorite Harbour Gold at the finishing post. However, as soon as the race ended, track stewards noticed white paint dripping from Fine Cotton's legs, exposing the illegal substitution. Less than half an hour after the horse crossed the finish line, he was disqualified and all bets were lost.

Emergency substitute
Fine Cotton's race lasted less than 90 seconds, but the entire plot began months earlier. Prison cell mates John Gillespie—who had a history of illegal horse gambling—and a relative of Haitana's passed their time discussing a possible ring-in scam. After his release, Gillespie purchased a fast galloper from Sydney, Australia, named Dashing Solitaire for $10,000 ($22,800 today). He then scoured

Hayden Haitana pictured with the real Fine Cotton. Haitana was prohibited from the sport for life for his part in the betting scam, but his ban was lifted in 2013.

See also: The Tichborne Claimant 177

The ring-in horse "Fine Cotton" is shown on the left, just beating the favorite to the finishing post.

I thought they were booing me because my ride was a roughie and I must've beaten the favorite.
Gus Philpot

racetracks for a slower look-alike. He chose the out-of-form Fine Cotton, which he purchased for $2,000 ($4,560 today), and hired Hayden Haitana as its trainer.

Days before the race, the syndicate suffered a catastrophic setback when Dashing Solitaire was injured. By this point, Gillespie had invested heavily in the scheme and was desperate for a payoff. So he paid $20,000 (4¢56,000 today)—with a check that later bounced—for the horse Bold Personality. There was one snag: he looked nothing like Fine Cotton. Bold Personality was lighter in color and had a white marking on his forehead. So, the night before the race, Gillespie and Haitana surreptitiously applied hair dye and paint to make him appear more like Fine Cotton.

Short odds
When "Fine Cotton" stepped onto the racetrack, betting escalated at a suspicious pace. The horse started with odds of 33-1, but they soon changed dramatically to 7-2. After "Fine Cotton" narrowly won, officials quickly spotted evidence of the ring-in and the horse was disqualified. Police began a manhunt for the culprits, but by then Haitana had fled. He was soon apprehended, however, jailed for six months, and banned from the racetrack for life. Six others, including Gillespie, were also banned. The horse's innocent jockey, Gus Philpot, was cleared.

The ring-in became one of the most notorious scams in the history of the sport. To combat similar plots, racehorses are now identified through microchips. ∎

Cheating in the "Sport of Kings"

A ring-in is not the only method cheaters use to make money illegally on the horse track.

Probably the best-known scam is to engineer betting odds by strategically placing large bets. Bookmakers now closely monitor betting patterns to identify any suspicious activity. Other tricksters have gone so far as to create fake winning tickets, but technological improvements now make it difficult for such crude practices to succeed.

Most of the cheating occurs on the other side of the rail, with unscrupulous trainers, jockeys, owners, and veterinarians attempting to alter races through collusion or by drugging horses with steroids and pain medication. Regular drug testing has made this more difficult, however. Crooked trainers and jockeys have also been known to use "buzzers," illegal devices that give the horses electric shocks and force them to run faster.

WHITE C
CRIMES

OLLAR

In France, the plunge in the value of the Mississippi Company, which is restructuring France's national debt, causes a **major financial crash**.

1720

In the US, the collapse of a **fraudulent investment scheme** set up by Charles Ponzi collapses, loses hundreds of investors' savings.

1920

In India, chemicals from the US-owned Union Carbide factory in Bhopal kill thousands, leading to accusations of **culpable homicide** against the company's CEO.

1984

1869

Speculators James Fisk and Jay Gould **manipulate the US gold market**, which endangers the economy.

1921–22

In the Teapot Dome scandal, US Secretary of the Interior Albert Bacon Fall **leases oil reserves in exchange for bribes**.

1990

In London, thieves **rob money broker messenger** John Goddard at knifepoint and seize £292 million (about $355 million today) in bonds.

White collar crime is fundamentally different from other types of illegal activity. The accountant who clandestinely siphons money from an employer, then cooks the books to conceal his activities, is often a skilled professional in a position of trust within a company. Invariably, financially motivated, white collar crime includes all kinds of fraud, insider trading, and embezzlement.

White collar crime often takes months or even years to uncover. If a member of the public witnesses murder, theft, or extortion—categorized by criminologists as "blue collar" crimes because they generally involve physical effort, often for low rewards—they would immediately recognize that a crime is taking place. However, a person tapping away at computer keys raises no alarm at all, because it does not fit society's stereotype of a criminal.

White collar crime is also hard to detect because it is often complex and difficult to understand. Without specialized knowledge, even a seasoned investigator is unlikely to notice anything untoward. It is difficult to even estimate the extent of white collar crime. For this reason, it may be far more prevalent than its blue collar counterpart.

Impact on society

From an economic standpoint, white collar crime can be devastating, on an individual, corporate, and even national level. The financial damage inflicted by the fraudster Bernie Madoff affected US citizens from all walks of life. More importantly, the impact of economic ruin can often run far deeper than the simple loss of money. According to research conducted by Oxford University, after the financial crash of 2008—which was partly precipitated and significantly worsened by mortgage fraud, investment scams, bribery, and unethical business practices—an estimated 10,000 Americans and Europeans committed suicide. The US economy and those of many European nations are still struggling to recover. Criminal psychologist Dr. Robert Hare, developer of the diagnostic tool known as the Psychopathic Checklist, once said that he should have conducted his research on Wall Street rather than in prisons. When asked about the relative impact of serial killers, he replied

US energy company Enron is exposed for a massive and **systematic accounting fraud**.

2001

US authorities fine German engineering giant Siemens for using **bribery to win overseas contracts**.

2008

Russian **malware developer** Aleksandr Panin is arrested for hacking millions of online bank accounts.

2013

2007–08

In France, **rogue trader** Jérôme Kerviel makes a number of unauthorized trades at Société Genérale and nearly brings down the bank.

2008

Wall Street investment advisor Bernie Madoff's Ponzi scheme collapses and **bankrupts thousands of people**.

2015

The US Environmental Protection Agency **uncovers emissions fraud** by the German car maker Volkswagen.

---

that serial killers devastate families, while white collar criminals destroy societies. Nonetheless, punishment for white collar crime tends to be more lenient than for violent crimes.

Apportioning blame

Criminologists identify two broad categories of white collar crime: "individual" and "corporate"—also known as "structural"—crime.

Individual white collar crime occurs when a person or persons working within a political or private organization exploits their position without the knowledge of the institution, and profits through their illegal activities. They may be in league with other members of the organization, or suppliers, or clients, but it is a small minority of employees that are corrupt rather

than the entire organization. The case of Albert Bacon Fall—who in 1922 was convicted of conspiracy and bribery while working as US Secretary of the Interior in what became known as the Teapot Dome scandal—typifies this behavior.

More troubling are corporate crimes such as the Enron scandal, Siemens scandal, and the Bhopal Disaster. Here, criminality is located, motivated, and enacted at an organizational level.

In cases like these, individuals may benefit from the wrongdoings of their company, but they are players in a larger conspiracy. Criminal activity is initiated or condoned at an executive level, often after a cost-benefit analysis. For example, if savings from illegal activities outweigh the cost of the possible fines, then breaking the

law can be perceived by some unscrupulous executives as a perfectly rational business decision.

In a situation when virtually everybody in the company is complicit in either illegal activity or a conspiracy of silence, it becomes extremely difficult to establish individual culpability beyond reasonable doubt, especially when the company employs accomplished defense attorneys.

In cases such as Jérôme Kerviel's, the official narrative of a lone wolf operating within an otherwise law-abiding company has been met with outright skepticism from many quarters. Critics argue that others higher up in the organization simply *had* to know, believing that not being aware of such systemic crimes would be functionally impossible. ∎

MONEY... HAS OFTEN BEEN A CAUSE OF THE DELUSION OF MULTITUDES
THE MISSISSIPPI SCHEME, 1716–20

IN CONTEXT

LOCATION
France

THEME
Financial bubble

BEFORE
1630s At the height of "tulip mania" in the Dutch Republic, speculators trade tulip bulbs for huge sums of money, until the market folds overnight.

1720 The British South Sea Company, which trades with Spanish America, takes over Britain's national debt. But it, and its shares, collapse, and thousands of people of all classes are ruined.

AFTER
1849 William Thompson commits a series of scams on strangers in the streets of New York City. His exploits lead a newspaper journalist to coin the term "Confidence Man," or "con man" for short.

In 1705, Scottish economist John Law proposed major reforms to the Scottish banking system designed to reduce public debt and stimulate the economy. These included the use of paper currency as money instead of gold. Law's theory was rejected, but in 1716, the Duke of Orléans, regent for the young King Louis XV, invited him to try it in France, which was near bankruptcy.

Law founded a national bank that accepted gold and silver deposits and issued banknotes in return. In 1717, he created a company with exclusive rights to develop France's US territories in the Mississippi River valley; by 1719, the company controlled all of the country's colonial trade.

He then undertook a radical restructuring of France's debt. He devised the "Mississippi Scheme," selling shares in his company, the value of which he had greatly exaggerated, in exchange for state-issued public securities. Investors flocked to buy shares, and their price rose sharply: issued at 500

There are good reasons to think that the nature of money is not yet rightly understood.
John Law

livres tournois each, a year later, they were worth 20 times as much. The value of the securities grew too. The scheme led to wild speculation, and stock markets across Europe boomed. The French authorities responded by printing money, but this caused rampant inflation and a loss in the value of currency and securities. In 1720, the value of the Mississippi stock plunged, causing a major financial crash. Law fled to Venice, where he died in poverty nine years later. ∎

See also: Charles Ponzi 102–07 ∎ Bernie Madoff 116–21

NOTHING IS LOST SAVE HONOR

BLACK FRIDAY GOLD SCANDAL, 1869

IN CONTEXT

LOCATION
New York City, US

THEME
Stock market manipulation

BEFORE
1792 In the fledgling United States, Assistant Secretary of the Treasury William Duer engages in speculation to drive up securities prices, leading to the "Panic of 1972," a national credit crisis.

AFTER
1986 Wall Street trader Ivan Boesky confesses to a US court that he acquired his $200 million personal fortune through illegal market manipulation and insider trading deals.

1992 Harshad Mehta uses forged bank receipts as a guarantee for loans of $740 million on the Bombay Stock Exchange. In an attempt to avoid prosecution, he then bribes politicians.

In late 19th-century America, the financial markets were unregulated, and some people known as "robber barons" engaged in shady practices to build huge fortunes. In 1869, financiers James Fisk and Jay Gould secretly stockpiled vast amounts of gold in a bid to corner the market. They planned to drive up the price, then sell for enormous profits. But they faced an obstacle. During the Civil War (1861–65), the Union government issued huge quantities of banknotes without the gold reserves to back them up. In 1869 Ulysses S. Grant's government provided the gold to effectively buy back the money. In so doing, the Treasury set the value of gold: when it sold its reserves, the price dropped; when it held on to them, the price rose. If speculators tried to manipulate the gold market, the government could do the same.

Fisk and Gould had to ensure government gold was kept off the market, which they did through political influence and bribery. They bought up gold, and the price soared. But Grant became aware of the plan, and so released $4 million ($72 million today) of Treasury gold. On September 24, 1869 (later called Black Friday), the inflated gold price dropped, and the market crashed. Meanwhile, Gould had secretly sold his gold, before the price fell. ■

James Fisk, unlike Jay Gould, did not sell his gold before the prices fell on Black Friday, and lost a significant portion of his investment.

See also: Charles Ponzi 102–107 ▪ Jérôme Kerviel 124–25

THE OLD GAME OF ROBBING PETER TO PAY PAUL

CHARLES PONZI, 1903–20

IN CONTEXT

LOCATION
Boston, Massachusetts, US

THEME
Ponzi scheme

BEFORE
1899 William "520 Percent" Miller runs a pyramid scheme in Brooklyn, New York, swindling investors out of $1 million with the promise of 10 percent interest per week.

1910 A man calling himself Lucien Rivier sets up a private bank in Paris and defrauds 6,000 investors of around 2 million francs (about $9 million today).

AFTER
2010 A whistle-blowing employee brings down Minnesota businessman Tom Petters's $3.65 billion scheme.

1991–2009 Texan Allen Stanford runs a $7 billion, 20-year scheme through his Antigua-based bank.

Charles Ponzi smiles for a police mugshot following his arrest for forgery in Montreal, Canada, in 1909. At the time, Ponzi went by one of his many aliases, Charles P. Bianchi.

I n July 1920, Charles Ponzi's grand financial scheme was collapsing. As the authorities tracked his every move, panicked investors crowded outside his Boston office demanding their money back. The details of his scam were splashed over the front pages of the Boston newspapers.

Confident and charming as ever, Ponzi seemed unfazed. Dressed in a designer suit, he faced the horde of angry investors with a smile. For the next three days, Ponzi placated the crowd, handing out more than $2 million ($23.7 million today) in cash. As well as these stacks of bills, he passed out coffee and donuts, smoothly convincing investors that they had no reason to worry. However, Ponzi's brazen display attracted the attention of the US Attorney for the District of Massachusetts. An audit was commissioned on Ponzi's finances, which unraveled one of the most notorious scams in US history.

A keen entrepreneur

Unlike some of his fraudster successors, Ponzi did not appear to start out with nefarious intentions. In 1903, at the age of 21, the Italian immigrant arrived in Boston with just $2.50 ($70 today) in his pocket.

Although he was broke, Ponzi had an enduring entrepreneurial spirit, and longed to make a name for himself. He picked up English quickly and traveled around the East Coast of America taking a number of temporary jobs, including working as a waiter and translator. Ponzi moved to Montreal in 1907, where he got a job at the Bank Zarossi and worked his way up to become a manager.

Early crimes

The bank he worked at failed, leaving Ponzi feeling desperate. He forged a check hoping to raise enough funds to return to the US, but was caught, and spent three years in a bleak prison facility on the outskirts of Montreal. Upon his release, he returned to the US, only to spend two years in an Atlanta prison for smuggling Italian immigrants into the country. Whether it was due to his circumstances or his character, being a crook soon became second nature to Ponzi.

After his release, Ponzi returned to Boston. He met a stenographer, Rose Maria Gnecco, and they married in 1918. For the next few months, Ponzi worked a variety of jobs, including one for his father-in-law, while all the time dreaming up ideas for businesses.

He hoped to make it big with a new venture, a trade magazine, but by 1919 this too seemed doomed to failure. Faced with not being able

I landed in this country with $2.50 in cash and $1 million in hopes, and those hopes never left me.
Charles Ponzi

See also: Bernie Madoff 116–21 ■ Jérôme Kerviel 124–25

> He is one of the best examples of misdirected energy in the annals of American crime.
> **The Washington Post**

to afford the following month's rent for his office, desperation was setting in again.

It was around this time that Ponzi received a letter from Spain with an unusual document inside. Similar to a self-addressed stamped envelope, the internal reply coupon (IRC) looked like money but was actually a system for prepaying international postage. It could be redeemed in various parts of the world, but the fixed prices did not reflect the dramatic postwar devaluation of some currencies. Ponzi realized that he could turn a profit if he bought the coupons in Italy, where they were relatively cheap, and exchanged them for more expensive stamps in the US.

Although Ponzi did not have a plan for converting the coupons into cash, he figured that he could make a profit of $2.30 ($31.50) for every $1 ($14) that he invested. Seeing the potential for a business

International Reply Coupons, which could be exchanged for postage stamps, inspired Ponzi's scam. This particular design was adopted by the Universal Postal Union in 1906.

venture, Ponzi obtained a loan and sent the money to family members back home in Italy. He asked them to purchase postal coupons and send them back to him in the US. He reportedly made more than 400 percent profit on some of his sales.

Generating investment

The scheme was not illegal—Ponzi was buying an asset at a lower price and selling it for a high price in a different market—but he had no idea how to redeem the coupons for cash. Undaunted, he promised friends and investors that he could double their investment in 90 days. He confidently explained that the fantastic returns on the postal reply coupons made profiting simple.

Many investors were paid as promised, receiving $750 ($10,300) interest on initial investments of $1,250 ($17,100). However, these profits did not come from trading in IRCs. Instead, Ponzi paid back his initial investors using money coming in from new investors, while all of his investors were kept unaware of his true methods. To add a sheen of legitimacy to his endeavor, Ponzi opened his own company. Word quickly spread about the returns he had produced, and an initial tiny pool of investors soon expanded into Boston's elite society, fueled by the impressive rates that initial investors were being paid.

Whether it was a scam from the beginning, or whether Ponzi intended to pay the investors once he figured out how to convert the coupons into cash, is unclear, but Ponzi made no effort to generate legitimate profits. Eventually, he stopped purchasing IRCs altogether and kept the money for himself. By June 1920, Ponzi had made $2.5 million ($29.6 million) from about 7,800 customers. His desk drawers overflowed with cash; money was »

A pyramid scheme promises high returns to investors, who are paid back through the investments of later investors. As with all pyramid schemes, Charles Ponzi's was mathematically unsustainable because each round needs to involve at least double the number of investors as the previous round.

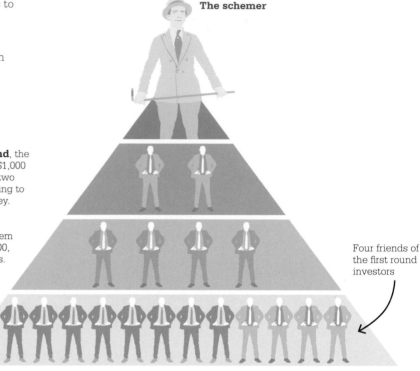

The schemer

In the first round, the schemer takes a $1,000 investment from two investors, promising to double their money.

In the second round, the schemer finds four more investors and gets them to invest $1,000 each. With this $4,000, he pays back the first round investors.

Four friends of the first round investors

In the third round, he needs $8,000 to pay the second round investors, and finds eight investors to invest $1,000 each. The first round investors are pleased with the results, reinvest, and tell their friends. The scheme grows and the schemer is able to make payments to himself.

even stored in his wastebaskets. Convinced of his genius, investors mortgaged their homes and invested their life savings with Ponzi. Most did not take their profits when offered, but instead reinvested, trusting him to increase their wealth even further. In February 1920, Ponzi was promising customers a 50 percent profit a mere 45 days after their investment. Soon, that number was raised to 100 percent, sparking even more investment.

Ponzi deposited the money in Boston's Hanover Trust Bank—in which he also bought a controlling stake. With the ever-increasing influx of cash, Ponzi reveled in his new life of luxury: he bought a mansion with a heated pool in Lexington, smoked cigars from diamond holders, and bought dozens of gold-handled canes for parading around town.

Questions raised

While Ponzi was making money, his operation was running at a tremendous loss, using money collected from new investors to pay the promised returns to earlier investors. This type of scheme, which "borrows from Peter to pay Paul," eventually came to be named after Charles Ponzi himself.

By the summer of 1920, Ponzi was making about $250,000 (£3 million) a day, but local newspapers began to investigate when a furniture dealer publicly claimed that Ponzi's checks had bounced. *The Boston Post* responded with a series of articles about Ponzi's money machine, noting that he himself was not investing with his own company.

Around the same time, the Commonwealth of Massachusetts got involved. Although Ponzi was questioned by state officials, he

steered them away from inspecting his books—his helpful offer to refuse new investments during their investigation calmed their suspicions. When the US Attorney for Massachusetts did look at the books, he just found a box of index cards bearing investors' names.

In July came another blow: the US Post Office confirmed that Ponzi could not possibly be making the returns he had claimed on the international postal coupons—there were not enough of them in circulation. The *Post* reported this, too, and Ponzi filed a suit against the newspaper, before spinning a yarn about purchasing coupons in Italy and selling and reselling throughout Europe.

He convinced nobody. On August 2, 1920, newspapers declared Ponzi to be hopelessly insolvent. As investors pulled out, Ponzi struggled to find the money to pay what they were owed. By August 9, his main bank account was overdrawn and the district attorney froze it. Knowing his arrest was imminent, Ponzi surrendered to federal authorities on August 12, 1920. He was charged with 86 counts of mail fraud.

Final years

Ponzi had lost approximately $20 million of his investors' money. While some were paid, Ponzi was short by $7 million. His arrest brought down six large state banks, including the Hanover Trust. Many investors were financially crippled, receiving less than 30 cents for each dollar they were owed.

The impulsive Ponzi used his bail release to flee to Florida, where he launched the "Charpon Land Syndicate," another Ponzi scheme selling swampland to investors with the promise of huge returns. Ponzi was arrested for fraud and sentenced to one year in prison, but he was freed on appeal.

In New Orleans, he was caught trying to flee to Italy by boat—despite shaving his head and growing a moustache to disguise himself—and was sent back to finish his original jail sentence in Boston. Deported to Italy in 1934, he tried a few more unsuccessful schemes in Italy before moving to Brazil, where he died, in 1948. ∎

A large crowd gathers outside Charles Ponzi's Boston office in July 1920 after *The Boston Post* published a number of articles questioning his business practices.

How Ponzi schemes impact the economy

Ponzi schemes inflict severe financial damage on investors and the economy by diverting money away from productive and legitimate investments. The bigger the scam, the more damage it causes, particularly once large banks become involved. When the scheme is revealed, investors can lose confidence in those institutions and are reluctant to invest in them again.

Discovering and closing down Ponzi schemes can be difficult. Often, neither the perpetrators nor the schemes themselves are regulated. And even in regulated institutions, Ponzi schemes may use technical language to hide their true nature.

Ponzi schemes that violate a number of financial laws may be investigated separately by more than one regulator, which makes it hard for the bigger picture to emerge. The financial significance of the institutions that have invested in the scheme can also make regulators reluctant to investigate, believing that the institutions are too big to fail.

YOU CAN'T CONVICT A MILLION DOLLARS

THE TEAPOT DOME SCANDAL, 1921–22

IN CONTEXT

LOCATION
Washington, D.C., US

THEME
Political corruption

BEFORE
1789–1966 The corrupt
leaders of Tammany Hall in
New York, a powerful
Democratic political machine,
allow mayoral candidates to
buy support and influence.

1912 In Britain, senior
members of the Liberal
government profit from inside
information about plans to
issue a lucrative contract to
the Marconi company.

AFTER
1975 The US Senate concludes
that American aerospace
company Lockheed paid
bribes to members of foreign
governments to guarantee
contracts for military aircraft.

Until Watergate, the illegal espionage operation that led to the resignation of President Richard M. Nixon in 1974, US political scandals were defined by the Teapot Dome incident of the early 1920s. It had nothing to do with tea, or a dome—it was about corruption, which was enough to taint a president's administration.

Early in the 20th century, the US Navy converted from coal to fuel oil. To ensure that it would always have sufficient supplies of fuel, President William Howard Taft designated several of the federal oil-producing areas as naval oil reserves—among them was a piece of land in Wyoming called Teapot Dome.

Politics and oil

In 1921, Taft was succeeded by President Warren G. Harding, who appointed a mixture of able politicians and old cronies to his cabinet. Among them was Albert Bacon Fall, secretary of the interior. In 1921, under pressure from Fall, President Harding issued an executive order that transferred supervision of the Teapot Dome oil

Bribery

A bribe is deemed to have taken place when an individual exchanges favors with another party to gain an illegitimate advantage over what should be a neutral process. It can take place at both corporate and governmental levels.

Even today, in countries with comprehensive antibribery laws, proving that an illegal *quid pro quo* has taken place—in which something is specifically given in order for something to be done in return—is a formidable task. This difficulty fuels much of the controversy around the large cash contributions lobbyists "donate" to politicians. Lobbyists hope these will have an effect on government policy, but proving that any eventual changes in policy were a direct result of their donations is nearly impossible.

Bribery investigations tend to reply on wiretaps or elaborate sting operations, in which both parties are tricked into explicitly stating what they intend to give and receive.

See also: The Mississippi Scheme 100

"Teapot Dome" became part of the political lexicon, a synonym for high-level corruption. It was pressed into play on campaign cards (left) during the 1924 presidential election.

field and two oil fields in California from the navy department to the department of the interior. Fall then covertly, and without competitive bidding, granted exclusive rights to Teapot Dome to Harry F. Sinclair of the Mammoth Oil Company. A similar deal was made with Edward Doheny of Pan American Petroleum and Transport Company for the Elk Hills reserve in California's San Joaquin Valley. In return, Fall received hundreds of thousands of dollars in interest-free loans from the companies.

Although these leases and contracts were technically legal, Fall's acceptance of the money was not. He attempted to keep the deals hidden and to cover his tracks administratively, but he was seen spending money lavishly on his New Mexico cattle ranch and other business ventures. Suspicions arose about his sudden prosperity.

The scandal blows open

In 1922, the US Senate launched an investigation into the leases and contracts negotiated by Fall, and his dishonesty was finally exposed. President Harding was ordered to cancel the leases, and the oil fields were shut down. Harding was not personally implicated in Fall's illicit deals, but as the scandal unfolded, his health began to suffer. In 1923, he died of a heart attack, before all the details of Fall's wrongdoings were made public.

Fall was found guilty of accepting bribes in the Elk Hills and Teapot Dome negotiations. He was fined $100,000 and sentenced to a year in prison, becoming the first cabinet member in US history to be convicted of a felony. His fine was waived, though, because he was destitute, and he was released after nine months on the grounds of ill health. The heads of Mammoth Oil and Pan American Petroleum were acquitted of all charges of bribery and criminal conspiracy.

Investigations initiated by Harding's successor, Calvin Coolidge, revealed that the Teapot Dome scandal had been one of many examples of corruption during Harding's tenure. His reputation was forever tarnished. ∎

I can take care of my enemies in a fight, but my friends, my goddamned friends, they're the ones who keep me walking the floor at nights!
President Warren G. Harding

President Harding **appoints several friends** to senior positions in his government

His friends **betray his trust** by accepting **bribes and embezzling** government funds

Secretary of the interior Albert Fall **leases public oil reserves**, including Teapot Dome, to private companies in return for **money and gifts**

A **senate investigation** into Albert Fall's activities begins but **President Harding dies** before it releases its findings

A Congressional investigation held after Harding's death finds that his administration was riddled with corruption

CITIZENS WERE DYING RIGHT, LEFT, AND CENTER

THE BHOPAL DISASTER, 1984

IN CONTEXT

LOCATION
Bhopal, Madhya Pradesh state, India

THEME
Industrial accident

BEFORE
1906 An explosion and fire at a French coal mine owned by the Courrières mining company kills 1,099 miners.

1932–1968 Methyl mercury dumped into Japan's Minamata Bay by chemical company Chisso Corporation contaminates shellfish, which in turn poisons local residents.

AFTER
July 31–August 1, 2014 A series of gas explosions caused by poorly maintained pipelines kill 32 people in Kaohsiung, Taiwan.

In the early morning hours of December 2, 1984, 40 tons of the deadly poisonous gas methyl isocyanate leaked from a pesticide plant owned by the Indian subsidiary of US firm Union Carbide Corporation (UCC) in Bhopal, Madhya Pradesh, India.

Half a million people were exposed to the gas cloud that floated across the packed shanty towns around the plant. Estimates of the number of casualties vary, but the government of Madhya Pradesh reported that several thousand people died immediately from the effects of the gas, and thousands more were left with permanent disabling injuries. It

See also: The Siemens Scandal 126–27 ▪ The Volkswagen Emissions Scandal 130–31

was the worst industrial accident in history. The name Bhopal became synonymous with death, corporate and government mishandling, and negligence.

Warning signs

In 1969, chemical manufacturer UCC built a plant on land leased to them by the Madhya Pradesh State Government to produce Sevin, a pesticide used throughout Asia. The Indian government owned a 49.1 percent financial stake in the operation.

But there were problems from the outset. The city of Bhopal was chosen for its good transportation infrastructure, but the plant's site was zoned for light industrial and commercial use, not for an industry with potential hazards. Although the plant was supposed to produce pesticides using chemicals prepared elsewhere, in order to cut costs and gain a competitive edge in the market, it began making the raw materials, too—a far more dangerous process.

In the early 1980s, widespread crop failures and famine across the Indian subcontinent meant farmers were unable to invest in pesticides, and demand fell accordingly. The Bhopal plant reduced its output while UCC looked for a buyer. In the meantime, the facility continued to operate with safety equipment and

The water caused a reaction that built up heat and pressure in the tank, quickly transforming the chemical compound into a lethal gas that escaped into the cool night air.
Union Carbide Corporation

Thousands of casualties, among them people whose eyes had been seared by the toxic fumes, assembled in the streets to await rudimentary treament. The local hospitals and mortuaries were quickly overwhelmed.

procedures that fell well short of the standards maintained in its US plants. India's government was aware of the safety issues but was concerned about the economic effects of closing a plant that employed thousands of local people.

Then came the terrible events of December 2–3, 1984. A strong wind quickly blew the poisonous gas plume from the plant through the city; it hugged the ground, and as victims inhaled it, their throats and eyes burned. Many died horribly, vomiting or foaming at the mouth. Chaos ensued as tens of thousands of terrified people tried to escape the city. Arjun Singh, the chief minister of Madhya Pradesh, was accused of fleeing to his palace outside Bhopal, leaving his constituents to fend for themselves.

The investigation begins

News of the disaster reached UCC's headquarters in the US, and Chief Executive Officer Warren Anderson flew to India with a technical team to help the government manage the aftermath. When Anderson arrived, he was placed under house arrest. Technicians began to assess the cause of the gas leak and delivered medical supplies and equipment to the local community. What they discovered was horrifying: the streets were littered with human and animal corpses.

Anderson was released after he promised to travel back to India to stand trial whenever he was » summoned. Ten days after the accident he appeared before the US Congress to report that his company had a commitment to safety. He promised to take action to ensure that a similar incident "cannot happen again." In the months that followed, UCC set up a $120,000 relief fund for their employees who had been affected by the tragedy, but that did not go far. By April 1985, it had increased the fund to $7 million.

The struggle for justice

The subsequent investigation into the Bhopal disaster lasted for years, and eventually revealed that a faulty valve had allowed 1 ton of water meant for cleaning internal pipes to mix with 40 tons of methyl isocyanate. This caused a chemical reaction that forced a valve to open and allowed the gas to escape. The investigators believed this was the result of sabotage: an employee must have tampered with the tank.

At first, UCC tried to avoid legal responsibility for the tragedy, but in 1989, it reached an out-of-court settlement with India's government and paid $470 million in damages.

> Medical experts report a high incidence of lung cancer, adverse outcomes of pregnancy, and respiratory, neurological, psychiatric, and ophthalmic problems among those exposed to the gas.
> **John Elliott**

However, some commentators felt that the company significantly underestimated both the long-term health consequences of exposure to the gas and the number of people affected. India's government and UCC paid for a hospital to treat victims which opened in 2001, and established a health insurance fund to cover the expenses of 100,000 people. Yet, chronically ill survivors and their dependents were still awaiting compensation more than 20 years after the disaster. And some group claims remain in litigation.

While no single saboteur was ever named, both civil and criminal cases were filed against UCC and dragged on for decades. In 2010, seven former executives of UCC, all Indian nationals, were convicted of causing death by negligence. Each was fined $2,000 and sentenced to two years in prison. Given the devastation the gas leak caused the punishment seems light, but it was the maximum allowed by Indian law.

In terms of public safety, it seems that some lessons are yet to be learned from Bhopal. In the years since the accident, India has undergone rapid industrialization, but activists say the government has been slow to regulate industry, continuing to put the health of the country's citizens at risk. Bhopal proved the need for preventative strategies to avoid similar events, enforceable international standards for environmental safety, and industrial accident preparedness.

A toxic legacy

Decades after the Bhopal disaster, estimates of the death toll vary from as few as 3,800 people to as many as 16,000. However, the Indian government now cites a figure of 15,000 people, which includes those who have died from illnesses related to exposure to the gas. Several thousand more survivors continue to battle life-limiting conditions, such as cancer, blindness, and neurological and immune disorders. A large number

Warren Anderson, CEO of UCC at the time of the disaster, was charged with manslaughter by the authorities in Bhopal in 1991. The US refused to extradite him to India to face trial.

Survivors' organizations and other local activists regularly stage protests demanding harsher punishment for those responsible for the tragedy, and more compensation for its victims.

of the children born after the disaster in the area around the plant suffered mental and physical deformities.

Human rights groups claim that birth defects have actually occurred in the area since the plant opened in 1969 due to groundwater contamination arising from the hazardous waste dumped in and around the plant. However, the government has not confirmed a link, and no long-term research has been carried out that proves the birth defects are directly related to the drinking of poisoned water.

Government apathy

Although UCC's 67-acre (27 ha) factory was closed down immediately after the disaster, the company was not permitted to decontaminate the site until the early 1990s. While litigation was in progress, the methyl isocyanate unit was considered "evidence" in the criminal case. In 2001, UCC was taken over by Dow Chemical Company, which has steadfastly refused to accept liability for the Bhopal accident. Dow says the legal case was settled in 1989, and that responsibility for the cleanup operation, as well as for ongoing medical care for victims and fresh claims for compensation, now rests with the authorities in Madhya Pradesh state, who assumed control of the site in 1998. Little has been done in recent years by India's government to resolve this impasse. And while local activists have no doubt that the toxic waste at the abandoned plant poses serious health risks for people living nearby, they have opposed government plans to remove and incinerate it, on safety grounds. However, in 2015, a small amount of waste from the site was burned in a trial incineration and the emissions were deemed to be within permissible limits. ■

The jury in the Robinson v. Reynolds case found that the tobacco giant had marketed its cigarettes as safe, knowing full well they were not.

Corporate negligence

It takes many forms, but generally, corporate negligence occurs when a company breaches its promise to a third party to do no harm. Whether it is done accidentally or intentionally to save money, a company can be held accountable for a negligent action, or a failure to act. A parent corporation may be found liable for the negligence of a subsidiary company, even if it played no part in the wrongdoing. Some landmark cases of corporate negligence include 79-year-old Stella Liebeck, who in 1994 successfully sued McDonald's for $2.86 million after spilling a cup of their scalding coffee in her lap and suffering serious burns. Today, most commercial hot drinks carry warning signs.

In 2014, a US jury awarded Cynthia Robinson $23.6 billion in punitive damages in her lawsuit against cigarette-maker R.J. Reynolds for the wrongful death of her husband, a smoker who died of lung cancer in 1996. She argued that the company was negligent in not informing consumers that its products are addictive and harmful to health.

THE WORLD'S BIGGEST MUGGING

THE CITY OF LONDON BONDS THEFT, MAY 2, 1990

IN CONTEXT

LOCATION
London, UK

THEME
Bond theft

BEFORE
1983 An armed gang steal £6 million (about $26.5 million today) in cash from a Security Express depot in London. Brothers Ronnie and John Knight are later convicted of masterminding the robbery.

AFTER
2006 Seven masked men brandishing guns burst into Securitas Cash Management Ltd.'s building in Kent, UK, tie up 14 members of staff, and in just over an hour steal £53 million ($110 million) in Britain's biggest cash robbery.

2007 Guards at a private bank in Baghdad, Iraq, steal $282 million in US dollars from its vaults.

For John Goddard, a 58-year-old messenger for money broker Sheppards, based in London's financial district, the working day on May 2, 1990, began just like any other. He left the Bank of England with a briefcase full of bearer bonds and headed toward a nearby finance house to deliver them. At 9.30 a.m., while walking along a quiet side street, he was approached by a man in his late 20s, who held a knife against his throat, grabbed his briefcase and wallet, and ran off.

An audacious heist

The mugger fled on foot and quickly disappeared into a busy subway tunnel. He had escaped with 301 bearer bonds—170 Treasury bills and 131 certificates of deposit from banks and building societies— mostly worth £1 million each. The mugger's total haul was worth an eye-watering £292 million ($355 million).

The Bank of England issued a global alert, notifying financial institutions of the bonds' serial numbers. The following day, the press reported the robbery as the work of an amateur opportunist thief who, without connections,

Life as an undercover cop: you're always one slip away from death or a breakdown.
UK police source

would be unable to cash the bonds. But City of London detectives soon discovered that the perpetrators were in fact an international fraud and money-laundering ring with links to organized crime in the US.

Police dispatched a 40-officer team to locate the mugger and, in a joint operation, worked with FBI agents who went undercover to infiltrate the crime ring. Both parties worked with urgency following the Bank of England's warning that the gang might be able to turn the bonds into cash.

Two months after the robbery, on July 31, there was a major breakthrough. Mark Lee Osborne, a Texas businessman, had tried

See also: The Great Train Robbery 30–35 ▪ D.B. Cooper 38–43 ▪ The Antwerp Diamond Heist 54–55

to peddle £10 million of the stolen bonds to a narcotics dealer in New York. Unfortunately for him, the potential buyer was undercover FBI Agent David Maniquis.

Following the money

Osborne cooperated with the FBI and turned on his co-conspirators, including British con man Keith Cheeseman, who was cornered by agents in a sting operation codenamed "Operation Soft Dollar." He pleaded guilty to laundering some of the bonds and was jailed.

However, when Osborne became an informant, he also became a target for organized crime operatives, who do not take kindly to snitches. In August 1990, despite being placed under FBI protection, Osborne was fatally shot twice in the head.

The stolen bonds were fenced worldwide. City of London police recovered a bag stuffed with undeclared bonds at Heathrow airport, and more were seized in Cyprus. During the summer of 1990, police traced all but two of

the bonds. They made 25 arrests, but Cheeseman was the only successful prosecution. The mugger is believed to have been 28-year-old Patrick Thomas, a petty criminal from London who shot himself in December that year. As for the messenger John Goddard, he only learned of the value of his briefcase after the event. At that time, money-market securities

After the mugging, in order to prevent similar crimes, the Bank of England (above) quickly developed a service to enable the electronic transfer of sterling securities.

worth billions were sent around the City of London by couriers who were not told what they were carrying. This risky delivery method was later discontinued. ▪

Pistone's cover was so convincing that before the operation ended, he was close to being proposed for membership of the Bonanno family.

Undercover police work

In order to gather evidence and intelligence about the ongoing and future illegal activities of groups and individuals, police forces use specially trained undercover operatives.

Their assignments include short-term stings that can last for just a matter of a few hours, to deep-cover, long-term investigations that mean months or years in the field. The personal risks can be huge, but the payoff— putting criminals behind bars— can outweigh them.

One man who understood that very well was undercover FBI agent Joe D. Pistone (1939–). In 1976, he infiltrated one of New York's five organized crime syndicates, the Bonanno family, as jewel thief Donnie Brasco. He lived and worked with them for six years, while collecting evidence that would convict more than 100 mobsters. The Mafia later put out a contract on his life, and he now lives under a secret identity. He wrote a book about his undercover work, which was the basis for the 1997 movie *Donnie Brasco*.

IT'S ALL JUST ONE BIG LIE

BERNIE MADOFF, 1990s–2008

IN CONTEXT

LOCATION
New York City, US

THEME
Ponzi scheme

BEFORE
April 6, 2007 Syed Sibtul Hassan, also known as the "Double Shah," is exposed by an investigative reporter for running a Ponzi scheme in Pakistan, which promised a 100 percent return on investments in only 15 days.

May 21, 2008 Lou Pearlman, the renowned American record producer and band manager, is sentenced to 25 years in prison for running a Ponzi scheme worth more than $300 million.

AFTER
June 7, 2011 Nevin Shapiro is sentenced to 20 years in prison and ordered to pay more than $82 million in restitution for a Miami-based Ponzi scheme worth over $880 million.

Bernie Madoff's elaborate Ponzi scheme evaded US financial regulators for decades. It delivered irresistible financial gains to thousands of investors before bankrupting people on five continents, leaving behind a trail of financial and emotional despair. Variously labeled a monster, a fraud, and a traitor, Madoff is seeing out the rest of his life with a 150-year sentence in jail.

It began like similar swindles—an individual or organization lures investors by promising unusually high returns. However, where most Ponzi schemes lure investors by offering high rates of returns, and then proceed to collapse quickly, Madoff's annual returns were incredibly consistent.

As news of the miracle investments spread, the enticing regularity of the scheme was a key factor in perpetuating the fraud, and Madoff could pick and choose from the scores of wealthy investors desperate for a piece of the action.

Humble beginnings

Madoff founded his Wall Street firm—Bernard L. Madoff Investment Securities LLC—in 1960, shortly after leaving college. He had saved up $5,000 from temporary jobs as a lifeguard and a sprinkler installer, and his accountant father-in-law, Saul Alpern, provided a $50,000 loan to help get the firm up and running.

The company initially dealt in penny stocks, which were traded outside of the New York Stock Exchange (NYSE) and American Stock Exchange (AMEX), so that Madoff could avoid their hefty fees.

Madoff is escorted into court in New York on March 10, 2009, where he was charged with 11 felonies, including securities fraud, mail fraud, wire fraud, money laundering, and perjury.

Madoff's firm took off. His first major investor—Carl Shapiro, the owner of a successful women's apparel company—gave Madoff $100,000 in 1960. This signaled both the start of their relationship as friends and business partners, and the first opportunity that Madoff could exploit. Over the next 50 years, Shapiro would come to see Madoff as a son, provide him with access to circles of wealthy investors, and eventually lose over half a billion dollars through his investments in Madoff's firm.

The firm was able to avoid scrutiny from the Securities and Exchange Commission (SEC) because Madoff seemingly had so few clients—it relied on an elite pool of wealthy investors. Saul Alpern initially helped Madoff recruit these clients for a commission, but later also acted as a conduit, investing money from

See also: Charles Ponzi 102–07 ▪ Jérôme Kerviel 124–25

several clients under his own name to make it appear that Madoff had fewer investors.

Family business

Madoff's firm continued to grow. By 2008, it was a multibillion-dollar family business: his niece was employed as a compliance officer, and his two sons, Andrew and Mark, were placed in charge of the company's legitimate operations outside of the private investment division. This division was a secret even within the company, and was highly illegal—clients' investments were deposited into Madoff's private accounts rather than being invested.

When investors asked for their money back, Madoff's firm would return their investment with interest, along with a fabricated list of trades based on real data. The money actually came from other investors' contributions. Perhaps because of the aura that developed around Madoff and his magic investments, most saw no reason to doubt the returns. One Madoff fund

> I certainly wouldn't invest in the stock market. I never believed in it.
> **Bernie Madoff**

for his investors' money focused on shares in the S&P 100-stock index. It reported a 10.5 percent annual return for 17 years. Even when the US stock market collapsed in 2008, the fund was up.

For decades, people trusted in Madoff's consistency—and not just the wealthy. Thousands of working people gave him responsibility for their life savings. His firm seemed legitimate, and he was, by all appearances, a trustworthy and credible businessman, who had

served on an SEC advisory committee and as nonexecutive chairman of the world's second-largest stock exchange.

When the scale of Madoff's deception was revealed, his hundreds of thousands of victims included Hollywood stars Kevin Bacon, John Malkovich, and Steven Spielberg, the French aristocrat and financier René-Thierry Magon de la Villehuchet, and the UK army veteran William Foxton. Tragically, de la Villehuchet and Foxton were driven to suicide as a result of their financial losses.

Investigations commence

The point at which Madoff began his Ponzi scheme is unclear. When he finally confessed in 2008, Madoff insisted that the fraud had started in the early 1990s, but federal investigators believe that it may have begun as early as the 1970s or mid-1980s. In fact, Madoff's investment operation may never have been legitimate—his financial operations were always highly secretive, to the extent that his »

Edward Snowden leaked classified information in 2013 which revealed previously unknown details about US-led global surveillance programs.

Whistleblowers

Whistleblowers are an important but controversial factor in the detection of crimes that might otherwise continue unchecked by bureaucratic processes. Despite the harassment and intimidation whistleblowers often experience, they are protected by the law.

After noting the due diligence of whistleblowers during Madoff's case, the SEC set up a specific whistleblowing fund intended to encourage financiers to come forward with vital information on financial crimes.

Whistleblowers, however, are also important in other fields, including education and healthcare, where workers are encouraged to speak up against negligence and poor conduct. In matters of state, whistleblowers can be extremely controversial. Former CIA employee Edward Snowden has been alternatively celebrated as a patriot and criticized as a traitor, while former US Army soldier Chelsea Manning was court-martialed and jailed for leaking confidential documents to condemn US foreign policy.

brother, Peter, who worked with him for over 40 years and was a codirector of the firm, was ignorant of the scheme's exact nature.

Suspicions as early as the 1990s that something was wrong were easily dismissed as the result of envy. In 2000, a financial analyst and independent fraud investigator, Harry Markopolos, told the SEC he could prove that it was legally and mathematically impossible to achieve the gains Madoff claimed. His findings were ignored for years, but others also arrived at the same conclusion. Apart from Madoff's private bank, JP Morgan, none of the major Wall Street firms would invest or trade with Madoff because they did not believe his numbers were real. JP Morgan would pay for their involvement— they were fined $2 billion in 2014 to compensate victims of his scheme.

The SEC had investigated Madoff before 2008, but missed the massive fraud. As early as 1992, they investigated and shut down

> The math was so compelling… unless you could change the laws of mathematics, I knew I had to be right.
> **Harry Markopolos**

Avellino and Bienes, a major "feeder fund" used to attract potential investors, but failed to see the signs that its malpractice was a part of Madoff's larger operation.

Subsequent investigations were plagued by incompetence, a lack of financial expertise, and failures in communication between SEC departments working separately on aspects of Madoff's firm. The

frequent but unproductive contact between the SEC and Madoff's compliance officers even led to the marriage of Madoff's niece and Eric Swanson, an SEC attorney leading investigations into the Madoff fund.

After years of incompetent investigations by the SEC, in late fall 2008 Madoff knew that his scheme, and the economy, were beginning to crumble. Clients suddenly requested a total of $7 billion in returns. Madoff had only $200–300 million left to give.

The truth comes out

On December 10, 2008, Madoff met with his sons to discuss year-end bonuses totaling millions of dollars. He explained that he wanted to give them earlier than scheduled. When his sons were suspicious enough to ask where the money was going to come from, Madoff admitted that it would come from a part of the business they were not involved in, and confessed to an

Respected Wall Street figure

Bernie Madoff had been secretly fooling investors, regulators, and the government since the early 1990s, when he first devised his Ponzi scheme.

1990
Madoff begins three years serving as chair of the NASDAQ stock exchange.

1960
Madoff founds Bernard L. Madoff Investment Securities LLC.

1986
Madoff sets up his firm's headquarters at 885 Third Avenue in New York.

1992
The SEC shuts down Avellino and Bienes, a "feeder fund" that recruited investors in Madoff's company, but fail to find a connection to Madoff himself.

Embroidered velvet slippers were included in an auction lot of Madoff's possessions sold to raise funds to compensate the victims of his $65 billlion Ponzi scheme.

elaborate Ponzi scheme. Instead of accepting the money, Madoff's sons reported him to federal authorities; FBI agents arrested Madoff the next day. Shortly after his arrest, Madoff was released on bail as he awaited charges and sentencing. He and his wife Ruth packed up some personal and family items, including jewelry, and mailed it to their sons.

In 2011, Ruth Madoff stated that she and her husband had attempted suicide together on Christmas Eve, 2008. Scared and acting on impulse, they took a cocktail of different pills—including what they hoped would be an overdose of sleeping pills—but woke up unharmed.

Tragic conclusion

On March 12, 2009, Madoff pleaded guilty to 11 different crimes, including securities fraud, investment adviser fraud, mail fraud, wire fraud, three counts of money laundering, giving false statements, perjury, and making false filings with the SEC.

On June 29, 2009, Madoff was sentenced to 150 years in prison— the maximum allowable sentence for his crimes. Just before he was sentenced, Madoff apologized to his victims, many of whom were seated on the benches behind him. In November 2009, the government began to sell and auction off Madoff's assets to repay his investors. These included a large yacht and two smaller boats; a property portfolio including a New York City penthouse, a beach house in Montauk, New York, and a Florida mansion; artwork by Picasso and Roy Lichtenstein; his wife's extensive jewelry collection, a Rolex collection, and a Steinway grand piano.

The unraveling of Madoff's scheme—the biggest Ponzi scheme in history—had a significant impact on hundreds of families across the US, and Madoff's own family would fall apart in the aftermath. His 46-year-old son, Mark, hanged himself on the second anniversary of Madoff's arrest, as a sad finale to a complex life lived under the constant but elusive authority of his father. ∎

2000
Harry Markopolos's first submission proving Madoff's guilt is submitted to the SEC but eventually rejected.

2005
Following concerns raised by Renaissance Enterprises, LLC, the SEC begins another ultimately unsuccessful examination of Madoff's firm.

2002
An anonymous hedge fund manager registers a detailed complaint with the SEC about Madoff's investments. Nothing comes of the investigation.

2008
Madoff confesses the Ponzi scheme to his sons. They immediately report their father to the FBI and Madoff is arrested.

I KNOW IN MY MIND THAT I DID NOTHING CRIMINAL
THE ENRON SCANDAL, 2001

IN CONTEXT

LOCATION
Houston, Texas, US

THEME
Accounting fraud

BEFORE
1991 The Bank of Credit and Commerce International (BCCI) is closed by regulators after it is implicated in a major money-laundering operation.

1998 Waste Management, an American trash disposal and recycling company, pays $457 million to settle a shareholder class-action lawsuit; the company's auditor, Arthur Andersen, is fined $7 million.

AFTER
March 2008 The US Securities and Exchange Commission (SEC) charges Canadian pharmaceutical company Biovail with engaging in fraudulent accounting schemes and fines the firm $10 million.

O nly 15 years after its formation, American energy company Enron had become America's seventh-biggest corporation, but the firm collapsed following a sensational scandal in 2001, during which it was revealed that the firm's success was built on fraudulent accounting practices.

The company was formed by businessman Kenneth Lay in 1985, after merging two fairly small regional energy companies, Houston Natural Gas and InterNorth Inc. By 2000, the Enron Corporation had grown remarkably,

claiming $111 billion in revenues and employing 20,000 workers in more than 40 countries.

Creative innovation
After Jeff Skilling impressed him as a consultant for McKinsey and Company, Lay hired him in 1990 as Chief Executive Officer of Enron Finance Corporation. He soon became Lay's second in command. Skilling began to implement an aggressive investment plan, earning the company the title of "America's Most Innovative Company" from *Fortune* magazine for six consecutive years from 1996–2001.

Skilling used a technique known as mark-to-market accounting to record an asset's projected profits rather than its real value. If the eventual revenue generated by the asset did not end up matching the projected profit, Skilling transferred the asset to a secret off-the-books company, concealing the loss. Enron's Chief

Sherron Watkins, a vice president at Enron, testifies at a Senate Committee in 2002. She raised concerns to Enron bosses in 1996 about financial irregularities but was reprimanded.

See also: Charles Ponzi 102–07 ▪ Bernie Madoff 116–21 ▪ Jérôme Kerviel 124–25

Kenneth Lay arrives at his fraud and conspiracy trial on April 26, 2006, under intense scrutiny from the media. He was convicted but died of a heart attack before he could be sentenced.

Financial Officer Andrew Farstow was instrumental in creating a network of companies to help hide the losses. To the public and the media, the company appeared to be growing rapidly.

It was only on August 14, 2001, when Skilling suddenly resigned on the day that Enron's broadband division reported a $137 million loss, that confidence began to fall in the company.

The penny drops

Shareholders only learned of the state of the company's finances on October 16, 2001, when Enron filed a $618 million third-quarter loss. It was later discovered that four days before, lawyers at Enron's auditor, Arthur Andersen, had destroyed almost all of Enron's files.

After the company's stock price spiraled from a peak of $90.75 per share in mid-2000 to less than $1 by the end of November 2001, Enron shareholders filed a $40 billion lawsuit against the corporation. The suit claimed that Enron executives had misled

Enron's board of directors and audit committee on the company's high-risk accounting practices.

The fallout

The suit prompted the SEC to investigate. On December 2, 2001, Enron filed for bankruptcy and Chapter 11 protection—at the time, the largest bankruptcy in US history. The US Senate convened a committee, which summoned

company leaders to hearings to explain Enron's collapse. The hearings revealed that Enron's aggressive accounting practices had been approved by the board of directors. The Senate committee also discovered that the company's financial statements were so complex that investors could not understand what they were looking at and did not understand the risks.

In June 2002, Arthur Andersen was charged with obstruction of justice for destroying Enron's documents. The decision was overturned by the Supreme Court but the damage to the company's reputation was irreversible.

Kenneth Lay and Jeffrey Skilling were each convicted of securities and wire fraud in a federal court in 2006. Lay died a month later. In total, 22 other Enron executives were convicted in the scandal. ∎

Forensic accounting

Forensic accounting is a specialized branch of accounting used to investigate, analyze, and interpret complex financial and business issues.

Forensic accountants are often employed by public accounting firms, law enforcement agencies, insurance companies, government organizations, and by financial institutions to examine allegations of fraudulent practices, and regularly give expert evidence in court.

The Enron scandal occurred at a time during the early 2000s when the number of corporate fraud cases investigated by the FBI surged by an incredible 300 percent, hugely increasing the need for forensic accountants.

The fallout from the scandal has led to more robust legislation and stricter regulation to improve corporate governance. Financial institutions and auditors also increasingly employ forensic accountants to prevent fraudulent activities from taking place within their organizations.

HE PUT IN PERIL THE EXISTENCE OF THE BANK

JÉRÔME KERVIEL, 2007–08

IN CONTEXT

LOCATION
Paris, France

THEME
Rogue trader

BEFORE
1992–95 The illegal trades of Nick Leeson, a futures trader based in Singapore, bring down Barings, Britain's oldest merchant bank. Leeson is sentenced to six and a half years in prison.

2004–06 Jordan Belfort, reputedly the real-life Wolf of Wall Street, serves 22 months in jail for securities fraud.

AFTER
2011 The unauthorized trading of UBS Global trader Kweku Adoboli costs the Swiss bank $2 billion. In 2012, Adoboli is convicted of fraud and jailed for seven years.

French trader Jérôme Kerviel's career in white-collar crime was relatively short-lived, lasting just over a year. In that brief period, the 31-year-old caused one of the leading French banks, Société Générale, to lose €4.9 billion ($5.4 billion). But who was really to blame?

The crime

Kerviel joined Société Générale's compliance department in 2000 and became a junior trader in 2005. He started to make unauthorized transactions late in 2006. His *modus operandi* was to make only small, occasional transactions, but

There was a tremendous culture … to take big risks in order to make the maximum profit.
Bradley D. Simon

over time these became larger and more regular, concealed by false hedge trading. Kerviel always closed his trades within three days, before the bank's control measures kicked in. He did not personally profit from these transactions.

In January 2008, Société Générale discovered that Kerviel had been making unauthorized deals. They asserted that Kerviel, anticipating a decline in market prices, made eight unauthorized trades in derivatives in December 2007 and January 2008 totaling €4.9 billion ($5.4 billion)—more than the total sum of the bank's stock and net earnings.

Kerviel was charged with breach of trust, forgery, and unsanctioned use of the bank's computer systems. His trial began on June 8, 2010.

During the proceedings, Kerviel admitted to entering sham trades and falsifying documents to obscure his actions, but claimed that his superiors at Société Générale had secretly condoned his behavior because it yielded significant profits. Kerviel's lawyers claimed that he earned the bank €1.4 billion ($1.55 billion) in the last quarter of 2007 alone.

See also: Charles Ponzi 102–07 ▪ Bernie Madoff 116–21

Jérôme Kerviel and his lawyer David Koubbi arrive at the Paris appeal court in 2012. Kievel lost this appeal, but a subsequent appeal in 2016 reduced the fine to €1 million ($1.1 million).

On October 5, 2010, Judge Pauthe sentenced Kerviel to three years in prison and ordered him to pay Société Générale €4.9 billion ($5.4 billion) in compensation.

Alternative opinions

Skeptics of the official narrative, including Kerviel's former work colleagues, have pointed out that the sheer scale of this unauthorized trading could not have escaped the bank's attention for so long. They also said that completing such large trades within three days would have been impossible. Furthermore, they argued, Kerviel's position in the company made it unlikely that he had worked alone.

Wrongful dismissal

In 2014, France's Court of Cassation reduced the repayment amount on the basis that Judge Pauthe's decision did not consider the role of the bank's own inadequate risk-management procedures. Kerviel was freed that same year.

However, Kerviel was determined to carry on his fight against the bank. In June 2016, he convinced a French labor tribunal that the termination of his employment from the bank had been unethical. In a strange paradox, the labor board ordered the bank to pay him €300,000 ($330,000) in compensation, including recompense for unused vacation and his 2007 performance bonus. In September 2016, Kerviel appeared in court to appeal his €4.9 billion ($5.4 billion) fine. He won the case and the fine was reduced to €1 million ($1.1 million).

Unfairly or not, Kerviel is seen as a martyr by some: a businessman pressured to compete unethically by a corrupt system that sacrificed him at the first sign of trouble. Regardless of the level of the bank's complicity, Kerviel has taken the opportunity for self-aggrandizement —he made a well-publicized pilgrimage to Rome in 2014 to discuss the "tyranny of the markets" with Pope Francis. ▪

The psychology of lying

In his book *The Honest Truth About Dishonesty*, Dr. Dan Ariely, a cognitive psychologist and behavioral economist at Duke University, North Carolina, proposes that the likelihood of an individual being dishonest increases when they: (1) can rationalize the lie; (2) have a conflict of interest; (3) have lied about the matter in the past; (4) observe others behaving dishonestly; (5) belong to a culture or subculture where dishonesty is normalized; (6) know others will benefit from their deceit; (7) are highly creative and imaginative; and (8) are tired or stressed.

In the case of Jérôme Kerviel, the first six factors certainly apply, while the last two are possible. Brain imaging has shown that lying and repeated deception reduces activity in the amygdala, the area of the brain where emotional responses are processed. This reduction can limit the feelings of shame or guilt that are often associated with lying, making it easier to continue lying.

BRIBERY WAS TOLERATED AND ... REWARDED

THE SIEMENS SCANDAL, 2008

IN CONTEXT

LOCATION
Washington D.C., US

THEME
Corporate corruption

BEFORE
1914 German company Siemens and British rival Vickers are exposed for bribing Japanese officials for warship contracts; Siemens employee Karl Richter is sentenced to two years in prison.

1985–2006 British defense group BAE Systems admits misrepresenting its dealings with Saudi officials in the Al-Yamamah arms-for-oil deal.

AFTER
2009 Executives at US engineering and construction company Kellogg Brown & Root are convicted for participating in a decade-long scheme to bribe government officials in Nigeria in return for $6 billion worth of contracts to build liquified gas facilities.

What do a cell-phone network in Bangladesh, a national identity card scheme in Argentina, a UN food-for-oil program in Iraq, and two new rail systems in Venezuela have in common? They are just a few of the lucrative public works projects awarded to German engineering giant Siemens by corrupt state officials, who were happy to accept "financial encouragement" when it came to choosing contractors.

Between March 2001, when Siemens was first listed on the New York Stock Exchange, and September 2007, when US officials intervened in the firm's operations, Siemens' staff ran a foreign bribery operation of unprecedented scale.

Allegations of bribery

The US stock exchange watchdog, the Federal Securities and Exchange Commission (SEC), brought a case against Siemens in

---

> Siemens sets aside **large pools of cash for bribery**

> **Governments** around the world **offer** private companies **contracts** to build **large-scale infrastructure projects**

> Siemens **bribes government officials** to bypass the public selection process and simply award the contracts to them

> **Competitors are shut out, and Siemens profits from the day-to-day running of railroad lines, energy grids, power plants, and other state projects**

See also: The Teapot Dome Scandal 108–09 ▪ The Enron Scandal 122–23 ▪ The Volkswagen Emissions Scandal 130–31

> The day is past when multinational corporations could regard illicit payments to foreign officials as simply another cost of doing business.
> **Cheryl J. Scarboro**

September 2008. It had discovered that between 2001 and 2007, 4,283 bribes and kickbacks totaling $1.4 billion were made by the firm to government officials in over 60 countries. A further 1,185 payments with a total value of $392 million were made to other third parties.

The SEC was not the only institution with allegations against Siemens. In Greece, prosecutors pursued the firm for complaints arising from contracts for security systems at the 2004 Athens Olympics. In subsequent months, fresh accusations were made about Siemens' activities in other parts of the world, from Norway to Slovakia and from China to Turkey.

Culture of corruption

For Siemens' management and staff, offering bribes when competing for foreign contracts was a standard business strategy. The US Department of Justice revealed that the firm had three "cash desks" in its offices. Staff would bring in empty suitcases and carry them away stuffed with banknotes. Up to €1 million ($1.1 million) could be "withdrawn" at a time to secure contracts for the firm's telecoms arm; few questions were asked and little paperwork was required. Between 2001 and 2004, approximately $67 million was taken out via the cash desks.

However, most of Siemens' illicit business practices were carried out rather less crudely: deniability was all. Special off-the-books bank accounts and "consultants" were widely used to hide the nature of the shady transactions. Accounting was kept deliberately sketchy. Managers would sign payment slips for bribes using Post-it notes, which would then be removed and disposed of at the very moment the authorized funds were transferred.

Siemens' apparent tolerance of these corrupt practices suggests that its staff must have felt, on some level, they were doing nothing wrong. This attitude was at odds with the fact that the firm's listing on the New York Stock Exchange meant it was subject to US anti-bribery laws. And although offering bribes to foreign officials was once

Reinhard Siekaczek was largely responsible for Siemens' accounting at the time of the scandal, but he helped expose the company's corruption and, as a result, received a lighter sentence.

legal in Germany, the practice had been outlawed in 1999. In December 2008, Siemens pleaded guilty in a US court; it was ordered to pay fines of $1.6 billion and to rehabilitate itself by reforming its internal culture. It has since set up anticorruption processes. ▪

Defining white collar crime

The term "white collar crime" was coined in 1939 by American sociologist Edwin Sutherland. His work attempted to shift criminology's focus away from the blue-collar street crimes committed by the working class —according to the prevailing theory, crime was intrinsically linked with poverty. Instead, he chose to study the financially motivated, nonviolent crimes committed by professional, often wealthy, businessmen and other pillars of society. His definition of a white-collar crime was one "committed by a person of respectability and high social status in the course of his occupation." Sutherland claimed that the offenses white-collar felons committed—including fraud, forgery, bribery, and money-laundering—were more likely to be seen as matters for civil rather than criminal law. And compared with their counterparts in the lower classes, they were far more likely to "get away" with them.

NOT JUST NERDY KIDS UP TO MISCHIEF IN THEIR PARENTS' BASEMENT
THE SPYEYE MALWARE DATA THEFT, 2009–13

IN CONTEXT

LOCATION
Moscow, Russia

THEME
Cybercrime

BEFORE
2000 RBN, a Russian Internet service provider that hosts illegal and questionable businesses, including malware distribution sites, becomes a major information highway for organized crime worldwide.

2007 Hackers steal at least 45.6 million credit card numbers from the servers of TJX, who own several US discount stores, and bring massive data breaches to public awareness.

AFTER
2010–13 Turkish hacker Ercan Findikoglu's cybercrime ring distributes debit card data to "cashing crews" around the world, who use it to syphon millions from ATMs.

I n recent years, the growth of the "hidden" part of the Internet has offered criminals a wider arena in which to operate. Behind the "surface web" of indexed sites accessed via search engines lies the "deep web." This is essentially all the unindexed data behind firewalls: intranets, archives, password-protected sites, and so on. The deep web also contains "the dark web," anonymously hosted sites that can be accessed only by using special software. Some of these sites are marketplaces for guns and drugs, or the release of computer viruses invented by criminal coders.

Data theft
Software programs designed to facilitate online fraud are one of the greatest risks to the security of billions of Internet users worldwide. Among the most damaging of these was SpyEye, a piece of malicious software used by hackers between 2010 and 2012 to secretly infect 50 million PCs and net confidential information from individuals and financial institutions worldwide.

Cybercriminals could purchase SpyEye's ready-made malware tool kit for between $1,000 and $8,000,

depending on whether they wanted a basic or premium version. Once in their hands, they could use it to infiltrate computers and log the keystrokes made by their owners. SpyEye's main selling point was its ability to identify and isolate data entered onto (supposedly) secure online banking pages, whisking it away before the protective software could encrypt it. Armed with the usernames, passwords, and PINs of their victims' online accounts, the hackers were able to steal funds.

The creator and administrator of SpyEye was a young Russian man called Aleksandr "Sasha" Panin, who worked out of an apartment in Moscow. Outwardly respectable and studious, he had an entirely different persona online, where he went by the alias "Gribodemon." Panin's partner in crime was Hamza Bendelladj—or "Bx1"—an Algerian computer-science grad who marketed the tool kit online.

The pair acquired a Robin Hood-style mystique when rumors circulated that Panin intended to invest his profits in technology research that could transform human life, and that Bendelladj had made generous donations to Palestinian charities.

See also: Frank Abagnale 86–87

Cybercriminals exploit the speed, convenience, and anonymity of the Internet to commit a diverse range of crimes that know no borders, either physical or virtual.

Finding the evidence

For law enforcement agencies in the US, catching the cybercrooks behind the anonymous screen names was a challenging task. The FBI hired the private computer security firm Trend Micro to identify the suspicious bytes that signal the presence of malware among the billions of streaming bits that make up computer code. The firm put 1,200 researchers on the case; for four years they mapped SpyEye's infrastructure. They found IP addresses and one infected computer in Atlanta, Georgia, which was used as a main server. It was remotely operated from Algeria by Bendelladj.

A team of researchers then impersonated cybercriminals to infiltrate the online forums used to distribute SpyEye. By June 2011, Trend Micro had evidence in place. The purchase of a SpyEye kit led it to Panin's money processor. Even after the online Gribodemon had been decisively linked to the real-world Panin, the FBI had to wait two more years for him to leave Russia—which has no extradition treaty with the US—before it could act. Panin was finally arrested in July 2013, when he incautiously took a vacation in the Dominican Republic. He was jailed for 9½ years. Bendelladj, captured six months earlier in Thailand, received a 15-year sentence. ∎

It's detective work—good, old-fashioned detective work.
**Rik Ferguson,
Trend Micro**

An anonymous hacker writes a **malicious software program**

↓

This program is offered for sale on the **dark web**

↓

Cybercriminals purchase the program and adapt it

↓

The data and identities of hundreds, thousands, or even millions of people can be accessed and stolen

The rise of cybercrime

Today, cybercrime—defined as any type of criminal activity that uses computers or the web as a tool to steal money, goods, information, or other assets—is expanding as rapidly as legitimate online activities. Cybercriminals can target individuals, corporations, institutions, and even government departments.

As more people conduct business online and utilize cloud storage, firms and individuals can be powerless when faced with the innovations used by hackers. In the case of hacking tool kits that automate the theft of credit card and bank details, even after their creators are apprehended, their software continues to circulate online. It can change form and name as easily as IP addresses.

The creator of a notorious piece of malware called Zeus, which inspired the creation of SpyEye, has never been caught, and his or her original source code has since been leaked, adapted, and further circulated by hackers.

THE IRREGULARITIES...
GO AGAINST EVERYTHING
VOLKSWAGEN STANDS FOR
THE VOLKSWAGEN EMISSIONS SCANDAL, 2015

IN CONTEXT

LOCATION
Worldwide

THEME
Software manipulation

BEFORE
2010 Cummins Inc., a motor vehicle engine company based in Columbus, Indiana, pays a $2.1 million penalty and recalls 405 engines after it ships more than 570,000 heavy-duty diesel engines without pollution control equipment.

AFTER
2016 In Japan, Mitsubishi Motors admits falsifying fuel economy tests for 157,000 of its own cars and for 468,000 vehicles that Mitsubishi produced for Nissan.

The Volkswagen emissions scandal is the greatest corporate scandal since the global financial crisis.
Peter Spence

In an unprecedented move in 2015, the US Environmental Protection Agency (EPA) accused German car manufacturer Volkswagen (VW) of installing prohibited "defeat device" software on diesel-powered vehicles sold in the US.

The software reduced nitrogen oxide emissions when the cars were placed on a test machine but allowed higher emissions and improved engine performance during driving. Once on the road, cars would pump out up to 40 times the permitted level of

Corporate punishment

The typical punishment for corporate wrongdoing is to levy fines against the corporation, treating it as a legal "person," rather than against its executives. The US—which established the concept of corporate criminal liability in the 19th century— investigates and prosecutes corporate wrongdoing most vigorously, but other countries are also embracing this concept. Recent trends have been to increase fines substantially, especially where internal controls are found to be lacking or companies have failed to cooperate with investigators.

In September 2016, Deutsche Bank, Germany's largest lender, faced a $14 billion demand from the US Department of Justice for mis-selling mortgages to investors during a housing bubble in 2005.

Critics claimed that such an enormous fine could cause international financial instability and argued that Deutsche Bank should be restructured and strengthened instead.

See also: The Enron Scandal 122–23 ▪ The Siemens Scandal 126–27

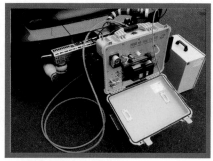

A portable emissions measurement system is shown attached to the exhaust of a car during tests performed by Germany's biggest independent technical testing agency.

Defeat device software put into 11 million VW engines to fool emissions tests

↓

During emissions test, car produces **low emissions** and passes the test

↓

On the road, engine emits nitrogen oxide at **40 times** the allowable level

↓

Testing at the University of West Virginia in May 2014 reveals the diesel dupe

↓

VW recalls millions of cars worldwide and agrees to pay $15 billion to settle claims in the US

nitrogen oxide. In September 2015, Volkswagen admitted that 11 million VW and Audi 2.0 liter diesel cars had been equipped with software used to cheat on emissions tests. The auto giant's chief executive Martin Winterkorn apologized and resigned.

The ringleader

US investigators reviewed 1.5 million documents as part of its criminal probe into the scandal. Key to the investigation was James Robert Liang, a German citizen who headed the Volkswagen Diesel Competence team in the US. He had been a member of the team of engineers that developed the so-called "clean diesel" engine in Germany. According to court documents, he and his colleagues concluded they could not design a diesel engine that would meet the strict US emissions standards, so they designed and implemented software that would cheat the emissions tests instead.

In June 2016, VW agreed to a separate civil settlement to pay regulators and consumers up to $15 billion. The deal, announced in August 2016, involved 652 US car dealers.

In September 2016, Liang pleaded guilty to US federal charges for his role in the scandal and agreed to cooperate with the investigation of other Volkswagen employees. It came out that Liang had answered questions from environmental regulators about the engines' test results, knowing they were false. Federal investigators further contended that Liang emailed colleagues in Germany about the software while committing the crimes in the US.

Liang faces up to five years in a US prison, deportation following his release, and a fine of up to $250,000. However, this is unlikely to be the end of the scandal: the company still faces criminal and civil litigation. ■

ORGANIZ

CRIME

A **smuggling ring** known as the Hawkhurst Gang plagues towns and villages in the southeast of England.

Mafia activity begins on the island of Sicily in the form of citrus fruit protection rackets.

During Prohibition in Chicago, the **Beer Wars** break out between **rival bootlegging gangs**.

1735–49

MID-1800s

1923–29

1761

The Heaven and Earth Society, the precursor to the **Chinese Triads**, forms in Manchuria in southeastern China.

1889–1908

Butch Cassidy's Wild Bunch holds up trains across the western states of the US. The outlaws are wanted "dead or alive."

The FBI defines organized crime as a category of offenses perpetrated by a group of people with a formal structure whose primary purpose is to obtain money through illegal activities. Such groups use violence, graft, and extortion to maintain their position, often bribing corrupt public officials to turn a blind eye or even lend their support.

Organized crime can be both a local issue and a worldwide phenomenon. In the late 1800s, Butch Cassidy's Wild Bunch, derided as two-bit outlaws by the lawmen they eluded for so long, was perhaps the most successful train-robbing gang in US history. At the other end of the scale are crime syndicates whose tentacles spread across the world, such as Japan's Yakuza, and the Sicilian Mafia.

Marginal groups

Crime groups often start out on the fringes of societies. The Triads were originally anti-Qing Dynasty revolutionaries who arose in 19th-century China; the Italian Cosa Nostra and its American offshoots evolved in the rural backwaters of Sicily; and the Hells Angels Motorcycle Club, which formed after World War II, mainly included disaffected war veterans. These organizations thrive on unlawful activities such as drug trafficking, prostitution, moneylending, gambling, and labor racketeering.

The American sociologist Robert Merton believed that individuals turned to organized crime when they were unable to obtain society's goals through socially accepted means because of class hatred and poverty. It is no coincidence that cocaine cartels emerged from the impoverished city of Medellín in Colombia, or that the Kray brothers and the Richardson crime family stemmed from deprived parts of south London. Modern Triad branches took root in the poorest areas of Hong Kong and Macau.

In many cases, such individuals have been blocked by racial prejudice. Prohibition-era mobs were largely made up of Italians, Jews, and the Irish, while 30 percent of Yakuza are Japanese-born Koreans, who face persistent discrimination. The crack cocaine epidemic was fueled by African-American street gangs. "Freeway" Rick Ross, who was illiterate and unable to land a job in 1980s' Los Angeles, built a multimillion-dollar empire selling crack cocaine.

The **Hells Angels** emerge in San Bernadino, California, and spread all over the world, fighting rival gangs and trafficking narcotics.

The **Medellín Cartel** begins its operations in Colombia and uses extreme violence to monopolize the cocaine trade and undermine the government.

1948

1972

1946

1960s

1980–95

In Japan, Kazuo Taoka becomes the boss of the Yamaguchi-gumi **Yakuza crime syndicate** and becomes known as the "godfather of godfathers."

The Krays and the Richardsons—rival gangs—rule the **criminal underworld** in the East End of London.

In Los Angeles, **"Freeway" Rick Ross** creates a multimillion-dollar market dealing crack cocaine.

Perhaps the strongest allure of organized crime is that the groups provide a sense of kinship to individuals estranged from their families or otherwise alienated from society.

Underground activities

Some organized crime gangs have been glamorized by the public, especially groups operating in the dim and distant past, such as during the Prohibition in 1920s America. Fast-forward to the street gangs of the 1980s and 1990s—who wreaked havoc on many poor communities with drive-by shootings, burglaries, vehicle thefts, and drug sales—and the public's attitude is less benign.

Sophisticated criminal groups became adept at operating under the radar and garnering public support as benevolent outlaws. Using both a populist platform and his savvy political maneuvering, the "King of Cocaine" Pablo Escobar even managed to win election to Colombia's Chamber of Representatives.

The Yakuza and the Triads have infiltrated white-collar positions all over Asia, from the most powerful corporations to the civil service and judiciary. However, unlike Pablo Escobar, who operated in the public spotlight, these groups have been successful precisely because of their ability to work behind the scenes, causing them to become almost invisible.

Until the last quarter of the 20th century, the Sicilian Mafia flourished by obscuring the fact that they were a highly organized criminal syndicate through the notion that mainland Italy simply did not understand the nuances of Sicilian culture.

Hells Angels and other biker clubs attempt to market themselves as rowdy but ultimately harmless throwbacks to an era of personal freedom exemplified by groups such as the Wild Bunch. In doing so, these groups exploit a collective, often misplaced nostalgia for a less centralized world.

Mobsters often associated with pop icons, such as crooner Frank Sinatra and the American Mafia, which helped to legitimize them. After all, they could not be such bad people, could they, if they socialized with such respected stars? For these organized crime groups, who were attempting to disguise what was actually going on, the ruse worked. ∎

THE MUST HAZARDUUS OF ALL TRADES, THAT OF THE SMUGGLER

THE HAWKHURST GANG, 1735–49

IN CONTEXT

LOCATION
South coast of England, UK

THEME
Smuggling

BEFORE
1735–1816 The Hadleigh Gang operates along the east coast of England. Two of its members are hanged for the murder of a dragoon.

AFTER
1799–1831 Jack Rattenbury, a smuggler on England's south coast, keeps diaries of his exploits. They are published with the help of a clergyman.

1817–26 A battle between the Aldington Gang, on England's Kent coast, and excise officers leaves five dead and 20 injured.

2014–16 NASCAR driver Derek White takes part in a major North American tobacco smuggling operation—selling tobacco bought in the US to Canada and evading $409 million in tax.

Smuggling in England peaked in the 18th century. When the government began to tax imports heavily in order to finance the country's military campaigns against France, the rise in the cost of goods—the price of tea alone rose by 70 percent in the mid-1700s—made smuggling lucrative. A band of smugglers known as the Hawkhurst Gang became the most well-known.

Taking their name from a town in southeast England, the gang plotted their exploits at the Mermaid Inn in Rye, Sussex, their pistols and sabers at the ready. The smugglers were notoriously violent, and did not hesitate to use force against revenue officers. In 1740, the gang ambushed excise officer Thomas Carswell and his dragoons on Silver Hill as they transported 1,650 lbs (750 kg) of tea seized from a barn in Etchingham. The gang shot Carswell dead, captured his men, and claimed the tea.

Dawn raid

In spite of such violence, the general public admired the gang for outsmarting the taxman and

The Robin Hood effect

The generally law-abiding public has long held popular outlaws in high esteem. It is an attitude that sometimes comes out of resentment against draconian laws imposed by the ruling class. At other times, it comes about when governments are unable or unwilling to protect their citizens and the resulting power vacuum is filled by organized gangs.

American sociologist Robert Merton theorized that when individuals cannot achieve their culture's goals through institutionalized means some pursue their goals illegitimately. Less bold citizens may idolize the scofflaw's flagrant rebellion and daring. However, when gang violence claims innocent victims, this admiration changes to outrage.

The murders of Daniel Chater and William Galley turned the public against the Hawkhurst Gang. The *London Gazette*, the government's newspaper, printed the smugglers' names and promised a royal pardon in return for information on them.

See also: Bonnie and Clyde 26–29 ▪ The Beer Wars 152–53

Shoemaker Chater and revenue officer Galley are kidnapped, tied to a horse, and flogged by members of the Hawkhurst Gang before their brutal murder.

giving them access to cheaper goods. However, this changed in October 1747, when the smugglers sought to recover £500 (about $70,000 today) worth of contraband tea, spirits, and coffee by attacking the custom house in Poole, Dorset, where the goods were held.

The gang had been smuggling the goods from Guernsey to Christchurch aboard *The Three Brothers* when their ship was intercepted by the *Swift*, a revenue vessel commanded by Captain William Johnson. Although the gang evaded capture by escaping in a rowboat, the goods were confiscated and taken to Poole.

Determined to recover their merchandise, in the early hours of October 8, gang leader Thomas Kingsmill and 30 armed men broke into Poole Custom House and absconded with more than 1.5 tons

> They are so immensely rich that they bribe ye private men … [who] at this time harbour the outlawed persons in their houses and are the support of the whole affair.
> **Mr. Pelham**

(1,500 kg) of tea. A £200 ($30,000) reward was offered for the capture of the smugglers, and former soldier William Sturt formed the Goudhurst Militia to stand up to the gang.

No one came forward to incriminate the smugglers. The following year, however, a comment made by Fordingbridge shoemaker Daniel Chater, who was acquainted with one of the gang, led to the arrest and imprisonment of John "Dimer" Diamond. Chater had been given a small bag of tea by Diamond as the gang passed through the town of Fordingbridge, drawing a large crowd of onlookers. Proud to be singled out by this gesture, Chater had bragged to neighbors about his friendship with Diamond.

Diamond was subsequently arrested and plans were made to take Chater to the court at Chichester to testify against the smuggler.

Alerted to the impending trial, fellow gang members William Jackson and William Carter

abducted Chater and customs officer William Galley from the White Hart Inn near Rowlands Castle, where the pair had stopped for refreshment on their way to Chichester. Tying the men to a horse, the smugglers took them to the Red Lion Inn at Rake and into nearby fields. They murdered them in cold blood, burying Galley alive and throwing Chater headfirst down a well.

Final retribution

The gruesome violence used against Galley and Chater turned public opinion overwhelmingly against the smugglers. The ringleaders were arrested, tried, and found guilty of raiding the custom house in Poole. On April 26, 1749, Kingsmill and three of his associates were executed by hanging at Tyburn gallows in London. Kingsmill's corpse was hung in chains at Goudhurst—a town he had once threatened to burn to the ground for turning against him. ▪

IN SICILY

THERE IS A SECT OF

THIEVES

THE SICILIAN MAFIA, MID-1800s–

IN CONTEXT

LOCATION
Sicily, Italy

THEME
Crime families

BEFORE
***c.*1800** The Camorra, a confederation of criminal families, emerges in the Kingdom of Naples; eventually, it controls the region's milk, coffee, and fish industries.

AFTER
1850s 'Ndràngheta forms in Calabria, southern Italy. By the late 1990s, it has become the most powerful crime syndicate in Italy. Its activities include extortion, money laundering, and drug trafficking.

Late 19th century The American Mafia emerges among Italian immigrant families in New York's East Harlem, the Lower East Side, and Brooklyn.

19th century mafiosi exchange fire with the carabinieri in the town of Vita in the province of Trapani in West Sicily, one of the region's six towns with a strong Mafia presence.

My name is Mori and I will make people die! Crime must vanish just as this dust carried away by the wind vanishes!
Cesare Mori

The Mafia has its roots in the 19th-century orange and lemon groves of western Sicily. Citrus fruits were a particularly lucrative commodity during this period, and if the yield was good, the owner of a Sicilian lemon grove could expect to turn a substantial profit. Unfortunately, lemon trees were vulnerable to temporary water shortages—something all too common in Sicily. The potential to reap significant profits combined with the fruit's precariousness gave rise to a particularly Sicilian form of crime: citrus fruit protection rackets.

Failed investigations

Dr. Galati of Palermo—the capital of Sicily and the Mafia's epicenter—was driven from his citrus farm by this type of racket. Although he complained to the police, they did nothing about it. This convinced the doctor that the investigators were working in tandem with his harassers. In 1874, Dr. Galati abandoned his business and moved his family to Naples.

Galati had learned that an influential gangster named Antonio Giammona, who was based in the village of Uditore, was running protection rackets to extort money from the owners of western Sicily's lemon groves. His goal was to develop a monopoly on the fruit. Giammona's influence not only extended to the police and local politicians but also to the cart drivers and dock workers who transported the goods. A member of the Italian parliament, Diego Tajani, asserted that the Sicilian Mafia was not intrinsically deadly and invincible; rather, it was its ability to collaborate with and embed itself in local governments that gave the Mafia great power.

In August 1875, Galati submitted the first known report of "Mafia" activities in Sicily to the Minister of the Interior in Rome, noting that although the population of Uditore was 800, there had been 23 murders in 1874 alone. Although nothing was done to help Galati, his memorandum forced the national government to look at the growing problem in the south.

From the 1800s to the end of World War I, government officials and scholars conducted further investigations into the Mafia, or "Cosa Nostra," often following a high-profile murder or a spate of killings. Although individual mafiosi (members of the Mafia) were indicted, the organization was never successfully systematically pursued or prosecuted. Meanwhile, the Mafia continued to conspire with municipal governments and police to exercise a subtle, profitable, and coercive influence on Sicilian life.

See also: The Triads 146–49 ▪ The Beer Wars 152–53 ▪ The Yakuza 154–59

Fascist enforcers

The most successful efforts to quash the Sicilian Mafia were initiated in 1925 by Cesare Mori, a prefect of Palermo operating under the Fascist government of Benito Mussolini. His tactics were simple—the use of authoritarian power in conjunction with strong-arm tactics. Mori, who did not believe that the Mafia were a unified structure, set up an "interprovincial" anti-Mafia police force and arrested 11,000 Sicilians, including many mafiosi and bandits but also innocent civilians. He processed them through mass trials, which he concealed from the press. Eventually, Mussolini could proclaim to the nation that organized crime had been crushed in Italy. During this time, approximately 500 mafiosi fled to the US, where they established the Sicilian mob in America.

The Allied invasion of Sicily in 1943 inadvertently restored the Mafia to power. When the fascist government was overthrown, a power vacuum ensued, particularly at municipal levels. This allowed the Mafia to step back into the positions they had occupied before Mussolini's rise.

Resolving disputes

During a 1957 trip to Sicily, New York mobster Joe Bonanno suggested that their European counterparts establish a committee to resolve disputes. Prominent mafiosi Tommaso Buscetta, Gaetano Badalamenti, and Salvatore Greco began drafting the rules, and the following year, the first Sicilian Mafia Commission was formed in Palermo. The commission intended to resolve disputes among families and individuals, to determine punishment for breaching the rules of the Mafia, and to control the use of violence against members of government, lawyers, and »

An Italian police handout of nine suspected Mafia members accused of drug trafficking in Sicily. The handout was part of a 2008 international operation codenamed "Old Bridge," which targeted 50 suspects in New York and 30 in Sicily.

journalists, as these murders brought unwanted attention to Sicilian organized crime as a whole. If a boss wished to order a person killed, it would have to be approved by the commission.

Warring mafiosi

For approximately 20 years the commission wielded little power, largely because regional bosses were accustomed to operating independently. The commission was unable to prevent the so-called First Mafia War which erupted in 1961 between the Greco and the La Barbera families, claiming 68 victims. The war culminated in the infamous 1963 Ciaculli massacre, in which seven police and military officers were killed while they tried unsuccessfully to defuse a car bomb intended for Salvatore Greco. The fallout for the Cosa Nostra was significant. Within ten weeks, 1,200 mafiosi were arrested.

The government established an Anti-Mafia Commission headed by Cesare Terranova, Palermo's former chief investigative prosecutor. Ultimately, although the investigation made many significant discoveries—such as

collusion between former mayor of Palermo, Salvo Lima, and the Cosa Nostra—the political will to act on the final report was lacking. The Sicilian Mafia temporarily dissolved their commission and hundreds of prominent members fled to other countries to avoid prosecution.

Beginning in the late 1970s, mafiosi from the village of Corleone made a successful bid for dominance of the Cosa Nostra in what would become known as the Second Mafia War (1981–83). Led by Salvatore "Totò" Riina, the Corleonesi successfully took over the largely ineffective Sicilian Mafia Commission and transformed it into a tool for exercising absolute power. Although uneducated, the Corleonesi more than made up for this deficit with deviousness and violence. Predictably, their rise was accompanied by a dramatic spike in the murder of public figures, a departure from Cosa Nostra's *modus operandi*.

In 1979, four establishment figures including Terranova were killed in separate incidents. The following year, the captain of Monreale's carabinieri, the president of the Sicilian region, and

> We are at war… The mafiosi are firing with machine guns and TNT. We can only hit back with words. There are thousands of them and only a few hundred of us.
> **Anonymous policeman**

Palermo's chief prosecutor were killed in Mafia hits. In 1982, the murder of Pio La Torre, an active member of the Anti-Mafia Commission, prompted a law that made it illegal to belong to a "Mafia-type association." Later that same year, General Carlo Alberto, a national hero, anti-Mafia advocate, and prefect of Palermo, was murdered alongside his wife when a dozen mafiosi sealed off the road on which they were traveling and emptied their machine guns into his car. His funeral was broadcast to weeping eyes all across Italy.

Legal offensive

For the first time, the Italian public and the government decided to act to break the Cosa Nostra's deadly grip on Sicily. A new law allowed the government to confiscate the wealth of convicts found to be mafiosi, hindering their ability to exercise power while in prison.

In July 1983, a car bomb detonated in Palermo, killing chief investigating magistrate Rocco Chinnici, his two bodyguards, and an innocent bystander. The violence spurred Antonino

Losing face

In Mafia nomenclature, *sfregio* (literally translating as "scar" or "insult") refers to a wound resulting in disfigurement, either in the form of a physical scar or through humiliation which causes the recipient to "lose face."

A common form of *sfregio* is the vandalism or theft of property owned or under the protection of another mafioso. This forces the victim to decide whether or not he should respond to the injury and, if so,

what the appropriate response should be. If he chooses not to respond, then he can be perceived as being weak and dominated by his aggressor. The exchange of insults may escalate to deadly levels.

One example of this is the 1897 executions of Olivuzza family members Vincenzo Lo Porto and Giuseppe Caruso, which were sanctioned by the heads of the eight families. They had unanimously agreed that the two men had inflicted an ill-conceived insult upon the leadership of their clan.

Caponnetto, a career magistrate who was planning to retire, to step in as Chinnici's replacement. Caponnetto developed a team of anti-Mafia magistrates. Going on the offensive, he announced that the authorities were now working with ex-Mafia informant Tommaso Buscetta, who was

> I obeyed orders, and I knew that by strangling a little boy I would make a career for myself. I was walking on air.
> **Salvatore Cancemi**

providing information that would finally prove the Cosa Nostra was a single unified organization. Caponnetto declared that the entire Mafia, rather than individual members or groups, was going on trial. Caponnetto's team went on to issue 366 arrest warrants on the strength of Buscetta's testimony. When further witnesses came forward, more arrests were made.

Fierce response

Rather than toning down their violence, the Corleonesi-controlled Mafia escalated it. As Italy had yet to develop an effective witness protection program, the Cosa Nostra gunned down informant Leonardo Vitale, Tomasso Buscetta's brother-in-law. Flying squad officer Beppe Montana, responsible for tracking down Mafia fugitives, was killed in July 1985. The next month, another flying

Sicilian police inspect the aftermath of the car bomb attack that killed Judge Paulo Borsellino and his police guards near the judge's mother's house in Palermo, Sicily, on July 20, 1992.

squad member, Antonino Cassarà, was riddled with 200 bullets while his wife looked on in horror.

The sheer scale of the violence triggered what was known as the "Palermo Spring." Students held anti-Mafia demonstrations in Palermo, an influential clergyman spoke openly of the "Mafia" for the first time and shamed the national government for not addressing the problem, as did the mayor of Palermo. Meanwhile, the anti-Mafia magistrates had accrued enough evidence to open a maxi-trial on February 10, 1986, in which 474 mafiosi and their allies were to face charges. On December 16, 1987, »

Mafia chain of command

Boss (king): Also known as a "Don," he is in charge of the organization.

Consigliere (rook): A trusted advisor to the boss. He can represent the boss in important meetings.

Underboss (queen): The boss's second in command. He is usually a family member who takes over if the boss is killed or incapacitated.

Caporegime (bishop): Usually shortened to "capo" (head), he leads a crew of soldiers. There may be anywhere between two and 20 in a family.

Soldier (knight): The lowest level of mobster attached to a gang. He is required to take *omertà*, the code of silence, and works in a small group.

Associate (pawn): An individual who has not yet become a "made" man, but works for a Mafia crew under the supervision of a soldier.

---

360 of the accused were found guilty and sentenced to a total of 2,665 years in jail. This was only the beginning: Caponnetto's team had already prepared for two more maxi-trials, and thanks to new information from informant Antonio Calderone, was poised to trigger another. In March 1988, 160 arrests were made. The Mafia responded by murdering Palermo appeal court judge Antonio Saetta and his son.

Administrative setbacks

When Caponnetto stepped down at the end of 1987, he was succeeded by the inexperienced Anthony Meli. He made countless clumsy decisions which endangered the entire project. Judges Paolo Borsellino and Giovanni Falcone of the anti-Mafia team spoke out

No one should provide the police or judiciary with facts that help uncover any crime whatsoever.
Niccolò Turrisi Colonna

against his incompetence but were ignored. To make matters worse, the anti-Mafia mayor of Palermo, Leoluca Orlando, lost his position in 1990. The bleakest moment came when Judge Corrado Carnevale, presiding over the Palermo Court

of Appeal, ruled that some of the maxi-trial convictions should be overturned based on technicalities.

In 1991, Giovanni Falcone was appointed Director of Penal Affairs in the Ministry of Justice. He united anti-Mafia police from various organizations in a single entity. New legislation allowed phone taps on Mafia members, combated money laundering, and dissolved municipal councils infiltrated by organized crime.

Again, the Mafia answered the threat with violence. In August 1991, they contracted the 'Ndràngheta to murder Antonio Scopelliti, a Court of Cassation prosecutor. Palermo businessman Libero Grassi, who campaigned against extortion rackets, was the victim of a similar homicide three weeks later.

Wanted posters for the Mafia's "boss of bosses" Bernardo Provenzano appeared in Palermo in 2005. They were based on a 1959 mugshot—the only photo of him then in existence.

New laws

On January 31, 1992, the Italian Supreme Court overturned Judge Carnevale's verdict, marking an unprecedented victory for the anti-Mafia cause in Italy. However, it drew a furious response from the Corleonesi. On May 23, 1992, Falcone and his wife were murdered in a car bomb attack. Paolo Borsellino and five members of his escort were murdered two months later by another bomb.

At this point, the government finally decided that enough was enough. They sent 7,000 soldiers to Sicily to take charge of day-to-day police duties, which freed up local forces to hunt down Riina and his men. The police were granted legal powers to infiltrate the Mafia and set up sting operations involving fake drug deals and money laundering. A significant new law also helped to protect informants by enabling them to change their identities.

Mafiosi informants

This law was passed at the perfect time. In the wake of the Court of Cassation's verdict, many mafiosi became informants. Based upon information provided by a captured mafioso, Riina was caught in 1993. Leadership of the Mafia passed to Leoluca Bagarella—who was, in turn, arrested in 1995—and then to Bernardo Provenzano.

The anti-Mafia efforts of the 1980s and early 1990s practically castrated the Cosa Nostra.

Provenzano wielded very little power, and the organization decentralized. Local Mafia leaders returned to small-time protection rackets, which were less profitable but allowed them to operate in relative secrecy.

On April 11, 2006, after an extensive manhunt, Provenzano was finally captured. In the years since, the Mafia has laid low, unlikely ever to be as powerful as they were during the second half of the 20th century. ∎

Giovanni Falcone

A self-described "servant of the state in the land of infidels," Judge Giovanni Falcone, more than any other politician before him, fearlessly and dutifully set about crushing the Sicilian Mafia.

Through his conversations with informant Tomasso Buscetta, he became the first Italian government official to learn about and document the structure of the Sicilian Mafia. When Falcone was targeted and killed by a Mafia bomb on May 23, 1992, along with his wife and three police officers, he was hailed as a hero to the Italian people.

Sicilians hung bedsheets from their windows emblazoned with "Falcone lives," and a tree outside his house was quickly transformed into a shrine adorned with photographs, flowers, and messages to the statesman who had exposed the Mafia.

Palermo's airport was even renamed Falcone–Borsellino Airport in honor of Falcone and his friend Paolo Borsellino, a fellow anti-Mafia judge who was murdered in a similar car bombing incident in Palermo just two months after Falcone.

THEY DARE DO ANYTHING
THE TRIADS, MID-1800s–

IN CONTEXT

LOCATION
China and worldwide

THEME
**International crime
syndicates**

BEFORE
1761–1911 The Heaven and
Earth Society is established
in southeastern China as a
secret sect; after 1911, it
evolves into the Triads.

AFTER
1850s The "Tong" brotherhood
originates among Chinese
expatriates in the US, and
acquires a reputation for
trafficking women.

1990 The Asian-American
street gang Jackson Street
Boys forms in San Francisco,
California, and becomes
involved in extortion,
racketeering, and narcotics
trafficking.

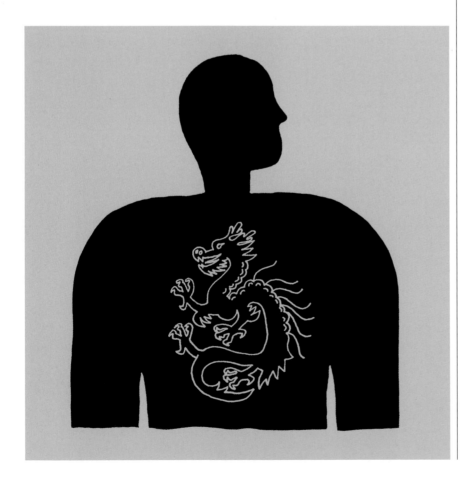

At the top-tier of the
Chinese criminal
hierarchy are the Triad
societies, with 250,000 members
worldwide and representation in
Macau, Hong Kong, Taiwan,
southeast Asia, and in Chinatowns
worldwide. Triad members range
from low-level thugs to those who
occupy positions in politics and
the criminal justice system.

The three most powerful Triad
societies are the Sun Yee On, 14K,
and Wo Shing Wo. Founded by
Heung Chin in 1919 in Hong Kong,
the Sun Yee On is the largest, with
approximately 55,000 members. Its
operations extend to southeast
Asia, Australia, Europe, and North

See also: The Sicilian Mafia 138–45 ▪ The Yakuza 154–59 ▪ The Medellín Cartel 166–67

The arrest of Samson Tan, a Chinese chemist, by Philippine police in 2008. Tan was charged with producing methamphetamine for Hong Kong-based Triad gangs.

and Central America. Since the late 2000s, it has acquired a reputation for trafficking methamphetamine (crystal meth), and for supplying Mexican drug cartels with the raw materials needed to produce it.

Sun Yee On's main rivals are the 14K. Founded in Guangzhou in 1945, the 14K moved its base to Hong Kong in 1949 and also formed a major branch in Macau during the 1970s. It is the second largest Triad, with 25,000 members.

The Wo Shing Wo emerged from Toronto's Chinatown in 1930 before it transferred its operations to Hong Kong in 1931; it also has a strong presence in London's Chinatown. The Wo Shing Wo is allegedly the top narcotics trafficker in Hong Kong.

Early origins
Most historians trace the origins of the Triads to the Heaven and Earth Society—a secretive fraternal organization founded in 1761 in southeastern China. Also known as the Hung Clan, the sect regarded the ruling Qing Dynasty, based in Manchuria, as "foreigners" and plotted their overthrow. Among their other activities during the 18th century, the Hung Clan conspired with foreign merchants to import opium. The English word "Triad" first appeared in reference to the triangular motifs that appeared on Hung Clan banners.

The Triads are believed to have been a driving force in the Xinhai Revolution of 1911. This finally ended Qing rule and led to the establishment of the Republic of China. After this time, the Triads found new purpose and gained significant wealth through illegal gambling and prostitution.

Triad hierarchy
Triads are devoted to the ancient rituals and symbols of their founders. As such, they rely on traditional Chinese numerology corresponding to the *I Ching* to structure their organization. The leader of a Triad, who makes the executive decisions, is known as the Dragon Head with the number designation 489. He is assisted by one or more office-bearing ranks, designated with the number 438, which include his Deputy and the Incense Master—usually a senior official in terms of rank and age. The lowest officer ranks—415, 426, and 432—include Enforcers, who work as military commanders. Non-office-bearing

ranks are known as "49ers". A special number—25—is used to denote spies, informants, or undercover police agents.

The traditional initiation ceremony for new recruits can last up to three days. It comprises 18 steps and historically involves drinking the blood of members and sacrificing a chicken. Modern ceremonies are much shorter; »

I like to describe Chinese organized crime as the flu virus because they're constantly mutating.
Kingman Wong

The Rank Structure of a Triad Society

489: Dragon Head ("Mountain Master")
The boss of the Triad.

438: Deputy ("Deputy Mountain Master")
The underboss, who leads the Triad if the Dragon Head
is incapacitated.

438: Ceremonies Officer ("Incense Master")
Organizes new recruits and the
induction ceremony.

438: Operations Officer ("Vanguard")
Assistant to the Incense Master.

415: Administrator
("White Paper Fan")
Advisor on financial and
business matters.

426: Enforcer ("Red Pole")
A military commander
overseeing a group of 49ers
and Blue Lanterns.

432: Liaison Officer
("Straw Sandal")
A coordinator between
different units.

49: Ordinary members ("49ers")
After passing the initation ceremony, a Blue
Lantern becomes a "soldier."

Uninitiated members ("Blue Lanterns")
Individuals not yet regarded as
full members have no number designation but
are connected to a Triad gang.

the chicken sacrifice is omitted and recruits are required to suck only their own blood from their finger.

The rise of the Triads

In 1916, following the death of the Chinese Republic's first president, Yuan Shikai, China split into a land of feuding warlords. In the ensuing chaos, the Chinese people turned to the Triads for protection and stability. This led to a surge in Triad power from the 1920s to the 1940s. Their hub during this period was Shanghai, where the gangster Du Yuesheng secured the city's opium trade by forcing "protection" on local opium traders. Bribing French authorities with $20 million, Du was allowed to freely smuggle opium into the city through the French Concession area.

Du became the leader of the 100,000 member Green Gang, a secret society originally formed in the early 1900s by grain shippers in Shanghai. The society soon became corrupt and dominated criminal activity in the city, especially in the opium trade.

By 1923 the Kuomintang—the Chinese nationalist republican army—allied with the Communists and ousted the warlords in an attempt to reunite China. However, the two former allies then turned on each other and fought for political control of the country.

The Green Gang entered the battle in 1927, when it was recruited by Kuomintang leader Chiang-kai-shek to fight the Communists. In a bid to protect their opium monopoly, the Green Gang sided with the democratic Kuomintang. On April 12, 1927, they conspired with the Kuomintang to perpetrate the White Terror Massacre, in which they stormed Shanghai's Chinese section and butchered 5,000 Communists. To reward the Green Gang for securing the city, Chiang-kai-shek made Du a general. Du later became an influential member of the chamber of commerce, and ironically, head of the opium suppression committee. Naturally, Du used his position to maintain the Green Gang's fortune by reselling the opium confiscated by the committee.

Du and the Green Gang suffered a major blow in 1937 when the Japanese invaded Shanghai. Du fled, but returned when Shanghai was liberated in 1945. However, his influence was significantly reduced. When the Communists seized power in 1949, Du fled again, leaving his gang to their fate.

Modern activities

Because the Triads had supported the Kuomintang when the Communists seized power in 1949, Chairman Mao Zedong began to implement measures that drove the Triads to the US, Taiwan, Canada, and British-controlled Hong Kong.

Hong Kong in particular became a hotbed for Triad activity, with around 50 gangs operating on the island. But in the 1970s, the British government clamped down on the Triads, and by 1997, the year in which the island was transferred back to Chinese rule, the number of reported crimes perpetrated by Triads in Hong Kong had been reduced to 5–10 percent of the total. Many gangsters subsequently moved their operations to Macau and to southern China.

In the 1950s, the Triads practically created the global market for heroin, selling it to US soldiers serving in Vietnam. However, in more recent decades, they have concentrated on human trafficking.

Poor Chinese families, who know that they can earn up to ten times as much money in the US, make a down payment to "Snake Heads"—traffickers of illegal aliens—to smuggle young males into the US. These men are then forced to work off the rest of the fee—typically up to $40,000—by laboring in kitchens or in sweatshops for next to nothing. Failure to do so inevitably results in bloodshed. ∎

Macau's casinos became the epicenter of the 14K Triad's criminal activity in the late 1990s following the police crackdown on the 14K's activities in Hong Kong in 1997.

Wan "Broken Tooth" Kuok-koi

Wan Kuok-koi was born in 1955 in a Macau slum. As a teenager he formed a street gang. He earned his nickname "Broken tooth" for an injury sustained crashing a stolen car. He was initiated into the notorious 14K Triad and rose through the gang's ranks until he controlled the city's underworld. He gained a reputation for his use of extreme violence. By the 1990s, 10,000 men were at his command.

Obsessed with his image, the snappy dresser spent $1.7 million to produce *Casino*, a film about his life as a gangster, starring Hong Kong actor Simon Yam.

Wan Kuok-koi was arrested on May 1, 1998 as he watched an advance screening of the film. He was charged with the attempted murder of Macau's Chief of police, Antonio Marque Baptista, as well as with loan sharking, money laundering, and operating a gang. Sentenced to 15 years in prison, Wan Kuok-koi continued to run his operations from behind bars. He was released in 2012 having served his time, and in 2015, he joined an important political advisory committee along with other powerful Macau businessmen.

Nu MoRE VILLAINOUS, RUFFIANLY BAND WAS EVER ORGANIZED

THE WILD BUNCH, 1889–1908

IN CONTEXT

LOCATION
Wyoming, Colorado, Utah, US

THEME
Outlaw gangs

BEFORE
1855 Thieves replace gold worth £12,000 (about $1.36 million today) on the London–Folkestone train with lead shot in "The Great Gold Robbery." The substitution is discovered when the crates arrive in Paris.

1877 Sam Bass and his men seize $60,000 in gold pieces from a train traveling from San Francisco in the Union Pacific Big Springs Robbery.

AFTER
1976 The Irish Republican Socialist Party steals £200,000 ($1.9 million) from a mail train in Sallins, Ireland.

Although Butch Cassidy's "Wild Bunch" was not as anarchic as its nickname suggests, the collective had none of the order of Cosa Nostra or the Triads.

In 1866, Butch was born Robert Leroy Parker to a Utah Mormon family. He adopted "Cassidy" from an older cowboy he worked for as a teenager, and picked up "Butch" during a brief stint at a butcher's.

Cassidy committed his first robbery with a small group of friends in 1889. They went down to the bars of Telluride, Colorado, one

Saturday and made off with $24,000 ($638,000 today) from the town's San Miguel Valley Bank on Monday. Robber's Roost was their hideout, a crag in the rugged "Canyon Country" of southeastern Utah.

Train robbers
Cassidy and his comrades lay low around the canyons for weeks or months at a time, in crude cabins and on ranches, before venturing out to rob trains across the Western states. The Wild Bunch were no idealists, but there was a utopian aura to their life of crime. Butch

The women of the Wild Bunch

The Wild Bunch took care to maintain good relations with the ranchers who owned the lands on which they lived. They were also notably welcoming of women. Josie and "Queen" Ann Bassett were sisters who worked on the family ranch close to Robbers' Roost. They became romantically and amicably involved with various members of the Wild Bunch, who protected the Bassett ranch when it came under attack from cowboys who wanted their land.

One of the woman in the Wild Bunch's circle would become a member in her own right: Laura Bullion. She was a bank- and train-robber who counted the Sundance Kid and Ben Kilpatrick—known in the gang as "The Tall Texan"—among her numerous lovers.

Historians have been intrigued by the involvement of women with outlaws, particularly by the apparent absence of ill-feeling as romantic attachments came and went.

See also: The James-Younger Gang 24–25 ▪ The Great Train Robbery 30–35

Members of the Wild Bunch, including Longabaugh (the Sundance Kid) on the far left and Cassidy on the far right, pose in a Texas photographer's studio in 1901.

claimed that he never killed a man, but an attack by gang members on the *Overland Flyer*, a Union Pacific train outside Wilcox, Wyoming, in 1899, certainly led to one death.

Sheriffs and deputies he regards with pity and contempt. He is a power unto himself.
San Francisco Call

The train was held up by two of the Wild Bunch standing on the tracks. The outlaws detached the main part of the train and forced the engineer to steam across a bridge with the lead cars which held valuables. After dynamiting the bridge to block the line, the outlaws took $30,000 ($884,000 today) in cash and jewelry and rode away.

A posse led by Sheriff Josiah Hazen traced them 75 miles (120 km) to the Castle Creek ravine. A shootout ensued, and the sheriff was killed by outlaw Harvey Logan. The rest of the gang escaped.

Wanted dead or alive
Working in groups of three or four, the Wild Bunch kept robbing and their notoriety skyrocketed. State authorities and private detectives wanted them dead or alive. Stray gang members were caught in shootouts and pursuits over a series of jobs, and the Wild Bunch's numbers steadily dwindled.

In 1901, Cassidy fled to South America along with Harry Longabaugh—famously known as "the Sundance Kid"—and Longabaugh's wife. Their last years are shrouded in romantic mystery, with reports of numerous heists and a final, fatal shootout in Bolivia on November 4, 1908. ▪

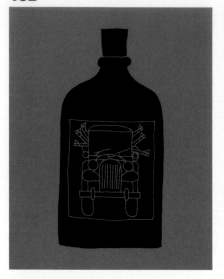

PROHIBITION HAS MADE NOTHING BUT TROUBLE

THE BEER WARS, 1923–29

IN CONTEXT

LOCATION
Chicago, Illinois, US

THEME
Gang warfare

BEFORE
1910: Chicago police arrest more than 200 gangsters from a crime family known as Black Hand in a raid in Little Italy.

January 16, 1917: The Illinois State Attorney indicts eight corrupt politicians and police officers, including the Chief of Police, for bribery and collusion with Chicago gangsters.

AFTER
July 29, 1932: John, Arthur, and James Volpe—Pittsburgh bootleggers—are shot in a coffee shop on the orders of local mob boss John Bazzano.

September 26, 1933: George Barnes Jr., alias "Machine Gun Kelly," is arrested in Memphis, Tennessee, for bootlegging and armed robbery.

O
n a rainy Friday night in Chicago, Illinois, six armed gangsters burst through the front doors of a saloon and attacked the bar owner, beating him senseless with the butts of their guns. A few days earlier, Jacob Geis had refused to purchase beer from the South Side O'Donnell gang, choosing instead to remain a loyal customer of the Saltis-McErlane gang.

In front of the saloon's patrons, O'Donnell gangsters threatened Geis, demanding that he purchase alcohol from them and them alone. The bar owner was left in a bloody heap with multiple skull fractures.

When I sell liquor, it's called bootlegging. When my patrons serve it on Lake Shore Drive, it's called hospitality.
Al Capone

The late night shakedown, which took place on September 7, 1923, was the beginning of Chicago's so-called "Beer War"— a gang war that left a trail of violence and death in its wake.

Territorial monopolies
This spate of gang violence had its roots in Prohibition. In 1920, federal Prohibition policies outlawed the sale of liquor across the US. Soon after, bootleggers emerged to fulfill the demand for illicit booze, smuggling alcohol from other countries and bottling their own concoctions. The Mafia was heavily involved in the bootlegging trade and rose to dominance as a result of its success in supplying liquor during Prohibition.

The most notorious criminal to profit from bootlegging was Chicago mobster Al Capone. Capone allegedly earned $60 million ($811 million today) each year from the industry. His success was thanks to the monopoly that his operation—the Chicago Outfit—held over the city's South Side. Capone worked under Johnny Torrio, who had divided the South Side of the city into territories. Each territory was controlled by

See also: The Hawkhurst Gang 136–37 ▪ The Sicilian Mafia 138–45

A police investigator stands amid containers of moonshine after a South Side raid in 1922. Gangsters often paid the police to raid rival breweries or to warn them of raids on their own.

a smaller gang, which supplied speakeasies—and a lucrative network of brothels and casinos—via Torrio's breweries. The North Side of Chicago was controlled by the Irish-American North Side Mob, with whom Torrio had agreed a truce.

The Outfit controlled all of Chicago's South Side except for one area under the jurisdiction of the Saltis-McErlane Gang. There was one other gang vying for a piece of the South Side—the O'Donnells, who controlled no territory but owned breweries. They were eager to fight existing gangs for a piece of the action.

City at war

The gangs of Chicago fought over customers, undercutting each other, threatening bar owners, and stealing from distributors. Their jostling over territorial boundaries often spilled blood. Gangsters met violent deaths—usually on

the wrong end of the "Chicago Typewriter," the Thompson machine gun, introduced to the city by Frank McErlane.

The Beer War raged between the O'Donnells and the Saltis-McErlanes, who also went to war with Capone allies, the Sheldon Gang. In late 1925, a Sheldon

member was murdered by a Saltis-McErlane mobster. Sheldons killed two Saltis gunmen in retaliation, escalating the gangs' rivalry.

The North Side truce also fell apart in the 1920s. North Side boss Dean O'Banion was killed in 1924, and Torrio retired after surviving an assassination attempt. He handed everything over to Capone, who inherited a bloody war for control of Chicago that culminated in the Saint Valentine's Day Massacre of 1929, in which seven North Side gangsters were killed.

Many of these bootleg gangs were folded into larger syndicates when Prohibition finally ended in 1933. Capone's organization, on the other hand, diversified into other rackets, such as gambling, prostitution, and narcotics trafficking, and would dominate Chicago for years to come. ▪

Prohibition, crime, and the economy

From 1920 to 1933, the ban on the production, transportation, and sale of alcohol had the unintended effect of creating a rise in mass disobedience.

Despite the Prohibition movement's expectation that outlawing alcohol would reduce crime, it actually led to a higher crime rate due to bootlegging. During Prohibition, crime rates in the United States increased by 24 percent, as criminal organizations supplied the black market in liquor sales.

Prohibition also had an effect on the US economy. During the 1920s, the cost of running the Bureau of Prohibition increased from $4.4 million to $13.4 million. Closing manufacturing plants and taverns also caused an economic downturn.

As a result of Prohibition, most large-scale alcohol producers were shut down, leading to a reversal in the technological advancements that had been made in the alcoholic beverage industry.

IF THE BOSS SAYS A PASSING CROW IS WHITE, YOU MUST AGREE

THE YAKUZA, 1946–

IN CONTEXT

LOCATION
Japan and US

THEME
Japanese criminal gangs

BEFORE
16th century *Kabukimono*, or "weirdo," gangs of roaming aristocratic samurai emerge during peacetime in feudal Japan. Sporting flamboyant fashions, they brawl and cause havoc in towns and cities.

AFTER
1950s Across Japan, groups of teenagers form motorcycle gangs who fight each other and race illegally. Police identify them as *bosozoku*, an "out-of-control tribe."

1972 In suburban Tokyo, "K-Ko the Razor" leads a female gang of 50 *sukeban*—girls who wear modified school uniforms and carry chains and razors with which they attack rival gangs.

Armed police stand guard after a 2016 raid at the Kobe Yamaguchi-gumi Yakuza headquarters. Investigators seized boxes containing evidence of drug trafficking activities.

T he Japanese mafia, known collectively as the Yakuza, comprises more than 100,000 members split into a small number of independent syndicates. Four syndicates—the Yamaguchi-gumi, the Sumiyoshi-kai, the Inagawa-kai, and the Aizukotetsu-kai—account for the vast majority of Yakuza members. The structure of these syndicates is complex and varied, but most are organized in a pyramid structure with a *oyabun* (boss) at the top, who is assisted by a number of senior advisers, each of whom control affiliated gangs. The Sumiyoshi-kai is an exception as it is made up of a confederation of gangs.

Traces of the Yakuza date back to the 17th century and two groups at the bottom rung of Japanese society. The first group, *tekiya*, were market traders who peddled their goods at festival events. Some *tekiya* hired themselves out as bodyguards to other *tekiya*, which led to the establishment of protection rackets.

The second group—gamblers known as *bakuto*— set up illegal casinos in temples on the edges of towns and villages, and ran loan shark operations.

Yakuza is a gambling term that owes much to the group's *bakuto* roots: in the Japanese card game *oichokabu*—in which the aim is to reach a score of 19 with three cards—*ya* means 8, *ku* means 9 and *za* represents 3. Together, they add up to 20 and form the worst possible losing hand. The word "Yakuza" became synonymous with something useless, which was later extended to refer to the gamblers themselves, denoting that they were useless members of society.

Structure and ritual

Although Yakuza groups have been involved in illicit activities from their inception, it has never been illegal to join a Yakuza group, and they are still not regarded as underground organizations.

In the mafia, blood relationships are pivotal, but for the Yakuza, the Japanese *senpai-kohai*, or senior-junior, mentor system is crucial. The system involves a foster parent figure, the *oyabun*, who has authority over his foster children, called *kobun*. Historically, this structure has provided the basis for the relationship between teacher and apprentice, and between Yakuza boss and follower. In the Yakuza, this system has established unity, strength, and devotion to the boss.

As in Japanese society as a whole, ritual holds Yakuza culture together. This is evident in the traditional *sakazuki* (sake saucer)

See also: The Sicilian Mafia 138–45 ▪ The Triads 146–49 ▪ Hells Angels 160–63

Once you make a pledge to the gang, the only way out is to cut off your fingers.
Yakuza member

ceremony, during which an *oyabun* drinks sake from the same cup as the *kobun*, to mark the *kobun*'s entry into the Yakuza group.

Yakuza syndicates developed stringent rules to preserve their secrecy, ensure adherence to the *senpai-kohai* system, and establish a ranking structure to determine each individual's status within the group. Beneath the *oyabun* is the *wakigashira* (underboss or first lieutenant) and the *shateigashira* (second lieutenant). The lieutenants command the senior-ranking *kyodai* (big brothers) and the lesser-ranking *shatei* (little brothers). The *oyabun* is also aided by the *saiko komon* (senior adviser) who leads a team of administrators, law advisers, and accountants.

Symbolic practices

Tattoos became a hallmark of Yakuza groups during Japan's feudal period (1185–1603). Originally, criminals were branded with black ring tattoos, but the Yakuza transformed the practice into complex, decorative badges of honor, which functioned as symbols of

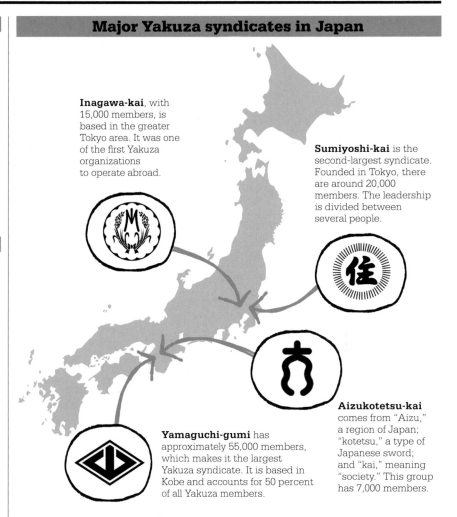

Major Yakuza syndicates in Japan

Inagawa-kai, with 15,000 members, is based in the greater Tokyo area. It was one of the first Yakuza organizations to operate abroad.

Sumiyoshi-kai is the second-largest syndicate. Founded in Tokyo, there are around 20,000 members. The leadership is divided between several people.

Aizukotetsu-kai comes from "Aizu," a region of Japan; "kotetsu," a type of Japanese sword; and "kai," meaning "society." This group has 7,000 members.

Yamaguchi-gumi has approximately 55,000 members, which makes it the largest Yakuza syndicate. It is based in Kobe and accounts for 50 percent of all Yakuza members.

strength, endurance, and status. A less artistic custom, called *yubitosome*, is the mutilation of one's own finger with a knife as penance to the *oyabun* for debt or disobedience. For a first offense, the left little finger is removed up to the knuckle and presented to the *oyabun*. A portion of the ring finger is removed for a second offense, followed by the middle finger, and, finally, the index finger. For the next transgression, the culprit moves to the next joint of the little finger. If an

entire finger is cut off a member's hand as a result of repeat offenses, it becomes known as a "dead finger."

The modern Yakuza

At the beginning of the 20th century, Japan underwent extensive economic modernization. The Yakuza expanded their activities accordingly, organizing labor forces of casual workers at dockyards and on construction sites. Yakuza bosses invested in legitimate businesses which » acted as shop fronts to conceal their racketeering. They also began to bribe police so that they would turn a blind eye to their crimes.

In 1915, the Yamaguchi-gumi Yakuza syndicate emerged from a dockworkers' union in Kobe on Honshu island. It rose to power in the postwar period, and profited from a growing black market. The Yamaguchi-gumi eventually became the largest and most influential Yakuza syndicate, involved in prostitution rackets, narcotics trafficking, gambling, arms dealing, and bribery.

The rise of the Yamaguchi-gumi is largely attributed to the leadership of the third *oyabun*, Kazuo Taoka, who between 1946 and 1981 transformed it into the world's largest criminal gang.

When Taoka died in 1981 and underboss Kenichi Yamamoto also died before he could take over, the syndicate underwent a bloody succession crisis. Hiroshi Yamamoto followed Taoka as temporary *oyabun* and Masahisa Takenaka became his underboss. However, when Takenaka was elected *oyabun* by a council of senior Yamaguchi-gumi members,

Mobs are legal entities here. Their fan magazines and comic books are sold in convenience stores, and bosses socialize with prime ministers and politicians.
Jake Adelstein

Hiroshi Yamamato split from the Yamaguchi-gumi to form the Ichiwa-kai syndicate, taking 3,000 members with him. In January 1985, Yamamato sent a team of assassins to the home of Takenaka's girlfriend and gunned down both Takenaka and his underboss. This was the start of what later became known as the Yama-Ichi War. Swearing vengeance, the Yamaguchi-gumi sought to wipe out the Ichiwa-kai. After four years and more than 200 gunfights, the Yamaguchi-gumi finally beat their rivals into

submission. A peace was moderated by the respected *oyabun* of the Inagawa-kai syndicate and the remaining Ichiwa-kai were allowed to rejoin the Yamaguchi-gumi. However, the war left the victors devastated. Many prominent Yamaguchi-gumi members were imprisoned and 36 Yakuza members had died in the conflict. The Japanese media provided extensive coverage of the conflict and kept a running tally of the body count.

Rival gang

The second-largest Yakuza syndicate is the Sumiyoshi-kai, which was founded in 1958. Unusually for the Yakuza, this confederation of smaller groups is less hierarchical than the Yamaguchi-gumi syndicate and has a less centralized leadership. The syndicate does have a nominal head, however, called Isao Seki. He was arrested in 2015 and received a suspended one-year jail sentence for election-law violations.

The Sumiyoshi-kai set up front companies—including real estate businesses—in Tokyo, which operated legitimately before turning to extortion and

---

Kenichi Shinoda

On July 29, 2005, the *oyabun* of the Yamaguchi-gumi, Kenichi Shinoda, also known as Shinobu Tsukasa, assumed leadership of the syndicate after Yoshinori Watanabe, the fifth *oyabun*, retired. Shinoda is most notable for expanding the organization's influence into Tokyo.

He began his criminal career in 1962 in a gang affiliated to the Yamaguchi-gumi. When the gang was dismantled in 1984, Shinoda worked with friend and Yakuza associate Kiyoshi Takayama to establish a successor organization called Kodo-kai. Shinoda's modest

demeanor—he famously took the train to his induction ceremony rather than arriving by chauffeur-driven limousine—conceals his capacity for violence; in the 1970s, he was sentenced to 13 years in jail for murdering a rival *oyabun* with a samurai sword.

Shinoda was jailed for firearms offenses in 2005 and released in 2011. In September 2015, in a bid to consolidate his leadership, he expelled thousands of Yamaguchi-gumi for showing him disloyalty; they promptly formed a new gang.

threatening their clients. Bitter rivals of the Yamaguchi-gumi, the two syndicates share a history of fierce conflict. In February 2007, this conflict nearly became an all-out turf war following the assassination of Ryoichi Sugiura, a senior member of a Sumiyoshi-kai affiliate.

Business involvement

The corrosive influence of the Yakuza has demonstrably affected both the entertainment business and the sporting arena—including sumo wrestling and the Pride Fighting Championships, a martial arts organization that held popular televised competitions from 1997 to 2007. In 2003, Australian martial arts manager Miro Mijatovic was abducted by an affiliate of the Yamaguchi-gumi syndicate. He was threatened with execution unless he signed a contract transferring the management of his world-class fighters to the Yakuza group. Mijatovic complied but later turned informant and told the police how the Yakuza had paid his fighters to fix fights by injuring themselves.

The Yakuza have been involved in the entertainment industry since the end of World War II, running talent agencies in order to extort money from celebrities. In 2011, the Tokyo Metropolitan Police Department revealed that a popular TV presenter, Shinsuke Shimada, had close connections to the Yakuza. Shimada was forced to resign, and the case led to a series of anti-Yakuza laws, such as the revised Organized Crime Group Countermeasures Law. This made it legal to arrest anyone believed to be involved in gang activities if he or she made unreasonable or illegal demands toward ordinary citizens.

Japanese author Tomohiko Suzuki—who worked undercover at the Fukushima nuclear power plant shortly after the triple-meltdown in March 2011—has claimed that the Yakuza were heavily involved in the Tokyo Electric Power Company (Tepco), which ran the plant. Suzuki asserted that Tepco went to elaborate lengths to mask safety violations at the Fukushima plant, doctoring film footage of broken pipes to avoid having to spend money on maintenance.

Shrinking membership

Internecine violence and serious crackdowns on the Yakuza saw membership decline by 14 percent between 1991 and 2002. Even as its membership continued to shrink, the Yakuza strove to assert their presence: in 2010, lawyer Toshiro Igari, a fierce anti-Yakuza crusader, was found dead in his Manila vacation home with his wrists slashed. Many believed that his death was a Yakuza hit staged to look like a suicide.

In September 2016, Japanese police arrested nearly 1,000 Yakuza members, greatly depleting their manpower and funds. Crucially, this action also halted an imminent war between rival syndicates, which authorities feared would outdo the bloody carnage unleashed by the Yama-Ichi War. ∎

To get your whole body tattooed, you need endurance.
Horizen

Yakuza tattoos

The unique Japanese form of tattooing known as *irezumi* began as early as the Paleolithic period. Over time, tattoos became associated with criminality. Starting in the Kofun period (250–538 CE), convicts were marked with tattoos to indicate both the nature and number of their crimes. From 1789 to 1948, tattoos were outlawed in Japan, but the Yakuza showed their contempt for the law by having their entire bodies tattooed. In keeping with traditional *irezumi*, the Yakuza have their tattoos completed *tebori* (by hand), via a steel spike attached to a rod. The process is slow and painful—the color red is created from toxic iron sulphate which causes illness—and a full body tattoo takes years to complete. The ability to endure this suffering is proof of toughness, while the financial cost demonstrates wealth. Since tattoos are connected so strongly with organized crime in modern Japan, people with them are frequently forbidden from using fitness centers and bath houses. The mayor of Osaka even pioneered a 2012 campaign to have companies dismiss tattooed employees.

WHEN WE DO RIGHT, NOBODY REMEMBERS. WHEN WE DO WRONG, NOBODY FORGETS

HELLS ANGELS, 1948–

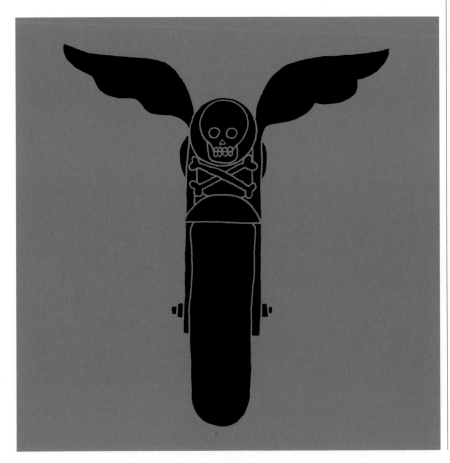

Ralph "Sonny" Barger was an ex-military man who, having forged his birth certificate to join the army at 16, had been discharged when his deception was discovered. In 1957, when Barger was 19, he began riding his motorcycle with a gang of bikers who bore a striking logo: a "Death Head" skull flanked by wings. The logo was brought from Sacramento by biker Don Reeves.

Inspired by their insignia, Barger's group referred to itself as the Hells Angels, unaware that there was already a group of loosely affiliated clubs in California with the same name. When they discovered these other clubs,

See also: The Triads 146–49 ▪ The Yakuza 154–59 ▪ The Medellín Cartel 166–67

The association of motorcycles with LSD is no accident of publicity. They are both a means to an end, to the place of definitions.
Hunter S. Thompson

Club members rise from "associate" to "prospect" to "full-patch" members. Only "full-patch" members may wear the Death Head logo and top "rocker" bearing the Hells Angels name.

Barger's group joined forces with them, and shared their Death Head logo. In 1963, after a meeting in Porterville, California, Barger's Oakland chapter assumed a position of authority within the wider Hells Angels—with Barger as the club's president.

Barger consolidated his power by establishing a new code of rules to replace the anarchy that previously prevailed. He drew up a charter for establishing a Hells Angels chapter: each new chapter had to be sponsored by an existing club, and required at least six "full-patch" members—the club's highest rank of membership. Within 50 years the Death Head adorned clubhouses all over the world, as new chapters sprang up. As with fraternities, each had its own territory and leadership, but was part of the larger organization, ascribing to Hells Angels ideology

and identity. The establishment of internal order, however, did not lead to greater harmony with the outside world. Better organized under Sonny's leadership, the Angels became increasingly involved in criminal activity.

Drug connections

At first, the Angels were chiefly consumers of narcotics—the horse tranquilizer PCP was referred to as "Angel Dust" due to the bikers'

fondness for it—but in the late 1960s, their business interests began to lean toward trafficking.

During the 1967 Summer of Love, the Angels became major pushers of LSD among the flower children of San Francisco, but the drug was too cheap to be profitable. Meanwhile, Angel Dust gained a reputation for "bad trips" and psychotic violence. However, methamphetamine (speed) seemed to offer no such drawbacks and »

Operation Black Biscuit

In 2002, undercover agent Jay Dobyns and two associates achieved a feat deemed impossible—they infiltrated a Hells Angels chapter. The agents worked for the Bureau of Alcohol, Tobacco, Firearms, and Explosives (ATF). During Operation Black Biscuit, the covert operatives posed as members of a Phoenix chapter of the Solo Angeles—a club allied with the Hells Angels. Dobyns then faked the murder of a member of the Mongols MC.

He presented the Hells Angels with a bloody jacket from the rival club, winning their trust, and over the 21-month mission, rose to become a "prospect" in the Angels organization.

The Hells Angels eventually disclosed drug- and gun-running techniques to the undercover agents. More than 800 hours of bugged conversations and 8,500 seized documents were gathered to prove that the Hells Angels operated as a criminal organization. As a result, in 2004, 16 Hells Angels were charged and brought to trial.

essentially sold itself. Smoked, snorted, or injected, this synthetic "upper" became the Hells Angels' best-selling product. Its abuse would reach near-epidemic proportions across North America.

In spite of this, it was not drugs but violence that caught the attention of the law. A report by

In the '60s we got a lot of publicity. It was all fun and games. In the '70s we all became gangsters.
Sonny Barger

California's attorney general had singled out the Hells Angels for the gang rape of a girl in Monterey by club members. The report pushed the club into the national spotlight, as stories of their violent acts circulated around the world.

One such notorious event took place in 1969, when club members were hired by the Rolling Stones as security at the Altamont Speedway Free Festival. The crowd was rowdy, and 18-year-old concertgoer Meredith Hunter drew a firearm and twice attempted to climb on stage. Hunter was fatally stabbed by Hells Angel Alan Passaro.

Years later, Rolling Stones tour manager Sam Cutler insisted that the fans were so out of control that without the Hells Angels, the band would have been trampled. Nevertheless, Altamont painted a different picture of the Angels: these men were dangerous outlaws.

The Hells Angels used extreme violence at Altamont on December 6, 1969. One Angel even knocked out Marty Balin, a member of the band Jefferson Airplane, during their set.

Their violence was not limited to the US. Barger incorporated the Popeyes motorcycle gang near Montreal, Quebec, in 1977, starting a new chapter. One of the founding members was 30-year-old serial killer Yves "Apache" Trudeau, who, two years later, founded the Laval "North" chapter in Quebec.

Rivals and conflicts
The Laval chapter gained a bad reputation for unparalleled use of violence. Its members were accused of taking the drugs they were supposed to be selling, and were also accused of cheating a Nova Scotia chapter out of money. Other chapters saw them as too

Worldwide reach of the Hells Angels

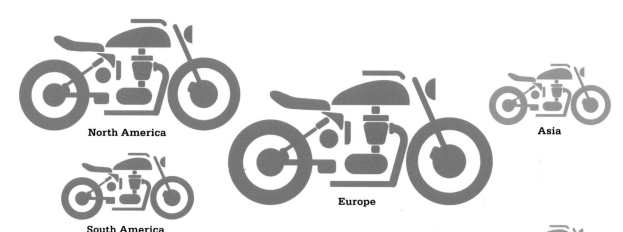

North America

South America

Europe

Asia

Africa

Oceania

Joining the club
Each "branch" of the Hells Angels is called a "chapter". In 2019, there were 466 chapters in 56 countries on six continents.

 20+ chapters   10–20 chapters   1–9 chapters

wild, and wanted them gone. In March 1985, five Laval Angels were invited to a clubhouse in Lennoxville, Quebec, by the Sherbrooke chapter. When they arrived, they were shot in the back of the head and dumped in the St. Lawrence River. It became known as the "Lennoxville Massacre." The massacre further cemented the Angels' reputation as violent—even by outlaw standards. Still, this reputation did nothing to slow the expansion of the club, or to prevent future violence.

By 1994, under the leadership of "Mom" Boucher, the Angels of Montreal were fighting a bitter war with a coalition of rival gangs for control of narcotics distribution. A similar conflict was fought in Scandinavia, where the Great Nordic Biker War saw the Hells Angels face off against the Bandidos MC and their allies in a struggle for hegemony over the northern European drug trade.

As a major crime syndicate, the Hells Angels have amassed their fair share of enemies. They have notable rivalries with the three other "big four" outlaw motorcycle clubs: the Pagans, the Outlaws, and the Bandidos MC. All four clubs are on government watchlists across the world. The Hells Angels, however, are arguably the most notorious, and the most often associated with criminal behavior. Since its founding, club members have been charged with a broad spectrum of crimes—from drug trafficking, extortion, and money laundering, to assault, murder, and prostitution. ■

"Mom" Boucher

Maurice "Mom" Boucher was born into poverty on June 21, 1953, in Quebec, Canada. He dropped out of high school to join a white-supremacist motorcycle gang, the SS, and eventually became its leader. Boucher joined the Hells Angels of Montreal in 1987 after serving 40 months in prison for sexually assaulting a 16-year-old girl.

Disgusted by the Hells Angels' Lennoxville massacre, Boucher's former SS friend, Salvatore Cazzetta, formed a gang—The Rock Machine— rather than join the Angels. When Cazzetta was arrested in 1994 for attempting to import 11 tons (11,000 kg) of cocaine, Boucher decided to monopolize narcotics in Montreal.

The resulting *Guerre des motards* (biker war) between the Hells Angels and the Rock Machine claimed the lives of 150 people. The conflict finally ended in 2002, after Boucher was convicted of ordering the murders of two corrections officers in a failed attempt to intimidate prosecutors.

THEY WERE THE BEST YEARS OF OUR LIVES

THE KRAYS AND THE RICHARDSONS, 1960s

IN CONTEXT

LOCATION
London, UK

THEME
Protection rackets

BEFORE
1930s-50s Notorious criminal Billy Hill commits smash-and-grab raids of London jewelry stores, including the high-profile Eastcastle Street Robbery of 1952.

AFTER
1980s–2000s The Noonan crime firm, led by brothers Dominic and Desmond Noonan, control organized crime in Manchester, UK, and allegedly commits up to 25 murders.

1980s The Clerkenwell Crime Syndicate, which specializes in drug trafficking, extortion, and murder in London neighborhoods, is established.

In 1960s' London, the notorious Brixton-based Richardson Gang and the Kray Firm led by East End twins Ronnie and Reggie, vied to dominate London's lucrative entertainment center, the West End. Both mobs came from impoverished backgrounds with absentee fathers and rose quickly before destroying themselves through mindless violence.

Reggie and Ronnie Kray were amateur boxers who idolized London mobster Billy Hill and were transfixed by gangster magazines and films. Their criminal empire was founded in the East End of London in 1954 when they took ownership of a billiard hall in Bethnal Green. When Maltese thugs attempted to collect "protection" money, Ronnie mangled them with a cutlass.

Partners in crime Reggie (left) and Ronnie (right) relax after questioning by the police about the murder of George Cornell. They appeared in an police lineup but witnesses could not, or would not, identify them.

See also: The Sicilian Mafia 138–45 ▪ The Yakuza 154–59 ▪ Jack the Ripper 266–73

The twins soon started a protection racket of their own. They allegedly had a personal bet to see who could make more money in a day, and earned a reputation for violence.

Reggie and Ronnie quickly established "The Firm" with Freddie Foreman, a powerful East End gangster, as their sometime enforcer. In 1957, they became owners of the Double R nightclub, then extended west, acquiring Esmeralda's Barn, a gambling club in Knightsbridge.

Bitter rivalry

Although the Krays' reputation has overshadowed the Richardsons', Charlie and Eddie were far more cruel and calculating. Charlie, labeled "vicious, sadistic, and a disgrace to civilization" by a judge, was the brains of the operation. His younger brother Eddie was the brawn. The gang tortured victims by nailing them to the floor, pulling out teeth with pliers, and chopping off toes with bolt-cutters.

The Richardsons' most feared enforcer was Frankie Fraser, who had earned the moniker "mad" after slashing the face of crime boss Jack Comer. "Mad" Frankie offered protection to pubs and clubs if they allowed the Richardsons' fruit machines into their establishments. Those who refused became the victims of vandalism or worse. The Richardsons also committed outright extortion as well as dealing in pornography and narcotics. They laundered their proceeds through their Brixton scrapyard and fruit machine business.

The first clash between the Krays and Richardsons occurred one night in a West End nightclub when Eddie Richardson and Frankie Fraser severely beat Kenny Hampton, a young man employed by Freddie Foreman. Swearing vengeance, Foreman walked into the club and reportedly jammed a .38 pistol into Eddie's nostril.

Tensions boiled over in March 1966 with "The Battle of Mr. Smith's" when members of the Richardson Gang and Kray associates shot, knifed, and beat each other in a club in southeast London. Both Fraser and Eddie Richardson were shot along with five others, while Kray cousin Dickie Hart was murdered with his own .45 gun. Fraser and Eddie Richardson were sentenced to five years in prison for affray. Charlie Richardson was arrested while watching the 1966 World Cup Final on July 30, and later sentenced to 25 years in prison.

Several days after "The Battle of Mr. Smith's," Ronnie Kray entered Whitechapel's busy Blind Beggar pub and was insulted by drunk Richardson gang member George Cornell. He fatally shot Cornell in the head. At an early Christmas

> Charlie [Richardson] is evil… in the nicest possible way. Evil people sometimes are.
> **John McVicar**

party on December 7, Reggie Kray repeatedly knifed drug dealer Jack McVitie in a dispute over money.

On May 8, 1968, the Krays were arrested by Detective Chief Inspector "Nipper" Read's Flying Squad, along with 15 other members of The Firm. The twins were sentenced to life without the possibility of parole for 30 years. Ronnie died from a heart attack in 1995; in 2000, Reggie's terminal cancer led to his compassionate release from prison. ∎

The Kray twins

The Kray twins grew up in the working-class community of Hoxton in East London. It was considered a "zone of transition" where criminal activity flourished. Both grandfathers—Jimmy "Cannonball" Lee and "Mad" Jimmy Kray—were renowned boxers in their day, as was the twins' aunt Rose.

The twins formed a unique bond, learning how to fight together, protecting each other from harm, and going into criminal business together.

Their sexuality has been the subject of intense speculation. Ronnie identified as bisexual in his 1993 book *My Story*, but the Kray family have denied claims by biographer John Pearson that Reggie also liked men. Pearson even claimed in a book written after the twins' deaths that they had engaged in incest.

The twins were only separated shortly after their convictions, when Ronnie was transferred to Broadmoor—a high-security psychiatric hospital—after being diagnosed as a paranoid schizophrenic.

ALL EMPIRES ARE CREATED OF BLOOD AND FIRE

THE MEDELLÍN CARTEL, 1972–93

IN CONTEXT

LOCATION
Colombia, Bolivia, Peru, Honduras, and the US

THEME
Drug cartels

BEFORE
1969 The Comando Vermelho (Red Command) is formed in Brazil by a group of convicts and political prisoners. It becomes the country's most dangerous cartel.

AFTER
1977–1998 The Cali Cartel separates from the Medellín Cartel and becomes one of the world's most powerful crime syndicates, controlling more than 90 percent of the global cocaine trade.

Mid 1980s Joaquín "El Chapo" Guzmán leads the Sinaloa Cartel in northwest Mexico, trafficking narcotics into the US; the organization is the most powerful drug trafficking cartel in the world.

The story of the Medellín Cartel's Colombian cocaine trafficking business is much more than just one of money-driven organized crime—it is part of a violent struggle for the governance of the country.

The Medellín Cartel was established in the early 1970s as a drug trafficking alliance between "The King of Cocaine" Pablo Escobar, "El Mexicano" José Gonzalo Rodríguez Gacha, Carlos Lehder, and the Ochoa family. At the height of the organization's power, it was earning at least $420 million a week through cocaine smuggling, at one point supplying up to 90 percent of the drug in the US and 80 percent worldwide.

Acting as a financier for the cartel, Jorge Luis Ochoa and his childhood friend Gilberto Rodriguez of the southern Colombian Cali Cartel acquired the First InterAmericas Bank in Panama, which both cartels used to launder drug money. For his part, Carlos Lehder purchased property on Norman's Cay, an island in the Bahamas which served as a major hub for drug trafficking from 1978–82. The cocaine was transported there from Colombia by jet, where it was then redistributed onto Lehder's personal fleet of small aircraft. These planes would then fly to the southeastern US to offload the narcotics, netting Lehder billions of dollars in profit.

Political influence

For the first ten years, the cartel operated more or less with impunity, uninhibited by the Colombian authorities. Then, in 1984, it ran up against Justice Minister Rodrigo Lara Bonilla. Lara—who suspected that Pablo Escobar's 1982 election to the Chamber of Representatives was the first move in a campaign to transform Colombia into a "narco-

Sometimes I am God, if I say a man dies, he dies that same day.
Pablo Escobar

See also: The Triads 146–49 ▪ Hells Angels 160–63 ▪ "Freeway" Rick Ross 168–71

Fabio Ochoa, a key figure in the Medellín Cartel, is escorted by two police officers at Bogotá's airport on October 13, 1999. He was extradited to the US in 2001.

state"—worked with the American Drug Enforcement Agency to oust Escobar from politics and proceed with criminal prosecutions against the cartel. Lara, however, was assassinated in 1984 on Escobar's orders. This was not the first or the last time that Escobar ordered the murder of a political opponent.

A particularly sensitive issue, which motivated Escobar and Lehder's decision to enter politics, was the government's support of extradition. Both men shrewdly employed anticolonialist rhetoric to oppose extradition legislation. Lehder founded the Movimiento Latino Nacional, which stirred up popular support by condemning US involvement in Latin America. He even claimed that cocaine was a means of liberation.

Police breakthrough

The dismantling of the Medellín Cartel came by way of intense collaborative efforts by the Colombian and American governments. The first kingpin to fall was Carlos Lehder, who was forced to abandon his base in Norman's Cay in 1983, when the Bahamian government seized his property and froze his bank accounts, causing Lehder to flee through the jungle. Escobar later brought Lehder back to Medellín by helicopter. Shortly after, he was captured at his farm by Colombian police, reportedly acting on a tip by one of Lehder's employees.

Lehder was extradited to the US in 1987 where he was sentenced to life without parole plus 135 years, a term that sent a strong message to the other cartel members. He then turned snitch in 1992 and agreed to testify against General Manuel Noriega of Panama, who had helped harbor cartel members. Lehder received a reduced sentence of 55 years.

Jose Gonzalo Rodríguez Gacha and Pablo Escobar refused to go peacefully. Gacha, his son Fredy, a bodyguard, and high-ranking cartel member Gilberto Rendón were killed in a firefight with Colombian military helicopters in 1989. Three years later, on December 2, 1993, Escobar was famously killed in a shootout with police in the backstreets of Medellín. ▪

War on drugs

In 1971, President Richard Nixon declared drug abuse "Public Enemy Number 1," and that to fight and defeat this enemy, an all-out offensive was required. This speech marked the start of the so-called "War on Drugs." By the 1980s, the American demand for cocaine was so high that an estimated 75 tons (68,000 kg) was being smuggled into the country every month. In the years since, breakthroughs have been made, from the destruction of the Medellín Cartel to statistics indicating a 46 percent decrease in cocaine use by young adults from 2006–11. However, leaders from Colombia, Mexico, and Guatemala have expressed their desire for a new antidrug strategy, noting the toll military intervention has taken on their countries. In recent years, the Portuguese model of drug control, which decriminalizes the possession of moderate amounts of narcotics and focuses on treatment rather than incarceration, has arisen as a viable alternative.

IT WAS ALWAYS ABOUT BUSINESS, NEVER ABOUT GANGS

"FREEWAY" RICK ROSS, 1980–95

IN CONTEXT

LOCATION
Los Angeles, California, US

THEME
Drug trafficking

BEFORE
1923 Miyagawa Yashukichi, a Japanese drug trafficker living in the UK, runs one of the largest drug rings of the 1920s. He sends huge amounts of heroin to Japan via London.

1960s–70s Frank Lucas, a heroin dealer in Harlem, cuts out the middle man by buying heroin directly from the Golden Triangle in Asia.

AFTER
2003 Thomas "Tacker" Comerford establishes an international drug trafficking network in England. He is caught and arrested, but dies of liver cancer before he can be brought to trial.

At the peak of his criminal career, "Freeway" Rick Ross—not to be confused with the rapper Rick Ross—earned up to $3 million per day. He sold crack cocaine in a trading empire that spread from South Central Los Angeles to more than 40 cities across the US, and evaded prison for nearly a decade.

Ross grew up in a Los Angeles ghetto at the end of a street that dead-ended against the Harbor Freeway—hence his nickname. Ross was a high-school tennis star, and some have suggested that he started his life of crime after he failed to get a tennis scholarship to college because he was illiterate.

See also: Hells Angels 160–63 ▪ The Krays and the Richardsons 164–65 ▪ The Medellín Cartel 166–67

At the age of 17, Ross dropped out of high school. Unable to read well enough to fill out job applications, he could not find work. Instead, he hit the streets, stealing cars and auto parts and working at a chop shop with a group of neighborhood friends who dubbed themselves the "Junkyard Freeway Boys."

Crack empire

Within a year of leaving school, Ross had tapped into the crack cocaine boom. Previously, cocaine had been considered an elitist drug only used by the rich. Now, in its inexpensive "crack" form, it became the inner city drug of choice. Crack differs from cocaine because it is made by mixing the drug with water and baking soda, drying it, then cracking it into rocks to be smoked.

Use of crack cocaine soared as Ross sold a seemingly endless supply at bargain prices. His primary sources were Oscar Danilo

At the age of 28, Rick Ross learned to read and write in prison. In 2014, Ross toured the US to promote his autobiography and to preach the importance of literacy.

Blandón and Norwin Meneses, who smuggled cocaine into the US from their native Nicaragua.

Ross saturated the inner city with the drug. Devastatingly addictive, crack cocaine wreaked havoc on poor urban communities, turning whole families into crackheads. Ross was initially unaware of the drug's serious side effects, which include respiratory problems, cardiac arrest, and psychosis. Instead, he approached the trade like an entrepreneur building a business. Because Ross purchased and produced large amounts of crack so cheaply, he was able to sell it for a low price while still making a huge profit. Sales went through the roof.

Ross used a network of runners and dealers to distribute the crack, and even employed people who did nothing but count the money he earned. According to the US Department of Justice, Ross became one of the biggest cocaine dealers in South Central LA.

Narcotics detectives with the Los Angeles County Sheriff's Department investigated his operation for eight years but Ross avoided capture by continually changing locations and cars. However, as he amassed more money, houses, vehicles, and a large crew, he came to the attention of federal investigators.

Law enforcement agencies formed a special task force to target Ross and other major drug dealers. It comprised officers and agents

with the US Drug Enforcement Agency (DEA), Los Angeles Police Department (LAPD), and the Sheriff's Department. As its focus centered on catching the elusive Ross, the group became known as the Freeway Rick Ross Task Force.

Expansion and detention

Between 1986 and 1990, Ross and his crew expanded into other cities, including St. Louis, Missouri, and Cincinnati, Ohio. Authorities in these cities were also drawn in to investigating his activities, with little success. In October 1986, Ross was arrested on federal charges for conspiracy to distribute cocaine in St. Louis, but the case was dismissed for lack of evidence.

However, Ross was indicted again on cocaine trafficking charges in Ohio and Texas, after drugs bound for Cincinnati were picked out by a sniffer dog at a bus station and traced to Ross. This time, the charges stuck and in 1990 he was sentenced. On completion of his federal sentence in Ohio, Ross immediately began serving »

[Ricky Ross] was a disillusioned 19-year-old... who, at the dawn of the 1980s, found himself adrift on the streets of South-Central Los Angeles.
Gary Webb

nine months in a Texas state prison for drug offenses. He was paroled in September 1994.

The sting

In the meantime, in 1992, Oscar Danilo Blandón, Ross's Nicaraguan source, was caught on wiretaps bragging about his cocaine dealings, including his trades with Ross. As a result, Blandón was arrested in San Diego, California, where he faced federal charges and a lengthy prison sentence.

Realizing they could use Blandón to catch Ross and other drug barons, the DEA presented Blandón with a deal. In exchange for working as an undercover informant for the DEA, they offered

Packed into sports bags, drugs were transported around Ross's empire, moving between those Ross paid to "cook" powder cocaine into crack, Ross's own crew, and local dealers.

him a reduced sentence, a green card on his release from prison, and even a $42,000 salary. Blandón served a year of jail time before he was released and began his work with the DEA.

His first assignment was to make one last drug deal with Ross under the eyes of DEA agents and San Diego police, who assisted in the sting operation. As the DEA listened in, Blandón contacted Ross to offer him 220 lbs (100 kg) of crack cocaine. Unaware of the setup, Ross arranged to meet Blandón in San Diego on March 2, 1995. The deal was made in a shopping-center parking lot in the suburb of Chula Vista, south of San Diego. Once the cash and drugs had been exchanged, officers closed in on Ross and arrested him.

The following year, Ross was tried in a federal court in San Diego, for conspiracy to distribute illegal drugs bought from a police informant. On consideration of his

> If there was one outlaw capitalist most responsible for flooding Los Angeles streets with mass-marketed cocaine, his name was Freeway Rick.
> **Jesse Katz**

previous drug convictions, Ross was sentenced to life in prison without the possibility of parole.

Scandal and conspiracy

Ross believed that Blandón had been arrested at the same time. However, just before his trial, investigative journalist Gary Webb visited Ross and told him of Blandón's betrayal. In 1996, after several interviews with Ross, Webb also wrote a series of articles, named the "Dark Alliance," in the

Suspected gang members are stopped by the LAPD during a crackdown on drug-related crime in Los Angeles in June 1988.

Life and crime in the ghetto

A crack cocaine epidemic rocked the US from the mid-1980s to the early 1990s. At its height, crack use was a serious problem in most major US cities: in particular, South Central Los Angeles.

Crack is approximately twice as pure as cocaine powder. This means that the high from smoking crack is strong and instant. The high causes feelings of euphoria, alertness, and invincibility. During the epidemic, crack cocaine was incredibly cheap. According to the DEA, in the early

1980s one hit of crack cost about $2.50 in many cities, so even those in poor communities could afford it.

Crack addiction drove users to violence and crime as they looked for money to feed their habits. Drive-by shootings, murders, muggings, and robberies skyrocketed in poor neighborhoods. By the late 1980s, the US government was forced to intervene and launched a new "war on drugs" to fight the epidemic.

<San Jose Mercury News.> His articles revealed that Blandón had long been working for the government as an informant. Webb's "Dark Alliance" narrative unlocked a whole new dimension to the case—the claim that the drug empire was connected to the CIA and the Contra army, who were fighting against the revolutionary government in Nicaragua.

According to Webb, the money Ross paid his Nicaraguan contacts was being used to fund and arm the Contras. The CIA, meanwhile, turned a blind eye as to the source of the funds.

Although major media outlets discredited Webb's findings, the CIA later acknowledged that it had worked with suspected drug runners and used funds from Ross's empire to arm the Contras. In a phone call from jail, Ross himself bemoaned the actions of the CIA. The government had exploited him, he claimed—just as he had exploited his own community.

Overturned conviction

Ross was determined not to live out his life in jail. While serving time in a federal prison, he taught himself to read and write, and studied law

Good people do bad things when there are no options.
"Freeway" Rick Ross

A heavily armed DEA agent takes part in an early morning drug raid on a suspected kingpin in Los Angeles. The war on drugs became increasingly militarized in the 1980s.

books in the prison library. He used these books to fight his sentence, which was based on the "three strikes" law that calls for a life term on conviction of a third felony. Ross argued that his convictions in Texas and Ohio related to the same federal offense and therefore counted as one crime, making a total of two convictions.

Although his own attorney dismissed the claim, in 1998 the Ninth Circuit Court of Appeal agreed with his reasoning. As a result, Ross's sentence was reduced to 16½ years from 20. He was released in 2009 after serving 14 years behind bars. ∎

KIDNAPP
EXTORT

NG AND
ON

In Jamestown, Virginia, Captain Samuel Argall kidnaps **Pocahontas**, the daughter of a paramount chief.

1613

US aviator **Charles Lindbergh's baby son** is kidnapped from the family home in New Jersey.

1932

1897

In a case known as the **Tichborne Claimant**, Arthur Orton claims to be the lost son and heir of Lady Tichborne.

Kidnapping is the illegal transportation of a non-consenting person through the use of force or fraud. In the US and UK, the majority of kidnap victims are taken by a loved one, such as a parent or spouse. Motives for kidnapping include securing custody of a child, monetary ransom, sexual abuse, and slavery.

None of the cases described in this book were designed to end with murder: the intent was either to extract a ransom payment or to keep the victim alive in sexual slavery. In cases where kidnap led to the death of the victim, such as the 1932 abduction of toddler Charles Augustus Lindbergh Jr., the son of the American aviator, evidence indicated that death resulted from the kidnapper(s) incompetence rather than design.

In the US, the botched kidnapping of the Lindbergh baby led to new laws to combat abduction. Later the same year, the US Congress passed the Federal Kidnapping Act 18 U.S.C. § 1201, known as the Lindbergh Law. This allowed federal officers to pursue kidnappers who crossed state lines with their victim or victims. The FBI could bring its experience, training, and overriding authority to bear on such cases, although parental kidnapping was excluded from the act. Until the revision of the law in the 1970s, convicted kidnappers could face the death penalty in some states if the victim had been harmed.

Stockholm syndrome

Even victims who are kept for a relatively short time may suffer psychological trauma such as anxiety attacks, phobias, or post-traumatic stress disorder (PTSD). The symptoms can be physical, mental, or both.

Being held over long periods of time can change the victim's character to the extent that they become unrecognizable to friends and family. This may occur as a result of Stockholm syndrome— a psychological phenomenon in which captives begin to identify with the motives of their captors. This famously happened in the 1974 case of American heiress Patty Hearst, who joined the cause of her kidnappers, the revolutionary Symbionese Liberation Army. Within 10 weeks of her kidnapping, most of which Hearst spent in a closet, she helped her captors rob a bank. A now-iconic photograph of Hearst appeared several months after she

Patty Hearst, daughter of US media tycoon William Randolph Hearst, is kidnapped by the Symbionese Liberation Army.

In Austria, **Natascha Kampusch** is imprisoned in the home of her abductor for eight years.

1974

1998–2006

1973

1976

Kidnappers seize **John Paul Getty III**, the 16-year-old grandson of billionaire Jean Paul Getty, from Piazza Farnese in Rome.

Twenty-six children are kidnapped and buried alive in a truck in Chowchilla, California.

---

was captured by the kidnappers. She was pictured holding an automatic weapon in front of the Symbionese Liberation Army's logo, and only repudiated her allegiance to the group once she had been separated from them for some time.

Of course, not all kidnap victims escape their kidnappers. Some are forced to adjust to their lives with their captors—as was the case for Pocahontas, the daughter of a 17th-century American Indian chief, who was kidnapped by English colonists in 1613 and never returned to her old life.

Technological advances

Uncovering the identities of anonymous abductors can be extremely difficult for police. Success often hinges on the ability of witnesses or the victim to give a physical description of their attacker after their release. Sometimes, kidnappers slip up and inadvertently provide clues that reveal the whereabouts of the victim's location.

The advent of forensic document identification, allowed in evidence in the US since the Supreme Court's landmark Bell v. Brewster ruling of 1887, which recognized the importance of handwriting as a means of identification, enabled police to employ trained experts to compare the writing on ransom notes with that of suspects. Marking the bills used to pay a ransom, or recording their serial numbers, are other ways in which abductors may be traced.

In recent years, advances in digital technology have made it significantly more difficult to commit kidnappings successfully. CCTV cameras play an important role in detection, while tracking software in cell phones can locate victims and their abductors. Removing or neutralizing tracking devices is of paramount importance to a kidnapper; otherwise, it is just a matter of time before police officers arrive at the abductor's door.

Such developments have led to a market for wearable GPS child-tracking devices. Most look similar to a wristwatch, and allow the child to contact a parent at the push of a button. However, many are clunky and easy for an abductor to spot. In theory, as man and machine become ever more interconnected, tracking technology could one day be incorporated into the human body—which raises important questions regarding civil liberties. ∎

HE VALUED HER LESS THAN OLD SWORDS
THE ABDUCTION OF POCAHONTAS, 1613

IN CONTEXT

LOCATION
Virginia, US

THEME
Political abduction

BEFORE
1303 The ambitious Pope Boniface VIII is kidnapped by an army of noble families. He refuses to abdicate and is sent back to Rome but dies soon after his release.

AFTER
1936 Chiang Kai-shek, leader of the Republic of China, is held hostage for two weeks by dissident officers who believe he is not using the full force of the army against Japan; Chiang complies but later has the rogue officers executed.

February 10, 1962 US pilot Francis Gary Powers is released in a prisoner exchange with the Soviets in Berlin, two years after he ejected from a damaged spyplane in Soviet airspace and was captured.

The short life of Pocahontas, the young American Indian "princess" who was a key contact between the first English settlers in the US and American Indian tribes, has long been romanticized in popular culture.

Born around 1596, Pocahontas was a daughter of Powhatan, paramount chief of some 30 Native American tribes in Virginia's Chesapeake Bay. As a young girl, she allegedly prevented her father's men from killing John Smith, the leader of Jamestown, an English colony founded in 1607 on land within Powhatan territory.

Jamestown's inhabitants co-existed fairly peacefully with the American Indian tribes until 1609, when Chief Powhatan brought all trade to an end in a campaign to starve the colonists out of Virginia. War soon broke out.

In spring 1613, mariner Sir Samuel Argall sailed up the Potomac River in search of new trading links with the Patawomeck tribe. He learned that Pocahontas was staying with Japazeus, their chief. Planning to use her to force the release of English prisoners and stolen tools and weapons, Argall abducted her.

A ransom note was sent to Chief Powhatan, and his daughter was held captive at Jamestown. The chief refused to meet all of Argall's demands, and Pocahontas remained with the English. In 1614, she became a Christian and married settler John Rolfe. She died in England in 1617, where royalty had welcomed her as a model for colonial relationships. ∎

Pocahontas arrives at Jamestown as a captive of the English—her abduction was an early example of the use of a prisoner as political leverage.

See also: The Kidnapping of Patty Hearst 188–89 ▪ The Abduction of Aldo Moro 322–23 ▪ The Kidnapping of Ingrid Betancourt 324–25

MARVELOUS REAL-LIFE ROMANCE
THE TICHBORNE CLAIMANT, 1897

IN CONTEXT

LOCATION
Hampshire, UK

THEME
Imposture

BEFORE
1487 Low-born Lambert Simnel, a pretender to the English throne, threatens King Henry VII's reign. He is defeated and later pardoned by the king, who believes Simnel was manipulated by nobles.

1560 In France, Arnaud du Tilh is executed after his 3-year impersonation of Martin Guerre is revealed when the real Guerre returns.

AFTER
1921 A man claiming to be Prince Ramendra Narayan Roy, one of the three cosharers of the extensive Bhawal estate in India's eastern Bengal, reappears 12 years after his supposed death and cremation. His claim is disputed but two trials rule in his favor.

Roger Tichborne, heir to the Tichborne baronetcy, was lost in the Atlantic in 1854, when the ship in which he was traveling sank off Rio de Janeiro, Brazil. His mother, Lady Henriette Tichborne, was devastated. However, after hearing a report that survivors had been rescued and taken to Australia, she held out hope that he was alive and placed advertisements around the world, asking for news of his whereabouts.

In 1866, a lawyer in Australia wrote to Lady Tichborne. A butcher in New South Wales calling himself Tom Castro had contacted him, claiming to be Roger. Overjoyed, Lady Tichborne sent for Castro, and when she met him later that year, claimed to recognize him.

An improbable prodigal
To the rest of the family, however, this "Roger" was obviously an impostor. A man who all recalled as being slight in stature, delicate in manner, his voice inflected by a boyhood in France, was now big and coarse in appearance and

The real Roger Tichborne (left), and Arthur Orton (right) looked very different, yet dozens of people swore that they were the same person.

unrefined in his speech. After Lady Tichborne's death, the family challenged his claim to the estate and title. The lengthy civil and criminal trials that followed caused a public sensation.

At their end, Arthur Orton, a Londoner who had left England, jumped ship in Chile, and ended up in Australia, was sentenced to 14 years for perjury. Orton tried to live off his dubious celebrity without much success. He died in poverty, still claiming to be Tichborne. ∎

See also: The Affair of the Diamond Necklace 64–65 ▪ Harry Domela 70–73 ▪ Frank Abagnale 86–87

ANNE, THEY'VE STOLEN OUR BABY!

THE LINDBERGH BABY KIDNAPPING, MARCH 1, 1932

IN CONTEXT

LOCATION
Hopewell, New Jersey, US

THEME
Child abduction

BEFORE
July 1874 Four-year-old
Charles Ross becomes the first
known American child to be
kidnapped for ransom.

AFTER
July 1960 Eight-year-old
Graham Thorne is abducted
for ransom after his parents
win Australia's Opera House
Lottery. His body is discovered
two months later.

May 1982 Nina Gallwitz,
eight, is freed by her captors
after 149 days, when her
parents pay the ransom of
1,500,000 deutsche marks
(about $1.2 million today).

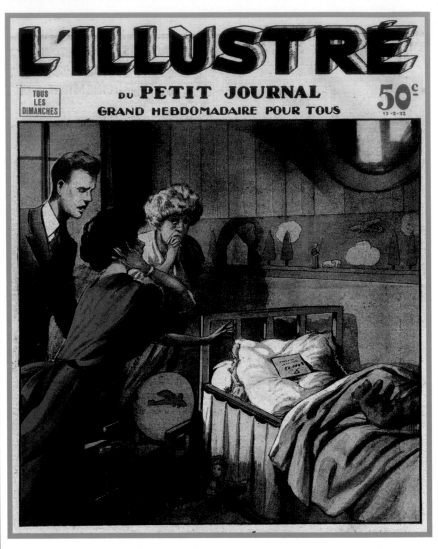

Around 10 p.m. on a rainy evening on March 1, 1932, nanny Betty Gow peeked into Charlie Lindbergh's nursery, where he had been sleeping since dinner. She had dressed him in a flannel sleeveless nightshirt and a pink sleeping suit and laid him down in his crib. Two hours earlier, she had checked on the boy and found him asleep. Now, however, the 20-month-old was gone.

Gow rushed downstairs to inform his parents—pioneering aviator Charles Lindbergh and his wife, Anne. They ran upstairs, where they discovered an open window and a ransom note propped up by the windowsill. In broken English, written in blue ink, the note demanded $50,000 ($868,000 today) for the baby's safe return.

Panic overtook the Lindbergh home. Family members and staff frantically searched the grounds of the Hopewell, New Jersey, mansion for the toddler, unwittingly trampling over evidence in the process. They found no sign of little Charlie. A groundskeeper phoned the Hopewell police who, within 30 minutes, had put up roadblocks and

The kidnap of the celebrity pilot's baby sparked international outrage. Sensational headlines and magazine covers about the story were published all over the world.

checkpoints across the area. Police also notified local hospitals that a toddler was missing.

Kidnapping confirmed
Police called to the scene soon determined that the kidnapper had used a homemade, three-piece extension ladder—broken and left lying 75 feet (23 m) away from the

Anne Morrow Lindbergh holds Charlie shortly after his birth in June 1930. Six months earlier, the pregnant Anne became the first woman to earn a first-class glider's license.

house—to climb up and in through the open second-floor window. Some rungs had snapped, which suggested the ladder might have broken when the kidnapper descended with the baby.

The police also found tire tracks and a chisel, and traces of mud on the nursery floor. Most importantly, they found two sets of footprints on the wet ground beneath the nursery window, which led away from the house in a southeasterly direction toward the tire tracks of the getaway car.

However, they did not take plaster casts of the footprints, nor did they measure the sets of footprints—which would have given them the opportunity to compare the prints with those of possible suspects. Newspapers reported that officers ignored protocol in their haste to find the baby and catch his abductor.

No usable fingerprints were found on the ransom notes, the crib, or the ladder, causing investigators to believe the crime scene had been wiped clean.

By 10:30 p.m., radio news bulletins about the kidnapping hit the airwaves and the world learned about the abduction. Over the next three days, a law-enforcement team of FBI agents and police officers from New Jersey and New York found no new clues.

Then, on March 5, a second letter arrived demanding $70,000 ($1.2 million). The note also told the Lindberghs to keep the police out of

the case. In a third note, the kidnapper gave instructions for dropping off the money.

Negotiations begin

Dr. John Condon, a 72-year-old retired educator, read about the kidnapping in a local paper. He wrote a letter to the editor, offering to act as an intermediary between the kidnapper and the Lindbergh family. Upon seeing the letter, the kidnapper wrote to Condon and agreed. They met in a cemetery and the kidnapper returned the pink sleeping suit as proof the boy was safe.

The Lindberghs were then told, through Condon, when and where to leave the money. After the kidnapper received the money, he would leave their baby on a boat named *The Nelly,* anchored near Martha's Vineyard off the coast of Massachusetts—between Horseneck beach and Gay Head near Elizabeth Island. The Lindberghs agreed to pay the ransom in order to get their son back safe and sound.

Under cover of night, Dr. Condon made the drop of $50,000, which Condon had negotiated down from the second request. Lindbergh waited in the car. The cemetery was dark and they could barely see the kidnapper, but his German-accented voice came across loud and clear. The man identified himself only as "John," and left with the Lindberghs' money. However, he did not hold up his end of the bargain: after an exhaustive search, during which Lindbergh repeatedly flew over the sea, the boat and child were nowhere to be found.

Investigators continued to look for the boy, but had no luck. When Charlie was finally found it was by chance—on May 12, 1932, a truck driver stopping for a bathroom break found a small body covered in leaves in a wooded area near the hamlet of Mount Rose, about 2 miles (3 km) from the Lindberghs' Hopewell estate.

Buried in a shallow grave, the body had already begun to decompose. Charlie Lindbergh, it seemed, had been dead since the very night he was taken. »

We warn you not to make anything public or notify the police. The child is in good care.
First ransom note

How the events unfolded

Charles Augustus Lindbergh Jr. disappears.

The family finds a ransom note demanding $50,000.

Police question household and estate employees.

The kidnapper sends a second, third, and fourth ransom note demanding $70,000.

A truck driver finds an infant's remains buried near the Lindbergh estate and summons the police.

The $50,000 ransom is handed over. There is no sign of the baby.

Go-between Dr. Condon meets with the kidnapper.

Medical examiners determined that the child had been killed with a blow to the head. Decomposition, however, made it impossible to officially determine even the body's gender. Staff at a nearby orphanage said the body was not one of their children. A discrepancy in the height of the remains raised further questions about the dead child's identity—Charlie Lindbergh was 29 inches (74 cm) long, but the body found was 33 inches (84 cm). His father and nursemaid, however, positively identified the body based on his hand-sewn flannel nightshirt and a deformed overlapping toe.

The Lindbergh Law
In the midst of the investigation, public outrage prompted Congress to swiftly enact the so-called Lindbergh Law in 1932: the Federal Kidnapping Act made kidnapping

a federal crime punishable by death. It intended to allow federal authorities to step in and pursue kidnappers as soon as they crossed state lines with their victims.

In September 1934, money from the ransom turned up at a gas station on Lexington Avenue in upper Manhattan. The attendant became suspicious when the driver of a dark blue Dodge sedan pulled out a $10 gold certificate—a form of

The Lindbergh's dog is pictured here in a stroller with Charlie. One especially curious feature of the case was that the dog, who usually barked at strangers, did not bark during the kidnapping.

paper currency issued by the US Treasury that had been withdrawn from circulation in 1933, when President Franklin D. Roosevelt removed the gold standard due to hoarding during the Depression.

Thinking that the gold certificate might be counterfeit, the gas station attendant jotted down the Dodge sedan's New York license plate number on the margin of the certificate.

When it reached the bank, a teller checked the note's serial number and discovered that it was part of the $50,000 ransom paid out to the kidnapper of toddler Charles Lindbergh Jr.

The bank notified the FBI, which traced the license plate back to a German immigrant named Bruno Hauptmann. He was a carpenter living in a quiet neighborhood in the Bronx, New York.

Hauptmann arrested

Police arrested Hauptmann on September 19, 1934, as he left his home. Inside his wallet was a $20 gold certificate, also from the Lindbergh ransom.

A search of Hauptmann's home turned up nearly $14,000 ($243,000 today) of the ransom money in an oil can, inside a package stuffed behind wooden boards in his garage. Hauptmann, however, insisted that he was innocent. He was holding the money, he claimed, for Isidor Fisch, a friend who had since died. Fisch, also German, had applied for a passport on May 12, 1932, the same day that Charlie Lindbergh's body was found. By December that year, Fisch had sailed for Leipzig, to visit family.

His friend, Hauptmann told police, had left a shoebox with some of his belongings inside.

Recreating the crime, officers stand outside the Hopewell mansion in an attempt to find clues. A long ladder, like the broken one found near the house, leads up to the open nursery window.

Hauptmann only learned that it contained money when he had a leaky roof and emptied the dampened box. Hauptmann said that he had kept the money, hoarding the gold certificates due to his fears about inflation.

According to news reports, the police did not believe him, referring to Hauptmann's claims as "the Fischy story." Fisch, who died of tuberculosis in Germany in 1934, never returned to America.

In Hauptmann's attic, investigators discovered a piece of yellow pinewood that matched the ladder used in the kidnapping. Handwriting experts were called in, and declared Hauptmann's script a match for the writing in the ransom notes.

The court proceedings attracted thousands of spectators and writers, who crammed into the tiny town of Flemington, New Jersey. **»**

Charles Lindbergh III

Lindbergh was born in Detroit, Michigan, in 1902, but grew up in Minnesota. His father, Charles August Lindbergh, was a member of Congress for Minnesota from 1907 to 1917. Lindbergh studied mechanical engineering in college for two years, but dropped out to begin flight training.

On May 20, 1927, he made history by flying solo from New York to Paris on his legendary monoplane *The Spirit of St. Louis*. After 34 hours of nonstop flying, he landed at Le Bourget Aerodrome, Paris, to win the $25,000 Orteig Prize. At only 25, the transatlantic feat changed his life completely, bringing fame and fortune.

On a goodwill flight to Mexico City, Lindbergh met Anne Morrow, whose father was ambassador to Mexico. The couple soon married and, in 1930, had their first of six children, Charles Jr.

After the Pearl Harbor attack in 1941, Lindbergh applied to join the Air Force, but was refused by President Roosevelt after a long-running spat between the two men. Lindbergh later helped the war effort by training pilots.

Some of the best-known journalists of the day—Walter Winchell, Damon Runyon, and Fanny Hurst—covered the trial.

Hauptmann, represented by flamboyant attorney Edward "Big Ed" Reilly, took the stand in his own defense and denied any involvement in the kidnapping. He told the jury that he had been beaten by police and forced to alter his handwriting to match the ransom notes. Meanwhile, Reilly attempted to arouse suspicion around Condon and his communication with the kidnapper.

Charles Lindbergh testified for the prosecution. He told the jurors that he recognized Hauptmann's voice as that of the man Condon had delivered the ransom money to years before.

Testimony ended in February 1935. Prosecutor David Wilentz, in his summation, asked the jury to find Hauptmann guilty of first-

> The trial of the century was probably the greatest fraud in the history of this country.
> **Robert R. Bryan**

degree murder with the death penalty imposed. The jury retired from the courtroom and deliberated in the jury room for more than 11 hours. At 10:45 p.m. on February 18, 1935, the jury of eight men and four women returned a verdict. When a bell tolled to announce that a verdict had been reached, the cheers of the crowd outside could be heard inside the courtroom.

Hauptmann, handcuffed between two guards, stood motionless as the foreman read the verdict. Perhaps under public pressure, the jury found Bruno Hauptmann guilty of first-degree murder. The judge sentenced him to death. Lindbergh, who attended every session of the 32-day trial, was not present for the verdict and sentencing.

Bungled investigation

The Lindbergh case had been an embarrassment to both the police force and FBI. It had also captured hearts across America.

Under New Jersey's capital murder statute, the prosecution did not need to prove Hauptmann intended to kill the baby—only that the toddler died as a result of the break-in. It was never determined whether the boy was hit over the head or died in a fall from the ladder as he was carried out of the house. After the verdict and sentence were read, Hauptmann declined to address the court.

Harold G. Hoffman, governor of the state of New Jersey, voiced doubts about the verdict and granted Hauptmann a 30-day reprieve, ordering New Jersey State Police to reopen their case. The Hauptmann investigation, he said, was one of the most bungled in police history.

The New Jersey State Police failed to find any new evidence, so Hoffman hired private investigators. They too came up empty-handed, and when the investigation was over, Hoffman's political career was so tarnished that he lost his bid for reelection as governor.

Newspapers announced the kidnapping to the world, making Charlie one of the most famous babies in America. This cover shows Charlie at his most defenseless, two weeks old.

They think that when I die, the case will die.
Bruno Hauptmann

Verdict challenged

For his part, Hauptmann's attorney appealed the conviction all the way to the US Supreme Court, but none of the appeals was successful. Still, Bruno Hauptmann proclaimed his innocence until his very last moment. He was executed in "Old Smokey," the electric chair at New Jersey State Prison on April 3, 1936.

The case did not end there, however. In 1981, Hauptmann's 83-year-old widow, Anna, sued the state of New Jersey for $100 million, claiming that it had wrongfully executed her husband. She asked that his case be reopened, but the court denied the request. Her attorney also asked the New Jersey

State Legislature to officially declare Bruno Hauptmann innocent. No action was taken.

The case has inspired more than a dozen books and two films. In 1982, the documentary, *Who Killed the Lindbergh Baby?*, written and narrated by British journalist Ludovic Kennedy, argued that Hauptmann was framed. In Gregory Ahlgren and Stephen Monier's 1993 book *Crime of the*

Police search Hauptmann's garage for clues that might tell them what happened to Charlie Lindbergh as hundreds gather outside Hauptmann's house during the search.

Century: The Lindbergh Kidnapping Hoax, they suggest that Charles Lindbergh accidentally killed his son and staged the kidnapping as a cover-up. Other authors have suggested there were multiple culprits, pointing to the use of "we" in the ransom notes, and the presence of two sets of footprints at the mansion.

In 2012, author Robert Zorn posited that "Cemetery John" was German grocery store worker John Knoll, and that he and Bruno Hauptmann performed the kidnapping together. While Zorn's theory has gained traction, particularly given the physical similarities between images of John Knoll and the artist's impression of "Cemetery John" based on Dr. Condon's description, we are still no closer to finding out what happened that night. ∎

Capital punishment

The American Civil Liberties Union contends that capital punishment is irrevocable, arbitrary, and permanent. It forever deprives the individual of the opportunity to benefit from new evidence or new laws. The International Commission Against the Death Penalty has noted that, while public support for the death penalty is linked to the desire to free society from crime, there are more effective ways to prevent crime than killing the perpetrators.

Those people and groups opposed to capital punishment point out that while it aims to deter killers, it instead mirrors the very behavior it seeks to prevent. They also argue that the death penalty promotes the idea that it is acceptable to kill as long as it is the government doing the killing.

The overwhelming majority of developed nations have abolished capital punishment either in law or in practice. The US remains the only Western country that still carries out capital punishment.

SINCE MONDAY I HAVE FALLEN INTO THE HANDS OF KIDNAPPERS

THE KIDNAPPING OF JOHN PAUL GETTY III, 1973

IN CONTEXT

LOCATION
Rome and Calabria, Italy

THEME
Kidnapping

BEFORE
1936 Ten-year-old Charles Mattson is kidnapped from his Tacoma, Washington, home and held for ransom. Negotiations break down and the boy is brutally murdered by an unknown culprit.

1963 Nineteen-year-old Frank Sinatra, Jr., son of the famous singer, is kidnapped from a hotel room by Lake Tahoe, Nevada, and freed three days later after a ransom is paid. Three men are later convicted.

AFTER
1983 In Amsterdam, Freddy Heineken—CEO of the family brewing company—and his driver are kidnapped. They are freed after a ransom of about $13 million is paid. All four kidnappers are later arrested.

John Paul Getty III, known as "Paul," was the rebellious grandson of J. Paul Getty, the famously miserly oil billionaire. At age 16, Paul was living a bohemian lifestyle in Rome, Italy—where he grew up. On a drunken night out with friends on July 10, 1973, he was kidnapped from Rome's Piazza Farnese. Due to his wild-child reputation, many assumed he had staged the kidnapping to extort money from his grandfather.

In fact, Paul had been driven 250 miles (400 km) south into Calabria by his kidnappers. They kept him on the move, changing their location regularly to throw off would-be pursuers. They forced him to write a letter to his mother telling her that he was being held by kidnappers who would cut off one of his fingers if they were not paid a ransom of $18 million ($96 million today).

Still unconvinced of the authenticity of the abduction, J. Paul Getty contracted ex-CIA agent Fletcher Chace to find his grandson. In the meantime, another letter arrived, again written by Paul under duress. The kidnappers included a threatening note giving the family 15 days to hand over the

This is Paul's ear. If we don't get some money within 10 days, then the other ear will arrive. In other words, he will arrive in little bits.
Ransom note

money, or else they would send another letter containing a lock of Paul's hair and one of his ears.

Paul's mother Gail contacted the kidnappers to tell them that she would find the money and meet them at a specific time and place. However, she never turned up.

Horrific package
Some weeks later, the kidnappers honored their gruesome threat. On November 10, the Italian newspaper *Il Messaggero* received a package containing a lock of Paul's auburn hair and his right ear. The kidnappers threatened to

See also: The Lindbergh Baby Kidnapping 178–85 ▪ The Kidnapping of Patty Hearst 188–89

remove his other ear unless they were paid $3.2 million ($17 million) within 10 days. Meanwhile, another package arrived at the offices of newspaper *Il Tempo*. Inside were photographs of Paul's scarred face.

Reluctant acquiescence

The photos finally prompted a response from J. Paul Getty. He contributed $2.2 million ($11.7 million)—the maximum amount that was tax deductible, according to his accountant—and loaned his son the remaining $1 million ($5.3 million), charging 4 percent interest. Chace handed over three sacks of cash on December 12. Two days later, Paul was released on a hillside outside Lagonegro in southern Italy and picked up by the police. He was malnourished and weak from the blood loss caused when his ear was severed.

Police arrested nine men, with links to the Calabrian Mafia. Seven received sentences of between four and ten years, while two were released. Only $85,000 ($453,000) of the ransom was found.

Scarred for life

A year after his ordeal, Paul married a German photographer. They moved to New York and had a son, Balthazar Getty, who became an actor. Paul never recovered from the psychological trauma of the kidnapping and descended into alcoholism and drug addiction. In 1981, at age 24, he suffered a stroke

> I can afford to say what I wish.
> **J. Paul Getty**

According to reports, John Paul Getty III, seen here after his ordeal, tried to speak to his grandfather to thank him for obtaining his release, but the elder Getty refused to take the call.

brought on by a cocktail of drugs. It left him paralyzed, almost blind, and practically speechless. His mother cared for him after his stroke, but she was forced to sue her ex-husband, Paul's father, to pay for his treatment and care. Paul and his wife divorced in 1993, and he died at his home in London in 2011, at age 54. ∎

Gershon Baskin, an expert on the Israeli-Palestinian conflict, helped mediate between Israel and Hamas in the 2011 deal to release Shalit.

Ransom rules

Different countries have varying policies about the payment of ransoms. The UK will not pay ransoms to terrorists because it believes it would encourage other abductions. The US has a long-standing policy against paying ransoms for hostages on the grounds that it puts its citizens at greater risk and funds terrorism. The US government will prosecute a US public company or private organization that buys the freedom of an employee in this way. However, it does permit

families to negotiate on their own. The French, Italian, and Spanish governments have a long record of directly paying ransoms, although the Italian government made a notable exception by refusing to negotiate in the kidnapping of former prime minister Aldo Moro (see pp. 322–23).

Israel has a different stance. It is prepared to negotiate for the release of captured citizens. For example, in 2011, more than 1,000 Palestinian prisoners were exchanged for a single abducted Israeli soldier, Gilad Shalit.

I'M A COWARD. I DIDN'T WANT TO DIE

THE KIDNAPPING OF PATTY HEARST, 1974

IN CONTEXT

LOCATION
Berkeley, California, US

THEME
Abduction and coercion

BEFORE
1874 Four-year-old Charley Ross is lured into a horse-drawn carriage outside his Pennsylvania home and abducted. His father cannot pay the ransom and the boy is not seen again.

1968 US student Barbara Jane Mackle is kidnapped from a hotel room by Gary Krist and Ruth Eisemann-Schier. They receive a $500,000 ransom from her wealthy father, and the girl is later found alive, buried in a wooden box.

AFTER
1996 Millionaire German businessman Jakub Fiszman is seized from his Eschborn office. His kidnappers take a ransom of $2 million, although they have already killed him.

O n the night of February 4, 1974, 19-year-old Patricia (Patty) Hearst, an heiress of the William Randolph Hearst media empire, was at her California apartment with her fiancé, Steven Weed. At 9 p.m., there was a knock on the door, and three armed men burst in. They beat up Weed, and dragged a screaming Hearst from her apartment, threw her into the trunk of a car, and drove off. The kidnapping made international headlines, and reporters camped out on the lawn of the Hearst family's San Francisco mansion.

An urban guerrilla

Two days later, the Berkeley radio station KPFA received a letter from a left-wing guerrilla group known as the Symbionese Liberation Army (SLA). Purporting to be a warrant for the arrest of Patricia Campbell Hearst, the missive included Patty Hearst's credit card and a warning that anyone attempting to interfere would be executed. It also ordered that all communications from the SLA be published in full in all newspapers and on radio and TV. On February 12, the radio station received a recording from the SLA. Hearst was heard telling her

Why'd they snatch Hearst? To get the country's attention, primarily. Hearst was from a wealthy, powerful family.
US Federal Bureau of Investigation

parents that she was fine, and was not being starved or beaten. She also said that the police should not attempt to find her. SLA leader, Marshal Cinque, whose real name was Donald DeFreeze, extorted $2 million ($9.6 million today) from Hearst's father in food aid for California's poor. But when the group sought a further $4 million ($19.2 million) from him, Hearst said he was unable to meet that sum. Negotiations broke down.

In the two months following Hearst's abduction, her captors seemingly transformed her into a willing accomplice. In another tape

See also: The Abduction of Pocahontas 176 ▪ The Lindbergh Baby Kidnapping 178–85
▪ The Kidnapping of John Paul Getty III 186–87

Patty Hearst poses with a gun in front of the SLA's flag in 1974. After 57 days of captivity, she joined the group, but whether she remained a victim or became a perpetrator remains unclear.

the heiress declared her allegiance to the SLA, saying that she had been given the option of either being released, or joining the SLA and fighting for the freedom of all oppressed people. Hearst claimed to have chosen to stay and fight alongside her captors.

In mid-April 1974, under her *nom de guerre* "Tania," Hearst took part in a bank robbery in San Francisco, during which the surveillance cameras captured a photo of her holding a rifle.

Bloody gunfight

A break in the case came on May 16, 1974, when two SLA members attempted to steal an ammunition belt from a Los Angeles store. They fled in a getaway van, which was later found by authorities at the group's safe house. The next day, police surrounded the house. A massive shootout ensued and the house erupted in flames. Six SLA members were killed in the fire, including DeFreeze, but Hearst was not among the dead. She and two other members had escaped and were watching the drama in a motel room via the first live TV broadcast of an unplanned event.

In September 1975, 19 months after her ordeal began, the FBI captured Patricia Hearst. In March 1976, she was tried and convicted of armed bank robbery and other crimes, and given a seven-year prison sentence. The jury had not found plausible the defense's theory that Hearst had been brainwashed

by the SLA, although today her case is regarded by many as a clear example of Stockholm syndrome. Hearst served just 21 months of her term. President Jimmy Carter commuted it to time served, on the grounds that had she not been subjected to degrading experiences as a victim of the SLA, she would

never have participated in the group's criminal acts. She was released in February 1979. Several other SLA members were captured with Hearst, who pleaded guilty to kidnapping the heiress. In 2001, in one of his final acts of his tenure, President Bill Clinton granted Hearst a full pardon. ∎

Stockholm syndrome

In August 1973, four employees of a bank in Stockholm, Sweden, were held hostage in its vaults for six days. Their captors were escaped prisoner Jan-Erik Olsson and his fellow convict Clark Olofsson, whose release Olsson had negotiated with the police. Strangely, although the victims feared for their lives during the siege, they also formed a strong sympathetic bond with their captors, even appearing to take their side against the police. When the standoff ended, the

hostages and convicts hugged, kissed, and shook hands. The victims' seemingly irrational attachment to their captors puzzled everyone, and soon after, a psychiatrist coined the term "Stockholm Syndrome" to explain this psychological response. It is now believed that in a hostage or kidnap scenario, bonding to a captor is a survival mechanism subconsciously adopted under extreme stress. The FBI's Hostage Barricade Database System states that about 8 percent of victims show signs of the syndrome.

I STILL SLEEP WITH A NIGHT LIGHT. I CAN'T RIDE A SUBWAY

THE CHOWCHILLA KIDNAPPING, JULY 15, 1976

IN CONTEXT

LOCATION
Chowchilla, California, US

THEME
Mass kidnapping

BEFORE
October 6, 1972 Two plasterers, Edwin John Eastwood and Robert Clyde Boland, abduct six students and a teacher from a school in the rural town of Faraday in Victoria, Australia, but the victims escape.

AFTER
April 14, 2014 Militant Islamist group Boko Haram kidnaps 276 students at Chibok Government Girls Secondary School in Nigeria. One girl is rescued in May 2016, and on October 13, 2016, 21 more students are released by kidnappers.

A buried removal van was used as a prison during the kidnapping. Here it is shown being excavated by workmen from the Livermore quarry, after the 26 children had escaped to safety.

J uly 15, 1976, was a typical summer day in California's Central Valley—hot, dry, and sunny, with the temperature approaching triple digits. It was an ideal time for children to play in the water, which is exactly what 26 summer school students from Chowchilla had been doing when bus driver Ed Ray collected them from the community pool just before 4 p.m. that afternoon.

Driving through fruit groves on the way back to the school, Ray came across a white van blocking an isolated stretch of Avenue 21 on the south side of town. When Ray slowed down, looking to see if the occupants were having trouble, he saw three men with guns and with women's nylon stockings covering their heads leap from behind the van. The men ordered him to stop and then commandeered his bus.

Terrifying journey

The group's intention was not simply to hijack the vehicle. This was a kidnapping plot. With Ray and the children still on board, the men drove to a nearby slough—an intermittent stream obscured by bamboo and other vegetation—where they crammed Ray and the children, aged between five and 14, into the back of two white vans. The kidnappers abandoned the bus in the dry streambed, and drove away in the two vans, with their victims huddled in the back.

It was a harrowing ride for the children. With no water, no bathroom breaks, and the windows blacked out so they could not see where they were going, the children endured an 11-hour drive.

Some of the younger children vomited due to motion sickness. The older ones sang popular songs to cheer them up, including "Boogie Fever," "Love Will Keep Us Together," and, ironically, the old summer camp standard "If You're Happy and You Know It Clap Your Hands."

He was a courageous man. He kept 26 scared children in line and made us feel safe.
Jodi Heffington-Medrano

See also: The Lindbergh Baby Kidnapping 178–85 ▪ The Kidnapping of Natascha Kampusch 196–97 ▪ The Zodiac Killer 288–89 ▪ The Kidnapping of Ingrid Betancourt 324–25

Buried alive

Finally, in the early hours of July 16, the vans came to a halt at a rock quarry in Livermore, about 100 miles (160 km) from Chowchilla. The abductors took the names of their captives and an item of clothing from each, then made them climb into an old Allied Van Lines removal van that was buried beneath the ground.

Ventilated by two tubes, the van was equipped with a few dirty mattresses and box springs. The only food provided—cereal, peanut butter, bread, and water—was barely enough for one meal. Once all the captives were inside, the kidnappers closed the opening in the van's roof, plunging the interior into darkness. They shoveled dirt over the roof, burying their hostages alive. The victims huddled together in the darkness of their metal box, the California heat making the smell of vomit and filth unbearable.

When the bus failed to arrive back at Dairyland Elementary School, parents began to call the school. Assuming the bus had broken down, school officials **»**

> It was like a grave, dark. Everyone had messed their pants, sweaty little bodies in 110°F (43°C).
> **Lynda Carrejo Labendeira**

Chowchilla kidnapping mistakes

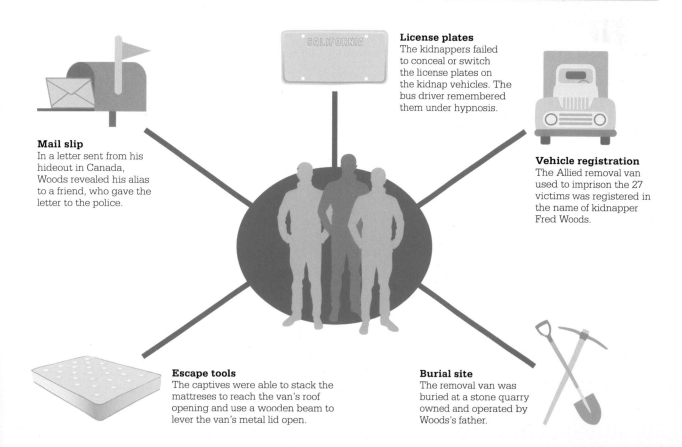

License plates
The kidnappers failed to conceal or switch the license plates on the kidnap vehicles. The bus driver remembered them under hypnosis.

Mail slip
In a letter sent from his hideout in Canada, Woods revealed his alias to a friend, who gave the letter to the police.

Vehicle registration
The Allied removal van used to imprison the 27 victims was registered in the name of kidnapper Fred Woods.

Escape tools
The captives were able to stack the mattresses to reach the van's roof opening and use a wooden beam to lever the van's metal lid open.

Burial site
The removal van was buried at a stone quarry owned and operated by Woods's father.

drove its route, but found nothing. By 6 p.m., the Chowchilla police and the county sheriff's office had been notified that something was amiss.

A deputy found the abandoned bus around 8 p.m., but no sign of the driver or children. Crime scene investigators found tire tracks leading away from the slough, but no other evidence to indicate how

After all of us were out, we started walking. A man drove up and said, 'Oh my God. You're those kids.'
Jodi Heffington-Medrano

27 people had simply vanished. Chowchilla went into crisis mode. Reporters flooded into the town and theories began to circulate about what might have happened— theories that included the Zodiac Killer (see pp. 288–89) and terrorism, as well as a simple kidnap and ransom demand.

Meanwhile, the kidnappers had retreated to a hideout to get some sleep. When they awoke on the morning of July 16, they planned to call the authorities in Chowchilla with a ransom demand of $5 million ($20.8 million today) and give the names of the driver and children. If further proof was needed, they would deliver the clothing samples to a place where authorities could easily find them. There was just one flaw in their plan: law enforcement telephone lines in Chowchilla were so jammed with calls from tipsters, reporters, and parents that the kidnappers could not get through.

The children are reunited with tearful parents in Chowchilla, as reporters and photographers crowd around them. All 27 victims arrived home on this Greyhound bus.

The great escape

Inside the van, 14-year-old Mike Marshall, the son of a rodeo cowboy, decided that he was not going to die without trying to escape. With the help of Ray and the other boys, Marshall stacked the mattresses high enough to reach the opening in the van's roof. Blocking the way was a steel plate, two heavy tractor batteries, and a pile of dirt 3 feet (1 m) deep. Using wooden beams salvaged from the box springs for leverage, they were able to move the plate, drag down the batteries, and dig upward through the dirt.

After 16 hours underground, the children of Chowchilla climbed out. They had not walked far before they were discovered by a quarry security guard, who recognized them immediately. Thirty-six hours after the bus was hijacked, the children were reunited with their families.

At first, authorities assumed that the abduction was committed by known criminals from the area. They fruitlessly scoured their records for anyone who might fit the profile. Ray, who had tried to remember details of the abduction, agreed to undergo hypnotism in order to aid the police effort. Under hypnosis, he was able to recall the entire license plate from one van and part of the second—enough to give authorities their first big break. They soon discovered that the old Allied removals van was registered to Fred Woods, the son of the quarry owner. The authorities could only guess at Woods's motives and accomplices.

Kidnappers Jim Schoenfeld, Fred Woods, and Richard Schoenfeld (left to right) sit together in the courtroom. All three received life sentences without parole for 27 counts of kidnapping.

Flawed plan

Wannabe movie moguls, the three men had wanted the ransom money to recoup their losses from a real estate project. Woods and his accomplices—Richard and James Schoenfeld, sons of a wealthy Menlo Park podiatrist—had imagined the kidnapping as a perfect crime, but now it was falling apart. Learning through the media that their captives had escaped, the men decided to run.

Woods flew to Vancouver and checked into a motel under a false name. Jim Schoenfeld planned to drive up and meet him, but his suspicious behavior prompted border guards to deny him entry into Canada. Rick Schoenfeld, meanwhile, returned home to the Bay Area and turned himself in. Learning that his brother was in custody, Jim also returned home and was soon arrested.

Woods, meanwhile, was arrested in Canada after penning a letter to a friend back home that contained his alias. All three men pleaded guilty to the kidnappings and were handed life sentences. ■

Criminally induced post-traumatic stress

According to the National Center for Victims of Crime, soldiers are not the only individuals who experience PTSD. The syndrome is also seen in victims of civilian trauma and criminal violence.

Symptoms of PTSD include flashbacks and nightmares, lethargy, detachment, anxiety, and anger. Appeals and parole hearings can trigger stress reactions in victims many years after the crime.

In the case of the Chowchilla Kidnapping, parents of the kidnap victims were reluctant to admit concerns about their children's mental health, so there was a delay of five months before they asked for help. A study conducted with 23 of the victims a year after the kidnapping—and again four years later—found that they all experienced PTSD. Five children who narrowly avoided being kidnapped—because they had only just been delivered home before the bus was attacked—were also traumatized. Now in their 50s, many of the victims report long-term anxiety, depression, and substance abuse.

I ALWAYS FELT LIKE A POOR CHICKEN IN A HENHOUSE

THE KIDNAPPING OF NATASCHA KAMPUSCH, 1998–2006

IN CONTEXT

LOCATION
Vienna, Austria

THEME
Child abduction

BEFORE
1984 Eighteen-year-old Austrian Elisabeth Fritzl is imprisoned by her father, Josef, in an underground dungeon at the family home. She remains there for 24 years, and gives birth to seven children, all fathered by Josef.

1990 In Japan, nine-year-old schoolgirl Fusako Sano is kidnapped by Nobuyuki Satō, a mentally disturbed unemployed man, and held for nine years.

AFTER
2013 Three American women, Amanda Berry, Michelle Knight, and Georgina DeJesus, escape from the home of Ariel Castro, who imprisoned, raped, and starved them for 10 years.

On the morning of March 2, 1998, 10-year-old Natascha Kampusch began the walk to school from her home in a suburb of Vienna. She never made it there.

Unemployed telecoms engineer Wolfgang Priklopil snatched the child from the street and took her to his home in the suburb of Strasshof, just a 30-minute drive away. After a 12-year-old witness reported seeing Natascha being dragged into a white minibus by two men, police launched a massive search of 776 vehicles—including Priklopil's. When interviewed, the 44-year-old told police he had been alone at home at the time of the abduction, and that he was using his van to remove rubble during construction work on his house. He was not questioned further, and his home was not searched.

A secret prisoner

For the next eight years, Priklopil held Natascha captive in a 54-square-foot (5-sq. m) soundproof, windowless cellar under his garage. The space was well hidden, and so secure that it took an hour to get inside it. Early on, Priklopil

---

The effects of long-term captivity

After being released from her long imprisonment, Natascha Kampusch received intensive treatment from doctors and psychologists to help her come to terms with her experience.

Prolonged captivity can have a profound psychological impact on victims, particularly if their abductor was also sexually abusive or violent. Experts say the will of anyone stripped of autonomy eventually breaks. As they experience trauma after trauma, they stop fighting their captors, and often surrender to powerlessness. Submission can be followed by depression, dissociative disorder, post-traumatic stress disorder, and anxiety. When victims are released from their confinement, psychologists say what they need most is time with their families or loved ones to recover, and to assimilate well in their home environment. Having an opportunity to talk about their experience, if and when they choose, also aids recovery.

See also: The Lindbergh Baby Kidnapping 178–85 ▪ The Kidnapping of John Paul Getty III 186–87
▪ The Kidnapping of Patty Hearst 188–89

> You saw my dungeon… You know how small it was. It was a place to despair.
> **Natascha Kampusch**

Natascha Kampusch later bought the house where she was kept in a cell (above), to prevent it from becoming a "theme park."

warned the child that he had a gun, and that he would use it to kill her if she tried to escape. He told Natascha that the doors and windows of the house were booby-trapped with explosives.

As the years passed and Natascha reached her early teens, she became less docile toward her captor. Priklopil responded by stepping up his efforts to cement his domination over her: he began regularly beating and starving her, and keeping her in darkness for long periods. He also brought her upstairs to clean his house. On a few occasions, he took Natascha with him on trips outside the house, during which the girl was too afraid to run away, or to reach out to the people she encountered.

Breaking free

On August 23, 2006, when she was 18, Natascha finally found a chance to escape. Priklopil had asked her to vacuum the interior of his car, which was parked in the yard. He took a call on his cell phone, and wandered off for a moment to get away from the noise. Natascha left the vacuum running to cover her and simply walked out the gate.

She then started sprinting down the street, begging passersby for help. At first she was ignored, but finally she convinced someone to contact the police. On the day of Natascha's escape, Priklopil went to a close friend and confessed his crime, saying: "I am a kidnapper and a rapist." He then killed himself by jumping in front of a train.

Once Natascha had emerged, Austria's police were criticized for failing to investigate certain leads in the wake of her disappearance. In the years that followed, rumors persisted that Priklopil had had an accomplice—fueled by the young witness's insistence that two men had taken Natascha. In 2012, a nine-month international probe, which included experts from the FBI, looked closely at the case and concluded that it was highly likely Priklopil had acted alone.

Natascha Kampusch's traumatic ordeal and her sensational escape made global headlines. In 2011, she wrote an account of her captivity, *3,096 Days;* in 2016, she published another book, *10 Years Of Freedom,* in which she reflected on her difficult adjustment to her new life amid constant public scrutiny. ▪

MURDER

CASES

The bludgeoned skull of a Neanderthal man found in a cave in Northern Spain is the **earliest evidence of murder**.

430,000 YA

French cloth merchant **Jean Calas is executed** for the murder of his eldest son, who was about to convert to Catholicism.

1762

The acquittal of murderer Daniel M'Naghten **on the grounds of insanity** sets a legal precedent in English law.

1843

Domestic maid Kate Webster, known as the **Dripping Killer**, is executed in London for murdering her employer.

1879

In the US, **prime suspect Lizzie Borden** is acquitted of the ax murder of her father and stepmother.

1892

In England, the Stratton brothers are convicted through **fingerprint** evidence and executed.

1905

Dr. Hawley Crippen is hanged at Pentonville Prison, London, for the murder of his wife, Cora.

1910

In Paris, an all-male jury cites **"unbridled female passion"** when acquitting Madame Henriette Caillaux of murder.

1914

Homicide is the killing of one person by another. Although not all homicides are murder, every murder is a homicide. Yet while homicide may be tolerated, or even championed, such as state-approved executions, murder is always condemned. It is usually defined as "the unlawful killing of a human being with malice aforethought."

Murder by degree

The law distinguishes between different types of murder, and these vary across legal jurisdictions. The degree of prior intent is critical. In the US, most states distinguish between premeditated murder; an intention to commit serious bodily harm that results in murder; a killing that results from extreme recklessness; and a murder committed by an accomplice during a felony. By contrast, in the UK, first degree murder involves premeditation, while second degree murder occurs in the heat of the moment, with a clear intent to kill but an absence of prior planning.

The case of woodworker Daniel M'Naghten in London in 1843 set a precedent for "not guilty of murder by reason of insanity." In English law, this can only occur if the defendant is able to clearly prove that "at the time of the committing of the act, the party accused was laboring under such a defect of reason, from disease of the mind, as not to know the nature and quality of the act he was doing; or if he did know it, that he did not know he was doing what was wrong." Most US states have a similar law regarding sanity.

Cold-blooded killers

Outside the criminal justice system, criminologists classify violence as being "reactive" or "instrumental" in nature. Reactive violence is hot-blooded, happens spontaneously, and characterizes most homicides. The murders detailed in this chapter are instrumental: cold-blooded, premeditated, and goal-driven. Their motivations differ widely, from profit (the Stratton brothers), sexual gratification (the Black Dahlia murder), to revenge (Roberto Calvi).

Historically, many middle- and upper-class women have been spared conviction for murder due to false assumptions about femininity and violence. The most shocking case was that of Madame Caillaux, caught red-handed for premeditated

Elizabeth Short, known as the **Black Dahlia**, is murdered and dismembered in Los Angeles by an unknown killer.

Charles Whitman carries out the Texas Towers Massacre, the **first mass shooting** on a US campus.

Mark David Chapman **shoots John Lennon dead** in New York.

Former football star **O. J. Simpson** is tried for the murder of his ex-wife, Nicole, and her friend Ron Goldman.

1947

1966

1980

1995

1948

1969

1993

1996–97

Sadamichi Hirasawa is found guilty of the **Teigin Incident**, a mass poisoning committed by a bank robber in downtown Tokyo.

In California, the cultlike **Manson Family** carry out nine murders over a five-week period.

Two 10-year-old boys become the **youngest convicted murderers** in British history for the murder of James Bulger.

In the US, rival hip-hop stars Tupac Shakur and Biggie Smalls are killed in separate **drive-by shootings**.

murder in early 20th-century France but acquitted because it was assumed that women could not control their emotions. Similarly, the trial of American ax murderer Lizzie Borden was governed by the belief that a lady was incapable of slaying with a hatchet. However, such attitudes did not protect 19th-century London maid Kate Webster—who murdered her wealthy employer—nor Lindy Chamberlain, whose unexpectedly calm reaction to her baby's disappearance led to her wrongful conviction for stabbing the child to death in Australia in the 1980s.

The social stigma and harsh legal penalties resulting from a wrongful murder conviction can devastate the life of an innocent person. Former US Marine Kirk Bloodsworth, spent nine years on death row before his acquittal. The Japanese artist Sadamichi Hirasawa, who was widely thought to be innocent in the Teigin Bank murder case, died behind bars without his name being cleared. Even being acquitted, however, leaves a stain on the character of the person accused—particularly when the defendant is a celebrity such as O. J. Simpson.

Mass murderers
Mass murders are considered a separate category and involve four or more victims killed in the same location: the Texas Towers massacre and the Teigin Incident are examples of this type of crime.

The Manson Family tend to be characterized as "spree killers"— alienated individuals or groups who embark on a deadly rampage. Although the number of victims in such killings are higher than in single, double, or triple homicides, they are invariably regarded as single events by the general public. In contrast to a serial killer, a spree killer does not return to the routine of their daily life, only to strike again at a later date. Typically, spree killers either never reoffend or, having crossed the line, continue to murder until they are killed or apprehended.

Technological advances in the field of forensic sciences—from DNA fingerprinting to forensic facial reconstruction—are allowing investigators to reopen closed and unsolved cases. These advances also make it increasingly difficult for guilty people to walk free, and correspondingly, for an innocent person to remain behind bars. ∎

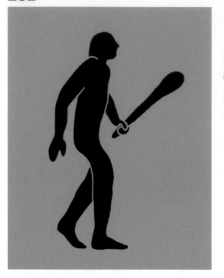

AN UNUSUALLY CLEAR CASE, LIKE A "SMOKING GUN"
THE NEANDERTHAL MURDER, 430,000 YEARS AGO

IN CONTEXT

LOCATION
Atapuerca Mountains, northern Spain

THEME
Earliest known murder

AFTER
5000 BCE In an early Neolithic settlement in southwest Germany, 500 people—babies, children, and adults—are killed and cannibalized.

392–201 BCE In Ireland, two men are tortured and killed as part of a ritual sacrifice and their bodies dumped in a peat bog. Their mummified remains are found by workmen in 2003.

c.367 CE At Vindolanda, a Roman fort near Hadrian's Wall in Britain, a 10-year-old child is killed by a blow to the head and buried in a pit in a barrack room floor. The skeleton is discovered in 2010.

Some 430,000 years ago, high in the Atapuerca Mountains of northern Spain, a lethal assault was committed. The victim, a young adult Neanderthal, received two blows to the head, just above the left eye. These were made by the same implement, but from different angles, suggesting two separate, deliberate strikes.

At some point after his or her death, the victim's corpse was dropped down a 43-foot (13-meter) vertical shaft into a pit within a cave complex. The remains lay undisturbed until an international team of archaeologists discovered the site—dubbed the Sima de los Huesos ("Pit of Bones")—in 1984.

Historic revelations

The victim's skull—known as Cranium 17—was found smashed into 52 fragments, among more than 6,500 bones belonging to at least 28 early human individuals unearthed from the underground cave. It is not clear how the bodies ended up there, but it is believed they may have been deliberately deposited in the pit after death by their peers. This suggests that early humans began burying—or at

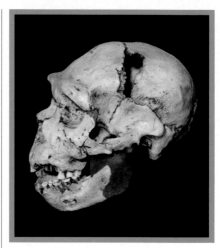

Modern forensic techniques were used to study the angle of the two fractures at the front of Cranium 17, and re-create impact trajectories. The results supported the murder theory.

least collecting—their dead far earlier than was previously thought. Scientific analysis of the victim's skull, which included a CT scan and a 3D model, led researchers to conclude that the owner of Cranium 17 had not died as the result of an accident, but by violence inflicted by a fellow Neanderthal. It may represent the first case of murder in human history. ∎

PERPETRATED WITH THE SWORD OF JUSTICE
JEAN CALAS, 1761

IN CONTEXT

LOCATION
Toulouse, France

THEME
Wrongful execution

BEFORE
1673 American colonial settler Rebecca Cornell dies in an accidental house fire. But her son Thomas, with whom she did not get along, is hanged for her murder after hearsay is offered as evidence at his trial.

AFTER
1785 Anna Göldi, a Swiss maidservant to a physician, is accused of witchcraft by her employer (and rejected lover) and executed. In 2007, the Swiss parliament declares the case a miscarriage of justice.

1922 In Australia, Colin Campbell Ross is hanged for the murder of a 12-year-old girl. The case is reexamined using modern forensic techniques, and Ross is posthumously pardoned in 2008.

One October night in 1761, Marc-Antoine Calas was found hanged in his father Jean's textile shop. Deep in debt, the Frenchman was believed to have killed himself. His untimely death was a personal tragedy for his family, but as Huguenots (Protestants) living in a resolute and unforgiving Roman Catholic country, their problems had just begun. Crowds gathered and suspicion ran rampant: it was said that Marc-Antoine had been on the brink of converting to Catholicism, and that his father must have killed him to prevent this. Jean Calas was arrested by the authorities, along with four other suspects.

A gruesome trial

The Toulouse magistrate asked witnesses to come forward. Their testimony was merely hearsay, but in 18th-century France, that was accepted as evidence. Calas's case went to an appellate court, which voted to convict and condemn him. The sentence called for Calas to be interrogated under torture, in the hope that he would confess and implicate his four coconspirators. But Calas steadfastly protested his innocence. He was then broken on the wheel, strangled, and burned.

Soon after, the philosopher Voltaire took up Calas's case, believing he had been wrongly executed. In a press campaign, Voltaire convinced many that the judiciary had allowed prejudice against Huguenots to influence the verdict. After a three-year crusade, Calas's conviction was overturned. ∎

It would seem that fanaticism is angry at the success of reason, and combats it ever more furiously.
Voltaire

See also: Sadamichi Hirasawa 224–25 ▪ Elizabeth Báthory 264–65 ▪ The Dreyfus Affair 310–11

NOT GUILTY BY REASON OF INSANITY
DANIEL M'NAGHTEN, 1843

IN CONTEXT

LOCATION
London, UK

THEME
Botched assassination

BEFORE
1800 James Hadfield tries to shoot Britain's King George III at a London theater. He is tried for high treason, but acquitted on grounds of insanity when doctors give evidence on his mental state. He spends the rest of his life in a hospital.

AFTER
1954 Monte Durham, a young man with a history of mental illness, is convicted of housebreaking in Washington, D.C. The appellate court finds that he is not criminally responsible because he is mentally ill, broadening the defense beyond one of knowing the difference between right and wrong. It is later reversed.

I n 19th-century England, it had for centuries been accepted in law that some criminal defendants should not be held responsible for their actions because of mental "defects." The courts also made a distinction between criminals who knew right from wrong, and those who did not. But in 1843, a case challenged the status quo and saw the formation of a new standard for evaluating the criminal responsibility of those defendants pleading insanity.

Mistaken identity
On January 20, 1843, Scottish woodworker Daniel M'Naghten set out to assassinate Britain's Tory Prime Minister, Robert Peel, in London. With murderous intent, he approached a man whom he believed was Peel walking toward Downing Street, site of the government's headquarters. He was, in fact, Edward Drummond, Peel's secretary. M'Naghten calmly drew a pistol and fired at point-blank range into Drummond's back. He was apprehended by a nearby police officer before he could fire a second shot. Drummond died a few days later, and M'Naghten was charged with his murder.

Daniel M'Naghten was almost certainly suffering from paranoid schizophrenia. His trial was a landmark in that it established a legal definition of criminal insanity.

Guilty but insane
At M'Naghten's trial the defense lawyers called nine witnesses who testified that he had been acting "suspiciously" and had paranoid delusions. The accused admitted his plan to murder Prime Minister Peel after being "driven to desperation by persecution." During the police interrogation, M'Naghten claimed to have been hounded by the ruling Tories who

See also: Jeffrey Dahmer 293 ▪ The Assassination of Abraham Lincoln 306–09 ▪ The Assassination of John F. Kennedy 316–21

followed him everywhere and wanted to murder him. The prosecution argued that, in spite of what they called his "partial insanity," M'Naghten was capable of knowing right from wrong. However, the jury found him not guilty on grounds of insanity, and he was sentenced to spend the rest of his life in a mental asylum.

The murderer's acquittal caused a huge outcry: even Queen Victoria, who herself had been the victim of assassination attempts, voiced her displeasure. There had never been such a high-profile case that accepted insanity as a defense.

Legal tests

Unable to disregard the volume of public and royal discontent, the government asked a panel of judges to answer a series of questions about the law of insanity as applied in the M'Naghten trial. Their responses established a specific test—known as the M'Naghten rule—to be applied by a jury in an insanity case. The rule holds that a criminal defendant is presumed to

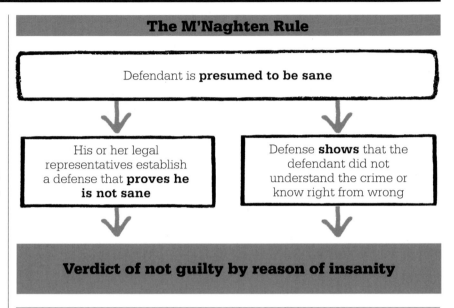

The M'Naghten Rule

Defendant is **presumed to be sane**

↓ His or her legal representatives establish a defense that **proves he is not sane**

↓ Defense **shows** that the defendant did not understand the crime or know right from wrong

Verdict of not guilty by reason of insanity

be sane, and for a plea of insanity to be accepted, it must be proven that the defendant has a mental defect or disease and was not aware that what they were doing was wrong. The rule is still used today in many countries. In the US, the rule has been modified by some states to include an "irresistible impulse" provision. A defendant

can be found not guilty by reason of insanity if they know the difference between right and wrong, but cannot stop themselves from committing a criminal act.

In almost all cases, a verdict of not guilty by reason of insanity leads to a sentence at a mental health institution for an indefinite number of years—even life. ▪

Lunatic asylums housed Britain's insane murderers until 1863, when Broadmoor, the first high-security psychiatric hospital, was founded.

Hospitals for the criminally insane

Institutions for the criminally insane have existed since the early 19th century. In Britain, they were established by the Criminal Lunatics Act of 1800 to prevent the criminally insane from being housed in regular prisons and asylums; however, they soon gained a reputation for poor treatment and bad conditions.

Institutions for the criminally insane ostensibly operate just like other mental health facilities, but, in fact, they often endanger patients and staff. In the US,

Bridgewater State Hospital in southern Massachusetts has been the subject of numerous controversies for inmate deaths, inmate abuse, and overuse of restraints by hospital workers.

On the other hand, staff are also at risk. Stephen Seager's *Behind the Gates of Gomorrah* gave a damning account of the chronic violence committed by a small number of patients that he witnessed when working as a psychiatrist at California's Napa State Hospital.

GAVE KATHERINE WARNING TO LEAVE

THE DRIPPING KILLER, 1879

IN CONTEXT

LOCATION
Richmond, Surrey, UK

THEME
Profit-motivated murder

BEFORE
1809 In England, Mary Bateman, the Yorkshire Witch, is hanged for the murder of Rebecca Perigo. She is one of the first criminals to be publicly dissected.

August 9, 1849 Maria Manning, a Swiss lady's maid, and her husband Frederick kill Maria's lover Patrick O'Connor and bury him beneath their kitchen floor. They are caught a few days later, tried, and executed on November 13, 1849, in London.

AFTER
1977–78 Scot Archibald Hall, dubbed the "Monster Butler," murders four people while in service to members of the British aristocracy. He is sentenced to life in prison.

The last time Henry Porter had seen his Irish friend Kate Webster, she had just been released from jail for larceny. Six years later, in March 1879, she visited him at his west London home, looking smart in a silk dress. Now called Mrs. Thomas through marriage, Kate explained that she had inherited a house in affluent Richmond, Surrey, but wanted to sell it and its contents. Did Henry know of a property broker? Henry introduced her to John Church.

Kate then enlisted Henry's son, Robert, to help her carry a hefty box from her Richmond home to the rail station. He was not concerned when, en route, she dumped the box into the River Thames.

Shocking discovery

Unfortunately for Webster, the box washed up downstream a day later, where it was spotted by a coal porter as he crossed a bridge. Hoping it might contain stolen goods, he fished it out and opened it up. Inside was a disemboweled female torso and two legs wrapped in brown paper. Horrified, he contacted the police, who quickly linked the grisly find to a severed human foot recently found nearby.

> I chopped the head from the body with the assistance of a razor which I used to cut through the flesh afterwards.
> **Kate Webster**

Meanwhile, at 2 Mayfield Cottages, Richmond, Mrs. Julia Thomas's neighbors were becoming anxious. The 55-year-old had not been seen for two weeks, although her maid, Kate, was still around. On March 18, moving vans arrived at the house, hired by John Church to buy Mrs Thomas's furniture for £68 (about $9,000 today). When asked who had hired them, the removal men said "Mrs. Thomas," and gestured toward Kate, who hurried away and caught a train to Liverpool.

Church realized that the "Mrs Thomas" with whom he had done the deal was an impostor. He called the police, who searched the house

See also: Lizzie Borden 208–11 ▪ Elizabeth Báthory 264–65

Anthropological criminology

During the 19th century, pseudoscience (theories and methods that were wrongly regarded as scientific) dominated academic debate in Europe and the US. Among these was Italian physician and criminologist Cesare Lombroso's theory of anthropological criminology. Misappropriating Darwinistic ideas, Lombroso argued that criminals were evolutionary throwbacks to primitive man, and could be identified by physical characteristics, such as gangly arms, a sloping forehead, jug ears, facial asymmetry, and so on.

Kate Webster came under similar scrutiny during her trial, with middle-class onlookers and the media commenting on her strong, "unfeminine build," without considering that this may have developed as a result of a life of manual labor. By the early 20th century, Lombroso's ideas had been discredited.

and found blood stains, charred finger bones in the hearth, and a copper laundry vessel clogged with human fat. Scotland Yard learned that Webster had fled to Ireland, and she was arrested there. On July 2, she stood trial for murder at the Old Bailey. The revolting details of the crime emerged over six days of witness testimony.

Webster entered the service of Julia Thomas in January 1879, but relations between them soon became strained. Julia was critical of the work of her heavy-drinking maid, and a month later, she fired her, giving her a few weeks' notice. On the afternoon of March 2, Julia

Hangman William Marwood used his newly perfected "long drop" technique, in which the condemned's neck was broken instantly at the end of the fall, to execute Kate Webster.

was at home preparing for a service at the local church and waiting for Kate to assist her. However, Kate came back late from the pub, and so Julia was delayed.

When Julia returned from the service, the two women argued. Kate claimed that in a fit of drunken rage she pushed Julia down the stairs, then strangled her to death with her hands to prevent her from screaming. Using a meat saw,

carving knife, and razor, she butchered the body, burning large sections of it in the kitchen.

Kate divided Thomas's body parts between a Gladstone bag and the box she later hurled into the river. Rather than trying to avoid capture, Webster took to wearing her late employer's clothes, assuming her identity, and selling Thomas's possessions. Some reports even said that Webster had boiled Thomas's body and made money selling the fat as dripping to local pubs. True or not, this story lead many to dub her the "Dripping Killer." Webster was found guilty and hanged on July 29, 1879. ■

LIZZIE BORDEN TOOK AN AX AND GAVE HER MOTHER FORTY WHACKS

LIZZIE BORDEN, 1892

IN CONTEXT

DATE AND LOCATION
Massachusetts, US

THEME
Unproven murder by a family member

BEFORE
1497 Giovanni Borgia, son of Pope Alexander VI, is stabbed multiple times and dumped in Rome's Tiber River. Rumors implicate rival families, political enemies, and Borgia's own brother, but the crime remains unsolved.

AFTER
1996 On December 26, six-year-old JonBenet Ramsey goes missing and a bizarre ransom note is found on the stairs of the family home in Colorado, US. She is later found strangled in the basement. Although no charges are filed, people speculate that her own parents are the killers.

On a hot August day in 1892, an assailant rained 19 blows on the back of Abby Borden's head with a hatchet before delivering 11 more to the face of her husband, Andrew, as he lay sleeping. A medical examiner later surmised that the couple had been killed roughly two hours apart.

At 6:15 that morning, the Bordens' live-in maid, Bridget ("Maggie") O'Sullivan arose to gather firewood from the basement of their home at 92 Second Street, Fall River. Ten minutes later, Abby came into the kitchen, and by 7 a.m., she had been joined at the breakfast table by her husband. Soon after, Andrew's youngest

See also: The Texas Tower Massacre 226–29 ▪ O.J. Simpson 246–51 ▪ Jack the Ripper 266–73

daughter, Lizzie, arrived, wearing a blue dress. Abby asked Bridget to wash the downstairs windows, then headed upstairs to change the pillowslips in the guest bedroom.

At 9 a.m., Andrew left to run some errands; when he returned, around 10:30, Bridget heard him struggling to unlock the main door, and hurried to assist. She saw that the spring lock had been fastened, and heard Lizzie laughing upstairs.

Andrew went into the sitting room, and the maid continued her work. Lizzie came down the stairs and spoke to her father. Bridget overheard her say that Abby, Lizzie's stepmother, had received a note from a sick friend and had gone to visit her. Bridget moved on to the dining room to wash the windows there, and was joined by Lizzie, who started ironing some clothes, chatting as she did so.

The nightmare begins

Feeling tired and nauseous, Bridget told Lizzie she was going to take a nap, and headed up the back stairs to her room. Lying on her bed, she heard the City Hall bell chime 11.

The Borden home at 92 Second Street in Fall River. Andrew was a rich man but chose not to live in the wealthiest part of the city, opting to live closer to his businesses.

Around 11:10 a.m., Bridget heard Lizzie call out to her: "Maggie, come quick! Father's dead. Somebody came in and killed him." Bridget rushed downstairs to find Lizzie standing in the rear hallway. She told her that Andrew's murdered body was in the sitting room and asked her to go find Dr. Seabury Bowen. Unable to locate him, Bridget soon returned.

In the meantime, the Bordens' neighbor, Mrs. Adelaide Churchill, had come by to see what all the fuss was about. She found Lizzie distraught and tried to comfort her. Lizzie explained that she had been in the barn when she had heard a groan coming from the house. On entering, she had found her father dead on the couch. When Mrs. Churchill asked about Abby, Lizzie told her that she was out visiting a friend. Shortly after, when Bridget

I'm going to burn this old [dress] up, it is covered with paint.
Lizzie Borden

suggested that she should try to find Abby, Lizzie said she thought she had heard her return. With Mrs. Churchill in tow, Bridget decided to check upstairs. As soon as her eyes were level with the landing, she saw Abby's bloodied corpse lying face down in the guest bedroom.

At 11:45, the first wave of police officers descended on the house and began to search it. They noted no signs of forced entry or burglary. The front and cellar doors were locked and, although there was blood on the victims, ceiling, and »

Defensive wounds

When a victim of violence is attacked they invariably raise their hands reflexively to deflect or protect themselves from the blows. The resulting injuries to their appendages are known as "defensive wounds." In a homicide investigation, a rule of thumb is that an absence of defensive wounds indicates the victim was unable to defend themselves—whether because they were bound, drugged, or because they trusted their attacker and were immediately

incapacitated in a sudden and unexpected attack. Neither Andrew nor Abby Borden had sustained defensive injuries.

In Andrew's case this was to be expected, because he was sleeping when he was attacked. Abby, however, was cleaning the guest bedroom, and appears to have been attacked on the side of the bed farthest from the doorway. It seems likely that either Abby's assailant sneaked up on her, or she was killed by someone she knew, who took her by surprise and struck her with the hatchet.

Murder 1

Abby Borden goes upstairs to clean a bedroom between 9 a.m. and 10:30 a.m.

↓

She is **struck with a hatchet** to the side of her head by an unseen assailant

↓

Abby turns and **falls face down** on the floor, causing major contusions to her face

↓

The killer sits on Abby's back and delivers **19 direct hits** to the back of the head

↓

Abby Borden's body is found at around 11:30 a.m. by live-in maid Bridget and neighbor Mrs. Churchill

Murder 2

Live-in maid **Bridget** opens front door to Andrew Borden at approximately 10:30 a.m.

↓

Bridget hears Lizzie Borden **laughing** upstairs as she opens the door

↓

Andrew Borden lies down on the couch in the living room for a nap. Lizzie claims she removes his shoes

↓

Andrew is assaulted with a hatchet and is **struck 10 or 11 times around the head**, causing fatal injuries

↓

Lizzie Borden raises the alarm at 11:10 a.m., when she calls for the maid, having found her father dead

A Venerable Citizen and His Aged Wife Hacked to Pieces in Their Home.
Fall River Herald

walls, there was none anywhere else. Bridget let an officer into the cellar where he came across a box containing two axes, one plastered with blood and hair, and a recently broken hatchet-head caked in ash.

Lizzie was questioned by Deputy Marshal Fleet about her movements. She said she had intended to spend the morning ironing clothes. When her father had come home tired, she had taken off his shoes while he napped on the sofa. She had gone to the barn for 15–20 minutes to look for lead to make fishing sinkers. And she had not seen Abby leave to "visit her sick friend." An officer inspected the barn to confirm Lizzie's alibi. It was humid and windless that day; given the stifling heat in the barn, he doubted she had spent as much time as she had claimed in there. The absence of footprints in the heavy dust supported his theory.

Arrest and acquittal

On August 11, Lizzie was arrested for the murder of her parents. Her alleged motive was that she suspected her father of writing her out of his will in favor of her stepmother. At first, it seemed as if the case might not go to trial, as at the inquest, it was reported that a passing peddler had spotted a woman walking from the yard to the side door of the house, seeming to support Lizzie's alibi. Secondly, a doctor from Harvard Medical School attested that the blood and hair on the ax belonged to a cow.

Suddenly, though, there was a reversal in Lizzie's fortunes. A prison matron claimed to have overheard her saying "Emma, you have given me away, haven't you?" to her older sister during a visit. Moreover, Lizzie's best friend told the inquest she had seen Lizzie burning a blue dress in the kitchen stove days after the slayings. This was sufficient to bring a murder charge against her.

Lizzie Borden's trial began in 1893. On June 20, after just 90 minutes' deliberation, the jury returned a verdict of not guilty. Lizzie used her inheritance to buy a house on the affluent side of Fall River. She died there in 1927.

The Bordens' unsolved murder remains a source of fascination. Many theories—some potentially possible, most just laughable— have been proffered as to who killed them, how, and why. Those who believe Lizzie was the culprit

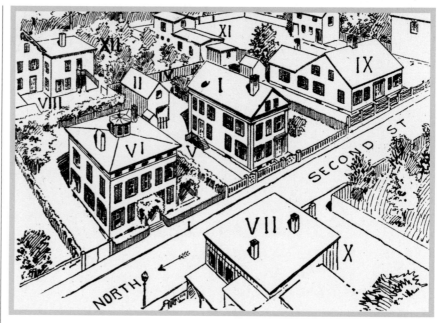

point to the evidence raised by the prosecution: her window of opportunity, the hot, dusty barn, at least 30 inconsistent statements, and the burning of the blue dress. However, two crucial pieces of evidence stand out: Lizzie was the only person to have stood on the landing while her stepmother lay dead in the guest room, a scene that Bridget and Mrs. Churchill had come across

The Bordens' side door, marked V, was unhooked from 9:30–10:30 a.m. Could an outsider have crept in, axed Abby, hidden for more than 90 minutes, then emerged to kill Andrew?

immediately after ascending the stairs. And although Lizzie insisted she had removed her father's shoes as he dozed on the sofa, in the crime scene photo he is still wearing them. ∎

Lizzie Borden

Lizzie Andrew Borden was a 32-year-old unmarried woman living with her wealthy but miserly father and his second wife, prominent residents of Fall River. Accounts of her character range from "kind Sunday School teacher active in local charities" to an "ill-tempered kleptomaniac who decapitated Abby's cat because it was annoying her."

Rumors have surfaced that Lizzie engaged in incest, whether consensual or not, with her uncle John Morse and her father—the locked door leading from her bedroom to Andrew's with a

bureau pushed against it is viewed as evidence of the latter. She was certainly a habitual thief. While he was alive, her father managed to protect her from prosecution, but she was later accused of shoplifting a painting. The matter was settled out of court.

The jury acquitted Lizzie on the grounds that the evidence against her was mainly circumstantial, but most likely also because the Victorian mindset could not comprehend that an upper-class spinster could commit such a brutal act.

FINGERPRINTING ALONE HAS PROVED TO BE BOTH INFALLIBLE AND FEASIBLE

THE STRATTON BROTHERS, 1905

IN CONTEXT

LOCATION
London, UK

THEME
Fingerprint evidence

BEFORE
1902 Burglar Harry Jackson is the first man to be convicted of a crime in the UK using fingerprint evidence. Police find his prints on a windowsill in a London home that had been robbed.

AFTER
1911 Murderer Thomas Jennings is the first person in the US to be convicted on fingerprint evidence.

2014 Police in Utah solve the 1991 murder of 78-year-old Lucille Johnson when they match fingerprints on Lego bricks with those of a man who played with them as a child while his father, John Sansing, killed Johnson in an adjacent room.

> Until the arrest of Alfred Stratton I had not been able to find any fingerprints that I tried which agreed with the print upon the cash box.
> **Detective Inspector Charles Collins**

When brothers Alfred and Albert Stratton robbed and murdered the husband and wife who managed a paint shop in south London in 1905, they left something behind: an oily fingerprint on an emptied cash box. This evidence became the cornerstone of the case against them, and paved the way for further development of fingerprint analysis.

A brutal robbery

Elderly couple Thomas and Ann Farrow lived in an apartment above their shop Chapman's Oil and Colour on Deptford High Street. On the morning of March 27, 1905, their assistant arrived to find Thomas dead in the parlor with terrible head injuries. Ann was found unconscious in the bedroom; she had been beaten around the head, and died a few days later. A tin cash box lay near her body; after a search, police found two masks made from stockings.

Detectives wrapped the cash box and took it to Scotland Yard's Fingerprint Bureau, which had been established four years earlier. On examination, they determined that the fingerprint was left by a thumb. It was compared to the victims' prints, those of the police at the crime scene, and more than 80,000 others on file at the bureau, but there was no match.

The tipping point

The police searched for witnesses. A milkman saw two men leaving the shop at the time of the murders, but he was unable to identify the Strattons. A breakthrough came on March 31 when another witness, Ellen Stanton, told police that she saw the two brothers running across the top of Deptford High Street while she walked to work on the morning of March 27. The brothers were arrested and on March 31 Stanton picked them out of a police lineup of 16 men.

The police also interviewed Alfred's girlfriend, who said he had borrowed stockings from her, and Albert's girlfriend, who claimed he had arrived home that day with unexplained money. The evidence against the brothers was highly circumstantial, but when their prints were taken, Alfred's matched the thumb print on the cash box.

A master stroke

During the trial, the prosecution counsel explained the new science of fingerprinting to the jury. In his testimony, Detective Inspector Collins of Scotland Yard showed an enlarged photograph of Alfred

Sir Melville Leslie Macnaghten co-led the police investigation. He had been on the Belper Committee (1900), which recommended that criminals' fingerprints be taken and classified.

See also: John Leonard Orr 48–53 ▪ The Lindbergh Baby Kidnapping 178–85 ▪ Colin Pitchfork 294–97

Stratton's thumb print alongside the thumb smudge on the cash box, and pointed out 11 characteristics that agreed in the prints.

The defense counsel, Mr. Rooth, attempted to cast doubt on fingerprinting as a scientific technique, and on the reliability of the work carried out by Collins's department. Rooth argued that the print taken at the crime scene did not match the one taken while Alfred Stratton was in custody.

In a stroke of genius, Collins offered to take the prints of a jury member to show the court that differing amounts of downward pressure could account for the deviation. The jury was convinced by his scientific demonstration and took less than two hours to deliver a guilty verdict. The brothers were later sentenced to death. It was the first murder conviction in the UK based on fingerprint evidence.

The high-profile media coverage caused one drawback: criminals became aware of the precautions they had to take to avoid detection by this new forensic tool. ▪

The up-to-date professional criminal now seeks to prevent the leaving of tell-tale prints by covering the finger-tips with thin india-rubber, gold-beater's skin, or silk finger-stalls.
The Mirror

Fingerprinting

Although it has been known since 200 BCE that each person's fingerprints are different from every other person's, Sir William James Herschel, a British magistrate in India during the 1850s, is credited with the first systematic use of fingerprints for identification. In 1891, English scientist Sir Francis Galton developed Herschel's findings.

Galton devised an efficient system that allowed fingerprints to be matched against each other. He discovered that every person has a different pattern of ridges and valleys on the pads of their fingers (and on their toes) that do not change with time and will even grow back in their original form if the digit is damaged. In his classic book *Finger Prints* (1892), Galton referred to the lines, ridges, and shapes of fingerprints as "little worlds in themselves."

Three types of fingerprints can be recovered from a crime scene. Patent prints can be made by blood, grease, ink, or dirt, and are easily visible to the naked eye. Latent fingerprints are not visible—they are impressions secreted on a surface or an object by sweat and oil on the skin surface. Plastic prints, which are visible to the naked eye, are 3D indentations that occur when a finger touches a soft, malleable surface.

Although fingerprinting has stood the test of time, since the 1990s, several court cases have challenged their interpretation. Tests have found a margin of error, and there have been "false positives"—two prints can be similar enough to fool experts. In 2002, a US federal judge ruled that fingerprint witnesses can no longer tell juries that two prints are a "definite match." Fingerprinting may soon be replaced with DNA tests.

The Henry system, used in most countries today, classifies fingerprints by four basic patterns—the arch, the loop, the whorl, and the composite. It is named for Sir Edward Richard Henry, who founded the Scotland Yard Fingerprint Bureau in 1901.

ARCHES
produce a wave-like pattern. Tented arches rise to a sharper point.

LOOPS
curve back on themselves to form a loop shape.

WHORLS
form circular or spiral patterns.

COMPOSITES
are a combination of arches, loops, and whorls.

THANK GOD IT'S OVER. THE SUSPENSE HAS BEEN TOO GREAT

DR. CRIPPEN, 1910

In February 1910, music hall singer Cora Crippen vanished. The wife of Dr. H.H. Crippen, she was last seen at a small party at their home on January 31. Asked about Cora's whereabouts, Dr. Crippen said that she had returned to the US, their birth country, and died unexpectedly. Cora's friends were suspicious, and convinced London's Scotland Yard to investigate. When interviewed, Crippen admitted that his wife had not died; rather she had left for the US with her lover, Bruce Miller. He had lied out of embarrassment.

On the run

A few days later, Crippen fled with his young mistress Ethel La Neve, who was disguised as his son. They boarded the SS *Montrose*, destined for Canada. The police searched his home and discovered a human torso—head and limbs missing—under the cellar floor. A pathologist was unable to identify the sex of the body, but concluded that it was Cora's, based on a scar she was said to have. The body also featured traces of a poison that Crippen had bought shortly before his wife's disappearance.

Meanwhile, the ship's captain, who had been following the case, spotted the couple on board and sent a wireless telegraph to England to alert the authorities. British police caught a faster ship to Quebec and arrested the couple on their arrival. Crippen was found guilty of his wife's murder and hanged in November 1910. ∎

Crippen and La Neve stood trial together. She was acquitted, and he protested his innocence to the end. In 2007, DNA tests on "Cora's" remains suggested that the victim was male.

See also: Lizzie Borden 208–11 ▪ O.J. Simpson 246–51

I WAS DRIVEN BY A WILL THAT HAD TAKEN THE PLACE OF MY OWN
MADAME CAILLAUX, 1914

IN CONTEXT

LOCATION
Paris, France

THEME
Crime of passion

BEFORE
1859 US politician Daniel Sickles shoots dead his wife's lover. He stands trial, but is acquitted on grounds of "temporary insanity."

1906 Albert Lemaître, a French racing driver, shoots his wife after she files for divorce. After an unsuccessful attempt at suicide, he is tried and acquitted of what is deemed a crime of passion.

AFTER
1955 London nightclub hostess Ruth Ellis shoots and kills her faithless lover. Her family unsuccessfully attempt to have her murder conviction reduced to manslaughter on the grounds of provocation. She is the last woman in England to be executed.

Gaston Calmette's *Le Figaro* was not the only Paris newspaper with doubts over the integrity of Joseph Caillaux. The left-wing politician (and former French prime minister) was dogged by allegations of corruption. But no other journal could match the zeal shown by *Le Figaro*'s right-wing editor, who led a smear campaign against him.

In December 1913, Calmette threatened to publish love letters exchanged between Caillaux and his second wife, Henriette, while he was still married to his first wife. On March 16, 1914, Henriette went to the newspaper's offices and shot Calmette six times; he died later.

During her testimony at her trial, Henriette Caillaux skillfully evoked the prevailing image of a woman as a creature of emotions. The all-male jury was convinced that she had shot Calmette without premeditation or criminal intent—that when she pulled the trigger on the Browning pistol she was a temporary victim of "unbridled female passions." Perhaps her crime

Henriette shot Calmette at point blank range. Afterward, she told police: "Since there is no more justice in France … I resolved that I alone would be able to stop this campaign."

had, in fact, been an act of "passive aggression" against a potentially restless husband. It certainly stalled Caillaux's public career, and quashed any realistic chance of a life beyond his marriage to the woman who claimed to have risked all to restore his reputation. ∎

See also: Phoolan Devi 46–47 ▪ O.J. Simpson 246–51

SHE WAS
VERY GOOD LOOKING WITH
BEAUTIFUL DARK HAIR

**THE BLACK DAHLIA MURDER,
JANUARY 15, 1947**

IN CONTEXT

LOCATION
Los Angeles, California, US

THEME
Unsolved murder cases

BEFORE
July 27, 1943 Ora Murray is beaten to death and left near the clubhouse at Fox Hills Golf Course, Los Angeles.

May 4, 1932 Lilly Lindeström is found dead in her apartment in Atlas, Sweden. The killer drains her blood, causing the case to be known as the "Vampire murder."

AFTER
January 17, 1996 Amber Hagerman, nine, is abducted while riding her bike. Her body is found four days later.

April 26, 1999 British journalist Jill Dando is shot outside her home in Fulham, London. Barry George is wrongfully convicted for the murder, and is later acquitted.

On a winter morning just after 10 a.m., Betty Bersinger went for a walk next to a vacant lot in a southwest Los Angeles suburb. She stumbled upon a disturbing scene. Lying next to the sidewalk at West 39th Street and South Norton Avenue—an area in Leimert Park known as lover's lane—was the mutilated body of a naked woman. The discovery on January 15, 1947, led the Los Angeles Police Department to launch the largest manhunt in the city's history.

The body had been cleanly severed at the waist, drained of blood, bathed, and positioned with the lower half 1 foot (30 cm) away from the upper half. The victim's greenish-blue eyes were open, and her hands were positioned by her head, with the elbows bent. Her legs were wide apart. Rope burns marked her wrists, ankles, and neck, while her arms, left thigh, and right breast all featured deep lacerations. Each corner of her mouth had been cut, creating the chilling impression that she was smiling. According to a report archived by the University of Southern California's College of

> She knew I was bashful and liked to see my face turn crimson. She would say, 'We ought to go out dancing together.' But she was a nice girl.
> **Bob Pacios**

Education, the letters "BD" had been carved into her thigh—however, the authenticity of this claim is still debated.

LAPD homicide detectives Finis Brown and Harry Hansen arrived and scoured the crime scene, but not before the press had arrived and taken photographs. However, despite the extent and severity of the injuries, the woman's body had been carefully scrubbed clean, so there was little physical evidence to be found. The victim was identified by her fingerprints as 22-year-old

Elizabeth Short

Elizabeth Short, known as "Beth" to her family and "Betty" to her friends, grew up in Medford, Massachusetts. Her father, who built mini-golf courses, abandoned the family soon after the Great Depression. Short suffered from asthma, so at 16, her mother sent her to Florida, hoping that the weather would improve her health. There, Short met Air Force officer Matthew Gordon Jr. In 1943, at 19, she went to Vallejo, California, to live with her father, but left his care that same year and moved to Santa Barbara. She was arrested there for underage drinking in September 1943, and a judge ordered her to return to Medford. Instead, Short went back to Florida.

Short told her friends that she and Gordon were engaged to be married. Gordon, however, was killed in August 1945, less than a week before the end of World War II. That year, Short returned to Medford, but soon became restless. In 1946, she moved to Los Angeles. After Short's murder, Gordon's wedding announcement—to another woman—was found among her possessions.

See also: The Dripping Killer 206–07 ■ The Manson Family 230–37 ■ Jack the Ripper 266–73 ■ Harvey Glatman 274–75

aspiring actress Elizabeth Short. The detectives surmised that she had been killed elsewhere and then driven to the vacant lot. Dr. Frederick Newbarr, the chief coroner for LA County, ruled that the cause of death was a brain hemorrhage due to concussion, combined with blood loss arising from the lacerations to her face.

Last movements
Beginning in May 1946, Short had for several months rented a room at a Hollywood home behind the Florentine Gardens nightclub, and worked as a waitress. Short had made contacts with a few people in the movie business, including Mark Hansen, her landlord, who, besides co-owning the nightclub, also part-owned movie theaters. Short's close friend, actress and model Ann Toth, told police that Short was promised a role in Florentine Gardens' burlesque revue. Short shared the

A collection of evidence in the Black Dahlia case, including Short's birth certificate and one of the threatening letters written by the person claiming to be "The Black Dahlia Avenger."

news with her mother in a letter dated January 2, 1947. It was the last correspondence Phoebe Short received from her daughter.

On Thursday, January 9, Short returned from a trip to San Diego with Robert "Red" Manley, a 25-year-old married salesman she had been dating. He dropped her off at the Biltmore Hotel, where she was to meet her visiting sister. Short, wearing a black tailored suit and matching suede high heels, was seen using a lobby telephone and then leaving the hotel on foot. She headed south on Olive Street and walked five minutes to the Crown Grill Cocktail Lounge where patrons recalled seeing her stop by, as if she were looking for someone.

Six days later, at dawn on Wednesday, January 15, a black luxury sedan driven by an unidentified driver briefly parked next to a vacant lot in Leimert Park. By late morning, Elizabeth Short's body had been discovered.

Mysterious letters
On January 21, the city editor of the *Los Angeles Herald-Examiner*, Jimmy Richardson, received a phone call from a man claiming to be Short's killer. The caller congratulated the paper for its work on the case, but suggested that it may have run out of material. The caller offered his assistance—he told the paper that he was going to turn himself in, but wanted the police to keep chasing him. He told Richardson to "expect some souvenirs of Beth Short in the mail."

On January 24, a US Postal Service worker came across a manila envelope featuring words and individual letters cut and pasted from the pages of a newspaper. On it was written "Los Angeles Examiner and other Los »

She'd come into our drug store frequently. She'd usually wear a two-piece beach costume, which left her midriff bare. Or she'd wear the black lacy things.
Arnold Landers Sr.

Elizabeth Short is **murdered** by a **heavy blow** to the head.

↓

Her face is **slashed** from ear to ear and her arms, thighs, and right breast are **lacerated**.

↓

Her body is **severed** at the waist, **drained of blood**, and carefully **washed**.

↓

Short's body is **transported** to a **vacant lot** between Coliseum Street and West 39th Street.

↓

The two halves of her body are placed a short distance apart with her intestines positioned under her buttocks.

↓

Her corpse is posed in a sexually degrading manner with her **arms raised** above her head and **legs spread**.

↓

Body found by Betty Bersinger.

Angeles Papers. Here is Dahlia's belongings. Letter to follow." Inside were Short's birth certificate, social security card, photographs, and an address book embossed with the name Mark Hansen.

Three more letters were received from a person identifying as the "Black Dahlia Avenger." The first was handwritten in ink on a postcard and declared "Here it is. Turning in Wed., Jan. 29, 10 a.m. Had my fun at police. Black Dahlia Avenger." The second letter, again in cutout letters, stated "Dahlia Killer cracking—wants terms." However, on January 29, a third letter indicated the killer's change of heart. Cut-and-pasted newspaper letters formed the message: "have changed my mind. You would not give me a square deal. Dahlia killing was justified."

Front page news

Early in the investigation, LAPD investigators interviewed more than 150 men as potential suspects. Ann Toth told detectives that Mark Hansen had tried to seduce Short, but had been rejected. With a plausible motive, Hansen became the number one suspect.

Next, police recovered Short's handbag and a shoe from the top of a trashcan 2 miles (3 km) from

Don't try to find the Short girl's murderer because you won't.
Unidentified caller

Chief suspect Robert "Red" Manley embraces his wife Harriet at the police station shortly after his release. He had an affair with Short soon after his wife gave birth to their first child.

where Short's body was found. The items had been wiped clean with gasoline, erasing any fingerprints. Mark Hansen identified the purse and shoe as belonging to Short but denied using the address book bearing his name. No charges were ever brought against him, though, and he was released. Attention turned to Robert Manley. He was officially named as a suspect, and, in interviews, initially denied knowing Short before changing his story. However, after twice passing polygraph tests, he was released.

For several months, the murder dominated the front pages of newspapers as the media sensationalized the life and death of Elizabeth Short. Following the established practice of assigning high-profile female murder victims a floral nickname, the papers called her case the "Black Dahlia murder" on account of Short's preference for black clothing and for the dahlia she wore in her dyed black hair.

Unsolved enigma

The murder investigation slowed until the summer of 1949, when 36-year-old Louise Springer, a beauty shop worker, was found garroted in the back seat of her husband's car on West 38th Street, one block from where Short's remains were discovered. Many

believed the Black Dahlia killer had struck again. The LAPD launched another manhunt, this time probing both murders, but concluded that the cases were not related.

Despite the long investigation, the Black Dahlia murder remains unsolved. Many attempts have since been made to profile the killer. Experts generally believe that the killer was medically trained, male, and craved the limelight.

One remarkable feature of the Black Dahlia case was the number of people—around 500—who voluntarily confessed to Short's murder. The vast majority of them were deemed to crave notoriety and all were discounted. Experts have also expressed doubts about the authenticity of the letters sent by the so-called "Avenger," suggesting that they were a ploy to sell more newspapers. Today, the Black Dahlia murder remains the most perplexing unsolved case in the history of the LAPD. ∎

Staged and posed murder scenes

Some criminals deliberately alter crime scenes to confuse forensic investigators. This practice is known as "staging." This differs from "posing," which is when a killer places the corpse in a specific position, marks something on a body, or takes a souvenir, such as a piece of jewelry or clothing. An offender might cover the face, wash the victim's hair or body, or tie ligatures using a unique knot. While posing can be a message to the police or to the public, it can also serve a killer's own fantasies. The Black Dahlia murderer placed Short's body in a sexually degrading pose, much like Jack the Ripper's signature posing, which represented complete control and humiliation even after death.

However, these practices assist criminal profilers, because they often provide insights into the characteristics, mindset, and behavioral patterns of the criminal that can help police to link a series of crimes together.

THE ARTIST WAS So WELL INFORMED ON CHEMICALS... IT WAS FRIGHTENING
SADAMICHI HIRASAWA, 1948

IN CONTEXT

LOCATION
Tokyo, Japan

THEME
Mass poisoning

BEFORE
1871 In Brighton, England, Christiana Edmunds buys chocolates from a confectioner, laces them with strychnine sourced from a local chemist, and returns them to the shop. Many people fall ill after eating the chocolates, including a four-year-old boy, who dies.

AFTER
1982 In Chicago, six adults and a 12-year-old girl die after taking Tylenol. Bottles of the painkiller had been removed from stores and pharmacies, laced with cyanide, and then returned to the shelves by an unknown hand.

On January 26, 1948, a man in his mid-40s wearing the armband of a municipal official entered a suburban branch of Teigin (Imperial) Bank in Tokyo. He told the staff that he was an epidemiologist from the Tokyo Metropolitan government who had been sent by the US occupation authorities to inoculate them against an outbreak of dysentery.

Each of the 16 bank employees and customers present took the pill and several drops of liquid the man offered. Soon, they were writhing on the floor in agony. Stepping around their dying bodies, the man plundered the bank, taking all the money he could find: a paltry ¥160,000 (about $6,600 today).

Manhunt for a poisoner

Had all of the victims poisoned with the cyanide compound died, this would have been the perfect crime, albeit not a very lucrative one. Miraculously, though, four escaped death and were able to provide a description of the perpetrator.

This was the third time in recent months that a lone man had used poison to rob a bank. In the first incident, he had offered staff a fake business card with the name

A man claiming to be a **health official** visits a bank in Tokyo

He offers **liquid cyanide** to 16 people, 12 die, and the poisoner escapes with cash and checks

Police track down Sadamichi Hirasawa through a **business card** and arrest him

Hirasawa pleads not guilty at the trial, but is convicted and receives the death penalty

See also: The Dreyfus Affair 310–11

After Hirasawa's death, his adopted son, Takehiko (right), fought to secure a posthumous retrial. Takehiko died in 2013, but his father's lawyers urged other relatives to continue the battle.

"Jiro Yamaguchi," while in the second he had produced a genuine card—that of Shigeru Matsui of the Ministry of Health and Welfare, Department of Disease Prevention. Cleared by alibi, Matsui told police that he had exchanged 92 of his cards. Fortunately, he made a note of the time and location of the exchange on the back of the cards he received. Using this data, police tracked down and cleared 62 of the card recipients. A further 22 were investigated and excluded from the investigation.

One recipient, an acclaimed artist named Sadamichi Hirasawa, stood out as suspicious. He was unable to provide the investigators with the card Matsui had given him as he said he had been pick-pocketed. Nor could his alibi be confirmed. Also, two surviving witnesses identified him as the poisoner, and more than ¥100,000 ($4,100)—the origins of which Hirasawa would not disclose— was discovered in his possession.

Arrested on August 21, 1948, Hirasawa protested his innocence. Soon after, however, he offered a confession in which he admitted to committing four prior bank frauds. He later retracted his statement.

By the time of his trial in 1950, Hirasawa had attributed his entire confession to coercion and mental illness. He was sentenced to die, but instead spent 32 years on death row until he died of pneumonia at age 95. It is thought that no Japanese politician would order his execution because there was widespread doubt about his guilt. ∎

Sadamichi Hirasawa

Sadamichi Hirasawa was a Japanese painter distinguished by his use of tempera—a fast-drying egg-based mixture that had been the most common form of paint until the advent of oils during the Renaissance. He was born in Tokyo in 1892, but when he was five, the family moved to Otaru on Hokkaido. Determined to become a painter, Hirasawa joined the art club at Otaru junior high school. Even at this young age, many claimed he was already better than his teacher. When he was 22, his painting *Ainyu Woman Drying Kelp* won a prize at a prestigious national exhibition, providing a solid start to his career as a professional artist. His works were selected to appear in the Imperial Art Exhibition on 16 consecutive occasions.

However, after World War II, his work became less popular. Following his murder conviction, his work was largely dismissed in Japan as being that of a degenerate criminal. During his decades in prison, Hirasawa passed the time working on a legal quest to exonerate himself, making hundreds of drawings and writing his autobiography.

I HAVE BEEN A VICTIM OF MANY UNUSUAL AND IRRATIONAL THOUGHTS

THE TEXAS TOWER MASSACRE, 1966

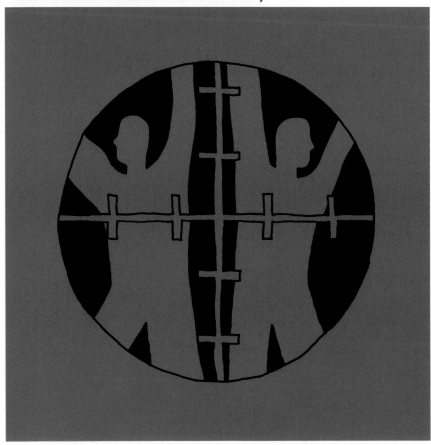

IN CONTEXT

LOCATION
Austin, Texas, US

THEME
Mass shooting

BEFORE
1897 In Borneo, Malaysia, a man called Antakin discovers his wife is having an affair and runs amok, stabbing people at random; 15 victims die.

AFTER
1999 Two male students go on a shooting spree at Columbine High School in Colorado. In less than 20 minutes they kill 13 people and maim 21 others.

2011 In Norway, Anders Breivik shoots 69 people at an island youth camp hosted by the country's Labor Party.

2012 Adam Lanza shoots 20 children and six staff at Sandy Hook elementary school in Newtown, Connecticut.

At around 11:30 a.m. on August 1, 1966, engineering student Charles Whitman entered the clock tower at the University of Texas at Austin dressed as a maintenance man. He hit the "27" button on the elevator and waited calmly as it rose to the highest floor. He exited, pulling a hand truck behind him. On it was a footlocker containing an arsenal of weapons and a cache of supplies.

He lugged the truck up four flights of stairs to the foyer of the observation deck, where he was greeted by receptionist Edna Townsley. Two strikes with a rifle butt knocked her unconscious. Whitman dragged her body behind

See also: The Murder of John Lennon 240 ▪ The Assassination of John F. Kennedy 316–21

An M-1 carbine, a sawn-off shotgun, knives, and a machete were among the stash of weapons Whitman took to the clock tower (right). His rampage was America's first mass college shooting.

a couch and left her for dead. Brandishing two rifles, he muttered a polite "hello" to Cheryl Botts and Don Walden as they came in from the observation deck; the couple thought he was there to shoot pigeons. After they left, Whitman built a makeshift barricade at the entrance to the reception area. As a family group climbing the stairs from the 27th floor approached it, he shot and killed two of them and wounded two others. Everything was now in place. Whitman walked out onto the observation deck and laid out his weapons.

Killer in the sky

At 11:48 a.m., shots started to ring out across an area that spanned the length of five city blocks, accompanied by clouds of gun smoke billowing from the clock tower. The first victim was a student who was eight months pregnant: she fell to the ground and when her boyfriend tried to help her, his body was pierced by a bullet.

Whitman then picked off other students and staff members who were walking around the campus. Several were killed outright, while the injured fell incapacitated or hurried for cover. He then trained his sights on a street that ran along the western edge of the campus, killing or wounding more people. Hundreds of tourists, pedestrians, and store clerks witnessed the carnage as they hid behind trees, cowered under office desks, or, if they had been hit, played dead.

The police were called just four minutes after Whitman began his killing spree, and were quickly at the scene. One officer took cover behind a columned stone wall, but Whitman sighted him in the space between the columns, and shot him with deadly accuracy. Active police officers in Austin were soon ordered to converge on the campus. They were joined by a number of off-duty officers, Texas Rangers, Travis County Sheriff's deputies, and citizens bearing hunting rifles. Twenty minutes after Whitman had killed his first victim, the people 231 feet (70 m) below him were beginning to return fire, and he was forced to seek refuge behind the thick walls of the observation deck. Whitman was able to continue shooting through the tower's waterspouts, but his range was drastically reduced. **»**

Charles Whitman

Charles Joseph Whitman was born in Florida in 1941. Although a good provider, his father was a disciplinarian who beat and berated his family. Charles was a polite and intelligent child who at the age of 12 became one of the youngest Eagle Scouts in Boy Scout history. In high school he was a popular student, but experienced medical problems.

After graduation, Whitman joined the Marines, where he earned several medals and a Sharpshooter's Badge. In 1961, he began to study mechanical engineering at the University of Texas at Austin, and married a year later. In 1963, he was recalled to Camp Lejeune to finish his five-year enlistment. There, he was court-martialed for keeping a personal firearm on base, and other infractions. Despite this, Whitman received an honorable discharge in 1964. Returning to the University of Texas, he started studying architectural engineering and did temporary jobs. By 1966, he was abusing amphetamines and suffering severe headaches.

As a police marksman struggled to target Whitman from a small airplane near the tower, the sniper turned around and fired at him, causing the plane to circle away.

Meanwhile, three policemen—Ramiro Martinez, Houston McCoy, and Jerry Day—decided to storm the clock tower. As they raced toward it they were joined by armed civilian Allen Crum, a bookstore manager and former serviceman whom they deputized immediately. The four men entered the building and took the elevator to the top floor. Working without a

From his shooting range atop the tower, Whitman had a bird's eye view of the campus and, given the lack of rapid-response law enforcement teams, plenty of time to kill and maim.

coordinated plan, the men decided to surround the sniper on the deck. When Crum's rifle discharged accidentally, drawing Whitman's attention to the northwest corner, Martinez began to unload his police revolver at him. McCoy raised his 12-gauge shotgun and fired twice at Whitman, blasting his head and neck full of buckshot. The officers checked the body for identification and learned the name of the man who had terrorized the town for more than 90 minutes.

In the immediate aftermath of the attack, investigators traced Whitman's movements that day. They found two more victims of his crazed behavior: his wife, who had been stabbed to death in the early hours of the morning as she slept in the couple's bed, and his mother,

Charlie could plug the eye out of a squirrel by the time he was sixteen.
Charles Whitman Sr.

killed in her apartment. Whitman had covered both bodies with sheets and left handwritten notes beside them. But it was Whitman's own suicide note, typed and handwritten at 6:45 p.m. on July 31, that would offer the most clues to

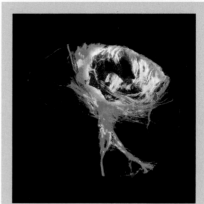

Brain damage and criminal violence

his state of mind. Among other things it said: "I don't really understand myself these days. I am supposed to be an average reasonable and intelligent young man. However, lately (I can't recall when it started) I have been a victim of many unusual and irrational thoughts. I talked to a Doctor once… and tried to convey to him my fears that I felt come (sic) overwhelming impulses. Since then I have been fighting my mental turmoil alone … to no avail."

After stating that he intended to kill his wife, Whitman continued: "I don't want her to have to face the embarrassment my actions would surely cause her… . I truly do not consider this world worth living in, and am prepared to die, and I do not want to leave her to suffer alone in it… .Similar reasons provoked me to take my mother's life… ."

In addition to his wife and mother, Whitman killed 14 people in cold blood and wounded 31 others that day; most of the casualties occurred in the first 20 minutes. Before the shooting, US police had no policies in place for responding to an attack by what

At a press conference after the shootings, Ramiro Martinez (left) and the other three police officers who had confronted Whitman showed a diagram of their haphazard strategy.

is known today as an "active shooter," and the event led to an overhaul of police procedures. Special Weapons and Tactics (SWAT) teams were formed nationwide, and these have swooped into action in the many similar atrocities that have taken place in the decades since 1966. ■

> **"**
> After my death I wish that an autopsy would be performed on me to see if there is any visible physical disorder.
> **Charles Whitman**
> **"**

The Whitman case is arguably most notable for being one of the first in which evidence of brain abnormalities could be definitively linked to violent behavior. After he was gunned down, Whitman's body was transported to the morgue, where the top of his skull was removed with a bone saw. When his brain was removed, the examiner noted a tumor, roughly the size of a nickel in diameter, sprouting under the thalamus, which is crucially involved in awareness and consciousness.

Most importantly, the tumor compressed the amygdala—a set of neurons located deep in the brain's medial temporal lobe that play a key role in the processing of emotions. Three decades prior to Whitman's rampage, US neuropathologist Paul Bucy and German psychologist Heinrich Klüver had discovered that fearlessness, dampened emotion, and a propensity to overreact were all associated with damaged amygdala in monkeys. Their findings provided a viable explanation for Whitman's seemingly senseless violence.

NOW IS THE TIME FOR HELTER SKELTER

THE MANSON FAMILY, 1969

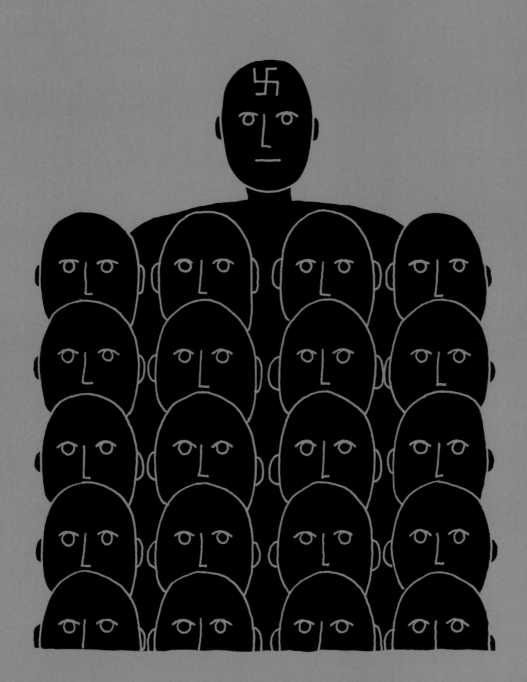

IN CONTEXT

LOCATION
California, US

THEME
Cult death plots

BEFORE
1955 Jim Jones founds the Peoples Temple cult, which ends with the mass murder-suicide of 918 people in Jonestown, Guyana, in 1978.

AFTER
1986–89 Believing that he has magical powers, drug dealer Adolfo Constanzo and his followers kill over 25 people in Mexico as human sacrifices.

1989 Leader Jeffrey Lundgren orders his followers to murder the Avery family for showing "disloyalty" to the cult in the barn of his Kirtland, Ohio, farm.

1997 The 39 members of the Heaven's Gate cult commit mass suicide in the belief that this will grant them entry to a passing UFO.

It was fun tearing up the Tate house… people were running around like chickens with their heads cut off.
Tex Watson

T he naked, bloody body of actress Sharon Tate was sprawled across her living room floor, a cross slashed into her eight-month-pregnant belly. The 26-year-old movie star had been stabbed 16 times. A rope around her neck connected her to the body of 35-year-old celebrity hairstylist Jay Sebring. On the front door of the house on Cielo Drive, just north of Beverly Hills, the word "PIG" was written in Tate's blood.

The bodies of Tate, Sebring, and four others were discovered by the housekeeper in the rented home of famed director Roman Polanski on August 9, 1969. On the house's front lawn lay the bodies of coffee fortune heiress Abigail Folger and Wojciech Frykowski, a financier and actor. In the driveway, Steven Parent, a teenager, was found shot to death in his car.

The crime appeared senseless, and police were baffled as to the motive, with some speculating the deaths were part of a satanic ritual. The next night, however, a wealthy couple, the LaBiancas, were butchered in similar fashion in the nearby Los Feliz neighborhood.

Initially, the second murders were believed to be the work of a copycat. By the end of the summer of 1969, however, the killers would be exposed as the followers of cult-leader Charles Manson.

Free love prophet

Two years before the murders, Manson was a 32-year-old aspiring musician who had spent half of his life in prison for theft and other crimes. Following his release on March 21, 1967, he moved to San Francisco where he established himself as a spiritual guru. Manson was charismatic, with an almost hypnotic ability to manipulate. Preaching a free-love philosophy that included some of the religious ideas he studied in prison, Manson soon established a group of mostly female followers.

Early followers

While living in Berkeley, California, Manson met a 23-year-old college graduate named Mary Brunner, who later gave birth to Manson's son, Valentine Michael. Manson moved into Brunner's home and soon 18 other women were sharing the property. Among them was 19-year-old hippie Leslie Van Houten, who later played a significant role in the "Family's" Los Angeles murder spree.

Toward the end of the summer of 1967, Manson and some of his followers piled into a converted school bus and traveled the country, partying and doing drugs. Among the women who joined Manson and his group was 19-year-old Susan Atkins, a California native.

Charles Manson wielded a spiritual and sexual influence over the Family, most of them young women. He would sleep with the women, then offer them to other men in exchange for favors.

See also: The Wild Bunch 150–51 ▪ Ted Bundy 276–83 ▪ The Assassination of Rasputin 312–15

In late spring 1968, Manson formed a brief friendship with Beach Boys' singer Dennis Wilson. While Wilson was driving around Southern California, he picked up two of Manson's followers, who were hitchhiking, and brought them to his house. One of the followers was 20-year-old Patricia Krenwinkel.

The next day, when Wilson returned to his home following a recording session, Manson met him in the driveway. Inside, a dozen of Manson's followers occupied the house. Wilson was fascinated by Manson and allowed the group to stay. He spent up to $100,000 in money, food, and clothing for them. Wilson was impressed with Manson's musical talent and the two wrote a few songs together. Wilson also introduced Manson to contacts in the entertainment business, including Doris Day's son, record producer Terry Melcher, who owned the home rented by Tate and Polanski. Melcher, however, did not advance Manson's career as much as Manson had hoped. Soon, Manson's violent tendencies and »

> I gave myself up to him and in return for that he gave me back to myself. He gave me… faith in myself.
> **Susan Atkins**

The Manson family was a group with no real organizational structure. Manson's magnetic personality was at the core of every relationship that drew people into the group.

Steve "Clem" Grogan was a ranchhand, drug user, and friend of the family, convicted in the LaBianca and Shea killings.

Mary Brunner was an accomplice in the Hinman killing. She was the first woman in the family to bear one of Manson's children.

Linda Kasabian was an accomplice in the Tate-LaBianca murders. Her remorse led her to testify against Manson. She described the murders in detail.

Lynette "Squeaky" Fromme kept a vigil outside the courthouse, although she was not involved in the murders.

Tex Watson was Manson's crazed right-hand man. A former honor student, he led the killings at Cielo and Waverly.

Leslie Van Houten at 19 was the youngest family member involved in the murders.

Charles Manson

Bobby Beausoleil murdered Gary Hinman during a drug deal. He was not a family member but regularly hung out with Manson.

Patricia Krenwinkel was devoted to Manson. She participated in the Tate-LaBianca killings. She stabbed Abigail Folger dozens of times.

Sandra "Blue" Good wanted to be at the Tate murders. She carved a cross into her forehead in support of Manson at his trial.

Susan "Sexy Sadie" Atkins first met Manson at a house party in 1967. She was involved in eight of the murders.

Ruth Ann Moorehouse was 16 when she ran away with Manson. She was charged with the attempted murder of Barbara Hoyt.

volatile nature began to make Wilson uneasy. Wilson abandoned both the group and the house, and, in August 1968, Manson and his followers were evicted by Wilson's manager.

The group moved to the deteriorating remnants of a Western movie set in the San Fernando Valley called Spahn Ranch. The owner allowed them to stay on the ranch in exchange for doing chores. While at the ranch the group became closer and started calling themselves the "Manson Family." They lived a communal life, regularly engaging in orgies and dropping LSD.

The Family was based at Spahn Ranch for much of 1968 and 1969, and their numbers continued to grow. Charles "Tex" Watson, a college dropout from Texas, joined the group, as did Linda Kasabian, a 20-year-old single mother with a 16-month-old daughter.

In December 1968, Manson visited a friend who played him the recently released Beatles' *White Album*. Manson became obsessed with the group. He believed that their songs contained hidden messages which warned the Family of an impending disaster. Manson believed he knew what this disaster would be.

Helter Skelter

On New Year's Eve 1968, as the Family gathered around a campfire at Spahn Ranch, Manson warned members of the Family that racial tensions between black and white Americans were growing, and that African Americans would soon rise up in rebellion across the country. He claimed that the whites were doomed due to a split between racist and nonracist whites.

Manson also told the group that the Beatles were sending messages about the race war to the Family,

Spahn Ranch was the perfect location for Western films—such as *Duel in the Sun* (1946)—with mountainous territory and plenty of open land. The Manson Family lived there until 1969.

who would be spared by hiding out in Death Valley. The Manson Family began preparing for the impending apocalypse, which the cult leader had termed "Helter Skelter," after the Beatles' song.

Initially, Manson's vision was to release an album like the Beatles had, with subtle lyrics that would trigger chaos. In early 1969, the Family left the desert and moved to a home in Canoga Park in order to monitor racial tensions in Los Angeles and write songs for their supposedly world-changing album.

By June, when the apocalypse failed to materialize, Manson started to tell the Family that he had to lead the way. He needed to show the nation how to start

"Helter Skelter" by murdering wealthy white people and framing African Americans for the crimes.

On July 25, Manson sent Family member Bobby Beausoleil, a young rock musician, along with Brunner and Atkins to the house of Manson's acquaintance, Gary Hinman. Manson believed Hinman had money that they could steal to fund an underground bunker.

After being held hostage for two days, however, Hinman still refused to give up the money. Angered, Manson slashed Hinman's ear off with a sword. On Manson's orders, Beausoleil stabbed Hinman to death. One member of the group wrote "political piggy" in Hinman's blood on the wall of his home. They also drew a Black Panther symbol on the wall, hoping the police would believe that the murder was committed by a member of the black nationalist organization.

The ruse was unsuccessful. On August 6, Beausoleil was arrested for the murder while out driving Hinman's car. Two days later, Manson declared that it was time to begin "Helter Skelter," and told them to start at the house currently occupied by Roman Polanski.

On the evening of August 8, 1969, Polanski's wife dined at her favorite restaurant, El Coyote, with Folger, Frykowski, and Sebring. Tate was just two weeks away from giving birth and had complained that day about Polanski delaying his return from London. At around 10:30 p.m., the four friends returned to Tate's property: a rambling house overlooking Benedict Canyon.

Deadly night

Just before midnight, Watson, Atkins, Krenwinkel, and Kasabian drove to the house. In the driveway, Watson shot and killed 18-year-old student Steven Parent who had been visiting the caretaker in the guesthouse. While Kasabian waited in the car, the others broke into the house and slaughtered all four occupants.

The bodies were discovered at 9:15 a.m. the next morning by Tate's maid, Winifred Chapman. The carnage sent her screaming into the street for help. A neighbor called the police. When the police arrived at the scene, they reported seeing looks of terror on the victims' faces. They were unable to save Tate's unborn child.

> I've done nothing I'm ashamed of. Nothing I couldn't face God with. I wouldn't kill a bug.
> **Charles Manson**

The murder sent shockwaves throughout the community, but Manson was displeased. The panic failed to ignite the race war that he had predicted.

The next evening, the four killers, Leslie Van Houten, and 18-year-old Steve "Clem" Grogan went with Manson to the home of Leno LaBianca, a wealthy 44-year-old supermarket executive. The Family entered the property on Waverly Drive in Los Feliz, Los Angeles. Manson roused the sleeping LaBianca from the living room couch at gunpoint. LaBianca's wife, Rosemary, was forced into the living room, and pillowcases were put over the couple's heads. They were told that they were being robbed, but would not be harmed if they cooperated.

Manson then left, instructing Van Houten and Krenwinkel to follow Watson's orders. Watson had been told to kill the LaBiancas. He stabbed Leno more than a dozen times with a chrome-plated bayonet and carved the word "War" onto his bare abdomen. Van Houten and Krenwinkel were told to kill Rosemary LaBianca, who was stabbed 41 times in the back and buttocks. Krenwinkel also wrote "Rise" and "Death to pigs" on the walls in the LaBiancas' blood. »

Charles Manson

Born to 16-year-old Kathleen Maddox in Cincinnati, Ohio, Charles Manson had a grim upbringing. Shortly after Manson's birth, Kathleen went to jail for robbery and he was sent to live with relatives in West Virginia. As a teen, Manson committed a string of petty crimes, robbing liquor stores and stealing bikes. After he robbed two grocery stores, aged 13, he was sent to a boy's school. Despite having a high IQ, Manson was illiterate and a caseworker deemed him aggressively antisocial. He was sent to a minimum-security institution in October 1951 and paroled in May 1954.

In 1955, Manson married hospital waitress Rosalie Jean Willis and the couple had a son, Charles Jr. After Manson was sent back to prison, the couple divorced. He was paroled in 1958, but soon returned to prison after attempting to cash a forged check. Manson was released in March 1967, and moved to San Francisco, where he established his cult.

Sharon Tate starred in Roman Polanski's 1967 movie *The Fearless Vampire Killers*, and married him in January 1968. Exactly 17 months later, the actress and model was murdered.

On the refrigerator door, she incorrectly spelled out "Healter Skelter." The killers then left the blood-soaked scene.

Around 10:30 p.m. on August 10, Rosemary LaBianca's son Frank Struthers returned from a camping trip and found Leno LaBianca's boat on the drive. Suspicious, he called his sister and her boyfriend. The men entered the house to find the LaBiancas' bodies.

Despite the similarity of the crimes, the Los Angeles Police Department (LAPD) did not initially connect the Hinman, Tate, and LaBianca cases.

The sheriff's department was handling the Hinman case, and the LAPD believed the Tate murder to be related to drugs. Investigators in each of the three cases found themselves at dead ends, partly due to the lack of communication between the authorities involved. However, the Manson Family's crime spree continued, and would provide the police with major leads.

Kitty Lutesinger, girlfriend of Bobby Beausoleil, was arrested for burning machinery in Death Valley,

California, near the Family's new hideout at Barker Ranch. Lutesinger snitched, and informed detectives that Susan Atkins had also been involved in the murder of Hinman, for which her boyfriend was already doing time.

Meanwhile, on August 16, in an unrelated case, the sheriff's office raided Spahn Ranch, which they suspected was the main base of an auto theft ring. Susan Atkins was arrested, and Manson, Watson, and a follower named Bruce Davis killed Spahn Ranch-hand Donald Shea, because they believed he had reported them to the police.

In jail on car theft charges, Susan Atkins told another inmate about her participation in the Tate and LaBianca murders. The inmate reported the claims and Atkins not only confessed to the crime, but agreed to testify against the others if the death penalty was dropped.

Family trials

Manson, Krenwinkel, and Atkins were each charged with seven counts of murder and one count of conspiracy. Because Van Houten had only participated in the LaBianca killings, she was charged with two counts of murder and one of conspiracy. Kasabian, who waited outside during the killings

They haven't made atonement to any one of my family members.
Debra Tate

Entering the courtroom in August 1970, Susan Atkins, Patricia Krenwinkel, and Leslie Van Houten all sport crosses they have carved into their foreheads.

and fled the Ranch after the murders, was granted immunity in exchange for her testimony.

The trial began on June 15, 1970. On the first day of testimony, Manson appeared in court with a cross carved into his forehead. In the days that followed, the other Family members at the trial—including the female defendants—followed suit, wearing the mark.

Throughout the trial, Atkins and her codefendants attempted to disrupt proceedings. They sang songs Manson had written as they were led in and out of the courtroom. Atkins giggled, snickered, and shouted insults. Family members loitered around the courthouse and held vigils on the sidewalk. Later, Manson and his codefendants all shaved their heads.

Their tactics did little to affect the trial's outcome. The prosecution argued the motive of the killings was to trigger Manson's race war, with the case hinging largely on the testimony of Kasabian. The defense, meanwhile, rested after three days without calling a single witness, which angered

Manson and his followers. As the trial concluded, with closing arguments pending, Van Houten's defense attorney, Ronald Hughes, disappeared during a weekend trip. His body was found months later.

The trial concluded in January 1971. Manson, Atkins, Van Houten, and Krenwinkel were found guilty of all 27 counts, and sentenced to death. In a separate trial in 1971, Watson was also found guilty and sentenced to death. The sentences were commuted to life in prison in

1972 when the death penalty was abolished in California. Manson followers Bruce Davis and Steve Grogan were convicted in 1972 for the murders of Hinman and Shea.

In 1971, Manson followers Catherine Share, Lynette Fromme, Dennis Rice, Steve Grogan, and Ruth Ann Moorehouse were convicted for plotting to kill Barbara Hoyt—a former Family member—to prevent her from testifying at the trial. Hoyt, Kasabian, and another former Family member Paul Walker all testified against Manson. Share later claimed that Manson had threatened to harm her if she did not testify on his behalf.

For decades after the killings, Manson remained in the news, giving interviews from prison. His case remains unique because he never actually killed anyone himself; instead, he used his powers of persuasion to convince his followers to do so. ∎

The psychology of cults

Contrary to stereotypes, 95 percent of the people who join cults are psychologically sound. Personality is also not a major factor in cult membership. Those who join cults do so in response to individual and circumstantial needs: a desire to belong, a search for answers to life's big questions, or an attraction to the insular, structured aspect of cult life.

Cult leaders play the most important role in recruiting and retaining members. These figures are usually incredibly charismatic and manipulative, and therefore exert significant influence over cult members.

Leaders encourage the group to embrace a collective identity, often ordering group activities such as prayer, manual labor, and orgies. Members follow rules set by the leader, who often forbids them from outside interaction. This makes it hard for them to leave, as they become isolated from support systems outside of the cult.

A DINGO'S GOT MY BABY!
THE DEATH OF AZARIA CHAMBERLAIN, AUGUST 17, 1980

IN CONTEXT

LOCATION
Uluru campsite, Northern Territory, Australia

THEME
Accused parents

BEFORE
1665 Anne Greene, an English servant girl, is hanged for the murder of her baby, conceived during rape. She insisted that the child was stillborn.

AFTER
1999 Sally Clark is falsely convicted of murdering her two infants after "expert" testimony on the improbability of two successive "cot deaths."

2015 Purvi Patel is sentenced to 20 years by an Indiana court after her "miscarried" 24-week fetus is found in a dumpster.

Michael Chamberlain's account of his wife's distress on realizing that their baby daughter Azaria had been taken by a dingo did not match her calm demeanor when she was interviewed by police. As they surveyed the couple's campsite in the shadow of Uluru (Ayers Rock), they felt that something did not add up.

Shreds of evidence
The police developed their own theory. They posited that Lindy, sitting in the front seat of the family car, had held her daughter Azaria in her lap and stabbed her with a pair of scissors until she died. This explained blood found on the car's dashboard, and the shredded bits

> I am here to tell you that you can get justice even when you think that all is lost.
> **Michael Chamberlain**

of clothing on the ground nearby. The absence of a body did nothing to make them doubt this version of events. The empty outback was the perfect place to hide a small body.

The police ignored evidence that did not support their theory. Other campers had heard a dog growl, and there were paw prints, dog hairs, and drag marks in and around the tent. Furthermore, Michael was a pastor and they had no motive for killing the baby.

A dingo in Australia. While attacks on humans and livestock have led to culls, their "vulnerable" status and ability to deter predatory foxes have led to calls for dingoes to be reintroduced.

See also: The Lindbergh Baby Kidnapping 178–85

The Chamberlains hold a picture of Azaria after the first coroner's inquest declares their innocence in 1981. State police rejected the verdict, and pushed for Lindy's conviction.

In the years following Azaria's disappearance, several serious dingo attacks were reported, some of which were fatal. In 1998, on Fraser Island, off the coast of Queensland, a father snatched his infant daughter back as she was being dragged away by dingoes; three years later, nine-year-old Clinton Gage did not survive his mauling on Fraser Island.

Once the idea that Lindy had killed her daughter had been established, all facts related to the case appeared to support a guilty verdict. The seeming impartiality of forensic analysis was in fact skewed to suit the preconceptions of the investigators. Both police and the public judged Lindy for the "unnatural" way she reacted. These views were unjust but deeply entrenched. It took other dingo attacks and new forensic evidence for the courts to completely exonerate the couple. ∎

Tests run by the court's forensic scientist Joy Kuhl endorsed the police view and, on October 29, 1982, Lindy was convicted of her daughter's murder and imprisoned. Michael, the court found, had been an accessory after the fact, helping his wife to conceal her crime. He was freed on bail.

Doubts were later cast on the conviction by the chance discovery of a baby's jacket outside a nearby dingo den in 1986. Consequently, Lindy Chamberlain was released on "compassionate" grounds. In 1988, the convictions against her and her husband were overturned, but even then an ugly question mark remained. It was not lifted by a fresh inquest in 1995, which returned an inconclusive "open" verdict on Azaria's death.

Not until 2012 was a coroner satisfied that the child had been killed by a dingo—the crucial evidence that Kuhl had identified as "fetal haemoglobin," a young baby's blood, in the family car was revealed through improved scientific testing to actually be a mixture of milk, copper oxide, and other chemicals spilled in the vehicle during manufacture. Furthermore, a "bloody" handprint on a scrap of baby clothing, which had damned Lindy in 1982, turned out not to be blood at all.

Dingo in the dock

Australia's native wild dog, the dingo, has never been considered harmless—dingo attacks on livestock mean farmers label them a pest. At the time of Azaria's disappearance, however, there were no recorded cases of dingoes hurting children. Perhaps the Australian public preferred to believe that a mother had killed her baby rather than that a part of Australia's national identity—the dingo—was something to fear.

No longer will Australia be able to say that dingoes are not dangerous.
Lindy Chamberlain-Creighton

I WAS MR. NOBODY UNTIL I KILLED THE BIGGEST SOMEBODY ON EARTH

MURDER OF JOHN LENNON, DECEMBER 8, 1980

IN CONTEXT

LOCATION
New York City, US

THEME
Celebrity stalker

AFTER
1981 John Hinckley Jr. enrolls at Yale in order to stalk actress Jodie Foster on campus. On March 30, he attempts to assassinate US President Ronald Reagan as a "love offering" to Foster.

1989 Robert John Bardo shoots actress Rebecca Schaeffer after stalking her for three years.

1995 Yolanda Saldívar stalks Tejano singer Selena in a bid to take over the running of her fan club. Selena fires her, and Saldívar kills the singer on March 31.

2004 Nathan Gale, a fan of the band Pantera, murders several people at a heavy metal concert. He is upset at the news that the band is splitting.

When Mark David Chapman fired bullets into John Lennon's back on December 8, 1980, he not only destroyed an icon of his generation, but also announced the arrival of a new kind of murderer: the celebrity killer. As a child in the Deep South, he was mesmerized by the Beatles, but would later turn against them.

Fixated on fame

Chapman had an unstable identity and was plagued by chronic feelings of worthlessness. At a low point, in 1977, he attempted suicide in Hawaii, but failed to end his life.

Chapman became obsessed with Beatles frontman John Lennon after reading his biography. At the time, he was also heavily influenced by J.D. Salinger's *The Catcher in the Rye*, and came to see Lennon as a "phony." For months, he stalked the star in New York City.

In December 1980, he finally made a move, ambushing Lennon as he returned to the Dakota Building from a recording session. Chapman shot Lennon five times

Fans pay homage to Lennon at the Dakota Building. News of the murder led to an international display of grief; at least three fans committed suicide in response to his death.

with a .38-caliber pistol. As the doorman took Chapman's gun, the killer did not try to escape. Instead, he sat and waited for police to arrive at the scene. Lennon was rushed to hospital, but was declared dead within 15 minutes of his arrival.

Chapman claimed that he shot Lennon to achieve notoriety. He was diagnosed as psychotic. In June 1981, he pled guilty to murder, and was sentenced to 20 years to life. He remains behind bars. ∎

See also: Madame Caillaux 217 ▪ The Murders of Tupac Shakur and Biggie Smalls 254–57 ▪ The Assassination of John F. Kennedy 316–21

WHO HAS SENT YoU AGAINST ME? WHO HAS TOLD YOU TO DO THIS THING?

MURDER OF ROBERTO CALVI, JUNE 17, 1982

IN CONTEXT

LOCATION
London, England

THEME
Mafia hit

BEFORE
1957 In New York, Albert "The Mad Hatter" Anastasia is murdered in his barber's chair on the orders of mobster "Don Vito" Genovese.

1980 Philadelphia crime boss Angelo Bruno is murdered and stuffed with dollar bills on the orders of his own *consigliere*, Antonio Caponigro, following a dispute about the meth trade.

AFTER
1986 Chicago Outfit boss Rocco Infelice orders the murder of Anthony Spilotro, who runs the Outfit's business in Las Vegas, and his brother.

1990 Lucchese family member Anthony DiLapi moves to California to escape the mob, but is found and gunned down on Anthony Casso's orders.

In 1975, Roberto Calvi became the chairman of the Banco Ambrosiano, a Catholic bank founded 75 years earlier to serve moral and religious organizations. Its main shareholder was the Vatican Bank—this connection led Calvi to be called "God's Banker." However, his actions as the bank's chairman were decidedly not holy.

Calvi made a number of shady moves: siphoning money to fund political parties; securing a controlling interest in the Banco Cattolica del Veneto; and creating

> There was the Vatican, the Mafia, Freemasons, and politicians. This trial is... just a part of all of these stories.
> **Luca Tescaroli**

offshore enterprises. He transferred billions of lire out of Italy, inflated the prices of shares, and took out a fortune in unsecured loans. In 1978, his activities came to the attention of the Bank of Italy, who began to investigate him.

Calvi was convicted, given a four-year suspended sentence, and released on bail. Heavily in debt, the bank owed huge sums to the Sicilian Mafia. The Banco Ambrosiano collapsed in June 1982, and that month, Calvi disappeared from his Rome apartment.

His body was found eight days later, hanging from scaffolding under London's Blackfriars Bridge. The banker had belonged to the P2 Freemasons, *frati neri* (black friars), and the name of the bridge did not escape notice. Initially ruled a suicide, prosecutors came to believe that the Mafia had killed Calvi to stop him revealing details of their dealings—or those of freemasons, politicians, and other powerful groups. Five suspects were charged in 2005, but were acquitted due to lack of evidence. ∎

See also: Bernie Madoff 116–21 ▪ The Sicilian Mafia 138–45 ▪ The Beer Wars 152–53 ▪ The Assassination of Rasputin 312–15

I WAS ON DEATH ROW, AND I WAS INNOCENT

KIRK BLOODSWORTH, 1984

IN CONTEXT

LOCATION
Rosedale, Maryland, US

THEME
Wrongful conviction

BEFORE
1950 Briton Timothy John Evans is convicted of the murders of his wife and daughter and is hanged. An inquiry held 15 years later determines that the killer was, in fact, Evans's co-tenant, John Reginald Halliday.

AFTER
1987 High school sophomore Tim Masters is convicted of killing Peggy Hettrick from Fort Collins, Colorado. A judge orders that Masters be released immediately when DNA evidence implicates the victim's boyfriend.

In 1984, 23-year-old former US Marine Kirk Bloodsworth was arrested and charged with the sexual assault, rape, and murder of nine-year-old Dawn Hamilton. The girl's body was found in a wooded area of a park in Rosedale, Maryland, near her home.

Bloodsworth was arrested based on the testimony of an anonymous caller, who told police that she saw him with the victim. Two other witnesses made positive identifications during a lineup. However, they had been instructed not to watch television—news

Kirk Bloodsworth holds a photograph of Dawn Hamilton, the young girl he was wrongly convicted of sexually assaulting, raping, and murdering in August 1984.

The Innocence Project

Founded in New York in 1992 by two prominent civil rights lawyers, the Innocence Project is a nonprofit legal organization that works to exonerate wrongly convicted prisoners through the application of DNA testing. The Innocence Project also works to advocate for major reform of the criminal justice system.

Despite the name of the group, self-confessed innocence is not in itself a legal basis upon which to overturn a conviction. Instead, it is normally necessary

for new evidence—such as a successful DNA test—to back up the victim's claim that there was a miscarriage of justice.

DNA testing was first introduced as a crime-fighting technique in 1989. As of early 2016, 340 people convicted of serious crimes in the US have been exonerated through DNA testing and about half of them have received some financial compensation for the time they spent in prison. Twenty of the inmates whose convictions were ultimately overturned had been sentenced to death.

See also: Colin Pitchfork 294–97

> If it could happen to me, it could happen to anybody.
> **Kirk Bloodsworth**

reports about Bloodsworth featured widely at that time—because it could affect their ability to recall exactly who they had seen. They did not listen, and both witnesses saw Bloodsworth on television before the lineup. Although no direct evidence connected him to the crime, Bloodsworth was convicted of rape and first-degree murder and sentenced to death.

In 1986, the Maryland Court of Appeals overturned Bloodsworth's conviction, finding that the prosecution had illegally withheld evidence that might have cleared him from the defense. They ordered a retrial, but Bloodsworth was convicted again and sentenced to two life terms.

Working in the prison library, Bloodsworth spent the next seven years trying to prove his innocence. In 1992, he read about a new technique—DNA fingerprinting. Hoping that DNA found at the crime scene might rule him out as the killer, Bloodsworth motioned the court. His tactic worked. In 1993, test results proved that the DNA evidence did not match Bloodsworth's genetic profile and he was set free. ∎

July 1984—The body of 9-year-old Dawn Hamilton is found in a park in Rosedale, Maryland.

August 1984—Police arrest and charge Kirk Bloodsworth, a former US marine.

March 1985—A jury convicts Kirk Bloodsworth of Dawn Hamilton's murder. He is sentenced to death.

July 1986—Maryland Court of Appeals overturns the conviction, stating that prosecutors withheld evidence. They order a retrial.

April 1987—A second jury convicts Bloodsworth of murder. He is sentenced to two life terms in prison.

April 1992—Baltimore County prosecutors release evidence from Bloodsworth's trial for sophisticated new DNA testing.

May 1993—A California lab reports that a semen stain on the victim's underwear could not have come from Bloodsworth.

June 25, 1993—The FBI accepts that the semen found on the underpants could not have been produced by Bloodsworth.

June 28, 1993—Kirk Bloodsworth walks out of the House of Correction in Jessup, a free man.

AN ACT OF UNPARALLELED EVIL
THE MURDER OF JAMES BULGER, FEBRUARY 12, 1993

IN CONTEXT

LOCATION
Merseyside, England

THEME
Child killers

BEFORE
1954 In Christchurch, New Zealand, Pauline Parker, 16, and Juliet Hulme, 15, murder Pauline's mother Honorah.

1968 In two separate incidents, 11-year-old Mary Bell strangles to death two little boys, ages three and four.

AFTER
1999 Lionel Tate, age 12, beats six-year-old Tiffany Eunick to death in Florida.

2001 Brothers Derek and Alex King, ages 12 and 13, beat their father to death with a baseball bat and then set their house on fire, in Florida.

On Friday February 12, 1993, two-year-old James Bulger was with his mother Denise at Bootle Strand shopping mall in Merseyside, England. At 3:42 p.m., she was buying food in a butcher's shop, while James waited by the door. The toddler was led away to a gruesome death by two 10-year-old schoolboys, who tortured and killed him on the local railroad tracks.

After paying for her goods, Bulger turned around to find her son gone. Panicking, she enlisted the help of security staff at the mall,

CCTV footage stamped 3:42 p.m. shows James Bulger trustingly holding the hand of one of his killers. Thompson and Venables took the two-year-old on a 2-mile (3-km) walk to his death.

who called for the boy over the PA system. Although they issued a description of James and the outfit he was wearing, the boy was nowhere to be found. At 4:15 p.m., Bulger called in the local police. At 5:30 p.m. when the shopping center closed for the day, James was still missing, and Merseyside police launched a major search operation.

See also: The Lindbergh Baby Kidnapping 178–85 ■ Lizzie Borden 208–11 ■ The Stratton Brothers 212–15 ■ The Death of Azaria Chamberlain 238–39

The biggest clue to James's disappearance came from the mall's CCTV cameras, which showed the two-year-old leaving the butcher's shop. Tracking his movements on video, the police also spotted him on the top floor, apparently following two boys. In the final sighting on the footage— the last image of James alive—it was apparent that one of the boys was holding James's hand, as the trio headed toward the Leeds and Liverpool Canal. Even with this information, however, the police still could not find James.

Kidnap becomes murder
Two days later, a young boy rushed into Walton Lane police station in a panic. He had found a body, severely mutilated, on the railroad tracks only a few minutes from the police station. James Bulger, it seemed, was no longer a missing child: he was now a murder victim. After identifying the body as James, the police turned their attention to finding their two prime suspects— the young boys from the video. They had a lucky break when a local woman was able to identify them as troublemakers who often visited her shop, and named them as Jon Venables and Robert Thompson.

Thompson and Venables were taken into custody, but the police found it hard to believe that they were capable of killing. The two boys were only ten years old, and James's injuries were many and terrible. Nonetheless, the police questioned the two suspects. In the course of these interviews, the boys' crime was slowly revealed.

Thompson remained eerily calm during questioning, but slipped up with a too-detailed description of what James had been wearing. Venables, on the other hand, became hysterical in the face of police interrogation. On February 19, he confessed to the murder of James Bulger, and on February 20, both suspects were arrested for the abduction and murder. Neither boy could explain their motive.

Children on the stand
The trial of the two young killers rocked the nation. A small platform was brought into the courtroom so that the boys could see out of the dock. As the country followed the proceedings with bated breath, a damning case against Thompson and Venables emerged.

Bulger's blood was found on one of the boy's shoes, while the bootprints of the other matched bruising on Bulger's face. A witness came forward to claim that the boys had tried to abduct her son that same day, and the court heard how, in his police interview, Venables had admitted to thinking about pushing a child into traffic, so that the murder seemed accidental.

> These are the ugly manifestations of a society that is becoming unworthy of that name.
> **Tony Blair**

The evidence mounted against them. While their attorney argued the boys were too young to be held legally responsible for their actions, a child psychiatrist testified that they knew the difference between right and wrong. Now age 11, Thompson and Venables were old enough to be charged, and on November 24 the two were found guilty and jailed for eight years.

The sentence was increased twice, but Thompson and Venables were released on parole in 2001. ■

The age of responsibility

In the mid-20th century, the courts ruled that the age of responsibility should be based on a child's emotional, mental, and intellectual maturity. Different countries set their own ages of responsibility. In the UK, that age is ten, while in other European countries it is 15. In the US, the age of responsibility varies between states and ranges from age six to 11.

Lawbreakers under the age of responsibility are treated differently. They cannot be charged with committing a criminal offense, but in some countries their parents can be held responsible for their crimes and the children may then be taken into care.

The UK considered raising the age of responsibility in 2014—a move opposed by James Bulger's mother. Had he been murdered a few months earlier, when Thompson and Venables were under the age of ten, they would not have been tried or punished by the courts.

I'M AFRAID THIS MAN WILL KILL ME SOME DAY

O.J. SIMPSON, JUNE 12, 1994

IN CONTEXT

LOCATION
Brentwood, Los Angeles, California, US

THEME
Celebrity defendants

BEFORE
December 2, 1954 Boxing promoter Don King guns down an alleged robber at his illegal gambling house in Cleveland.

October 12, 1978 Punk rocker Sid Vicious stabs and kills his girlfriend, Nancy Spungen. He is charged with murder, but dies of a heroin overdose before trial.

AFTER
January 22, 2001 Former NFL player Rae Carruth is convicted of conspiracy to murder his pregnant girlfriend, Cherica Adams.

February 14, 2013 Oscar Pistorius, a paralympic runner, fatally shoots his girlfriend, Reeva Steenkamp.

Nicole Brown Simpson at the premiere of her husband's movie *Naked Gun 33⅓: The Final Insult* on March 16, 1994. She and O.J. had reconciled following their divorce in 1992.

O n the front doorstep of a condo in Brentwood, Los Angeles, a barefoot woman in a black dress lay face down in a pool of blood. Beside her the remains of a 25-year-old man were tangled in the bushes. At about 12:10 a.m. on June 13, 1994, a neighbor stumbled onto the ghastly tableau. He had found the bodies of Nicole Brown Simpson and Ron Goldman. Both victims had been dead for some time.

The deep slash wound on Nicole's neck left her nearly decapitated. Goldman's shirt was pulled over his head, exposing a torso riddled with stab wounds. The neighbor flagged down a passing patrol car and soon the condo on South Bundy Drive was swarming with detectives.

The gruesome crime was not typical for the affluent Brentwood neighborhood. But the murder investigation took on a frenzied pace when police learned the dead woman was Nicole Brown Simpson, the ex-wife of famed football star turned actor O.J. Simpson.

Background to tragedy

On the night of her murder, Nicole had dined at the restaurant Mezzaluna with her mother and children. Nicole's mother phoned the restaurant at 9:35 p.m. to report that she had left her eyeglasses behind. Nicole followed up with a call of her own, asking her waiter friend, Ron Goldman, to bring the glasses to her home that evening. Goldman finished his shift around 9:50 p.m, and headed to Nicole's. Just over two hours later, both were found dead. Nicole's children, fast asleep upstairs during the murder, awoke to a tragedy.

Once both of the victims were identified, detectives went to Simpson's Rockingham estate, where they discovered a white Ford Bronco marred with bloodstains. Without a warrant, but claiming that he feared for Simpson's safety, Detective Mark Fuhrman scaled the estate's walls and let his team in. Outside the house, Fuhrman discovered a bloody glove, which was later determined to be a match to one found at the murder scene. DNA testing revealed that the blood on the glove came from both Nicole and Goldman.

Later, three drops of Simpson's blood were found near the gate of his home, from an open wound on Simpson's hand. The discovery of the glove, plus the blood evidence at both scenes, was enough for an arrest warrant to be issued against Simpson for double murder.

Dramatic surrender

While his lawyers negotiated a planned surrender on June 17, 1994, Simpson fled. His friend Al Cowlings picked him up in his Ford Bronco and drove Simpson up and down the freeway. Intermittently, O.J. put the gun against his head and threatened suicide.

I'm absolutely, 100 percent, not guilty.
O.J. Simpson

See also: Dr. Crippen 216 ▪ The Manson Family 230–37 ▪ The Murders of Tupac Shakur and Biggie Smalls 254–57

The white Ford Bronco is chased at a slow speed along an LA freeway in the gathering dusk. The televised chase was a cultural phenomenon, and raised interest in the Simpson case.

By 2 p.m., the Los Angeles Police Department had issued an all-points bulletin for Simpson's arrest. Early that evening, the Bronco was spotted. One officer approached the car but, because Simpson had a gun to his head, decided to back off. This ignited a low-speed chase, with up to 20 police cars and nine helicopters following the car. Thousands of spectators packed the overpasses to cheer on the white Bronco, some holding homemade signs urging Simpson to keep running. Television stations interrupted regularly scheduled programming, and the chase was seen by some 95 million viewers.

After 50 miles (80 km) on the freeway, the chase ended at 8 p.m. at Simpson's Brentwood estate. In exchange for a peaceful surrender, Simpson was allowed an hour in the house to speak to his mother.

Meanwhile, officers searched the Bronco and found $8,000 in cash, clothes, and a disguise—a fake goatee, mustache, and makeup kit—as well as family photos and a loaded handgun.

Courtroom personnel

Simpson was arraigned on June 20, and pleaded not guilty to both murders. He was ordered to be held without bail. In a controversial decision, the prosecutors chose to file charges in downtown LA, which would result in a jury pool with a majority of people of color.

Veteran LAPD detective Tom Lange led the murder investigation. Prosecutor Marcia Clark, a Deputy District Attorney, was designated lead prosecutor; acting as cocounsel was Deputy District »

O.J. Simpson

Born Orenthal James Simpson, O.J. Simpson grew up poor in the housing projects outside San Francisco, California. Simpson discovered a passion for football and won a football scholarship to the University of Southern California. In 1968, he won the prestigious Heisman Trophy.

After college, Simpson was drafted to the NFL and played 11 seasons with the Buffalo Bills and San Francisco 49ers. In 1973, he became the first player to rush more than 2,000 yards (1,800m) in a season, and was later inducted into the Football Hall of Fame.

After he retired from the NFL, Simpson began a career as a football broadcaster and actor, and appeared in several movies including *The Towering Inferno*, *Capricorn One*, and *The Naked Gun* trilogy.

Simpson met 18-year-old waitress Nicole Brown in 1977, and the two were married in 1985. They had two children: Sydney and Justin. After a tumultuous marriage rife with claims of spousal abuse, Nicole filed for divorce on February 25, 1992. Two years later, Simpson was accused of her murder.

O.J. Simpson in court beside one of his attorneys, Johnnie Cochran Jr. Cochran was criticized by Deputy DA Christopher Darden for emphasizing possible racial discrimination at play.

Attorney Christopher Darden. Simpson, meanwhile, hired a team of high-profile lawyers including F. Lee Bailey, Robert Kardashian, Robert Shapiro, Alan Dershowitz, Johnnie Cochran Jr., and Barry Scheck. The defense, dubbed the "Dream Team," cost Simpson between $3 and $6 million.

Controversial trial

The trial began on January 24, 1995, and lasted 134 days; viewers watched live via a closed-circuit camera in the courtroom. The case turned the detectives, attorneys, and even Judge Lance Ito into celebrities; the proceedings were dubbed the "Trial of the Century."

Part of the fascination stemmed from a deep societal divide over whether or not Simpson was guilty. While 77 percent of white people polled believed that he had done it, the African American community thought otherwise: 72 percent believed he should be acquitted. The defense argued that Simpson had been set up by racially biased cops, then took another shot at the

LAPD, claiming that the DNA evidence had been contaminated due to sloppy police work.

One officer admitted that he had taken home Simpson's shoes and left them unattended in his trunk for at least six hours, breaking the chain of custody. Furthermore, the forensics team were found to have mishandled the blood samples— one vial was carried around in a jacket for hours before it was taken

to the lab, and some of Simpson's blood was purportedly spilled by technicians in the very lab where they tested the evidence samples.

Detective Fuhrman also came under scrutiny. During cross-examination, F. Lee Bailey pressed Fuhrman, who had found the second glove, about his history of racist rhetoric. Fuhrman denied it, but audiotapes were discovered of him repeatedly using racial slurs. The tapes became a cornerstone of the defense team's argument that the detective's testimony lacked credibility. Charged with perjury, Fuhrman invoked his right to remain silent when asked if he had planted evidence.

On June 15, 1995, defense attorney Cochran goaded Darden into asking Simpson to put on the leather glove. The glove appeared too tight for Simpson's hand. In his closing arguments, Cochran used the glove demonstration to quip, "If it doesn't fit, you must acquit."

Maintaining a chain of custody

When evidence is collected at a crime scene, it must be handled in a scrupulously careful manner to prevent contamination and to prove it has not been tampered with. To preserve the integrity of evidence and ensure it can be used in court, law enforcement establishes a chain of custody— chronological documentation showing its seizure, control, transfer, and analysis.

Recording a chain of custody establishes that evidence is connected to the crime, instead of from another source, or planted in an attempt to frame an innocent party. To maintain the chain of custody, each item of evidence must be labeled with the initials of everyone who handles it. Prosecutors use chain of custody documentation to prove that evidence has not been tampered with, and that it was discovered at the scene of the crime. If there are any discrepancies, or if a chain of custody is broken, evidence can be declared inadmissible.

Not only did we play the race card, we dealt it from the bottom of the deck.
Robert Shapiro

The jury was quick to make their decision. After only four hours of deliberation, they voted to acquit O.J. Simpson—to the shock of the nation. Critics attributed the jury's decision to its racial makeup. Jury members themselves cited LAPD incompetence and an unconvincing case by the prosecution.

Civil punishment

In 1997, Ron Goldman's parents sued Simpson in civil court for wrongful death. Nicole's father also filed a suit. A civil suit could not land Simpson any prison time, but it could make him pay a price. He lost badly in the civil suit, and was ordered to pay $33.5 million to the victims' families.

In 2007, Simpson once more found himself in legal trouble. On September 13, he and his friends threatened a memorabilia dealer at gunpoint in a Las Vegas hotel room, demanding the return of items that Simpson believed had been stolen from him. On October 3, 2008—13 years to the day after he was acquitted of murder—O.J. Simpson was sentenced to 33 years in prison, on 10 felony counts. Many believe this sentence was a way to bring him, at last, to justice. ■

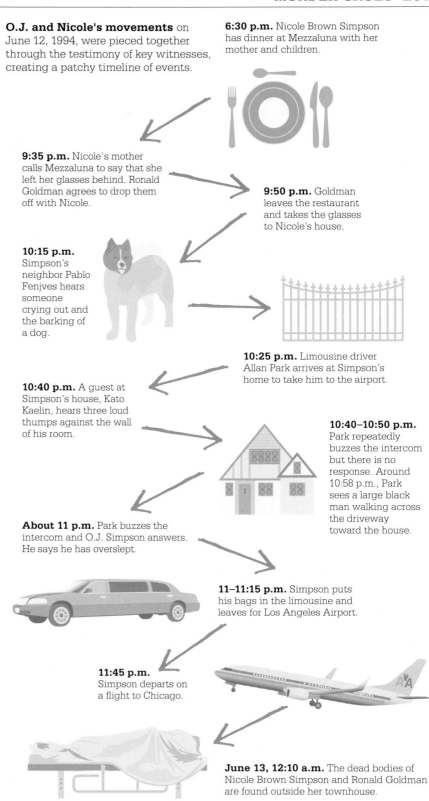

O.J. and Nicole's movements on June 12, 1994, were pieced together through the testimony of key witnesses, creating a patchy timeline of events.

6:30 p.m. Nicole Brown Simpson has dinner at Mezzaluna with her mother and children.

9:35 p.m. Nicole's mother calls Mezzaluna to say that she left her glasses behind. Ronald Goldman agrees to drop them off with Nicole.

9:50 p.m. Goldman leaves the restaurant and takes the glasses to Nicole's house.

10:15 p.m. Simpson's neighbor Pablo Fenjves hears someone crying out and the barking of a dog.

10:25 p.m. Limousine driver Allan Park arrives at Simpson's home to take him to the airport.

10:40 p.m. A guest at Simpson's house, Kato Kaelin, hears three loud thumps against the wall of his room.

10:40–10:50 p.m. Park repeatedly buzzes the intercom but there is no response. Around 10:58 p.m., Park sees a large black man walking across the driveway toward the house.

About 11 p.m. Park buzzes the intercom and O.J. Simpson answers. He says he has overslept.

11–11:15 p.m. Simpson puts his bags in the limousine and leaves for Los Angeles Airport.

11:45 p.m. Simpson departs on a flight to Chicago.

June 13, 12:10 a.m. The dead bodies of Nicole Brown Simpson and Ronald Goldman are found outside her townhouse.

FOUL PLAY WHILE IN THE SPY CRAFT STORE
CRAIG JACOBSEN, AUGUST 1997

IN CONTEXT

LOCATION
Las Vegas, Nevada

THEME
Desert murder

BEFORE
1978 The bodies of siblings Jacqueline and Malcolm Bradshaw are discovered by a sheep herder near the desert town of Barstow, California.

1984 William Richard Bradford strangles 15-year-old Tracey Campbell to death at a remote campsite in the Mojave Desert, and leaves her body there.

AFTER
2009 The remains of 11 women are found buried in the sands of Albuquerque's West Mesa. Some may have been there since 2001.

2013 Joseph and Summer McStay, who along with their young sons have been missing since February 2010, are found murdered in the desert near Victorville, California.

In August 1997, the body of backup singer and dancer Ginger Rios was unearthed from a shallow grave in Arizona's portion of the Mojave Desert. The 20-year-old had last been seen four months earlier, on April 4, at a Spy Craft store near the University of Nevada, Las Vegas.

Rios had gone there to purchase a book on cleaning up her credit report. While her husband, Mark Hollinger, waited in the car, Rios ran into the shop. According to Hollinger, she planned to be gone just a few minutes. Rios, however, never emerged from the store. The owner, Craig Jacobsen, who used the alias John Flowers, took her into the back room and delivered a swift uppercut to her nose that proved fatal. He then put her body in a trash bag, moved her to the back of his van, cleaned up the back room with strong bleach, and drove Rios's body to Arizona.

Jacobsen's wife, Cheryl Ciccone, was with her husband when Rios walked into the store. She saw Rios's body, and accompanied Jacobsen to Arizona. Fearing for her life, however, she later went to the authorities, and four months later guided police to Rios's body.

A second victim
A month after Rios's death, another Las Vegas woman went missing: chiropractor's daughter Mary Stoddard. On May 10, hunters chanced upon the body of a young woman in a desert grave in Pinal County, Arizona. A forensic facial reconstruction was ordered, but nobody claimed the victim, who became Jane Doe 2278DFAZ.

Craig Jacobsen looks unkempt in his 1997 mugshot. Jacobsen confessed to murdering Ginger Rios, claiming to have killed her because he had snapped when she "got in his face."

See also: Dr. Crippen 216 ▪ The Death of Azaria Chamberlain 238–39 ▪ Ian Brady and Myra Hindley 284–85

Pinal County, Arizona is a land of remote desert valleys—one of which became a burial ground for Jacobsen's victims. The graves were found near Florence, a town southeast of Phoenix.

The graves of Doe and Rios were in close proximity to each other, and both graves were covered with concrete caps, which suggested the two shared a killer.

Arrest and detention

In August 1997, Jacobsen was arrested in Los Angeles, California, by a fugitive law-enforcement task force—he was wanted in Florida for battery and counterfeiting. Under interrogation, as well as admitting that he killed Rios, Jacobsen confessed to killing a second woman in Las Vegas and burying her in Arizona.

Jacobsen identified the woman as Mary Stoddard, which seemingly solved the mystery of Jane Doe's identity. However, the Arizona authorities had reburied Jane Doe in a county cemetery, but the location of the plot was not on the paperwork. Without the body, prosecutors had to focus their case on Ginger Rios. Jacobsen was convicted in 2000 and sentenced to at least 25 years behind bars.

Third victim

In a strange twist of events, in 2010, the remains of Jane Doe were relocated and identified by the Doe Network. She was not Mary Stoddard. Jane Doe was actually 15-year-old Christina Martinez, who disappeared in May 1997 on her way to a local laundromat in Phoenix, Arizona—two blocks from another store owned by Jacobsen.

In 2014, a grand jury charged Jacobsen with the murder of Martinez. The body of Stoddard has not been recovered, despite searches near the other graves. ▪

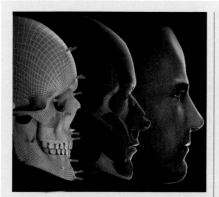

Facial reconstruction software
creates a photo-realistic image based on the skull and other known data, such as age, ethnicity, or weight.

Forensic facial reconstruction

Advancements in computerized 3D technology have vastly improved the field of forensic facial reconstruction. It is now possible to scan a skull from multiple angles to create a precise digital reconstruction, instead of having to build a model by hand from clay. The technique is particularly useful for crimes that involve unidentified remains.

Reconstructed images may be shown to potential victims' family members, run through police databases, or sent to the Doe Network, a US nonprofit organization dedicated to connecting missing and unidentified persons with John and Jane Doe cases. The US has a 50 percent success rate in making identifications from forensic facial reconstruction.

The technique of forensic facial reconstruction has also been used to create realistic images of historical figures—such as Tutankhamun, King Richard III, and Copernicus—based on their remains.

PEOPLE ARE AFRAID AND DON'T WANT TO TALK TO US

THE MURDERS OF TUPAC SHAKUR AND BIGGIE SMALLS, 1996 AND 1997

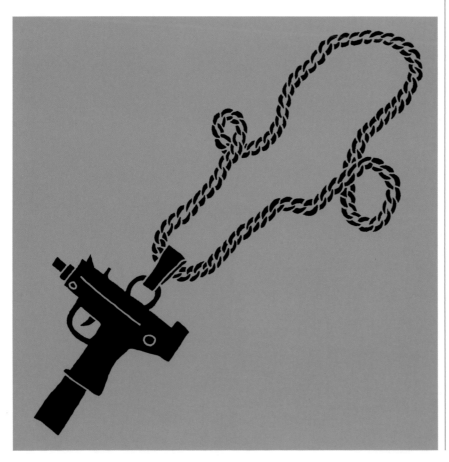

I n the late 1990s, two of hip-hop's biggest stars, Tupac Shakur and Biggie Smalls, were gunned down in eerily similar drive-by shootings.

Shakur, working on the West Coast, and Smalls, who performed as The Notorious B.I.G. on the East Coast, were modern-day American storytellers pursuing similar musical careers. When Shakur traveled to New York, he regularly invited Smalls on stage to rap, which furthered Smalls's career. In the years before their deaths, however, the two rappers were embroiled in a bitter feud that became known as the East Coast-West Coast hip-hop rivalry.

See also: The Assassination of John F. Kennedy 316–21 ▪ The Abduction of Aldo Moro 322–23

Bad blood between Shakur and Smalls began in Manhattan in 1994 when Shakur was ambushed and shot at Quad Studios by three men. They stole $35,000 worth of jewelry from him and his crew and then escaped. Smalls was recording in the building at the time, and Shakur was convinced that Smalls and his record producer, Sean "Diddy" Combs, had set him up. The two men never reconciled.

> I don't think the powers that be give a damn that another little ghetto kid gets killed in the streets. It's not important to them to solve this case.
> **DJ Shay**

Biggie and Tupac hang out at the Royalty Hotel in May 1994, and are filmed freestyling by Dream Hampton, in one of the few videos of the two rappers together.

On September 7, 1996, Tupac Shakur, just 25 years old, was shot in a car-to-car shooting on his way to a party in Las Vegas, Nevada. He died six days after the shooting.

Six months later, on March 9, 1997, 24-year-old Smalls was shot four times in a car-to-car drive-by attack as he left a party at the Petersen Automotive Museum in Los Angeles, California. He died within 30 minutes of the shooting.

Shocking scenes

On September 7, 1996, Shakur attended a boxing match between Mike Tyson and Bruce Seldon at the MGM Grand Hotel in Las Vegas. As he left the bout with his entourage—which included friends, backup singers, and Death Row Records producer Marion "Suge" Knight—the crew spotted »

September 7, 8:30 p.m.
Shakur and friends leave the Tyson/Seldon boxing match at the MGM Grand Hotel, Las Vegas

8:30–9 p.m.
Shakur and his bodyguards are involved in a physical altercation with Orlando Anderson outside the hotel

11:15 p.m.
Shakur is shot at close range at a Las Vegas intersection, in his BMW 750 sedan

September 8–9
Shakur undergoes three operations at the University Medical Center of Southern Nevada

**September 13, 4.03 p.m.
Shakur is pronounced dead due to respiratory failure**

Gang identity and turf wars

Gang warfare—which can have violent consequences even for innocent bystanders—usually occurs within low-income communities. The Los Angeles Police Department believes that there are five main reasons that individuals in such communities join gangs. Some are attracted to the increased social status, or the sense of brotherhood. Others want protection from rival gangs, or want to engage more easily in criminal activity. Some are simply coerced into joining.

Gangs use signifiers of identity to create a sense of exclusivity, such as tattoos, clothing, and hand signs.

Gang rivalries usually occur between two sides seeking control of a particular territory. One of the deadliest rivalries is that of the Bloods and Crips in Los Angeles. It began in the 1970s over control of the neighborhood of Compton and accounted for a high percentage of the gang-related murders in southern Los Angeles.

Orlando Tive "Baby Lane" Anderson, a member of the Southside Crips Gang.

Knight was affiliated with the rival Pirus Bloods street gang. Upon seeing Anderson, Knight's friend Trevon "Tray" Lane told Shakur that Anderson was part of a posse that snatched a Death Row gold necklace from Lane's neck a month earlier. Shakur pounced on Anderson, and his whole entourage joined in stomping and kicking him, not caring that their actions were being captured on the casino's surveillance videotape. However, Anderson declined to press charges, and they all went their separate ways.

Shakur shot
After Anderson's beating, Shakur's group got into a convoy of cars to head to a party. At 11:15 p.m., at the intersection of Flamingo Road and Koval Lane, a white Cadillac with California license plates pulled

up next to Knight's black sedan, in which Shakur and Knight were riding. As the Cadillac came alongside, a man in the back seat rolled down the window, stuck out his arm, and opened fire. Shakur was shot three times, once in the chest; Knight was hit with shrapnel at the base of his skull.

Two bicycle officers with the Las Vegas Metropolitan Police Department heard the shots from

inside a parking garage next to the intersection and hurried down to street level. They followed Knight's sedan as it made a U-turn to evade the gunman. The driver of the Cadillac turned onto another street and disappeared into the night.

For the next seven days, Shakur remained in a coma in a critical condition. He also underwent several surgeries and medical procedures to stop the bleeding in his chest. On the afternoon of September 13, however, he died from his injuries.

Shakur's shooting sparked a five-day gang war on the streets of Compton, California, between the Bloods and the Crips. In the end, three men were dead and 10 were wounded. The Compton Police Department attributed the war to retaliation by the Bloods against the Crips for the Shakur shooting.

Biggie gunned down
Five months later, in February 1997, Biggie Smalls—whose real name was Christopher Wallace—traveled to Los Angeles to promote his

Funeral cars pass down St. James Place, Brooklyn, toward the home of Biggie's mother Voletta Wallace on March 18, 1997. Press and crowds gathered to pay tribute to the rapper.

> I don't think my son's death was connected to Tupac. And I don't think Christopher had anything to do with Tupac's death.
> **Voletta Wallace**

second studio album and film a music video for the album's lead single, "Hypnotize." On March 7, Smalls appeared at the Soul Train Music Awards to present an award to singer Toni Braxton, but was booed by some members of the audience due to his feud with the late Tupac Shakur.

On March 8, Smalls, with record producer Sean Combs and an entourage, attended a party hosted by *Vibe* magazine and Qwest Records at the Petersen Automotive Museum on Wilshire Boulevard, Los Angeles. Smalls told his mother he had canceled a flight to London so that he could attend the party.

A fire marshal closed the party early due to overcrowding, and at 12:30 a.m., Smalls and his entourage left the museum in two GMC Suburbans. Smalls sat in the front passenger seat. When his SUV stopped at a red light behind Combs's vehicle at the corner of Wilshire Boulevard and South Fairfax Avenue, a Chevrolet Impala drove up alongside.

The events that unfolded mirrored the fate that had befallen Shakur. A man in a button-down shirt and bow tie rolled down the driver's window of the Impala and fired at Smalls with a 9 mm blue-steel pistol, hitting him four times.

The driver of the Impala sped away, while Smalls's entourage rushed him to hospital. Despite the doctors' efforts, Smalls was pronounced dead 30 minutes later.

Unsolved crimes

Police investigations into Shakur's death did not lead to any formal murder charges. In his affidavit chronicling the investigation, Detective Timothy Brennan of the Compton Police Department's gang unit named Anderson as Shakur's likely killer. However, Anderson was killed in an unrelated shootout in Compton in 1998 and could not be charged. Brennan was also assigned to the taskforce working to find Smalls's killer. There, too, the police were unable to bring the killer to justice.

Multiple conspiracy theories surround the murders of both rappers, but none have been substantiated. Rumors persist that Smalls had Shakur killed, but there is no evidence to back up the theory. Investigators also found no proof that the murder of Biggie Smalls was linked to the East Coast-West Coast rap war. Still, some claimed that Sean Combs hired Anderson to take out Shakur, and others said Suge Knight ordered the hit on Smalls.

The most plausible theory, said the Los Angeles police, was that Smalls was shot over a financial dispute with Crips members who had acted as his bodyguards—and that it was unrelated to the murder of Shakur. Nonetheless, new books, biopics, and theories continue to flourish, with even the police assigned to the cases now writing about the mysterious deaths of Tupac Shakur and Biggie Smalls. ∎

March 9, 12:30 a.m.
Biggie Smalls and his entourage leave the Petersen Automotive Museum in Los Angeles

Smalls's Suburban stops at a red light near the museum; a Chevrolet Impala pulls up alongside

The driver of the Impala fires four shots into Smalls's chest at close range

Smalls is rushed to the Cedars-Sinai Medical Center in Los Angeles

**1:15 a.m.
Biggie Smalls is pronounced dead as a result of his gunshot wounds**

SERIAL K

ILLERS

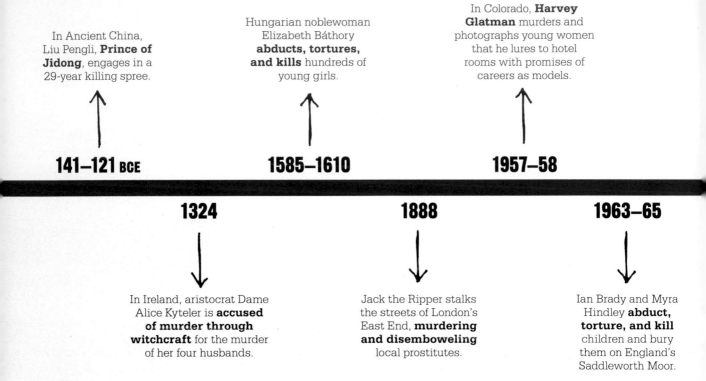

In Ancient China, Liu Pengli, **Prince of Jidong**, engages in a 29-year killing spree.

Hungarian noblewoman Elizabeth Báthory **abducts, tortures, and kills** hundreds of young girls.

In Colorado, **Harvey Glatman** murders and photographs young women that he lures to hotel rooms with promises of careers as models.

141–121 BCE

1585–1610

1957–58

1324

1888

1963–65

In Ireland, aristocrat Dame Alice Kyteler is **accused of murder through witchcraft** for the murder of her four husbands.

Jack the Ripper stalks the streets of London's East End, **murdering and disemboweling** local prostitutes.

Ian Brady and Myra Hindley **abduct, torture, and kill** children and bury them on England's Saddleworth Moor.

The term "serial murder" was coined in 1930 by Ernst Gennat, director of the Berlin police, in reference to Peter Kurten, who killed nine people in and around Düsseldorf. Forty-four years later in America, FBI behavioral scientist Robert Ressler adopted the term "serial killer," specifically to describe a person who commits three or more murders on separate occasions, with each one separated by a "cooling-off period."

Ressler's definition distinguished serial killing from mass murder, during which at least four victims are slain in a single location, as at the Teigin Bank incident in Tokyo, and the spree killings of Charles Whitman. Ressler is credited with bringing the phrase "serial killer" into popular use.

In the years since, individuals and agencies have sought to revise the definition of the term serial murder. Some specify a minimum of four victims, while others apply the term to cases with just two. The phrase "cooling-off period" was also felt to be ambiguous. The FBI has revised its own definition of serial murder to be "the unlawful killing of two or more victims by the same offender(s), in separate events." This new criteria allows police departments who have identified the early stages of a homicidal pattern to approach it in the specific manner necessary to investigate a series of murders.

Noble killers

Although many argue that serial murder is a product of the modern age, the reality is that serial killers have existed for many centuries. The cases of Liu Pengli, a prince in ancient China, Dame Alice Kyteler in 14th-century England, and the Hungarian Countess Elizabeth Báthory at the turn of the 17th century seem to indicate that it was only considered worthy of note when killings were committed by those of high social station.

This may be the reason why a member of the British Royal Family became a suspect in London's Whitechapel Murders of 1888. Jack the Ripper, more than likely a working-class man, operated in the right place at the right time in history to ignite the public imagination. The rise of modern policing in London after the establishment of the Metropolitan Police in 1829 and the proliferation of print media meant that the

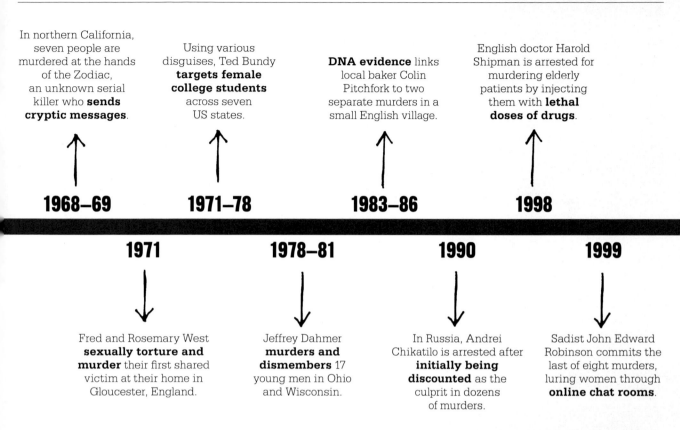

In northern California, seven people are murdered at the hands of the Zodiac, an unknown serial killer who **sends cryptic messages**.

Using various disguises, Ted Bundy **targets female college students** across seven US states.

DNA evidence links local baker Colin Pitchfork to two separate murders in a small English village.

English doctor Harold Shipman is arrested for murdering elderly patients by injecting them with **lethal doses of drugs**.

1968–69 **1971–78** **1983–86** **1998**

1971 **1978–81** **1990** **1999**

Fred and Rosemary West **sexually torture and murder** their first shared victim at their home in Gloucester, England.

Jeffrey Dahmer **murders and dismembers** 17 young men in Ohio and Wisconsin.

In Russia, Andrei Chikatilo is arrested after **initially being discounted** as the culprit in dozens of murders.

Sadist John Edward Robinson commits the last of eight murders, luring women through **online chat rooms**.

city's bloodiest, most gruesome crimes began to be documented, disseminated, and commercially exploited. *The Penny Dreadful*, a cheap 19th-century publication featuring sensational stories of the most grisly murders, appeared in weekly installments and was devoured by the British public.

Diaries and records

By the 1950s, cameras and recording devices were widely affordable, and serial murderers could create their own record of their crimes. Aroused by the images of bound, scantily clad women on the covers of detective magazines, serial murderer Harvey Glatman abducted, tied up, photographed, and then murdered at least three women in California. Once apprehended, Glatman's

pictures were reprinted in the very detective magazines that had nurtured his own deviant fantasies. Similarly, in England, in the 1960s, "Moors Murderers" Ian Brady and Myra Hindley, became the first known compulsive killers to make audio recordings of a victim. The recording was played at their trial and the court listened in silence to harrowing evidence of the pair's torture and abuse of 10-year-old Lesley Ann Downey.

Serial killer cases continued to be covered in the media. Shortly after this, on the west coast of the US, a killer calling himself "the Zodiac" sent proof of his crimes to newspapers in the San Francisco area, accompanied by strange codes and letters threatening to commit further carnage if he did not receive front page coverage.

Five years after the Zodiac's last letter in 1974, the televised trial of Ted Bundy—the superficially charming killer of American college girls—shattered popular notions of serial killers as ugly monsters. Bundy looked like the kind of upright, young man many parents would want their daughter to meet. Bundy's trial overlapped with the pioneering research of the Ressler-era Behavioral Science Unit in Virginia, which began to offer serial killer profiles to police agencies across the western world.

By the 1980s, serial murder rates were at an all-time high. The most notorious cases of the late-1980s and 1990s included Andrei Chikatilo in Russia and Jeffrey Dahmer in the US, as well as Fred and Rosemary West and Harold Shipman in the UK. ∎

MURDERING PEOPLE... FOR SHEER SPORT
LIU PENGLI, 144–121 BCE

IN CONTEXT

LOCATION
Jidong, China

THEME
Thrill-seeking serial killers

BEFORE
313 BCE In ancient Rome, rumors circulate of a mass poisoning by Roman matrons after several men drop dead. Some 170 women are arrested. They claim that their potions are medicinal but two of them die when they are made to drink their own concoctions.

AFTER
2007 In Russia, Alexander Pichushkin is brought to trial for the murder of at least 48 people between 1992 and 2006. Known as the Chessboard Killer, Pichushkin claims that he wanted to kill 64 people—the number of squares on a chessboard. Moscow's Bitsa Park, where Pichushkin played chess, is the scene of many of his murders.

Serial killers are by no means a modern phenomenon. Centuries before Jack the Ripper, Rosemary and Fred West, or Ted Bundy murdered their victims, Prince Liu Pengli slaughtered dozens of men, women, and children in ancient China.

Liu Pengli, one of five brothers, ruled over the principality of Jidong during the second century BCE. It was a tempestuous time of rebellion and political machinations that led to the banishment of Liu Pengli's father, the once-beloved younger brother of Emperor Jing.

Soon after coming to power in Jidong, Liu assembled a gang of slaves and young men on the run. Together, they went out at night to terrorize anyone they found. The people lived in fear of their ruler. Liu killed his subjects and stole their possessions, with no higher motive than pleasure.

In the 29th year of his rule, the serial killer's run came to an end when the son of one of his victims went to the only person who could stop the wave of terror—Liu's uncle,

He was arrogant and cruel, and paid no attention to the etiquette demanded between ruler and subject.
Sima Qian

Emperor Jing. Investigations finally brought Liu Pengli's crimes to light, and he was found responsible for at least 100 murders.

Under pressure from his courtiers, who demanded Liu Pengli's execution, the emperor acknowledged the severity of the crime, but was reluctant to kill his own nephew. Instead, he stripped Liu Pengli of his royal status and banished him to another province. The sentence was considered the next best thing to execution. ∎

See also: Ted Bundy 276–83 ▪ Fred and Rosemary West 286–87 ▪ Harold Shipman 290–91 ▪ Jeffrey Dahmer 293

THE SAID DAME ALICE HAD A CERTAIN DEMON
ALICE KYTELER, 1324

IN CONTEXT

LOCATION
Kilkenny, Ireland

THEME
Witchcraft and sorcery

BEFORE
1317 Hugues Géraud, Bishop of Cahors, France, is flayed alive and burned after an ecclesiastical court finds him guilty of using sorcery in an attempt to assassinate Pope John XXII.

AFTER
1597 In Scotland, the Great Scottish Witch Hunt, which began in the 1560s, concludes with the trial and conviction of 200 people for witchcraft. Confessions are extracted through torture, or their guilt is decided by witch prickers, who pierce the accused with a sharp implement. If they fail to bleed, they are found guilty.

To lose one husband is unfortunate; to lose four in rapid succession is bound to raise eyebrows, especially if all the men are wealthy. When the death of Dame Alice Kyteler's husband, John le Poer, left her a widow for the fourth time, local people accused her of witchcraft.

Devilish accusations

In the 14th century, Catholic orthodoxy did not generally take the idea of sorcery seriously—the great European witchhunts took place in the 16th and 17th centuries. However, the Catholic church frowned on heresy, and some members of the clergy were prepared to define this broadly.

Dame Alice had repeatedly clashed with Kilkenny's Bishop of Ossory, who resented her wealth and connections among Ireland's

Kilkenny's Kyteler's Inn, reputedly established by Dame Kyteler herself, continues to operate, bolstered by its connection to the first person convicted of witchcraft in Ireland.

elite. When le Poer's children came to him with stories of finding satanic powders, the body parts of unbaptized babies, and the toenails of corpses boiled up in a robber's skull, the bishop did not probe too deeply. Dame Alice was brought to trial and convicted. Delays in procedure allowed Kyteler to escape to England, but her maidservant, Petronilla de Meath, was condemned for being her accomplice, and was burned at the stake on November 3, 1324. ∎

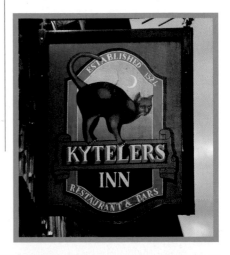

See also: Lizzie Borden 208–11 ∎ Dr. Crippen 216

THE BLOOD OF MAIDENS WILL KEEP HER YOUNG

ELIZABETH BÁTHORY, 1585–1610

IN CONTEXT

LOCATION
Kingdom of Hungary

THEME
Murderous women

BEFORE
47–42 BCE Prior to her five-year reign as the first queen of Sri Lanka, Anula of Anuradhapura poisons her son and four of her husbands.

AFTER
1876–96 Nurse Amelia Elizabeth Dyer murders an estimated 400 infants in Caversham, England.

1988 While inquiring about a missing tenant, police find seven bodies buried in the yard of a California boarding house run by serial killer Dorothea Puente.

1989–90 Former prostitute Aileen Wuornos shoots and kills seven men in Florida at point-blank range. She receives the death penalty, and is executed by lethal injection.

Brick by brick, stonemasons walled a 50-year-old woman into a windowless suite inside Cachtice Castle, Slovakia, with only small slits for air and food. For close to five years, the "Blood Countess" remained trapped there in solitary confinement—a bleak end to the life of the most prolific female mass murderer of all time.

Countess Elizabeth Báthory de Ecsed came from one of Hungary's most distinguished and powerful families. At 15, she married Count Ferenc Nadasdy in a ceremony attended by European royalty. The couple was gifted Cachtice Castle.

Nadasdy was the commander of the Hungarian forces fighting against the Ottoman Empire. Called the "Black Hero of Hungary," he was particularly known for torturing the soldiers he captured. His wife seemed like any other noblewoman; attending parties, opening an etiquette school for aristocratic ladies, and providing a haven for destitute war widows.

Dark obsessions

Elizabeth was drawn to the occult. She began consorting with women who claimed to be witches, and began to torture her servant girls.

The shadows will envelop you and you will find time to repent your bestial life.
Count Gyorgy Thurzo

When Nadasdy died in 1604, Báthory grew even more sadistic. Taking advice on torture from her children's governess, one of Báthory's many sexual conquests, the countess began to abduct girls to torture and kill. At first, she took the daughters of local peasants, some of whom were lured by the promise of work. Later, she turned to wealthy girls who had come to her school to learn etiquette.

By this time, rumors were circulating about the countess. A prominent Lutheran minister denounced Báthory as a villainess. In 1610, one of Báthory's victims escaped from Cachtice Castle.

See also: The Dripping Killer 206–07 ▪ Lizzie Borden 208–11 ▪ Ted Bundy 276–83 ▪ Ian Brady and Myra Hindley 284–85

The girl's testimony prompted the King of Hungary, Matthias II, to order that Count Gyorgy Thurzo start an investigation.

On December 30, 1610, Count Thurzo ordered a raid on the castle. The investigators found at least one dead girl, drained of blood, and another dying. Further searches uncovered several girls—still alive—in the dungeons, and about 50 buried beneath the castle.

At a trial led by Thurzo, Báthory and her servants were accused of torturing and killing hundreds of women between 1585 and 1609: beating, burning, freezing, and most notably, draining victims' blood. One servant claimed to have seen Báthory's records, which detailed more than 650 victims.

Báthory's four conspirators were beheaded and cremated. Báthory, however, was saved from execution by her noble status, and died in confinement in 1614. Some have suggested that the powerful widow was a victim of a conspiracy by the ruling Hapsburg emperor—or perhaps even her own children. ▪

Elizabeth Báthory is often called the "blood Countess" or "female Dracula." Her infamy has persisted since her death, with stories that she bathed in the blood of virgins to retain her youth.

Medieval torture

From the 12th century, torture experienced a revival in Europe, both as a popular method to make suspects confess to their crimes and as punishment for wrongdoing.

In 1252, Pope Innocent IV authorized his inquisitors to use torture to gain confessions from suspected heretics. These confessions made under duress were especially useful for prosecuting people for crimes of belief—a growing category of crime in the religious unrest that plagued Europe's medieval period.

Public torture aimed to dissuade criminals and preserve social order. The medieval era was beset by wars, famine, and disease, and crime was a menace that societies could do without.

Common techniques included burning, mutilation, and beheading. Often, torture became a public spectacle. Townspeople regularly witnessed public floggings, with criminals chained in iron collars. As a punishment, torture was often just a prelude to public execution, after which corpses, heads, and body parts were impaled on stakes on the city walls.

I WILL SEND YOU ANOTHER BIT OF INNARDS

JACK THE RIPPER, 1888

IN CONTEXT

LOCATION
Whitechapel, London, UK

THEME
Serial murder of prostitutes

BEFORE
1866 French warehouse porter Joseph Philippe murders six prostitutes in Paris. He claims to have been in a state of "erotic catalepsy," some sort of sexual trance or blackout.

AFTER
1975–80 "Yorkshire Ripper" Peter Sutcliffe kills 13 women, some of whom are sex workers.

1982–98 Gary Ridgway, known as the "Green River Killer," kills at least 48 sex workers in Washington state.

1983–2002 Robert Pickton murders a number of prostitutes—between six and 49—and buries some at his family's pig farm in Vancouver, British Columbia.

Attacks a **prostitute** at night in the sidestreets around a pub where she picks up clients

↓

Slashes the victim's throat and repeatedly **stabs her** in the stomach

↓

Eviscerates her body and **cuts off pieces** of her organs as souvenirs

↓

Displays the victim's body in a **humiliating position**

↓

Disappears into the Whitechapel sidestreets to find another victim

---

Around 3:30 a.m. on Tuesday, August 7, 1888, cab driver Albert Crow returned home to the George Yard Buildings on London's Whitechapel Road, between the areas of Whitechapel and Spitalfields. Crow found what he thought was a female vagrant passed out on the first-floor landing, her green skirt and petticoat hiked up. At 5 a.m., tenant John Saunders Reeves discovered the truth: the mystery woman had been murdered.

Dr. Timothy Killeen, who performed the autopsy, concluded that the victim had been stabbed nearly 40 times in her throat and abdomen. She was identified by her husband as 39-year-old Martha Tabram, who earned her living as a prostitute. Investigators learned that Martha's body had not been on the landing when tenants Joseph and Elizabeth Mahoney returned home at 2 a.m. The killer must have committed the crime at some point between 2 a.m. and 3:30 a.m.

Establishing a pattern
The grisly murder of a second woman, 24 days later, bore striking similarities to the Tabram slaying.

This victim was found by two workers outside a stable on Buck's Row at 3:40 a.m. on August 31. Her genitals were exposed. Arriving at 4 a.m., surgeon Henry Llewellyn discovered two fatal slashes running from left to right across her throat. There were also multiple postmortem incisions to the abdomen. The warmth of her body and legs led Llewellyn to conclude that she had not been dead for longer than half an hour. A laundry mark on her petticoats from a Lambeth workhouse identified her as Mary Ann "Polly" Nichols.

See also: The Black Dahlia Murder 218–23 ▪ Elizabeth Báthory 264–65 ▪ Ted Bundy 276–83

At 6 a.m. on September 8, market worker John Davis discovered the body of a third woman in his backyard, at 29 Hanbury Street in Spitalfields. Whoever had done the grisly deed had eviscerated the victim, draping her intestines over her shoulders. Like the first two victims, Annie Chapman worked as a prostitute. Her body had been posed to allude to this, with legs splayed to degrade her even in death.

Dr. George Bagster Phillips, arriving half an hour later, noted that her handkerchief had been tightened around her neck, causing asphyxiation. Once again, the killer had slashed his victim's throat from left to right. A more thorough examination revealed that a portion of the uterus had been excised. Phillips estimated the time of death at 4:30 a.m. or earlier.

Early clues

Scant clues emerged about the three murders, but at an inquest, witness Elizabeth Long testified she had seen Chapman speaking with a man at 5:30 a.m. near the crime scene. She described the figure as around 40 years old, with dark hair and a foreign, "shabby-genteel" appearance. The man Long described wore a brown deerstalker cap and overcoat. The police also found a leather apron at the scene of Chapman's death.

Local gossip transformed these details into the tale of "Leather Apron," a homicidal Hebrew who preyed upon English prostitutes. John Pizer—a Polish Jew and boot-maker with the misfortune of having the nickname "Leather »

Policemen discover a victim of Jack the Ripper in this 1891 illustration from *Le Petit Parisien*. The mysterious killer became notorious not just in the United Kingdom, but across the world.

Apron"—was named by the media as a suspect in the killings. On September 10, Pizer was arrested despite the lack of evidence against him. When Pizer was able to give an alibi for two of the murders he was released. He later sued a local newspaper for libel.

With few leads, the people of Whitechapel took matters into their own hands. Local businessmen, concerned about the effect the murders were having on commerce, organized the Whitechapel Vigilance Committee to patrol the streets after dark. They elected a local builder, George Lusk, as the committee's chairman. Each night the group convened at 9 p.m. at the Crown pub to inspect patrollers—

underemployed men who were paid a pittance to walk the beat armed with nothing but a cudgel.

The double event

All was quiet for a while, and the people of Whitechapel began to relax. The increased police attention and vigilantes probably deterred the killer from striking again. Then, on September 30, 1888, came the "double event." Two new victims were discovered within an hour of each other.

At 1 a.m. in east Whitechapel, a steward of the worker's club, Louis Diemschutz, drove his pony-drawn cart into Dutfield's Yard. When the animal began to act strangely, the steward struck a

> I am down on whores and I shant quit ripping them till I do get buckled.
> **Jack the Ripper**

match and crept into the darkness. There, in the flickering light, he beheld the body of a woman in a pool of blood. Her dead hand clutched a packet of cachous—

September 8, 6 a.m., Annie Chapman discovered at 29 Hanbury Street

August 31, 3:40 a.m., Mary Nichols discovered at Buck's Row Stables [now known as Durward Street]

Spitalfields

November 9, 10:45 a.m., Mary Kelly discovered at Miller's Court, off Dorset Street [now known as White's Row car park]

Whitechapel

August 7, 3:30 a.m., Martha Tabram discovered at George Yard Buildings [now known as Gunthorpe Street]

The City

September 30, 2 a.m., Catherine Eddowes discovered in Mitre Square

September 30, 1 a.m., Elizabeth Stride discovered at Dutfield's Yard [now known as Henriques Street]

Whitechapel and neighboring Spitalfields are areas of east London. In the 19th century, Whitechapel was home to the working class, migrants, and Jews, all crowded into cheap accommodations.

The "Dear Boss" letter was sent to London's Central News Agency on September 27, 1888, suggesting that the killer wanted notoriety. He even gave himself a name: Jack the Ripper.

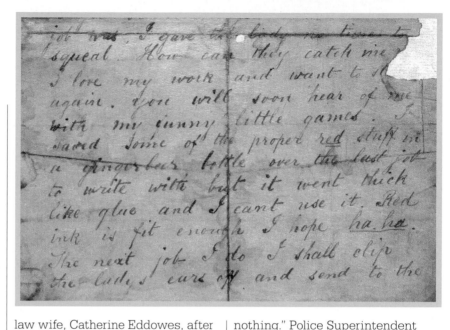

sweets used to freshen the breath. Obviously, the attack had been swift and unexpected. Later, Diemschutz testified that he believed the killer was still lurking in the yard when he came upon the body. The victim was Elizabeth Stride, a 44-year-old-prostitute.

However, the night's bloodshed had just begun. Within an hour, the body of a second woman was found in the south corner of Mitre Square, a 15-minute walk from Dutfield's Yard. Dr. Frederick Brown attended the scene at 2 a.m.

Like Annie Chapman, her bowels were strung over her right shoulder and her legs were spread. This time the Ripper had used his blade on her face, slicing off the tip of her nose and eyelids, and carving triangular incisions into her cheeks. During the autopsy, Dr. Brown discovered that the left kidney and part of the womb were missing. John Kelly identified the second victim as his 46-year-old common-law wife, Catherine Eddowes, after reading in the paper about two pawn tickets found on her person.

Notes and graffiti
Searching along Goulston Street at 3 a.m. on the night of the double event, PC Albert Long happened upon a bloodied piece of apron discarded in a stairwell. A cryptic message was scrawled in white chalk on the wall: "The Juwes are the men that will be blamed for nothing." Police Superintendent Thomas Arnold was among the first to arrive at the scene. Fearing that the graffiti would spark antisemitic rioting, he ordered the "Goulston Street Graffito" to be washed away.

The high level of attention that the killings received in the media led to numerous hoax letters being sent to the investigators. While initially considered to be another hoax, a letter sent on September 27, written in red ink, would come to take a particular hold on the investigation—it claimed to come from the killer, and promised to "clip the ladys ears off" the next victim. When the autopsy of Catherine Eddowes revealed a mutilated earlobe, the police took the implications of the red letter seriously. They distributed copies of the letter among the public through handbills, hoping to get a lead. The letter signed off with the first use of the nickname "Jack the Ripper," which soon captured the public's imagination.

More clues were forthcoming. On October 16, a package arrived at the doorstep of George Lusk, **»**

Prostitutes as victims

Social stigma around sex work often means that prostitutes have tenuous family bonds and poor relationships with police. Their disappearances are not typically met with the same outrage as those of other women. Their transient lifestyles mean they may travel from city to city without telling anybody, and are therefore not reported missing until it is too late.

Their profession may provide a twisted moral justification for killers. When speaking with police about the women he murdered, "Green River Killer" Gary Ridgway said, "I thought I was doing you guys a favor, killing prostitutes."

Sex workers are frequently placed in vulnerable positions with strangers. The damaged egos of their clients, who are often unknown quantities, can put prostitutes at risk. The correlation between sex work and substance addiction also means that some are led by the desperation of their situation to lower their guard or take risks they normally would not take.

the Chairman of the Whitechapel Vigilance Committee. It contained a letter signed "From hell" and a human organ. Examining the organ, Dr. Thomas Horrocks Openshaw, a surgeon at London Hospital, concluded that it was a human kidney preserved in spirits. On October 19, the *Daily Telegraph* reported that the kidney belonged to an alcoholic female in her mid-forties, but Dr. Openshaw himself claimed that this was impossible to determine. Ultimately, most of the police and surgeons attributed the kidney to a morbid prank perpetrated by medical students.

Final victim

The last act in the Ripper's spree occurred on November 9, 1888, at 13 Miller's Court: the home of a 25-year-old Irish prostitute named Mary Kelly. Thomas Bowyer, a rent collector for Kelly's landlord John McCarthy, stopped by the address at 10:45 a.m. with orders to obtain 29 shillings in back rent from the tenant. After knocking on the door and receiving no answer, he peered through the makeshift curtains and swiftly recoiled. Kelly's naked body lay sprawled across her bed,

hacked beyond recognition. At 1:30 p.m., Superintendent Arnold instructed his men to forcibly enter the dwelling.

Upon examining the corpse's state of decay, doctors Thomas Bond and George Bagster Phillips both concluded that the murder had occurred between 2 and 8 a.m. The level of mutilation was unparalleled: the victim's skin had been stripped from her legs, her breasts and internal organs removed and arranged around her remains, and her face disfigured by countless gashes. Only one organ—her heart—was unaccounted for.

Kelly's mutilations were far worse than those of the other victims, and she was considerably younger. While police at the time investigated her murder as a Ripper case, it has since been suggested that Kelly was killed by someone attempting to pass off the murder as the Ripper's work—perhaps even her boyfriend, Joseph Barnett. However, Barnett was questioned by police for hours after Kelly's death and released without charge. The police were yet again unable to find any useful clues as to the true identity of Jack the Ripper.

I send you half the Kidney I took from one women ... tother piece I fried and ate it was very nice.
Jack the Ripper

Then, as suddenly as they had begun, the killings stopped. Although some similar subsequent murders were suspected to be the Ripper's work—such as the slaying of Frances Cole in February 1891—Kelly is usually considered to have been the final Ripper victim.

Difficult investigation

Today, it seems inconceivable that the Ripper would be able to elude the authorities for more than a few weeks, let alone an eternity. The investigations were hampered, however, by a lack of evidence and eyewitnesses—the murders being committed so late at night in a dangerous area—and also by the interference of the press.

Initially, the police believed the "Whitechapel murders" to be the work of local gangs—largely due to the death of Emma Smith, who was attacked by a gang on April 3, 1888, and erroneously included in Scotland Yard's Ripper files.

The police investigation was frustrated at every turn. In September 1888, Scotland Yard sent in Frederick George Abberline, a policeman who had worked in Whitechapel for 14 years before being promoted out of the area. They hoped he would be able

Pioneering policing

If Jack the Ripper gave birth to the modern serial killer, law enforcement must be credited for creating the serial killer's arch nemesis: the criminal profiler. Following the murder of Mary Kelly, Dr. Thomas Bond, surgeon to the Metropolitan Police's "A" Division, submitted a report on the deaths of the "Canonical Five"—Nichols, Chapman, Stride, Eddowes, and Kelly—to Scotland Yard. The document has been recognized as being ahead of its time.

Bond employed what is now termed "linkage analysis," identifying signature techniques to establish the likelihood that a series of crimes were committed by a single individual.

From the way each woman was lying down when they were murdered, each with their throat cut, Bond saw the murders as erotically motivated mutilations committed by one person. His focus on the psychology of the killer was a big improvement on the phrenological approaches to criminal profiling that were popular at the time.

Painter Walter Sickert (left), Prince Albert Victor, Duke of Clarence (center), and Sir William Gull (right) have all been suggested as suspects by modern "Ripperologists" due to their poor alibis.

to use his knowledge of local criminals to get some information about the killer. This was not the case—it is unlikely that the Ripper was a known Whitechapel criminal, and the man worked alone. None of the criminals in the area were able to provide any useful leads for Abberline's investigation.

The Ripper was also a press sensation. Not only did articles about the murderer create more work for the police—who had to deal with false leads, copycats, and terror in the community—but journalists also went to extreme lengths to investigate the murders. Some followed policemen around as they investigated; others went so far as to dress up like prostitutes and wait for the Ripper to appear.

In the more than 125 years since, countless detectives, writers, and armchair sleuths have proffered suspects from the Duke of Clarence

and his physician, Sir William Gull, to psychologically tortured wretches like Polish hairdresser Aaron Kosminski. Today, we are no closer to discovering the Ripper's identity than we were in 1888.

At the inquest into Annie Chapman's death, Dr. Phillips put forward the opinion that the Ripper may have been a medical man, due to the anatomical knowledge displayed in his removal of the victims' organs. However, Dr. Bond disagreed, stating after the Kelly murder that the killer did not even have a butcher's accuracy when it

The murderer is likely to be a quiet, inoffensive-looking man.
Dr. Thomas Bond

came to cutting into his victims. The image of him as a doctor or surgeon has persisted, however, thanks to reports of the Ripper carrying a Gladstone bag, often used by medical professionals.

Profiling the Ripper

Modern social scientists largely agree that the Ripper was a resident of London's East End. Although we may never know the Ripper's real name, advances in our understanding of serial killers can provide strong indications as to the kind of person he was.

There is a strong likelihood that he suffered from chronic or episodic impotence, which may have caused or resulted from his abnormal, and violent, sexual impulses. Like his fellow "rippers" Andrei Chikatilo and Robert Napper, he was probably aroused by stabbing, cutting, or mutilating his victims. An alienated individual, it is likely that he struggled to form intimate interpersonal relationships— particularly with women. These deductions may perhaps explain why he targeted prostitutes. ■

THEY'D RATHER BE DEAD THAN BE WITH ME

HARVEY GLATMAN, 1957–58

IN CONTEXT

LOCATION
Los Angeles, California, US

THEME
Trophy killers

BEFORE
1950s Wisconsin farmer Ed Gein, inspiration for Robert Bloch's novel and subsequent Hitchcock movie *Psycho*, made everyday items such as bowls out of his victims' body parts.

AFTER
1969 Police arrest serial killer and shoe fetishist Jerome Brudos in Oregon. He is later sentenced to life in prison for murdering three women.

1996 In the Ukraine, police capture Anatoly Onoprienko, responsible for killing 52 people. Onoprienko, who targets isolated properties and then murders everyone inside, keeps the underwear of his victims—both male and female—as souvenirs.

Locked in a toolbox in the apartment of Harvey Glatman was a collection of photographs. Some of the pictures showed women with their hands bound behind their backs, eyes wide with terror. Others showed the same women dead, their bodies set in particular poses.

The photographs were the personal signature of one of the most terrifying serial killers of the 1950s. They ultimately led to his conviction.

Teenage rapist

Raised in Colorado, Harvey Glatman was a skinny loner with buck teeth. As a child, he began to exhibit antisocial behavior and bizarre sexual tendencies. In his teens, he started to break into women's apartments, where he tied them up and raped them, and then took pictures as mementos.

In 1945, Glatman was caught as he broke into a house and was charged with burglary. While on bail, he raped a woman, serving eight months in prison as a result.

Following his release, Glatman moved to Albany, New York, where he was soon convicted of a series of muggings. He was imprisoned

Photographs models posing in bondage positions

↓

Photographs **the same models** as he binds and **assaults** them

↓

Photographs the models in positions of his own choosing after **strangling** them to death

↓

Keeps all of the photos to relive each stage of the crime

See also: Jack the Ripper 266–73 ▪ Ian Brady and Myra Hindley 284–85 ▪ Jeffrey Dahmer 293

Los Angeles police officers question Glatman following his arrest for his assault on Lorraine Vigil near Santa Ana, Orange County. Glatman readily confessed to all his crimes.

and diagnosed as a psychopath. However, Glatman was also a model prisoner, and he was granted parole in 1951. For the next seven years, he worked as a television repairman in Denver, Colorado.

Photographic bait
In 1957, Glatman moved to Los Angeles. Using pseudonyms, he posed as a photographer to attract pretty young women with the promise of a modeling career.

He trawled modeling agencies for victims and lured the women to hotel rooms, where he paid them to pose in bondage positions for pictures he claimed were for publication in detective magazines. Two of those models, Judith Dull and Ruth Mercado, were bound and sexually assaulted by Glatman as he photographed them. He then strangled them, photographed their bodies, and dumped them in the desert. A third victim, Shirley Ann Bridgeford, met Glatman through a classified advertisement.

On October 27, 1958, a motorcycle cop discovered Glatman attempting to abduct a woman named Lorraine Vigil. The officer saw a car pulled over at the side of the road. Inside the car, a man was aiming a pistol at a woman's head and attempting to tie her up. The officer quickly intervened and arrested Glatman.

Conviction and sentence
Knowing that investigators would soon find the incriminating photographs of his victims in his apartment, Glatman confessed to the three murders and eventually led police to the toolbox containing the images. He was found guilty of two counts of first-degree murder and sentenced to death. On September 18, 1959, Glatman was executed in the gas chamber at San Quentin State Prison.

Psychiatric study of Glatman's desire to collect souvenirs of his victims changed how serial killings are investigated in America—the FBI's Violent Crime Apprehension Program was founded to look for serial patterns in violent crime. Glatman's obsessions largely explained the serial nature of his offenses, and he was later classified as a "serial killer." ▪

Souvenir killers

Many serial killers keep mementos of their murders. Often they are trophies, used to revisit the pleasure derived from the murder. Psychiatrists say the act is a twisted deviation of the impulse that motivates collectors of mundane items, such as baseball cards, coins, or stamps.

Some of the most notorious killers have collected souvenirs. In Victorian times, Jack the Ripper was alleged to keep human remains of his victims.

A number of serial killers have, like Glatman, photographed their victims' final moments.

In a bizarre twist to this strange urge to record such gruesome crimes, there is also a market for "murderabilia:" items related to murderers. These might be the clothes worn by murderers when they committed their crimes, weapons that were used, or postcards or letters sent from jail. The online company eBay banned the sale of murderabilia in 2001, although buyers and sellers are still active on other e-commerce sites.

I JUST LIKE TO KILL

TED BUNDY, 1961–78

IN CONTEXT

LOCATION
Seven US states, from Washington to Florida

THEME
College student killer

BEFORE
1966 Richard Speck receives life imprisonment for strangling and stabbing eight student nurses in Chicago.

1973 Known as the Co-ed Killer, Edmund Kemper receives concurrent life sentences for the murders of at least six female students in California, as well as those of his own mother and best friend.

AFTER
2004 Derrick Todd Lee is convicted of murder after DNA evidence links him to a string of murders committed around Louisiana State University.

ed Bundy was a good-looking law student. He seemed charming and bright. No one would ever take him for a serial killer, like Charles Manson or Dennis Nilsen. Ted's many victims were different, too. They were mostly pretty, white, middle-class college students, and not the vulnerable women serial killers usually preyed upon.

Ted Bundy's 30 known victims did not realize they were vulnerable. They often became victims because they stopped to help him out in some way. Bundy would pose as a young man in need—wearing a fake cast on his arm, with his arm in a sling, or hobbling on crutches—eager for help with a sailboat or his schoolbooks. Once he had lured them close to his Volkswagen Beetle, Bundy reached under the car for his tire iron and hit them on the head. He then bundled them into the car and handcuffed them.

Theatrical psychopath
Bundy loved the playacting, the setup. He would also enter apartments—and even a sorority

Smooth operator Ted Bundy (center), in consultation with the Assistant Public Defender Ed Harvey (left) and a Leon County police officer, during his trial in 1979.

house— at night to abduct and kill. He was particularly drawn to college girls with long, brown hair parted in the middle. It was the style of the day, but some wondered if he was unconsciously taking his revenge on a girlfriend who had worn her hair that way. Perhaps, they speculated, she dumped him or belittled him.

See also: Jack the Ripper 266–73 ▪ Harvey Glatman 274–75 ▪ Colin Pitchfork 294–97

I don't feel guilty for anything. I feel sorry for people who feel guilt.
Ted Bundy

Disturbed child

Bundy's family background was complicated. He grew up in Philadelphia believing that his grandparents were his parents and that his real mother, Eleanor, was his sister.

From a very early age, Teddy—then Theodore Robert Cowell—enjoyed scaring people. His family later revealed how, as a three-year-old, he had delighted in placing large, sharp kitchen knives around his teenage aunt as she slept. When his aunt awoke, she was terrified, and her reaction thrilled the laughing toddler.

Dr. Dorothy Otnow Lewis, a psychiatrist who has researched the mental makeup and motives of serial killers and got to know Bundy when he was on death row, described this behavior as "extraordinarily bizarre" for such a young child. It suggests Bundy may have endured trauma at a very young age: perhaps he experienced abuse himself, or witnessed extreme violence between members of his family.

Whether it was because of the incident with the knives, or for other reasons, Teddy and Eleanor

Bundy **attracts sympathy** by wearing a sling, putting on a fake cast, or using crutches

↓

He **asks a young woman for help** gathering his books or crossing the road

↓

He **lures** the woman to his Volkswagen car

↓

He **hits the woman with a tire iron**, handcuffs her, and drives her away

↓

Murders the woman and drives her corpse to a mountainous area for burial

were sent away when Bundy was four or five. They went to Tacoma, Washington, as far west as possible, to live with an uncle. Eleanor began to use her middle name, Louise, and passed herself off as a widow or a divorcée.

In 1951, Eleanor met and later married a hospital cook named Johnnie Bundy. Together they had four children. Ted now had to share what little emotional connection he had with his mother with two brothers and two sisters. In an attempt to tighten the family ties and make Johnnie Bundy a father figure for the young Teddy, he was renamed Theodore Robert Bundy.

However, Teddy was missing something—and it was more than a father, a mother who wanted him, or a home life devoid of violence. Teddy was missing empathy. He was missing an ability to form **»**

Murder is not about lust and it's not about violence. It's about possession.
Ted Bundy

emotional bonds with his fellow human beings. He was missing a conscience.

A taste for murder

Bundy's first victim may have been eight-year-old Ann Marie Burr, who disappeared from her home in Tacoma, Washington, in the early morning of August 31, 1961. She was never found. Bundy was only 14 years old when Burr vanished and always denied having anything to do with her disappearance. However, detective Robert Keppel's claim that Bundy never revealed the name of his first victim has fueled speculation that he did kill the girl.

There is good reason to think that Ann was Bundy's first victim. Ted and his mother lived with family members in the Burr's neighborhood before his mother married. Bundy continued to visit those relatives after they moved. Although Tacoma police dismissed the speculation about Ann Burr's disappearance, her parents did not. Furthermore, Dr. Ronald Holmes, a professor in the Department of Justice Administration at the University of Louisville who interviewed Bundy in prison, claimed he admitted committing his first murder at the age of 15.

Bundy's VW, the scene of many of his crimes, was later bought by Lonnie Anderson, a former Salt Lake County sheriff's deputy, for $925, and later displayed at the US Crime Museum.

Bundy's first acknowledged murder was in January 1974. He was 27 and had graduated with a degree in psychology from the University of Washington in Seattle two years earlier. Bundy abducted 21-year-old Lynda Ann Healy, a student at the same university, from the basement bedroom of a house she shared with friends. Just over a year later, in March 1975, her skull was found on Taylor Mountain, east of Seattle.

After Healy's murder, Bundy was unstoppable. Between February 1974 and August 1975, with brief breaks of just a few weeks between murders, he killed more than a dozen young women.

Bundy's Florida victims included 21-year-old student Margaret Bowman (right), who was murdered in her bed, and 12-year-old Kimberly Leach (far right), who was abducted from school.

During this time, Bundy moved to Utah to at the University of Utah Law School.

First arrest

Bundy's first arrest came in August 1975. It was 3 a.m., and he was driving his VW through the suburbs of Salt Lake City when a highway patrol officer, Sgt. Bob Hayward, noticed that Bundy had not turned on his headlamps. When Hayward tried to pull Bundy over, a chase through residential streets ensued, which ended when Hayward cornered Bundy in an abandoned gas station. Asked by Hayward to account for his movements that night, Bundy explained that he was a Utah law student and had lost his way after leaving the local drive-in movie. Dressed in a black turtleneck and trousers, Bundy looked the part, but Hayward knew that his claim to have watched *The Towering Inferno* was a lie, because that movie was not showing locally. During a search of the vehicle, Hayward found a torn pantyhose, a crowbar, rope, and a ski mask. Although Bundy was calm and provided an explanation for having each of these items, a highly suspicious Hayward booked him for avoiding arrest.

However, it was an incident that had taken place the previous year that clinched Bundy's conviction. In November, 1974, 18-year-old Carol DaRonch was approached by Bundy in Murray, Utah. Pretending to be a police officer, Bundy claimed her car was stolen and told her to go with him to the station to fill out a report. DaRonch got into his VW, but when she pointed out that Bundy was driving away from the police station, he became aggressive and tried to handcuff her. As DaRonch struggled with Bundy, he mistakenly fixed both cuffs round the same wrist. »

Ted Bundy

When Bundy's mother, 22-year-old Eleanor Louise Cowell, found herself unmarried and pregnant in 1946, she traveled to the Elizabeth Lund Home for Unwed Mothers in Burlington, Vermont, to give birth. Her father Samuel was a violent and abusive man, dominating his children and his wife. Eleanor was unable to confirm the identity of her unborn baby's father, and rumors began to circulate that Samuel Cowell was the father.

On November 24, 1946, Theodore Robert Cowell was born. Eleanor went home, leaving her baby son at the facility. It was his first abandonment. In 1947, Eleanor returned to collect the baby at the insistence of her father. They called him Teddy.

For years, Bundy believed that Eleanor was his sister and that his grandparents were his parents. One of his high school teachers later suggested that Bundy "snapped" when, at 15, he found out he was illegitimate. After his mother married in 1951, her husband, Johnnie Bundy, legally adopted her son. But Ted, unimpressed by his stepfather's low intelligence, never bonded with him.

DaRonch escaped capture and went to the police. She described her attacker as a fairly good-looking man driving a VW and wearing a smart pair of shiny shoes.

Luckily, Detective Jerry Thompson, who was investigating the disappearances of several girls in the area, matched the appearance of the man booked by Hayward in Salt Lake City with the description that Carol DaRonch had given of her kidnapper in Murray the previous year.

A subsequent police search of Bundy's apartment found evidence that he had visited several of the towns from which girls had disappeared. When his car was examined, strands of the girls' hair implicated Bundy further. When DaRonch identified Bundy in a lineup, he was arrested for kidnapping and assault. Detectives suspected him of murder but needed hard evidence.

This came when hairs from murder victim Caryn Campbell were found in his car. On June 30, 1976, Bundy was placed in Utah State Prison, Colorado. In October, he was charged with Campbell's murder, and taken to Pitkin County Courthouse in Aspen for trial.

Escaping justice

Taking advantage of his law studies, Bundy served as his own attorney. During a break in proceedings, he was granted permission to use the court's law library. Left on his own, Bundy jumped out of a library window and made a run for Aspen Mountain. For six days, Bundy roamed hiking trails and campsites until police discovered the fugitive in a stolen car. Bundy was placed in Garfield County jail, Colorado.

His second escape involved months of preparation: Bundy got hold of the prison's floorplan and a hacksaw from fellow prisoners, cut through the ceiling of his cell, and lost enough weight to squeeze through the gap. After practicing his escape route several times, Bundy broke out of prison on December 30, 1977. He stole cars, hitchhiked, boarded planes, and traveled by train to Tallahassee, Florida, where he rented a room near Florida State University. A week after he arrived in town, Bundy crept into Chi Omega

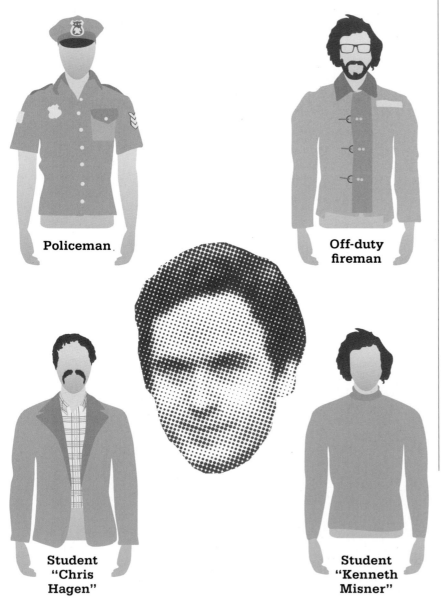

Policeman

Off-duty fireman

Student "Chris Hagen"

Student "Kenneth Misner"

Bundy took pleasure in dressing up and assuming other identities, and would flick through local telephone directories for inspiration. With the aid of various hairstyles, fake moustaches and moles, glasses, and clothes, Bundy developed a range of alteregos.

During Bundy's trial, Nita Jane Neary said she saw Bundy leaving the Chi Omega sorority house at Florida State University on the morning two students were murdered.

Several appeals for new trials and for a stay of execution were denied. In his last days on death row, Bundy confessed to 36 murders of which he was suspected, and gave details of others that had not previously been associated with him, linking him to some 50 murders in all. However, a court-appointed psychiatrist put the number of victims at around 100, and Bundy himself told Dr. Ronald Holmes that he had committed 300 murders across 10 states. Bundy offered to give more details about other missing women if his execution was postponed for a few months, but Florida Governor Bob Martinez refused to "negotiate with a killer."

On the evening of January 24, 1989, 42-year-old Ted Bundy died in the electric chair. The answer to why he killed so many women may be deduced from one of the last explanations that he gave: "I just liked to kill. I wanted to kill." ∎

sorority house late one night and attacked four young women, killing two of them. He then attacked a fifth woman in a nearby apartment.

A couple of weeks later, Bundy abducted 12-year-old Kimberly Diane Leach from in front of her school. Her body was later found in a pigpen. Within a week of her disappearance, Bundy was arrested for driving a stolen vehicle. Witnesses placed him at the sorority house and at Kimberly's school. There was also physical evidence that linked him to the murders. Convicted of all three murders, Bundy was sentenced to death.

Death row

For nine years and six months Bundy corresponded from Florida's death row with dozens of people, including Beverly Burr, the mother of Ann. He married a loyal friend,

Carole Boone, and became a father—they reportedly bribed a guard to look the other way. He "consulted" with police about other serial killers, and cooperated with authors writing about him.

Interviews with killers

Scientists researching criminal pathologies, investigators hoping for a lead, and journalists out for a sensational scoop have all been granted permission to conduct interviews with serial killers in prison. As a consequence, hundreds of hours of interview footage exists, much of it now available on the Internet.

However, the study of these interviews does not necessarily offer many insights into the mind of a serial killer. Given

a chance to present themselves and their behavior to the public outside the prison walls, serial killers are theatrical, often playing up to the interviewers' desire to gain an understanding of their subjects and to be shocked by them. From Ted Bundy's cold pretense of remorse to Charles Manson's wilfully insane diatribes and Jeffrey Dahmer's astonishingly candid responses, the performances of these men make a convincing psychological portrait of a serial killer seem increasingly elusive.

CALCULATED, CRUEL, COLD-BLOODED MURDERS

IAN BRADY AND MYRA HINDLEY, 1963–65

IN CONTEXT

LOCATION
Saddleworth Moor, near Manchester, UK

THEME
Toxic relationships

BEFORE
January 29, 1958 Teenagers Charles Starkweather and Caril Ann Fugate are arrested after a 60-day road trip across the American Midwest, during which they kill 11 people. Only 14 at the time of the spree, Fugate later claims to have been Starkweather's hostage.

AFTER
February 17, 1993 Canadian rapist and killer Paul Bernardo is sentenced to life in prison. His wife, Karla Homolka, participates in the murders, but strikes a deal with the police for a reduced sentence.

On July 12, 1963, 16-year-old Pauline Reade was on her way to a dance near Manchester in northwest England, when killer Myra Hindley pulled over in her car and convinced the teenager to get in.

Hindley, 21, drove the girl to a nearby rural area, with her boyfriend Ian Brady following closely behind on his motorcycle. Brady then raped, tortured, and sexually abused Reade, before slitting her throat and burying her body in the bogs of Saddleworth Moor.

Monstrous obsession

Reade was the couple's first victim—but she would not be their last. Between 1963 and 1965, Brady and Hindley abducted, abused, tortured, and killed four more children in a case known as the Moors Murders. Four of their victims were discovered buried on Saddleworth Moor. One of them has never been found.

Myra Hindley was 18 years old in 1961, when she began to date Ian Brady. He was 22. Despite regularly being dominated and abused by her boyfriend, Hindley became obsessed with him. In an attempt to please Brady, she began

I would always be covered in bruises and bite marks. He threatened to kill my family. He dominated me completely.
Myra Hindley

to procure vulnerable children for him to assault sexually, torture, and strangle.

Months after Pauline Reade's murder, on a Saturday afternoon in November 1963, the pair abducted 12-year-old John Kilbride. Brady raped him and then strangled the boy with a string.

Now jointly reveling in Brady's depravity, the couple abducted their next victim, 12-year-old Keith Bennett, while the boy was on his way to visit his grandmother in Manchester. On June 16, 1964, Brady and Hindley drove Bennett to Saddleworth Moor and buried him.

See also: Ted Bundy 276–83 ■ Fred and Rosemary West 286–87 ■ Colin Pitchfork 294–97

These iconic images of Ian Brady and Myra Hindley were taken during their trial for multiple murders in April 1966. Their volatile relationship caused the deaths of five innocent children.

Despite extensive and systematic searches of the moor, his body remains undiscovered.

On December 26, Brady and Hindley visited a fairground, where they approached 10-year-old Lesley Ann Downey and asked her to carry some packages. They abducted Downey, bound her with rope, and forced her to pose for pornographic photographs. The pair also made a 13-minute audio recording of Downey screaming and pleading for her life. She was then strangled and buried.

Admission and downfall

By then, Brady had grown arrogant and confided his murderous secrets to David Smith, Hindley's 17-year-old brother-in-law. In October 1965, after luring engineering student Edward Evans, also 17, to their home, Brady sent Hindley to fetch Smith, hoping to involve him in the murders. Brady then bludgeoned Evans with an axe, while Smith watched in horror. He helped Brady and Hindley to clean up, then ran home to his wife. The Smiths called the police from a telephone booth, and led them to Evans's body.

Both Brady and Hindley were arrested. During the search of the couple's home, police found the pornographic photos and audio recording of Downey, along with a large collection of pictures that were taken on Saddleworth Moor. As many as 150 police officers were assigned to conduct an extensive search of the moor. There, they discovered the bodies of Lesley Ann Downey and John Kilbride.

In 1966, Ian Brady and Myra Hindley were both found guilty of three murders. Following their conviction, they also confessed to the murders of Pauline Reade and Keith Bennett.

Aftermath

In 1987, after a 100-day-long search, Pauline Reade's decomposed body was found buried in a shallow grave on the moors. One of her killers, Myra Hindley, died in prison on November 15, 2002, at the age of 60. In 1985, Ian Brady was declared criminally insane and confined to a high-security hospital. He claims that he has no desire to be released and has repeatedly asked to be allowed to die. ■

Serial killers in abusive relationships

Throughout history, women with no previous criminal past have participated in gruesome crimes with their boyfriends and husbands. In some of these cases, the women later claimed that they were dominated and manipulated by their partners.

In an abusive relationship, a manipulative partner may attempt to isolate their lover and destroy their self-esteem. In some situations, this could lead to physical, emotional, verbal, mental, and sexual abuse. The dominant partner will attempt to control their victim, while denying them of the right to make their own decisions.

Whether this was the case with Myra Hindley is fiercely debated. The victims' families contend that she was a willing participant in the murders. However, in several interviews Hindley claimed that she did not have a compulsion to kill and that she was emotionally manipulated and physically abused by Ian Brady.

MORE TERRIBLE THAN WORDS CAN EXPRESS

FRED AND ROSEMARY WEST, 1971–87

IN CONTEXT

LOCATION
Gloucester, UK

THEME
Killer couples

BEFORE
1890–93 Australian couple
John and Sarah Jane Makin
run an orphanage at their
home. They take payments
from unwed mothers, but kill
the babies in their care and
bury them on their property.

AFTER
1986–89 An elderly couple,
Faye and Ray Copeland, kill
drifters whom they hire to
work as farmhands on their
Missouri ranch.

January–February 1987
Michigan couple Gwendolyn
Graham and Cathy Wood
kill five elderly women in the
nursing home where they both
work. They perform necrophilic
acts on their victims.

Pick up female hitchhikers in their car	**Invite** friends and prostitutes to their house for parties	Turn on their own **children**

Trap victims in their house for extended sessions of sexual torture and abuse

Kill victims if they threaten to leave the house or report the Wests' crimes

Dismember victims' bodies and bury them in their garden and local fields

In October 1972, 17-year-old Caroline Owens met Fred and Rosemary West while she was hitchhiking out of Gloucester. The Wests picked her up in their gray Ford Poplar, got chatting, and soon offered her a job as a nanny for their children. Owens moved in the next day. However, profoundly disturbed by invitations to join the couple's "sex circle," Owens quit her job and left the Wests' house within weeks.

In December, the Wests saw Owens walking alone again. They asked her to come home with them for a cup of tea, to apologize for their earlier indiscretion. Owens accepted. The couple then

See also: Ted Bundy 276–83 ▪ Ian Brady and Myra Hindley 284–85 ▪ Colin Pitchfork 294–97

subjected her to a horrifying 12-hour ordeal in which they bound and raped the 17-year-old. After the assault, Owens broke down in tears. This had some effect on Fred West, who said that she could leave, provided she promised to return and continue working as their nanny.

Traumatized, Owens fled back to her mother's house and called the police. However, Owens was too ashamed to report the rape, and so in 1973, the Wests were charged at Gloucester Magistrates Court with the lesser offense of indecent assault, fined £100 ($1,350 today), and released.

Continuing nightmare

This initial case merely hinted at the criminal depravity that went unnoticed inside the Wests' home at Cromwell Street, Gloucester, for almost 20 years. The couple "harvested" their victims by hiring teenage girls as nannies, renting rooms to young women, and abusing their own children.

In the summer of 1992, social workers and police officers once again visited the Wests' home, alerted by reports of both child

> I met Rose at sixteen and trained her to what I wanted.
> **Fred West**

An artist's impression of Fred and Rosemary West at Gloucester Magistrates Court on June 30, 1994. Fred was charged with 12 murders, but Rosemary was only charged with 10.

abuse and a missing girl. They searched the house and removed five children from the home, placing them in foster care.

However, another year elapsed before social workers called police to report comments from the rescued children about 16-year-old Heather West—daughter of Fred and Rosemary. During the search of the house the children indicated that Heather was "under the patio." This began what became the investigation of Britain's most notorious killers.

Police excavated the garden at 25 Cromwell Street and discovered not only the remains of Heather and Fred West's eight-year-old daughter Charmaine, but also the skeleton of Charmaine's mother, Catherine Costello. Charmaine is believed to have been the Wests' first victim, killed by Rosemary in 1971 in order to sever links with Costello, who was Fred's first wife. Costello was subsequently killed by the couple when they feared she suspected

what they had done to Charmaine. Fred and Rosemary's daughter Heather suffered a lifetime of molestation and beatings and was eventually murdered in June 1987 by Rosemary in her husband's absence, after a "blazing row."

In total, nine bodies were found buried at 25 Cromwell Street. One more was discovered at the Wests' previous home in Gloucester, and two others were buried nearby in a remote field. The couple were accused of collectively killing 12 people in the span of 20 years.

Fred West confessed his guilt, but used a blanket from his cell to asphyxiate himself 10 months before his trial. Rosemary maintained her innocence, but she was eventually convicted of 10 murders and sentenced to life imprisonment. ▪

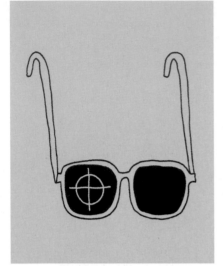

THIS IS THE ZODIAC SPEAKING

THE ZODIAC KILLER, 1968–69

IN CONTEXT

LOCATION
San Francisco, California, US

THEME
Expressive/transformative serial homicide

BEFORE
1945–46 William Heirens, the so-called "Lipstick Killer," leaves messages in lipstick at the scenes of his crimes in Chicago.

AFTER
1976–77 Serial killer David Berkowitz leaves handwritten letters signed "Son of Sam" near the bodies of his victims in the Bronx, New York.

1990–93 Heriberto Seda, a copycat Zodiac Killer, kills three people in New York.

July 4, 1969, should have been a wonderful night for Michael Mageau. Fireworks were exploding over San Francisco Bay, and he had a date with beautiful 22-year-old Darlene Ferrin. The two were sitting in Darlene's car at Blue Rock Springs in Vallejo, when a vehicle pulled up. The driver got out, shone a flashlight into their car, and began to fire a pistol at them. Ferrin died but Mageau survived. Soon after, a man phoned the Vallejo police department saying, "I want to report a murder. If you will go 1 mile east on Columbus Parkway, you will find kids in a brown car. They were shot with a 9-mm Luger. I also killed those kids last year. Goodbye."

Coded messages

On July 31, letters and coded messages arrived at the *San Francisco Chronicle*, *San Francisco Examiner*, and *Vallejo Times-Herald*. They contained a sinister threat: if the ciphers did not appear on the newspapers' front pages by the following afternoon, the author would go on a killing rampage. The letters claimed responsibility for Ferrin's murder and another double

Expressive/transformative violence

Drawing upon social psychology, criminologist Lee Mellor's expressive/transformative theory of violence proposes that offenders who communicate with the police—whether through letters, leaving messages at a crime scene, or by symbolically posing a victim's body—are engaged in a process of identity negotiation. Due to social inadequacies, the offender cannot establish an acceptable sense of self and therefore suffers from a perpetual crisis of identity. He seeks to unite his fragmented personality in the guise of a murderer, even going so far as to wear a costume and use a moniker such as "Zodiac." In his sample of 10 expressive/transformative offenders, Mellor found that 90 percent were single at the time of their offenses, and that a majority felt that they had never really grown up, were unstable in their masculinity and vocation, and obsessed with police and/or military culture.

See also: The Lindbergh Baby Kidnapping 178–85 ▪ The Black Dahlia Murder 218–23 ▪ Ted Bundy 276–83

San Francisco police circulated this composite of the "Zodiac" killer based on the accounts of three witnesses interviewed shortly after the murder of Paul Stine in October 1969.

homicide committed in Vallejo in December 1968, which had an identical *modus operandi*.

After some hesitation, the papers printed their portions of the cipher. A second letter arrived at the *Herald* on August 4, in which the author referred to himself as "the Zodiac."

Fatal finale

By August 8, 1969, a couple living in Salinas decoded the 408 symbol cryptogram, in which the author said that he hunted people. The Zodiac described killing as a thrilling experience and claimed that, after his death, the victims would be his slaves in the afterlife.

On the afternoon of August 27, Bryan Hartnell and Cecelia Shepard were relaxing at Lake Berryessa in Napa when they were approached by a gunman in a strange black mask and costume. He bound them with rope and stabbed them repeatedly. Hartnell survived to recount the details but Shepard died. Before leaving, the killer drew the Zodiac symbol on their car door.

The final murder definitively linked to the Zodiac occurred in San Francisco on October 11, 1969. That night, cabbie Paul Stine was shot in the head by a passenger with a pistol. The killer ripped away a bloodstained section of Stine's shirt, stole his wallet and keys, and wiped the car down. He was spotted by three witnesses, but a dispatcher's misreporting of their descriptions ensured that the killer was never arrested. Although police recovered a bloody fingerprint and black gloves from the taxi, the killer remained unidentified. The killer sent a letter to the *Chronicle* two days later with a bloody piece of Stine's shirt. The letters continued until 1978, but the Zodiac killer was never caught.

Prime suspect

Of all the names to surface in the hunt for the killer, that of Arthur Leigh Allen has been the most mentioned. When questioned in 1969, Allen admitted that his mother had recently given him a Zodiac brand watch, featuring a crossed circle symbol. A friend of Allen's claimed that after he received the watch, Allen mentioned a desire to murder random couples and taunt police with letters signed with the Zodiac symbol. Allen lived within minutes of the 1968–69 murders and owned the same ammunition that was used in the 1968 attack.

In 2002, 10 years after his death, Allen's DNA was compared to a saliva sample taken from a Zodiac envelope. They did not match, so he was excluded by police. It was later discovered that Allen asked others to lick envelopes for him, because he claimed that the taste of the glue made him feel nauseous. ∎

The case against Arthur Leigh Allen

Was given a **Zodiac brand wristwatch** by his mother, which featured the cross-in-the-circle symbol

Told friends he would like to **murder** random couples and taunt police with coded letters

Lived only a few minutes from the **scenes of the crimes**

Owned the same brand of **ammunition** as those used by the **Zodiac**

IN HIS OWN EYES, HE WAS SOME SORT OF MEDICAL GOD
HAROLD SHIPMAN, 1975–98

IN CONTEXT

LOCATION
Hyde, near Manchester, UK

THEME
Medical homicides

BEFORE
1881–92 Dr. Thomas Neill Cream, a Scottish-Canadian medical practitioner, poisons multiple US and British women with chloroform.

1895–1901 Jane Toppan, a Massachusetts nurse, poisons at least 30 victims, including her patients and family.

1970–82 "Angel of Death" Donald Harvey murders between 37 and 57 patients in various hospitals, using an extensive range of methods.

AFTER
1988–2003 Charles Cullen kills 40 patients during his time as a nurse in New Jersey.

2001–02 Colin Norris, a male nurse, kills many of his elderly patients in Glasgow, Scotland.

Married since the age of 20, and a father of four, Dr. Harold Shipman was seen as a kindly doctor. There had been a blip in 1975 when he was caught forging prescriptions to sate his pethidine addiction, but after he paid the £600 ($5,665 today) fine and went to rehab, his indiscretion soon passed out of memory.

Nevertheless, the frequency with which his patients died suddenly and unexpectedly did not entirely escape notice. Observing that an unusually high number of female senior citizens in Shipman's care chose cremation for their end, a funeral parlor employee voiced her suspicions to Dr. Linda Reynolds of Brooke Surgery in Hyde, who in turn passed them on to the South Manchester District coroner. However, after a cursory check, the police found no evidence of any wrongdoing.

Vanished reputation
John Shaw was a cabbie who regularly drove Shipman's patients to his office in Hyde, and became friends with many of them. In March 1995, the sudden death of Netta Ashcroft left Shaw feeling that something was amiss. Well aware of the doctor's good reputation in the community and convinced that the police would not believe him, Shaw maintained a tortured silence as more and more of Shipman's patients died. It was not until August 1998 that Shaw was convinced that Shipman had murdered 21 of his patients—and finally voiced his concerns to the police.

The harmless looks of Dr. Harold Shipman in this police mugshot taken at the time of his arrest belie the reality of his terrible crimes. The doctor's activities went unnoticed for years.

See also: Burke and Hare 22–23 ▪ John Edward Robinson 298–99 ▪ The Poisoning of Alexander Litvinenko 326–31

By that time, Shipman had already slipped up. On June 24, 1998, 81-year-old Kathleen Grundy, the wealthy former mayor of Hyde, was discovered dead in her home. When Grundy's daughter, lawyer Angela Woodruff, read the will—which declared that all Grundy's wealth was to be given to her doctor, Harold Shipman, instead of to her family—Woodruff immediately alerted the authorities to the forgery. Grundy's body was exhumed and traces of the analgesic diamorphine, an opioid used for pain relief, were found in her system. Shipman, who had listed her cause of death as "old age," was arrested on September 7. A typewriter of the same make used to forge Grundy's will was recovered from Shipman's office, and his fingerprints were found all over the document.

Arrogance and denial

Following these revelations, police brought charges against Shipman for the murder of 15 other female patients. On January 31, 2000, he was convicted on all counts. Rather than obtaining £386,000 ($764,500 today) from Kathleen Grundy's will, Shipman received 15 concurrent life sentences. In a subsequent enquiry, he was found responsible for a minimum of 218 deaths. The real number may exceed 250.

Despite overwhelming evidence of his guilt, Shipman refused to confess. He turned his back on police interviewers throughout hours of extensive interrogation. However, one day before his 58th birthday, Shipman hanged himself from his cell window. A fellow prisoner explained that Shipman had recently received a letter from his entirely supportive wife, Primrose, asking him to tell her "everything, no matter what."

The notion that Shipman was addicted to holding power over life and death has largely been accepted as his motive, because his clumsy attempt at financial benefit actually precipitated his downfall. However, of the 100 items of her jewelry seized by police, Primrose could only prove that 66 items belonged to her. ▪

He simply … enjoyed the feeling of control over life and death.
Coroner John Pollard

Shipman **visits** his patients **at their home**

⬇

Injects patients with a **lethal dose** of heroin

⬇

Provides **fake** causes of death and advocates **cremations**

⬇

Murders at least 218 patients before he is caught by authorities

---

Victimization of the elderly

In 2006, British criminologist David Wilson pointed out that the elderly represent a large part of the victim demographic in the UK. The figure, however, was vastly inflated by Harold Shipman's many killings.

Wilson noted that the old—particularly those estranged from their family or without one—often endure invisible lives in which weeks or months might pass without anybody checking on them. Due to inadequate social services, impoverished retirees often occupy dwellings that are easy to break into in places where there is often little sense of community. Deaths of the aged are also more likely to be attributed to natural causes than those of other citizens and they are therefore less likely to be investigated.

It is notable that the vast majority of Shipman's victims were working or lower-middle class men and women. Only the death of a wealthy, high-profile citizen finally aroused suspicion.

A MISTAKE OF NATURE
ANDREI CHIKATILO, 1978–90

IN CONTEXT

LOCATION
Union of Soviet Socialist Republics (USSR)

THEME
Serial mutilators

BEFORE
1944 Los Angeles resident Otto Wilson kills and eviscerates prostitutes to satisfy a perverse erotic desire.

AFTER
1985–99 Peter Dupas murders at least three women in Melbourne, Australia. He removes the breasts from his victims as souvenirs.

1992–93 Robert Napper sexually attacks dozens of women in Plumstead, UK, and kills three of them. He keeps body parts from his victims as trophies.

The official party line was that there were no serial killers in the USSR—but from early 1983, when the mutilated bodies of numerous young women and children were found in the wilderness around Rostov-on-Don, the authorities were forced to reassess. The wound patterns were so striking that police were forced to admit that a single predator was responsible for at least six murders.

Following extensive surveillance, a detective arrested Andrei Chikatilo. He was carrying a knife and rope, and resembled a man suspected of murder. They obtained a sample of his blood, but it was found to be Type A; the killer's semen indicated a blood type of AB, so Chikatilo was released.

In 1990, a spike in the killings encouraged the police to step up their activity. On November 6, Chikatilo was spotted leaving the woods near Donleskhoz station. His knees and elbows were stained and his cheeks smeared red. The undercover officer looked over his earlier papers and filed a report.

Soviet serial killer Andrei Chikatilo, during court hearings in 1993, which revealed the full horror of his 52 brutal killings to a stunned Russian public.

When a young woman's body was found in the same woods, Chikatilo's name resurfaced. He was arrested and a sample of his semen taken. It was discovered to be type AB—Chikatilo was a rare individual whose blood type differed from that of his semen. Chikatilo confessed and was executed in February 1994. ∎

See also: Jack the Ripper 266–73 ▪ Ted Bundy 276–83 ▪ Colin Pitchfork 294–97

I WAS SICK OR EVIL, OR BOTH

JEFFREY DAHMER, 1978–91

IN CONTEXT

LOCATION
Ohio and Wisconsin, US

THEME
Killer necrophiliacs

BEFORE
1947–52 Ed Gein steals
bodies from graves in
Wisconsin and makes
keepsakes from the remains.

1964–73 Edmund Kemper
embarks on a crazed spree
of necrophilia, serial killing,
and cannibalism in his
native California.

1978–83 Dennis Nilsen
strangles and kills around 12
men at his home in London,
England. He stores some of the
bodies under the floorboards.

AFTER
1994–2004 Sean Gillis rapes
and murders eight women in
Louisiana. He is unable to
account for the brutality of
his mutilations.

Just before midnight on
July 22, 1991, a distraught
young man with a handcuff
dangling from his wrist approached
two Milwaukee police officers. He
said that some "freak" had tried to
restrain him. The three men headed
back to the aggressor's apartment.
They were greeted at the door by
the tenant, Jeffrey Dahmer.

Dahmer tried to talk his way out
of the situation, but the appalling
stench of death gave him away. In
Dahmer's bedroom, an officer found
Polaroid photos of nude male bodies
in varying stages of dismemberment.
The background in the photos
indicated that they had been taken
in that very same room. Dahmer
was immediately arrested. The
police then searched his apartment
and discovered boxes, a 57-gallon
(260-liter) drum, a freezer, and a
fridge filled with human body parts.
Painted skulls and a complete human
skeleton hung from his shower head.

Back at the police station,
Dahmer confessed to the murders
of 17 young men, and engaging in
necrophilic acts with their corpses.

Dahmer also admitted that he had
experimented with cannibalism, by
eating the body parts of his victims.

Trial and death
Dahmer's trial began on January 30,
1992. The purpose of the trial was to
determine whether or not he was
criminally responsible for his actions.
Despite persuasive arguments from
both sides, he was declared sane,
and received 15 life sentences. He
was beaten to death with a metal bar
by fellow prison inmate Christopher
Scarver on November 28, 1994. ■

I acted on my fantasies
and… everything
went wrong.
Jeffrey Dahmer

See also: Jack the Ripper 266–73 ▪ Ted Bundy 276–83

A DANGER TO YOUNG WOMEN

COLIN PITCHFORK, 1983–86

IN CONTEXT

LOCATION
Leicestershire, UK

THEME
DNA convictions

BEFORE
1968–72 Samuel P. Evans of Seattle is convicted for two murders 39 years after the crimes were committed, in the oldest cases ever solved using DNA evidence.

AFTER
1987 Serial rapist Tommie Lee Andrews is the first criminal in the US to be convicted as a result of DNA evidence.

1988 Virginian Timothy Wilson Spencer becomes the first US murderer convicted as a result of DNA testing.

2003 Steven Avery of Wisconsin is exonerated by DNA evidence, and released after 18 years in prison.

O n August 2, 1986, the small English village of Narborough was shaken by the discovery of the body of a 15-year-old girl. Dawn Ashworth had vanished two days earlier on her way home from a friend's house. She had been assaulted, raped, and strangled to death. Her body was found in a field near the footpath she had taken. Forensic analysis was able to identify a semen sample, which proved that the criminal was a male with type A blood and a rare enzyme profile.

Three years before Dawn's murder, on November 21, 1983, Lynda Mann's body had also been found on a Narborough footpath.

See also: The Stratton Brothers 212–15 ■ Kirk Bloodsworth 242–43
■ Harvey Glatman 274–75

Like Dawn Ashworth, she was 15 years old and a victim of assault, rape, and strangulation. Police had never solved the crime, but a semen sample taken at the time matched the blood type and enzyme profile of Dawn Ashworth's killer.

The similarities between the circumstances of the girls' deaths, as well as this genetic link, led police investigating the murder of Dawn Ashworth to believe that both crimes were committed by the same man. Headlines in local newspapers reflected the villagers' fear that it was only a matter of time until the murderer claimed his third victim: "If we don't catch him, it could be your daughter next."

Colin Pitchfork, depicted by a court artist, appeals against the length of his sentence at the Court of Appeal in London in May 2009. His 30-year sentence was commuted by two years.

Genetic fingerprinting

Local police contacted the geneticist Dr. Alec Jeffreys about the murders of the two girls. They hoped to use his recently discovered "genetic fingerprinting" technique to further their investigations. They had a suspect in custody, 17-year old Richard Buckland, who had learning disabilities. Buckland's confession confused the police. He admitted to committing the first murder, but not the second. However, at the time »

DNA and forensic evidence

Deoxyribonucleic acid (DNA) is a molecule that stores and carries all our biological information. Every individual has a different pattern. In 1981, Professor Alec Jeffreys, a British geneticist from the University of Leicester, was studying hereditary diseases in families when he discovered the technique for genetic fingerprinting—a crucial way for modern criminologists to identify individuals from forensic evidence.

Nazi war criminal Josef Mengele (pictured below) fled to South America at the end of World War II. He died in 1979, at age 67, when he had a swimming accident in Brazil. However, repeated sightings of Mengele reported around the world led to doubts about his death and calls for him to be brought to justice for his crimes. It was only when Jeffreys compared DNA from a thigh bone of Mengele's exhumed skeleton with DNA from his son, Rolf, that the so-called "Angel of Death" could be conclusively confirmed as deceased.

of Lynda Mann's murder, Buckland was just 14 years old. Of course, the police realized that children sometimes kill other children—however, they delayed charging Buckland until they learned more about the second murder. Could it be the work of a copycat?

Dr. Jeffreys compared the genetic profiles of the semen samples from both murders against that of a blood sample from Buckland. This proved conclusively that both girls were killed by the same man—and that man was not Buckland, who was released. The police launched a manhunt, asking 5,000 men in three surrounding towns to give a sample of their blood or saliva. Jeffreys was amazed at the trust the police put in him, and in the new science of DNA fingerprinting. It took six months to process the 5,000 samples. No match was found.

The course of justice

Local man Colin Pitchfork, a baker, had previously been questioned by the police about his whereabouts on the night that Lynda Mann was killed. He truthfully informed them

that he had been with his son, and was released from further questioning. As one of the 5,000 men tested by the police, Pitchfork gave a DNA sample. His sample, like many others, did not match the killer's. However, months after all the DNA had been checked, a colleague of Pitchfork's named Ian Kelly was overheard bragging during a drunken conversation at a local pub. Kelly claimed that he had taken the DNA test on Colin Pitchfork's behalf.

Kelly was asked to take the test as a favor to Pitchfork, who falsely claimed to have taken it already in the name of a friend who had a conviction for indecent exposure. Kelly accepted the illegal invitation. Pitchfork doctored his passport to allow Kelly to enter one of the testing stations using Pitchfork's identity.

After six weeks, a woman who overheard the conversation in the pub went to the police. As a result of her evidence, Pitchfork was immediately arrested. Dr. Jeffreys compared Pitchfork's DNA with that of the semen found on the two

> I have no doubt whatsoever that Buckland would have been found guilty had it not been for DNA evidence.
> **Professor Sir Alec Jeffreys**

victims. It was a perfect match. Instead of going to trial, Pitchfork pleaded guilty to both rapes and murders. His claim to have been with his son on the night of Lynda Mann's murder was true—but he had left his son in the car while he committed the crime.

Evolution of a killer

After interviewing Kelly, the police and judge said that his immense gullibility made it "just about" possible to believe that Kelly was taken in by Pitchfork's lie. When Pitchfork was eventually convicted, he would receive an additional charge for perverting the course of justice by manipulating Kelly.

During questioning, Pitchfork revealed his development from flasher to killer. He relished the fact that he had exposed himself to hundreds of women and girls, a compulsion that began in his early teens. Pitchfork had no problem describing some of the girls he exposed himself to in order for the police to verify his

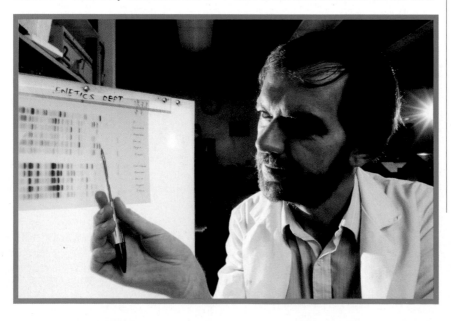

British geneticist Professor Sir Alec Jeffreys studies DNA codes in his laboratory at Leicester University. His groundbreaking technique has transformed criminal investigations.

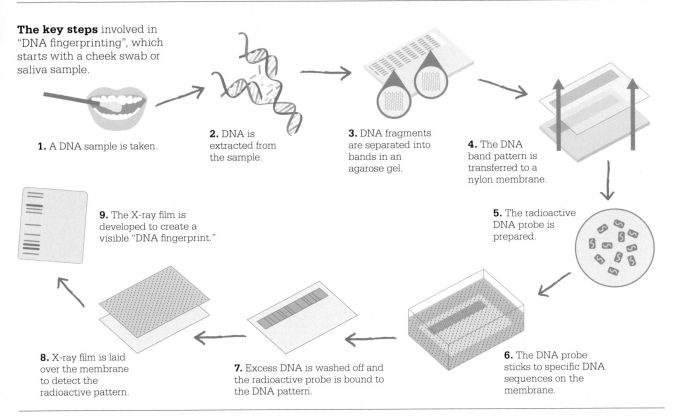

The key steps involved in "DNA fingerprinting", which starts with a cheek swab or saliva sample.

1. A DNA sample is taken.

2. DNA is extracted from the sample.

3. DNA fragments are separated into bands in an agarose gel.

4. The DNA band pattern is transferred to a nylon membrane.

9. The X-ray film is developed to create a visible "DNA fingerprint."

5. The radioactive DNA probe is prepared.

8. X-ray film is laid over the membrane to detect the radioactive pattern.

7. Excess DNA is washed off and the radioactive probe is bound to the DNA pattern.

6. The DNA probe sticks to specific DNA sequences on the membrane.

claims. Two further counts of sexual assault were brought against Pitchfork as a result of his willingness to provide details of his crimes.

Pitchfork revealed that soon after he started flashing girls, he also began to follow them. The rapes of Lynda Mann and Dawn Ashworth insidiously developed out of this tendency—the result of pure opportunism as Pitchfork spotted them in a secluded area. The state of the teenagers' bodies indicated that Pitchfork had beaten them before he strangled them to death.

During questioning, Pitchfork was totally unwilling to accept the violent brutality of his behavior, and exhibited a psychopathic lack of empathy. Pitchfork claimed that he strangled both of his victims purely to protect his identity.

Colin Pitchfork was the world's first killer to be convicted of murder based on DNA fingerprinting. He was sentenced to life in prison, with a minimum term of 30 years. It was evident from the trial that Pitchfork was compulsively violent toward women. There was every chance that he would murder again, given the opportunity.

Appeal for clemency

In 2009, Pitchfork appealed his sentence. The court heard how well Pitchfork had adapted to prison life. He had spent his time training to transcribe printed music into Braille and promised to help the blind when he was released. He had studied and become well educated, had never been in trouble while in custody, and was trusted to help fellow inmates adapt to prison life. His victims' families

were unimpressed. "Life should mean life," said the mother of one of the girls.

Pitchfork's sentence was reduced to 28 years, with the caveat that "the safety of the public is assured." While in prison, he also became an artist. One of the sculptures he produced was exhibited at the Royal Festival Hall in London in April 2009. Entitled "Bringing the Music to Life," it depicted a miniature orchestra and choir, made in meticulous detail by folding and tearing the score of Beethoven's "Ninth Symphony." It was sold for £600 (about $750). However, when British newspapers heard about it, the public was outraged and the sculpture was removed from display.

In 2016, thirty years after Dawn Ashworth's murder, Pitchfork was denied parole. He was, however, moved to an open prison. ∎

READ YOUR AD. LET'S TALK ABOUT THE POSSIBILITIES
JOHN EDWARD ROBINSON, 1984–99

IN CONTEXT

LOCATION
Kansas and Missouri, US

THEME
Classified ad killers

BEFORE
1900–08 Belle Gunness kills dozens of the suitors she meets through classified ads.

1947–49, Martha Beck and Raymond Fernandez, known as the "Lonely Hearts Killers," meet their victims through classified lonely heart ads.

AFTER
2005 In Osaka, Japan, Hiroshi Maeue seeks sexual gratification by strangling three people that he meets via an online suicide club. He receives the death sentence.

2011 Preacher Richard Beasley and his 16-year-old accomplice Brogan Rafferty kill three middle-aged men whom Beasley lured into the Ohio wilderness with a Craigslist ad for a job on a cattle ranch.

I n 1984, 19-year-old Paula Godfrey accepted an offer to work as a sales representative for Equi-II. The balding founder of the company, John Edward Robinson, arrived at the Godfreys' home on September 1 to pick up Paula for training in San Antonio, Texas. Two days later, a handwritten letter, allegedly from Paula, was delivered to her parents. It stated that she was safe, but her father was suspicious and went to the police. Paula was put on the missing persons' list, until a second letter, also from "Paula," arrived at the police department. This letter claimed that she did not wish to see her family; believing the letter to be genuine, police dropped the case.

Three more victims
That same year, Robinson accepted $2,000 to arrange an adoption for his childless brother and sister-in-law. Masquerading as "John Osborne," he lured 19-year-old Lisa Stasi and her baby, Tiffany, to a motel on January 10, 1985. The following day, Robinson met his brother and sister-in-law at the airport and handed the baby over to them along with a set of forged adoption papers. Lisa Stasi simply disappeared.

John Edward Robinson used online forums for BDSM—bondage and discipline, dominance and submission, sadism and masochism—in order to select his murder victims.

In 1987, Robinson struck again. After answering a newspaper job advertisement, Catherine Clampitt, 27, left her child behind in Texas and moved to Kansas City. Her family never saw her again.

From 1987 to 1993, Robinson served time for a number of fraud convictions. At Western Missouri Correctional Facility, Robinson befriended prison librarian Beverly

See also: Harvey Glatman 274–75 ▪ Ted Bundy 276–83 ▪ Andrei Chikatilo 292 ▪ Jeffrey Dahmer 293

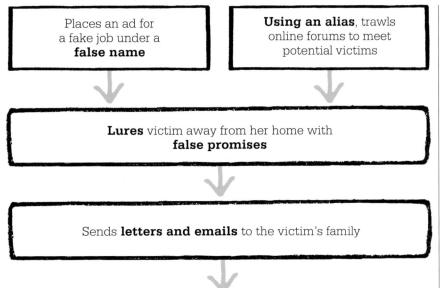

Places an ad for a fake job under a **false name**

Using an alias, trawls online forums to meet potential victims

Lures victim away from her home with **false promises**

Sends **letters and emails** to the victim's family

Murders the victim, steals her identity, and continues to cash her checks

Bonner. When he was paroled in 1993, the 49-year-old Bonner separated from her husband and moved to Kansas to work for one of Robinson's companies. Once her mother began to forward her alimony checks to Robinson's P.O. box, Bonner also disappeared.

The move online

In the early 1990s, Robinson was part of a secret sadomasochist group called the International Council of Masters, and he turned to the same type of community when his hunt for victims moved online. Under the username "Slavemaster," he searched Internet messageboards for women who classified themselves as sexual submissives. In 1994, he met 45-year-old Sheila Faith on a forum. Claiming to be wealthy, he offered

Sheila a job and promised to pay for her wheelchair-bound daughter Debbie to have medical treatment.

Sheila believed she had met her dream man. That summer, she and Debbie went to Kansas City to meet Robinson. Their social security checks were soon redirected to a P.O. box in Kansas. At Christmas, Sheila's sisters received typed letters with Sheila's signature, but she was already dead.

Robinson continued to lure women to Kansas City with job offers and a slave/master sexual relationship. Some women balked at signing blank stationery, or escaped when Robinson's behavior in the bedroom crossed over from dominance into outright sadism.

Others were less lucky: first, Polish immigrant Izabela Lewicka, then 27-year-old Suzette Trouten

both fell prey to him. Suzette, however, would be Robinson's downfall. She had agreed to keep in regular phone contact with her mother, but on March 1 her calls were replaced by emails. These emails sounded nothing like Suzette, and her sister, Dawn, called the police on March 25, 2000.

Robinson's ruse was soon discovered. Searches of his trailer and storage locker revealed it all: financial papers belonging to Lisa Stasi, Beverly Bonner, and the Faiths; blank paper presigned by Suzette; photographs of Izabela in bondage; videos of Robinson and his victims engaging in BDSM; slave contracts, and more.

The following morning, a K-9 police dog search of Robinson's Linn County farm revealed Suzette and Izabela's bodies in big plastic drums. Beverley Bonner's and the Faiths' remains were found soon afterward in a storage locker in Raymore, Missouri. Although Stasi, Godfrey, and Clampitt were never found, Robinson was convicted of eight counts of murder and sentenced to death. ▪

Anyone could create an email account and sign it as you. If you would telephone, I would feel much, much better.
Andrew Lewicki

ASSASS
AND POL
PLOTS

NATIONS
TICAL

The Praetorian Guard in imperial Rome stab Emperor Pertinax to death and award the role of emperor to the highest bidder.

193 CE

Actor and Confederate supporter John Wilkes Booth **assassinates Abraham Lincoln** at a theater in Washington, D.C.

1865

In Russia, Grigori Rasputin, mystical adviser to the imperial family, is **poisoned, shot, and dumped** in the Nevka River.

1916

1100s–1200s

A militant order of Shia Muslims known as the **Hashashins** assassinate Seljuk Turks and other Sunni opponents.

1894

French Army captain **Alfred Dreyfus** is convicted of passing secrets to the Germans.

While the methods of political plotters and assassins have changed over time, their motives remain the same. Political plots are typically undertaken with the goal of attaining power. They can be protests against poor leadership or controversial policies, or attempts at censoring a powerful voice. When the Praetorian Guard overthrew Pertinax in 193 CE they were able to choose the next ruler of the Roman Empire.

The political plots in this chapter all had far-reaching consequences. The removal of one important figure can be enough to transform a place or an organization for the better, or cause widespread chaos. It is often achieved through assassination—the targeted murder of an influential figure.

Assassinations are typically planned in secret. For conspirators to succeed, they must be discreet, and the element of surprise is often key to their success. Historically, when a conspirator has been caught before the plot is executed, the consequences have been severe. Guy Fawkes, who failed to blow up the British Parliament in the 1605 Gunpowder Plot, was hanged, drawn, and quartered for his part in the treasonous plan.

Some of the major turning points in history have hinged upon assassinations: the death of Archduke Franz Ferdinand by the clandestine society Black Hand, for example, is often cited as the catalyst for the start of World War I. Other assassinations achieved the opposite of the intended effect by making the victims martyrs.

Global consequences
Political plots are very rarely hatched by a lone figure with a personal vendetta. Even when a single killer is involved, bigger forces are generally at work behind the scenes. These can be underground organizations— radical groups, guerrillas, or terrorists—but sometimes they are government agencies or the power bases of other politicians.

Just as there is infrequently only one plotter, there is rarely just one victim. An assassination can have far-reaching consequences. In Italy, the death of former prime minister Aldo Moro, 55 days after he was kidnapped by a group of Red Brigades terrorists, ended a proposed compromise between the Italian Communist Party and Christian Democratic Party, while

In Rome, the former
Italian prime minister
Aldo Moro is ambushed
and shot dead by the
left-wing paramilitary
Red Brigades.

Former **Russian spy
Alexander Litvinenko**
is poisoned with
radioactive polonium
at a London hotel.

1978

2006

1963

2002

Lee Harvey Oswald
**shoots US President
John F. Kennedy** as
he rides through Dallas
in an open-top car.

One-time Colombian
**presidential candidate
Ingrid Betancourt** is
kidnapped by guerrillas.

the poisoning in 2006 of former
Russian spy Alexander Litvinenko
in a London hotel, which was
believed to be perpetrated by
fellow Russians, led to a tit-for-tat
expulsion of diplomats from
Russian and British embassies.

Protective measures

Bringing political plotters to justice
is often difficult. While authorities
can arrest an individual perpetrator
once an assassination has been
committed, the shadowy nature
of their plots may make it hard
to identify coconspirators. Lee
Harvey Oswald apparently worked
alone when he shot President
John F. Kennedy, but numerous
conspiracy theories suggest he
may have been the puppet of other
bodies, such as the CIA or the
Soviet Union. Likewise, the truth

behind the murder of Alexander
Litvinenko is not fully understood,
although evidence does point
strongly to Andrey Lugovoi, whose
extradition was requested by the
British government in May 2007
but refused by Russia.

These days, technological
advancements help government
agencies, such as the FBI, the CIA,
and the National Security Agency
(NSA), to uncover and prevent
political conspiracies. While the
world's secret services once relied
on spies to intercept documents
and source physical evidence of
assassination plots, they can now
also call upon techniques and
equipment, such as surveillance
drones and wire-taps.

Most nations have not enacted
specific laws to prevent political
plots. Instead, laws focus on

prohibiting the means the
perpetrators use: murder, bribery,
and kidnapping, for example, are
all illegal, as are conspiracies to
commit them. Assassination has
always been illegal because it is
murder, but there are usually
harsher penalties for killing people
in positions of power.

Most nations around the world
do, however, have treason laws,
which punish those acting against
the nation or the crown. In Britain,
for example, the monarch was free
to determine what constituted
treason until 1351, when the
Treason Act defined the offenses
deemed treasonous. In the US,
Article III of the US Constitution—
ratified in 1788—limited treason to
either levying war against the state
or providing enemies of the state
with aid and comfort. ■

INSATIABLE AND DISGRACEFUL LUST FOR MONEY
THE ASSASSINATION OF PERTINAX, 193 CE

IN CONTEXT

LOCATION
Rome, Italy

THEME
Assassination of a head of state

BEFORE
44 CE Roman dictator Julius Caesar is assassinated by members of the Senate, the Roman Republic's governing and advisory council, who are unhappy with his social and political reforms.

AFTER
1610 Henry IV of France is killed by François Ravaillac, a Catholic fanatic who does not trust the Protestant king's conversion to Catholicism.

October 31, 1984 India's prime minister, Indira Gandhi, is killed in a hail of bullets fired by two of her Sikh bodyguards, in retaliation for an attack that she ordered on the holy Sikh shrine at Amritsar on June 6 of that year.

Helvius Pertinax became ruler of the Roman Empire in January 193, after the murder of Emperor Commodus. The disastrous reign of his predecessor had left the empire's finances so depleted that Pertinax initiated cuts to state spending. The move was unpopular, especially with the Praetorian Guard—soldiers of the emperor's household—who plotted to remove Pertinax from the throne.

Sale of the empire

The Praetorian Guard thought the sums Pertinax gave in exchange for their service were too small. They refused to believe that treasury funds were insufficient to offer more, and on March 28, they mutinied. Some 300 men stormed the palace, and although he was warned to leave, Pertinax decided to confront them. He hoped to quell the uprising, but instead, he was stabbed to death.

In the power vacuum that followed, the Praetorian Guard decreed that no new emperor would be chosen without their approval. Pertinax's father-in-law, Flavius Sulpicianus, offered the soldiers 5,000 drachmas each if they would appoint him emperor. Instead, they decided to sell the throne to the highest bidder. Consul Didius Julianus saw his chance. He went to the guards' camp, and when asked to wait outside, he shouted his monetary offer from the foot of the rampart. He won the auction, and the empire was sold for 6,250 drachmas per soldier. Julianus became emperor, but just 66 days later, he too was murdered. ∎

I see that you need a ruler, and I myself am best fitted of any to rule you.
Didius Julianus

See also: The Assassination of Abraham Lincoln 306–09 ∎ The Assassination of John F. Kennedy 316–21

MURDERING SOMEONE BY CRAFT
THE HASHASHIN, 11TH–13TH CENTURIES

IN CONTEXT

LOCATION
Persia and Syria, southwestern Asia

THEME
Assassination for political and religious motives

AFTER
1336–1600 In Japan, covert agents called ninja, or *shinobi*, are hired as spies, surprise attackers, and assassins.

1948 Mahatma Gandhi, leader of the nationalist movement against British rule in India, is assassinated by a young Hindu with extremist links.

1965 Civil rights activist Malcolm X is assassinated by three members of the Nation of Islam while giving a speech in New York. He had a falling out with the leaders of the African American movement—which blended elements of Islam with black nationalism—a few years earlier.

The Hashashin, also known as the "Assassins," was a military religious order founded by Hassan-i-Sabbah in Persia (modern-day Iran). Sabbah was the leader of Shia Islamic sect, the Nizari Ismailites. In 1090, he decided to expand Nizari interests and oppose the Seljuk Turks—Sunni Muslims who had conquered Persia. Sabbah traveled to the ancient castle of Alamut, in the mountain kingdom of Daylam, a province of the Seljuk Empire. Once inside, he secretly converted prominent residents to his cause, and captured the fortress in a bloodless coup from within.

From Alamut, Sabbah sent missionaries into enemy territories to find further Shia converts. When the missionaries were unable to turn one *muezzin*, they killed him so he could not report their efforts. However, the *vizier* soon found out, and executed the missionaries' leader. In response, Sabbah sent an assassin to murder the official using the Hashashin's weapon of choice—the quiet dagger. He was

Hasan-i-Sabbah issues orders to two of his assassins at the castle of Alamut. The Hashashin assassinated at least 14 high-profile individuals, including royalty.

the first of many prominent Seljuks, Persians, and later, Crusaders, to be killed for opposing the order.

Assassination was employed as a political tool by the Hashashin throughout their history. After the Mongols swept into Persia in 1228, the order's power began to ebb. ∎

See also: The Assassination of Abraham Lincoln 306–09 ∎ The Assassination of John F. Kennedy 316–21 ∎ The Abduction of Aldo Moro 322–23

SIC SEMPER TYRANNIS!

THE ASSASSINATION OF ABRAHAM LINCOLN, APRIL 14, 1865

IN CONTEXT

LOCATION
Washington, D.C., US

THEME
Political assassination

BEFORE
336 BCE Philip II, king of Macedonia, is assassinated by one of his bodyguards, Pausanias, for reasons that are unknown. He is succeeded by his son, Alexander the Great.

AFTER
1995 Israeli prime minister Yitzhak Rabin is assassinated by a Jewish extremist while attending a peace rally.

2007 Benazir Bhutto, the former prime minister of Pakistan, and two dozen others are killed by a suicide bomb at a political rally during an election campaign.

Maryland native and well-known actor John Wilkes Booth became an advocate of slavery after working in Virginia. When the American Civil War broke out in 1861, Booth supported the Southern cause and became a Confederate sympathizer. During his tours of the nation's theaters, he worked undercover to smuggle supplies to Confederate troops. As the conflict deepened, so did Booth's loathing of the abolitionists of the northern Union states, and President Abraham Lincoln in particular.

In March 1865, as the Civil War entered its final throes, Booth and several associates in Washington, D.C. hatched a plot to kidnap the president and take him to the

See also: The Assassination of John F. Kennedy 316–21 ▪ The Abduction of Aldo Moro 322–23

Armed with a derringer pistol and a hunting knife, Booth arrived at Ford's Theatre at about 9:30 p.m. He had a drink in a nearby saloon and then fatally shot the president.

Confederate capital, Richmond, Virginia. Their plan was foiled on April 9, 1865, when Confederate General Robert E. Lee surrendered what was left of his army to Union forces led by Ulysses S. Grant and effectively ended the Civil War. Booth heard the news of the Confederacy's collapse three days later and was filled with a burning desire to destroy the president.

Death at the theater

On the morning of April 14, Booth found out that Lincoln would be attending a performance of the comedy *Our American Cousin* that evening at Ford's Theatre. Rounding up his coconspirators, he told them about his audacious plan to create chaos at the heart of government: the simultaneous assassination of Lincoln, Vice President Andrew Johnson, and

Secretary of State William Seward. Booth himself would deal with the president and two of his associates would kill the other politicians.

That evening at Ford's Theatre, Booth made his way to the private box above the stage where Lincoln and his wife, Mary Todd Lincoln, were watching the play with two guests. He found it unprotected—John F. Parker of the Washington police had escorted Lincoln to the venue, but he was not standing guard when Booth arrived. Some accounts suggest that Parker may have slipped off for a drink. At about 10:15 p.m., Booth went into the box and barred the door. **»**

Motives for Assassination

The term "assassination" refers to the murder of a person (often a high-profile, public figure) by a surprise attack. When political leaders are assassinated, the motive is their removal from power, so assassins often act in response to tyrannical rule.

Assassinations therefore often occur in societies with deep social and ideological rifts, with lone assassins rising up from the populace to violently express their dissatisfaction with the status quo.

While many assassins work alone, others operate within insurgent groups with the intention of causing disorder.

Some assassins target high-profile figures with whose beliefs they disagree. James Earl Ray had racist motives for shooting civil rights activist Dr. Martin Luther King Jr. in 1968. Others, however, do not have a personal or ideological vendetta: they are simply guns for hire, paid by powerful individuals or groups to eliminate their enemies.

The ballot is stronger than the bullet.
Abraham Lincoln

Booth plans to **abduct** President Lincoln in exchange for the release of Confederate soldiers → He **fails** to enact his kidnap plan

Booth is angered when Lincoln makes a speech supporting limited black suffrage

Lincoln is **reelected** in November, 1864

In April 1865, **the South surrenders** to the Union, ending the American Civil War → **Booth comes up with a plan to assassinate President Lincoln**

At the very instant an amusing scene in the play prompted a loud laugh from the audience, Booth fired a single shot from his .44-caliber derringer into the back of Lincoln's head. The bullet entered behind the president's right ear and lodged behind his right eye. Booth, ever the actor, dropped his pistol and shouted in triumph, "Sic semper tyrannis!" The Latin phrase, meaning "thus always to tyrants"—and short for "thus always I bring death to tyrants"—was the motto of his

adopted state of Virginia. Other members of the audience claimed he also cried: "The South is avenged!"

The dramatics gave those in the box time to react. One of Lincoln's guests lunged at the assassin. Booth stabbed him in the arm with a knife, then leapt from the box onto the stage, falling awkwardly as his boot spur caught on a flag, and breaking his left shin. He was able to reach the alley outside, and rode away on his horse, which had been held for him by his theater worker accomplice, Edmund Spangler.

President Lincoln's body, meanwhile, was taken across the street, where his family and six doctors maintained a vigil at his bedside. He never regained consciousness and died at 7:22 a.m. the next morning, nine hours after Booth had shot him.

As the nation mourned, a huge manhunt was launched for Booth, backed by a $1,000,000 reward.

John Wilkes Booth, a member of a famous theater dynasty, was one of America's most acclaimed actors, known for his energetic performances and his habit of stealing the show.

The assassin was already on the run. First, he visited Dr. Samuel Mudd, who set his broken bone. As troops searched the land around Washington, D.C., Booth and David Herold, a fellow conspirator, hid for days near a swamp in Maryland. Later, they moved on to Virginia.

Famous fugitive
While in hiding, Booth read the newspapers, which were brought to him each day. He had expected some public sympathy for his actions, and was disappointed to read descriptions of himself as a savage, rather than a hero. Booth

soon learned that some of his fellow plotters had been arrested. George Atzerodt, assigned to kill the vice president, had lost his nerve and got drunk instead, and Michael O'Laughlen, who was to kill secretary of war Edwin Stanton, failed for the same reason. Lewis Powell, assigned to assassinate William Seward, caused severe wounds to the secretary of state's face and neck, but did not manage to kill him. Booth was the only one of the assassins to succeed.

The authorities set to work tracking Booth down through his known associates. A boarding-house kept by Mary Surratt was identified as having been used by the conspirators, and, by chance, Lewis Powell arrived at Surratt's door as she was being questioned. Both were taken into custody.

On April 26, Booth and Herold were traced by federal troops to a tobacco barn on a farm outside Port Royal, Virginia. Herold surrendered,

> I have too great a soul to die like a criminal. Oh may [God] spare me that and let me die bravely.
> **John Wilkes Booth**

but Booth chose to remain inside the barn. The authorities responded by setting the barn on fire, hoping to flush Booth out.

As the blaze grew fiercer, one of the soldiers shot Booth in the neck, reportedly because the assassin had raised his gun as if to shoot. Whoever fired the final shot, it is known that Booth was dragged from the barn, and died hours later.

Trial and execution

In May and June 1865, the eight people accused of President Lincoln's murder were tried by a military commission. Several of them had been involved in the failed plot to abduct the president, but their role in the assassination itself was less apparent. Over seven weeks, 371 witnesses testified, and seven of the accused were found guilty of at least one charge.

Mary Surratt, Lewis Powell, George Atzerodt, and David Herold received the death penalty for their part in the conspiracy. Dr. Samuel Mudd was sentenced to life in prison, as was Michael O'Laughlen, who died of yellow fever after two years behind bars. Edmund Spangler received a six-year sentence. ∎

Four of Booth's coconspirators were executed by hanging on July 7, 1865. Among them was Mary Surratt, the first woman to be put to death by the federal government.

DREYFUS IS INNOCENT. I SWEAR IT! I STAKE MY LIFE ON IT—MY HONOR!
THE DREYFUS AFFAIR, 1894

I n 1894, Alfred Dreyfus was a captain in the French army. Born in Alsace, a German-speaking area of France, he was Jewish by descent. What became known as the "Dreyfus Affair" began when a French spy at the German embassy in Paris discovered a large torn-up note written on tissue paper. This was a *bordereau*—a detailed statement in which an anonymous French officer offered to sell military secrets.

Suspicion immediately fell on Captain Dreyfus, who often visited his family in German-held Mulhouse. The French army's intelligence service, the *Section de Statistique*, called in a graphologist to examine the handwriting in the note. He pronounced that the writing was so unlike that of Dreyfus that it must amount to a "self-forgery"—that is, a deliberate attempt by Dreyfus to disguise his own hand. In spite of this distinctly dubious claim, Dreyfus was arrested. The case set off a wave of acute antisemitism, both among the public and in the press.

Dreyfus was court-martialed and found guilty of passing secrets to the Germans, but was never allowed to see the evidence against

> Show me at least the proofs of the infamous act you pretend I have committed.
> **Alfred Dreyfus**

him. The government made sure that the people of France witnessed his humiliation. Dreyfus was paraded in front of a crowd that shouted, "Death to Judas, death to the Jew," before he was sentenced to life in prison at the infamous Devil's Island, off French Guiana.

Inconclusive evidence
From the start of the affair, people were divided into those convinced that Dreyfus was a spy, and those who thought there had been a rush to judge him because he was Jewish. Two years after Dreyfus was convicted, the new head of the army's intelligence unit, Georges

See also: Jean Calas 203 ■ Lizzie Borden 208–11

Captain Alfred Dreyfus is escorted to prison after his wrongful conviction for treason, Paris, 1895. His humiliation included the tearing of his military decorations from his uniform.

Picquart, uncovered evidence implicating another French military officer, Major Ferdinand Walsin Esterhazy, as the real traitor. Picquart was silenced, quickly moved overseas, and imprisoned on trumped-up charges. However, the rumblings about Esterhazy's possible guilt grew louder, and in 1898 he was court-martialed in secret, quickly found not guilty, and allowed to flee the country.

At this point, author Émile Zola took up the cause of Alfred Dreyfus. He wrote an open letter to the President of France, detailing Dreyfus's innocence and boldly accusing the Army of both a cover-up and antisemitism.

Second court-martial

The Paris newspaper *L'Aurore* published Zola's piece on its front page, with a banner headline reading *"J'Accuse…!"* ("I accuse"). Zola wanted the government to arrest and prosecute him, so that the facts of the Dreyfus case could come out. He got his wish: Zola was arrested and convicted of libel, but he escaped to England—where he continued to defend Dreyfus— before he could be sent to prison.

In 1899, under pressure from Zola and other intellectuals, Dreyfus was given a second court-martial. He was once again found guilty by the court, but this time with "extenuating circumstances."

To save face, the new French President Émile Loubet offered Dreyfus a pardon: he would be freed, on the proviso that he did not speak about his innocence, but he would not be reinstated in the army. Unwilling to return to Devil's Island, Dreyfus went home to his family.

Dreyfus was still officially guilty, but the threads of injustice began to unravel. Finally, in July 1906, a civilian court annulled the Dreyfus verdict and completely cleared the officer. He was never acquitted by his fellow officers in a military court. However, on the exact spot where he had been stripped of his uniform and sword, Dreyfus was reinstated into the Army and in 1918 was promoted to become an officer of the *Légion d'Honneur*. ■

Courts martial

Courts martial are military courts that dispense justice and discipline. They date back to ancient Rome, where some of the earliest military trials took place to instill discipline within the Roman army. In the US, the court martial is the oldest court of law, dating back to before the American Revolution. Congress adopted the Articles of War, based on Britain's military code, in 1775. In Britain, military conduct was regulated for centuries via individually convened cases in the Court of the High Constable and Earl Marshal; the "Court Martial" only became a permanent standing court in 2009.

Courts martial are more common during times of war, when they often try soldiers for actions in the field. General Charles Lee was court-martialed for cowardice in the 1778 Battle of Monmouth. More recently, during the Vietnam War, Lieutenant William Calley was court-martialed for presiding over the massacre of innocent Vietnamese civilians at My Lai.

IF THEY SHED MY BLOOD, THEIR HANDS' WILL REMAIN SOILED

THE ASSASSINATION OF RASPUTIN, 1916

IN CONTEXT

LOCATION
St. Petersburg, Russia

THEME
Anarchic assassinations

BEFORE
1909 Anarchist Simón Radowitzky kills Argentina's national police chief, Ramón Lorenzo Falcón, with a homemade bomb.

1911 A left-wing revolutionary, Dmitry Bogrov, assassinates the Monarchist Russian Prime Minister Pyotr Stolypin at the Kiev Opera House. Stolypin's death is a precursor of the Russian Revolution.

AFTER
1919 German Nationalist Anton Arco-Valley kills Kurt Eisner, leader of the Bavarian socialists. Counter to Arco-Valley's hopes, this leads to the formation of the short-lived Bavarian Socialist Republic.

O n December 19, 1916, the body of Grigori Yefimovich Rasputin was found 460 feet (140 m) west of the Bolshoy Petrovsky Bridge in St. Petersburg, Russia. The death of the mystic healer would devastate the tsarina, and was soon followed by a grisly end for Nicholas II and his family.

As a young man, Rasputin was considered reclusive and odd; he was accused of excessive drinking, fist fights, and groping village girls. However, he also possessed the ability to calm hysterical animals, and once even identified a horse thief using what appeared to be clairvoyance. At the age of 23, Rasputin left his home to stay at

See also: The Assassination of Pertinax 304 ▪ The Dreyfus Affair 310–11 ▪ The Poisoning of Alexander Litvinenko 326–31

Grigori Yefimovich Rasputin came from Siberian peasant stock, but used his sexuality, charisma, and skills as a faith healer to rise to a position of great influence in Russian society.

a monastery in Verkhoturye, where he taught himself to read and write, and experienced a religious conversion. Henceforth, he became a *strannik*, or religious wanderer.

Meanwhile, the reign of Tsar Nicholas II, last of the Romanov dynasty, was proving to be particularly turbulent. His troubles began in 1896 with the Khodynka Tragedy, during which 1,389 revellers were trampled to death at an outdoor coronation banquet. Nicholas wanted to miss a ball at the French embassy out of respect for all those who were killed, but his uncles pressured him to attend. Predictably, the public viewed this as evidence that the tsar was cold

and uncaring. His popularity tumbled again when he refused to negotiate with those who believed that Russia should become a constitutional monarchy.

Irresistible rise
Rasputin arrived in St. Petersburg in 1903. Gurus and mystics were in vogue at the time, and he secured invitations to society parties, where Rasputin impressed aristocratic women with his spirituality.

Nicholas's fortunes, however, continued to sour. Russia was defeated in the 1904–05 Russo-Japanese war, lost its entire navy, and conceded Manchuria. Then, on Sunday January 22, 1905, soldiers of

the Imperial Guard fired at unarmed demonstrators marching toward the Winter Palace, killing approximately 1,000. The event, dubbed "Bloody Sunday," resulted in a rash of armed uprisings, mass strikes, and suicide bombings. Nicholas's decision to handle the fallout with violent suppression further damaged the tsar's fragile reputation.

Nicholas and Rasputin finally met in 1905, when the mystic healer was introduced to Tsarina Alexandra. She had turned to faith healing and spiritualism in the hope of finding a cure for her son, Alexei, who had been born with hemophilia. Using his powerful charisma, Rasputin quickly endeared himself to the Romanovs. When he claimed that he could heal the tsarevich, however, Rasputin became indispensable. The tsarina was particularly entranced, sending Rasputin gushing letters which »

The appearance of Grigori Rasputin, and the influence he exercised, mark the beginning of the decay of Russian society.
Mikhail Rodzianko

Nicholas II's family were the last of the Romanov dynasty. The Tsar and Tsarina were executed along with their son Alexei and daughters (left to right) Marie, Olga, Tatiana, and Anastasia.

were later interpreted as sexual in nature. Rasputin habitually bragged of his special relationship with the Romanovs and flashed around Alexandra's letters in public.

Because of this, Rasputin soon became a scapegoat for all of Russia's problems, and was portrayed as wielding a sinister and corrupting influence over the royal family. During the summer of 1914, in the belief that he was the Antichrist, a woman named Chionya Guseva slashed Rasputin across the stomach with a knife, leaving a 14-inch (36-cm) wound that exposed his intestines.

While Rasputin recovered in hospital, tensions mounted in Europe—war between the Triple Entente and the Central Powers seemed imminent. Rasputin sent an ominous telegram to the tsar warning of a whole ocean of tears.

Rasputin prophesied that they would all drown in blood. Ignoring the mystic's words, however, the tsar went to war with Germany and Austria-Hungary on August 1. Millions of Russian soldiers were killed as their enemies advanced in the east. Again, the Russian public blamed Rasputin.

Rasputin's mystical predictions continued. By 1916, Rasputin was convinced of his impending death. He wrote an impassioned note to the Romanovs on December 7, prophesying that, should he die at the hand of one of their family members, none of their children or relations would outlive him by more than two years.

Uncanny prescience

Nine days after the letter was sent, Prince Felix Yusupov, who was married to the tsar's only niece, arrived at the Rasputin family residence. The prince called upon Rasputin for help—his wife, the Princess Irina, was experiencing terrible headaches and required immediate treatment. Rasputin agreed to leave with Yusupov, despite earlier warnings from the Minister of the Interior, Alexander Protopopov, to stay inside his home. The minister had heard of several plots against the mystic.

When they arrived at Yusupov's home, the Moika Palace, the prince led Rasputin into the "games room." It was actually part of the wine cellar, but had been decorated to look as though it was in regular use. Yusupov told Rasputin that his wife was hosting a party and offered him some Madeira wine

Toxicology

Pioneered by Paracelsus in the 16th century, toxicology is the study of poisons and drugs. Toxicology reports can give the authorities clues to determine a victim's cause of death, and either corroborate or undermine a suspect's statements.

Forensic toxicology, studied postmortem, differs from clinical toxicology, which tests living patients who exhibit drug or toxin-related symptoms. Forensic toxicology exams test samples of urine, as well as blood from different parts of the body. Blood from the femoral vein may yield a different concentration of a toxin to blood from the heart, so this allows toxicologists to get a complete picture. Tissue samples can be collected from the liver, brain, kidney, and vitreous humor (in the eyeball chamber). Stomach contents and bile are also examined. Different techniques including immunoassay, in which antibodies search out toxins, are then used to screen all samples and determine the concentration of each substance.

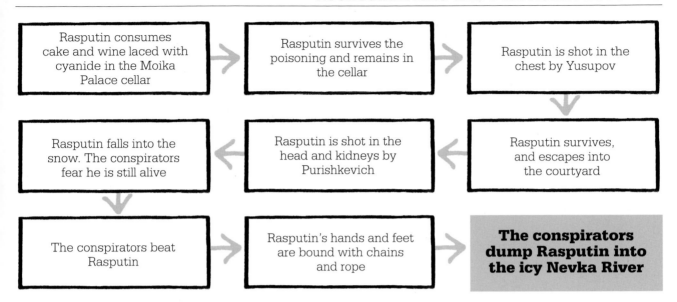

Rasputin consumes cake and wine laced with cyanide in the Moika Palace cellar

→

Rasputin survives the poisoning and remains in the cellar

→

Rasputin is shot in the chest by Yusupov

↓

Rasputin falls into the snow. The conspirators fear he is still alive

←

Rasputin is shot in the head and kidneys by Purishkevich

←

Rasputin survives, and escapes into the courtyard

↓

The conspirators beat Rasputin

→

Rasputin's hands and feet are bound with chains and rope

→

The conspirators dump Rasputin into the icy Nevka River

---

and cakes while he waited. However, the food and drink had been laced with cyanide—and the only guests in the house were Yusupov's coconspirators: Grand Duke Dmitri Pavlovich, politician V. M. Purishkevich, and Dr. Stanislas de Lazovert. All wanted to murder Rasputin to end his influence over the Romanovs.

Yusupov left Rasputin in the room, but the mystic was still alive when he returned. The poisoning had failed. Yusupov excused himself again and went upstairs, where the Grand Duke handed him a revolver. Yusupov returned to the cellar and shot the mystic through the chest. Rasputin fell to the floor. Exuberant, Felix raced upstairs and announced that Rasputin was dead.

The joyous men descended into the cellar only to find Rasputin gone. They tracked him into the courtyard where he was limping toward the gate. Purishkevich took aim with the revolver and fired four times, piercing one of Rasputin's kidneys. When he fell into the snow, one of the conspirators shot him

through the head. The four men battered Rasputin's body, then tied him up and dumped him into a hole in the half-frozen Nevka River.

Prophecy fulfilled

The next day, Rasputin's daughter, Maria, contacted the tsarina to inform her that her father had disappeared after going to Moika Palace to treat Irina's headache. Alexandra, however, knew that Irina was not even in the city. An investigation was quickly launched to find the missing mystic.

During a search of Moika Palace, police found traces of blood near the back door, which Yusupov claimed belonged to a dog. More blood was discovered on a parapet by Bolshoy Petrovsky Bridge, along with one of Rasputin's galoshes. On December 18, a Uhlenhuth test— used to determine the species of a blood sample—revealed the blood on the back steps to be human. Yusupov and Grand Duke Pavlovich were placed under house arrest.

Rasputin's body was found on December 19. The autopsy showed that he had died instantly when the

third bullet penetrated the frontal lobe of his brain. However, his body showed no evidence of the supposed cyanide poisoning.

A week later, Nicholas II sent Yusupov and Pavlovich into exile without trial. While they succeeded in murdering Rasputin, they failed to save the Romanovs. In 1917, Nicholas was forced to abdicate, and the Bolsheviks seized power that October. The Romanovs were held in a house in St. Petersburg until July 17, 1918, when they were shot by a firing squad. Rasputin's dark prophecy had come to pass. ∎

Without Rasputin, there could have been no Lenin.
Alexander Kerensky

THERE HAS TO BE MORE TO IT

THE ASSASSINATION OF JOHN F. KENNEDY, NOVEMBER 22, 1963

IN CONTEXT

LOCATION
Dallas, Texas, US

THEME
Shootings of US presidents

BEFORE
1881 Four months after taking office, President James A. Garfield is shot dead by Charles J. Guiteau, a writer and lawyer from Illinois.

1901 Leon Czolgosz, a former steel worker from Michigan, shoots and kills President William McKinley. He is executed later the same year.

1912 While campaigning for a second term, former president Theodore Roosevelt is shot by saloon-keeper John F. Schrank. The campaign speech notes in his pocket save his life.

AFTER
1975 Sara Jane Moore fires a shot at President Gerald Ford, but narrowly misses due to a faulty sight on her new gun.

At 12:30 p.m. on November 22, 1963, President John Fitzgerald Kennedy rode through Dallas's Dealey Plaza in an open-topped limousine with the First Lady, Texas Governor John Connally, and Connally's wife, Nellie. Rumblings of hostility toward the president in Texas made his two-day visit an important one, and Kennedy was keen to allay as many fears as possible. As his motorcade crawled down Elm Street, shots rang out. One bullet struck Kennedy in the neck, then another blasted open his skull. Kennedy was pronounced dead at 1 p.m. at Parkland Memorial Hospital. Although millions later witnessed the shocking events—thanks to Abraham Zapruder's home movie footage—speculation still surrounds Kennedy's death.

Authorized account

The official narrative is that Howard Brennan, a witness seated across from the Texas Schoolbook Depository, noticed a man with a rifle firing from the building's sixth-floor corner window. Within minutes of the shooting, Brennan approached police officers to inform

> My God, they're trying to kill us all!
> **Governor Connally**

them of what he had seen. He was joined by fifth-floor Depository employee Harold Norman, who had heard gunshots and cartridges being ejected from the floor above. The sixth floor was unoccupied, as new flooring was being laid.

These tips led the Dallas Police Department to seal off the building some time between 12:30 and 12:50 p.m. At around 1:03 p.m., a roll call of Depository employees was taken. This revealed that temporary employee Lee Harvey Oswald—a former defector to the Soviet Union, who had last been seen in the building as late as 12:33 p.m.—was absent.

Lee Harvey Oswald

Depending on who you ask, Lee Harvey Oswald was a naive fall guy, a psychologically disturbed attention-seeker, or a secret operative carrying out a plot by a government agency. Oswald was born on October 18, 1939, in New Orleans. Between his birth and the age of 17, Oswald lived in 22 different locations and changed schools 11 times.

At 17, Oswald joined the Marine Corps, where he worked as a radar operator. His childhood had been unhappy, but life in the Marines was no better; he was court-martialed twice and

demoted for accidentally wounding himself with an unauthorized .22 pistol.

In October 1959, Oswald arrived in the Soviet Union. He hoped to get a warm welcome in return for secrets he had learned as a Marine. However, he soon tired of his marginalized life in Belarus and returned to the US in 1962. In 1963, he allegedly decided to express his Marxist political views by shooting right-wing General Edwin Walker. This assassination attempt failed—but his attempt on the president did not.

Nine minutes after the roll call, investigators discovered three empty cartridge cases near the southeast window on the sixth floor. At 1:22 p.m., Carl Day noticed a Mannlicher-Carcano bolt-action rifle hidden among some boxes.

They've killed Jack! They've killed my husband!
Jackie Kennedy

In the meantime, at 1:15 p.m., Dallas police officer J.D. Tippit was shot dead on East 10th Street in the Oak Cliff neighborhood. Witnesses observed the gunman fleeing the crime scene and ducking into the Texas Theatre without stopping to buy a ticket.

Acting on a tip, police entered the theater, where they found a man who fitted the suspect's description sitting in one of the back rows. When Officer McDonald drew near, the suspect leapt up and struck him, then attempted to draw a pistol. He was unsuccessful. Officer Bentley grappled him from behind and the police officers managed to restrain and handcuff the suspect. The contents of his wallet identified him as Lee Harvey Oswald—the employee who had

Classic footage from the Zapruder home movie of the killing shows Jackie Kennedy, in pink, tending to her mortally wounded husband in the back of the presidential limousine.

been conspicuously absent from the Schoolbook Depository a little earlier that day.

Fatal ambush

Oswald was immediately arrested and formally charged at 7:10 p.m. for the murder of Officer Tippit. By 1 a.m. the following day, he was also charged with killing President John F. Kennedy. On the morning of November 24, Oswald was ambushed in the underground parking lot of the Dallas Police Department headquarters as he was being transferred to the »

Jack Ruby steps out from the throng of press reporters and photographers waiting for Oswald in the Dallas parking lot. One captured this image of Ruby shooting Oswald.

county jail. Nightclub operator Jack Ruby shot him point-blank through the abdomen, and Oswald died just days after his world-famous victim, by the same method.

Ruby alternately claimed that he had assassinated Oswald to spare the former First Lady Jacqueline Kennedy from having to attend a harrowing trial; because he was angry at Oswald; and to redeem the city of Dallas. Ruby was convicted of murder. The conviction was later overturned, but Ruby died behind bars of a pulmonary embolism before his new trial began.

Aftermath

Lyndon B. Johnson was sworn in as president on board Air Force One immediately after Kennedy's death. During his first days as commander-in-chief, speculation abounded about the events in Dallas. Johnson quickly appointed the Warren Commission to investigate the assassination and satisfy the public. After 10 months of investigation, the Commission

The right rear portion of the head was missing. It was lying in the rear seat of the car. His brain was exposed.
Clint Hill

concluded that Oswald acted alone, using his Mannlicher-Carcano bolt-action rifle to fire three shots in less than eight seconds from the Depository window. All three shots had been fired from behind: the first missed; the second entered the president's upper back and exited through his throat; and the third struck him in the back of the head and killed him. The public, however, remained unsatisfied.

Conspiracy theories

Kennedy's murder is arguably the most widely and hotly contested case of the 20th century—perhaps of all time. A 2013 poll conducted by the Associated Press found that 59 percent of Americans believe there was a conspiracy to murder the president involving multiple people, while 24 percent are of the opinion that Lee Harvey Oswald was solely responsible. Ten years earlier, a Gallup poll indicated that 75 percent of the nation favored a

conspiracy explanation. Even the US government remains divided on the issue.

In 1979, the US House of Representatives Select Committee on Assassinations (HSCA)—which was assembled to investigate the murders of Kennedy and Dr. Martin Luther King Jr.—reached a slightly different conclusion to the Warren Commission. Although they agreed with much of the Commission's report, the HSCA determined that a fourth shot had been fired by somebody other than Oswald—suggesting a wider plot.

Conspiracy theorists point to a number of supposed flaws in official accounts of the assassination. One major theory casts doubt on the government's claims that all of the shots were fired from behind by a single gunman. To many, the Zapruder film shows the President's head moving back and to the left, indicating that the fatal shot came from the front right-hand side.

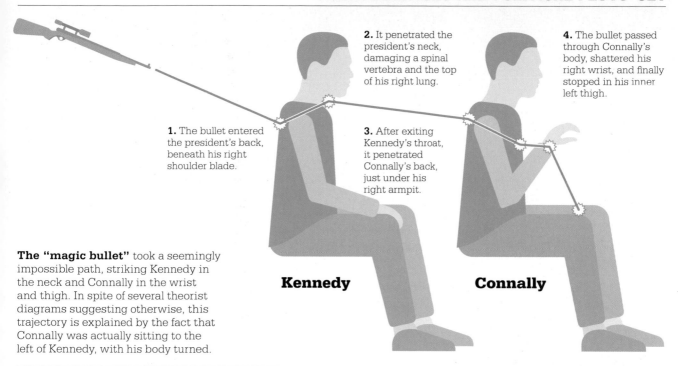

2. It penetrated the president's neck, damaging a spinal vertebra and the top of his right lung.

4. The bullet passed through Connally's body, shattered his right wrist, and finally stopped in his inner left thigh.

1. The bullet entered the president's back, beneath his right shoulder blade.

3. After exiting Kennedy's throat, it penetrated Connally's back, just under his right armpit.

Kennedy

Connally

The "magic bullet" took a seemingly impossible path, striking Kennedy in the neck and Connally in the wrist and thigh. In spite of several theorist diagrams suggesting otherwise, this trajectory is explained by the fact that Connally was actually sitting to the left of Kennedy, with his body turned.

Some theorize that there was a second shooter, on the "grassy knoll" of Dealey Plaza. Theorists also claim that the second bullet—which hit Kennedy and Governor Connally—would have been a "magic bullet" because it seemed to defy the laws of physics.

Theorists' protestations are supported by quotes from eight doctors who opined that they had observed an entry wound in the

The public must be satisfied that Oswald was the assassin.
Nicholas Katzenbach

lower front area of Kennedy's throat with an exit wound in the back of his skull. This belief was affirmed by an emergency room nurse, a radiographer, and two autopsy technicians, who worked at a trauma center in Texas where gunshot victims were often treated and would have been accustomed to assessing bullet wounds.

Secret Service Agent Clint Hill, who was riding in the motorcade when Kennedy was shot, originally reported to the Warren Commission that: "There was so much blood you could not tell if there had been any other wound or not, except for the one large gaping wound in the rear portion of the head." Hill later changed his mind about the possibility of a second wound.

Some theorists do believe that Oswald was a lone shooter, but still believe in a conspiracy. The CIA, the Secret Service, and foreign governments have all been accused of orchestrating the murder. ∎

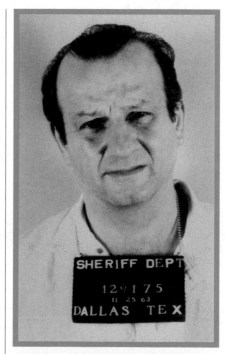

A police mugshot of Jack Ruby, who gunned down Lee Harvey Oswald. Theorists believe he shot Oswald to prevent him from revealing information about a larger conspiracy.

I KISS YOU FOR THE LAST TIME

THE ABDUCTION OF ALDO MORO, MARCH 16, 1978

IN CONTEXT

LOCATION
Rome, Italy

THEME
Murder by radical groups

BEFORE
March 1881 Russian Tsar Alexander II is killed by a bomb thrown by members of a group known as *Narodnaya Volya*, the "People's Will."

June 28, 1914 The assassination of Archduke Franz Ferdinand of Austria by "Black Hand" anarchist Gavrilo Princip in Sarajevo is a major catalyst for World War I.

AFTER
October 1986 Gerold von Braunmühl, a West German diplomat, is assassinated by a guerrilla organization known as the "Red Family Faction."

August 1989 Huey Newton, Founder of the Black Panther Party, is killed by a member of the Black Guerrilla Army in Oakland, California.

O n March 16, 1978, four members of the Red Brigades ambushed Aldo Moro's car in Rome. The armed terrorists fired 91 bullets from a submachine gun toward the car escorting Moro; more than 40 of the bullets hit the bodyguards and police officers, killing them all. Kidnapped at gunpoint, Moro was taken alive.

Moro was Italy's longest-serving postwar prime minister. He held office five times between 1963 and 1976. In 1978, he was working to end a government crisis, and had proposed a coalition between his Christian Democratic Party and the rival Italian Communist Party. This so-called "Historic Compromise" enraged both sides of the Italian political spectrum, but Moro remained a favorite to win that year's election and become prime minister once more.

The Red Brigades was a far-Left terrorist group hoping to start a communist revolution in Italy, by

What was the prime minister's life worth?

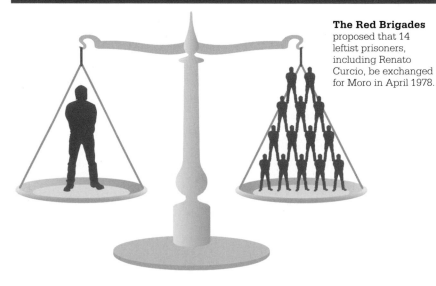

The Red Brigades proposed that 14 leftist prisoners, including Renato Curcio, be exchanged for Moro in April 1978.

See also: The Lindbergh Baby Kidnapping 178–85 ■ The Assassination of Abraham Lincoln 306–09
■ The Kidnapping of Ingrid Betancourt 324–25

Aldo Moro stands in front of the flag of the Red Brigades on March 17, 1978. That day, the group held a "people's trial" of Moro, timed to coincide with the trial of Brigadist prisoners in Turin.

way of a campaign of bombings, assassinations, and abductions. Following the arrest of founding Red Brigades members such as Renato Curcio, the well-liked Moro became their next target. The Brigadists waylaid Moro's convoy on its way to the Chamber of Deputies and kidnapped him.

Fruitless demands

One week after the abduction, the group claimed responsibility for Moro's kidnapping and threatened to kill him if their demands were not met. In a controversial decision, the Italian government staunchly refused to negotiate. The Italian Communist party notably disavowed the terrorists, and declared that they would not enter into a coalition if the demands were met.

Moro himself wrote many letters pleading with the government to save his life—as did his family, supporters, and even Pope Paul VI. Hundreds of suspected terrorists were arrested as police scoured the country for Moro but they failed to find solid clues to his whereabouts.

On April 15, the Red Brigades announced that they had sentenced Moro to death. Knowing that he was going to die, Moro sent a final letter to his wife. Abandoned in his time of need, he also requested that no one from his political party attend his funeral. Two days later, on May 9, 1978, Moro was murdered by the Red Brigades leader, Mario Moretti. Thanks to an anonymous tip, police found Moro's corpse, riddled with bullets, in a truck near the historic center of Rome. He had been shot in the heart 11 times.

Finding the killers

In the aftermath of Moro's death, many more suspected terrorists were detained. Embarrassed by the whole affair, the Italian government introduced new measures in 1980

He knew it was over. I didn't deceive him. All I told him was to get himself ready because we had to go out.
Mario Moretti

to capture those responsible for Moro's murder. They introduced lighter penalties for *pentiti*—those who decided to "repent" and inform on their former comrades.

Despite these measures, the apparent mastermind behind Moro's execution was not caught until April 1981. Mario Moretti was finally arrested at a farm between Milan and Pavia during a massive sweep operation conducted across northern Italy. He received six life sentences for his crimes. ■

Protecting politicians

Bodyguards protecting high-ranking politicians, public officials, or soldiers, take an oath of commitment to safeguard an individual by risking their own lives. All major politicians are protected by security details—these are usually assigned by their departments, but some also hire private bodyguards, especially after their time in office ends.

Some countries have dedicated security corps to protect their most powerful citizens—for example, the US Secret Service, which guards the president, or the Swiss Guards, who protect the Pope.

Bodyguards plan escape routes, scout venues for escape routes and potential threats, and escort their client on their day-to-day activities. In peak physical condition, bodyguards are often members of law enforcement or former members of the military. They are usually trained in firearms, combat, and first aid, and some bodyguards also specialize in fields such as bomb detection.

BARBARITY WAS ALL AROUND US

THE KIDNAPPING OF INGRID BETANCOURT, 2002–08

IN CONTEXT

LOCATION
Colombia, South America

THEME
Political abductions

BEFORE
October 1970 James Cross, a British diplomat, and Quebec politician Pierre Laporte are kidnapped by militants of the Front de Libération du Québec. Laporte is killed, but Cross is released in December 1970.

August 1973 South Korean politician Kim Dae-jung, who later serves as president of South Korea, is kidnapped and held hostage for 42 days.

December 1981 Members of Italian group the "Red Brigades" (see pp. 322–23) kidnap US General James Dozier in Verona.

AFTER
May 2010 Diego Fernández de Cevallos Ramos, a Mexican politician, is held for seven months by leftist rebels.

Deep in the Colombian jungle, during a brutal guerrilla war, a group of revolutionary armed forces—the Fuerzas Armadas Revolutionaries de Colombia (FARC)—hid from the world, plotting their next attack.

For six years, the jungle was also a prison camp for former Colombian presidential candidate Ingrid Betancourt. She was kept there alongside her campaign manager Clara Rojas and a small group of other hostages. The captives were kept in cages, slept on tarps in the mud, and bathed in the rivers, surrounded by giant snakes, insects, and deadly predators. They survived on meager meals of rice and watery soup, which left them malnourished. Despite the horrifying conditions, however, Betancourt never lost hope that she would one day be rescued and returned to her family.

Distinguished history

Betancourt, who grew up in France and settled in Colombia in 1989, was the daughter of diplomat Gabriel Betancourt—a former Education Minister and assistant

Surviving captivity

Whether captured by a terrorist group, lone kidnapper, or enemy army, experts say that a few fundamental survival principles can help keep hostages alive. The highest priority is to obey the captor. Complying quickly with orders can curry favor. Violating the captor's rules, however arbitrary, can lead to harsh punishment.

Although the body can usually handle extreme physical challenges, mental strength is an equally essential element.

To survive the mental stress of captivity, hostages may seek out secret, small victories against their captors, or send encrypted messages when allowed to speak or write to their families.

While confined, hostages often endure severe emotional trauma that can have long-lasting mental effects. Unlike Betancourt, some hostages experience Stockholm Syndrome, where they develop an overwhelming dependency on their captors, and even resist authorities who would try to rescue them from captivity.

See also: The Abduction of Pocahontas 176 ■ The Kidnapping of Patty Hearst 188–89
■ The Abduction of Aldo Moro 322–23

Ingrid Betancourt looks thin and unhealthy during her time in the jungle. This still, taken from a video of the camp, was confiscated from a captured guerrilla in 2007.

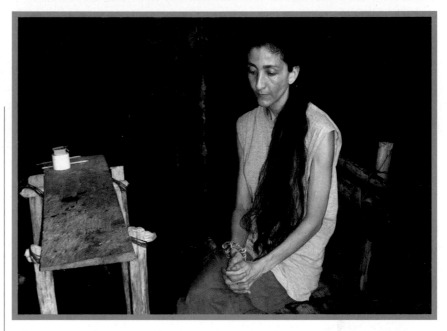

director of UNESCO. Ingrid was a pacifist, dedicated to fighting corruption in Colombia. She was elected to the Chamber of Representatives in 1994, and had created her own political party, the Green Oxygen Party, in 1997. In a landslide victory, she became a senator in 1998, and launched her campaign for the Colombian presidency in 2001.

Captured campaigners

Despite advice, Betancourt took her campaign into rebel territory in February 2002. There, she and Rojas were kidnapped by FARC guerrillas. Forced to abandon their vehicle, they were chained by the neck to other prisoners and led from the main road into the remote villages, where they traveled by foot into the rainforest.

During her six years in captivity, Betancourt tried to escape three times, swimming down the rivers and hiking through the rainforest

It was a battle, not only with the guerrillas, but with ourselves.
Ingrid Betancourt

for days before being recaptured. While in captivity she was beaten, underfed, forced on epic marches at gunpoint, and often threatened with death.

Betancourt nearly died from hepatitis and malaria. Her health was so poor that in July 2003 FARC told Betancourt's family that they would release her, due to her condition. However, the promised handover never happened.

False dawn and release

An abortive French rescue bid failed to bring Betancourt home, and angered Colombian authorities who had not been consulted about the mission. As her health declined, only irregular videos and missives from the rebels told her family that she was still alive. Her husband, Juan Carlos Lecompte, feared that an armed rescue attempt by the Colombian government would result in the hostages being killed. The six years passed slowly.

Meanwhile, in the jungle, Clara Rojas began a relationship with one of her captors, and nearly died giving birth by Caesarean in the jungle, with scalpels sterilized over candles. Accused by other hostages of sleeping with the enemy, Rojas was eventually freed in January 2008.

Betancourt's own freedom soon followed. On July 2, 2008, a Colombian military team entered rebel territory. Disguised as guerrillas—even wearing iconic Che Guevara T-shirts—they flew into the jungle camp in a civilian helicopter. They claimed to be taking the hostages for a meeting with a rebel leader, and managed to fly Betancourt and three Americans to safety without bloodshed.

As the Colombian government promised to secure the release of the remaining hostages, Betancourt returned home, and became a symbol of the country's brutal guerrilla war. ■

BARBARIC
AND RUTHLESS

THE POISONING OF ALEXANDER LITVINENKO, NOVEMBER 2006

IN CONTEXT

LOCATION
London, England

THEME
Espionage

BEFORE
September 1978 After his defection from Bulgaria in 1969, Georgi Ivanov Markov is assassinated in London—stabbed in the leg with an umbrella point containing ricin.

April 1983 American CIA agent and spy Robert Ames is killed in the bombing of the US embassy in Beirut, Lebanon.

April 2006 Denis Donaldson, a volunteer in the Provisional Irish Republic Army, is killed by the IRA after he is exposed as an informant for the police and MI5.

AFTER
August 2010 MI6 agent Gareth Williams is found dead in suspicious circumstances at a safe house in London.

O n November 1, 2006, 44-year-old former Russian spy Alexander Litvinenko met with two men from Moscow at the Millennium Hotel in London. By the time Litvinenko arrived at the hotel, at around 3:40 p.m., the Russians were already seated toward the back of the Pine Bar in the hotel lobby—a blind spot in the hotel's CCTV coverage.

One of the men, Andrei Lugovoi, had ordered green tea, and three empty mugs were placed around the table. Lugovoi offered the remaining tea to Litvinenko, who poured himself half a cup. It was sugarless and cold, and Litvinenko swallowed just a few sips before leaving the rest.

Litvinenko proceeded to talk briefly with Lugovoi and his companion, Dmitry Kovtun, about a possible business venture. Although he had no way of knowing it as he left the hotel, Litvinenko was already a dead man. He had just consumed a radioactive poison known as polonium-210—the tea had been laced with it. At this point, not even the most gifted medical team in the world could have saved him.

That night Litvinenko felt sick and began to vomit. He was admitted to Barnet General Hospital on November 3. His condition rapidly deteriorated, and Litvinenko was moved to University College Hospital on November 17. Initially, his doctors thought Litvinenko had been poisoned with thallium, and Scotland Yard sent detectives to investigate. Under an armed police guard, Litvinenko spent his final days in a series of interviews with the police, using his detective skills to solve his own murder.

A defiant Andrei Lugovoi claims his innocence during a press conference in Moscow. Still wanted by the British authorities, Lugovoi is now a deputy in the Duma, Russia's lower house.

Enemy of the state
A former officer of Russia's Federal Security Service, Litvinenko defected to London after exposing corruption in President Vladimir Putin's regime. In 2000, he received political asylum in the United Kingdom, where he was recruited to work for the British foreign intelligence agency, MI6.

There, Litvinenko also became one of Putin's most vocal critics. By the time Litvinenko met with the

If you want some tea, then there is some left here—you can have some of this.
Andrei Lugovoi

See also: Sadamichi Hirasawa 224–25 ▪ Harold Shipman 290–91 ▪ The Assassination of Rasputin 312–15

two men from Moscow, he had lived in London for six years. He joined them at the hotel that fateful afternoon because he was under the impression that they could become business partners. Although Litvinenko felt slightly suspicious after the meeting, he did not realize then that Lugovoi and Kovtun were Russian spies.

Deathbed testimony

On November 18, two detectives from the Metropolitan Police Specialist Crime Unit, Detective Inspector Brent Hyatt and Detective Sergeant Chris Hoar, interviewed Litvinenko in the critical care unit on the 16th floor of University College Hospital.

Over the next three days, Litvinenko participated in 18 interviews which lasted nearly nine hours. At times, he was forced to stop speaking as his condition grew more painful and serious.

An experienced detective, Litvinenko became a significant witness in the case against his killers. He drew up a list of

suspects, at the top of which were the Moscow men he met for tea— Andrei Lugovoi and Dmitry Kovtun. Their strange meeting at the hotel had unnerved Litvinenko.

After the first four or five hours of interviews, the investigation began to gather momentum. Litvinenko directed detectives to critical documents he kept on Russian gangs and Putin; he was convinced that ultimately the Russian president had given the order to assassinate him. Litvinenko also phoned his wife, who located photographs of Andrei Lugovoi that Litvinenko had at home. Lugovoi became Scotland Yard's prime suspect.

Litvinenko did not initially disclose his status as an MI6 informant to the police. When Hoar and Hyatt inquired about some unaccounted time in his rundown of the week, Litvinenko was unwilling to explain whom he had met, or why. Instead, he gave the detectives the phone number of his handler. The handler, "Martin," visited University College Hospital,

> Later on, when I left the hotel, I was thinking there was something strange. I had been feeling, all the time, I knew that they wanted to kill me.
> **Alexander Litvinenko**

and began looking into the two mysterious Russians. MI6's findings, whatever they were, remain classified.

Russia's secret service—the KGB and later FSB—has a long history of poisoning its enemies. Under Boris Yeltsin's regime, Moscow's secret poison lab had all but ceased operation, but when Putin became president, his critics began to die in strange ways.

Litvinenko knew that, even if he could be proved responsible, it was highly unlikely that Putin would be prosecuted, because of his position as a world leader. However, he was hopeful that at least Lugovoi and Kovtun could be caught and punished for their actions. Wanting to get his story out to the world, on November 19 Litvenenko gave an interview to *Sunday Times* journalist David Leppard.

The next day, Litvinenko's condition deteriorated rapidly; his heart rate was irregular and his organs were failing. As he lay gravely ill, Litvinenko gave one final interview to the police. His death now seemed inevitable. **»**

Alexander Litvinenko

Born in Russia, Alexander Litvinenko was drafted into the Ministry of International Affairs at 18. In 1986, he was recruited to the counterintelligence unit of Russia's security agency (KGB).

In 1997, Litvinenko was promoted to the Federal Security Service (FSB). While working for the FSB, Litvinenko discovered that organized crime and corruption had penetrated Russia's government. He made numerous attempts to discuss the corruption problem with

officials, including President Vladimir Putin. Seeing that his discussions were fruitless, however, Litvinenko held an unauthorized press conference, in which he accused supervisors of ordering the assassination of Russian business tycoons.

Litvinenko was dismissed from the FSB and arrested for exceeding the authority of his position. After he was acquitted in November 1999, he fled Russia and was granted asylum in the UK, where he worked as a journalist, writer, and MI6 consultant up until his murder.

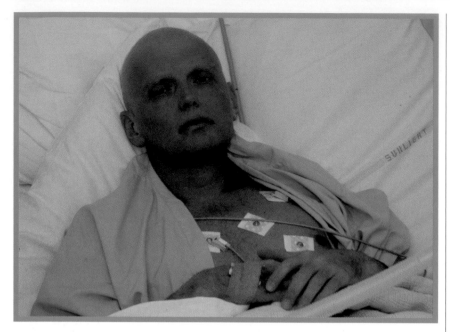

You may have succeeded in silencing one man but the howl of protest from around the world will reverberate, Mr. Putin, in your ears for the rest of your life.
Alexander Litvinenko

On November 20, he allowed press photographer Natasja Weitsz to take a last photograph of him, to show what Putin's men had done.

By then, the medical team had realized that the poison was not thallium, but something worse. While many of his symptoms fit the criteria, he lacked a key indicator of thallium poisoning—numbness or pain in his extremities. A new urine test revealed the presence of

This haunting image of Litvenenko on his hospital death bed shows a bald, gaunt, yet defiant man, staring directly into the camera lens. It was published in newspapers around the world.

the radioactive isotope polonium-210—a rare and expensive poison that is deadly when ingested. The doctors, however, believed this result to be anomalous, and proposed five different theories on

what was killing their patient. Still, to be sure, they sent a sample of Litvinenko's urine to the UK's atomic weapons establishment at Aldermaston in Berkshire to test.

On November 22, Litvinenko drifted in and out of consciousness in the intensive care ward. By midnight, he had suffered two cardiac arrests. He was unconscious and on life support for most of the following day, but had a third arrest and was pronounced dead at 8:51 p.m. on November 23. That same day, test results from Aldermaston officially identified the poison as polonium-210.

Forensic trail

After Litvinenko's death, suspicion around Lugovoi and Kovtun intensified. The police tested a number of premises for traces of polonium. At the Pine Bar of the Millennium Hotel, officers found the substance everywhere. Traces were discovered on the floor, chairs, and tables where the Russians had met, as well as in the teapot and dishwasher. The teapot had unknowingly been reused, but fortunately had not caused any further deaths.

Extrajudicial killing

These murders are carried out by agents operating on the orders of a government, in the interests of the state. They operate outside the law of that state, in that the victim is put to death without being allowed a trial. Extrajudicial killings are usually conducted as secret missions by highly trained assassins working for the army, intelligence services, or secret police. Such killings occur when a government wishes to eliminate or silence a political opponent—often, this is because a trial would lead to the exposure of information that the government does not want made public. In extreme cases, extrajudicial killings are used to eliminate a regime's critics; this usually occurs under particularly oppressive regimes, as a means of censorship.

There are many alternate, subjective terms for extrajudicial killings that attempt to spin them as a necessary evil, especially as targeted killing is increasingly gaining legitimacy as a counterinsurgency tactic.

The objects that came into direct contact with polonium-210

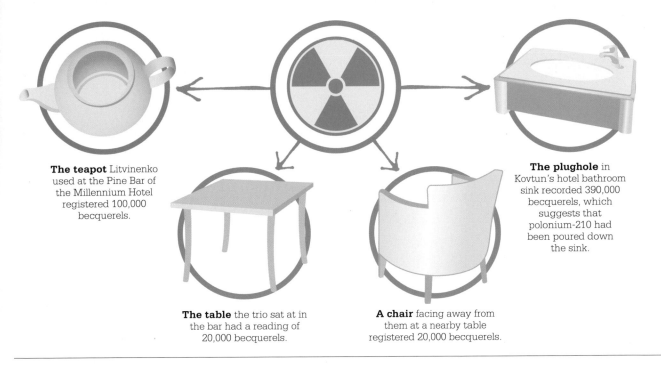

The teapot Litvinenko used at the Pine Bar of the Millennium Hotel registered 100,000 becquerels.

The plughole in Kovtun's hotel bathroom sink recorded 390,000 becquerels, which suggests that polonium-210 had been poured down the sink.

The table the trio sat at in the bar had a reading of 20,000 becquerels.

A chair facing away from them at a nearby table registered 20,000 becquerels.

In Kovtun's room, several floors above the Pine Bar, police forensic teams took apart the bathroom sink and found a clump of debris containing 390,000 becquerels of polonium. Ingested, 10,000 becquerels of polonium is enough to kill a man. After the meeting, it seemed, Kovtun had returned to his room and slipped the rest of the poison down the sink, to dispose of the murder weapon.

In spite of these findings, Lugovoi and Kovtun denied any responsibility for Litvinenko's murder, and held a press conference in Moscow claiming they were innocent. Kovtun never explained the polonium found in his bathroom. Following a two-month investigation, Scotland Yard detectives recommended that Andrei Lugovoi be charged with murder. Moscow officials, however, declared that Lugovoi would not be sent back to London because the constitution prevented the extradition of Russian citizens.

Diplomatic consequences

For eight years, the transcripts of Litvinenko's interviews were kept secret, marked restricted by Scotland Yard. They were finally released in 2015. In January 2016, a public inquiry concluded that

President Putin probably approved, if not directly ordered, the assassination of Litvinenko.

The murder of Litvinenko, an M16 contractor, on British soil clouded relations between London and Moscow. In July 2007, these tensions were made manifest with the expulsion of four Russian embassy officials from Britain. Russia retaliated in kind by expelling British diplomats from its embassies.

The UK subsequently broke off its links with Russian security services. While evidence clearly pointed to Kovtun and Lugovoi, no one has ever been brought to justice for Litvinenko's murder. ∎

Marina Litvinenko holds a copy of the 328-page report investigating her husband's death, in which former high court judge Sir Robert Owen blamed Russia's President Putin for the murder.

DIRECTO

RY

DIRECTORY

No society has managed to eradicate crime completely. The more sophisticated the society—and the more elaborately developed its code of rules—the greater the scope for infraction there has been. Many of the most infamous crimes in history have already been discussed in this book, but no database is large enough to categorize every notorious offence. The criminals below all occupy a special place in the history of crime, and deserve further exploration—whether for their ingenuity, depravity, audacity, or even their ridiculousness. The victims, methods, and motives represented here provide an eerie index of the many forms criminality has taken, and demonstrate that sometimes, true crime really is stranger than fiction.

ASSASSINATION OF JULIUS CAESAR
March 15, 44 BCE

Roman ruler Julius Caesar's prestige soared after his military victories in Gaul, and many in the Senate saw him as a threat to the existing order. Calls for him to be crowned emperor brought things to a head and on the Ides of March he was assassinated by senators, who stabbed him over 20 times on the Senate steps. His death plunged the empire into civil war.
See also: The Assassination of Pertinax 304 ▪ The Abduction of Aldo Moro 322–23

RICHARD OF PUDLICOTT
April 24, 1303

Driven to recklessness by his large debts, London wool merchant Richard of Pudlicott stole the contents of Edward I's Westminster "Wardrobe treasury," which was filled with the king's personal treasures. With the assistance of corrupt clergymen, Richard broke into the crypt beneath Westminster Abbey's chapter house and helped himself to gold and jewels worth up to £100,000 ($103 million today). When the treasures began to flood London's pawn shops, investigators traced them back to Pudlicott. At trial, he falsely claimed to have worked alone, saving the clergymen from punishment. Pudlicott was hanged and skinned for his crime.
See also: Thomas Blood 18 ▪ The Hatton Garden Heist 58–59

ASSASSINATION OF GIULIANO DE' MEDICI
April 26, 1478

A leading member of Renaissance Florence's famous Medici family, Giuliano was cut down during Easter Mass in the city's cathedral by nobleman Francesco de' Pazzi and other members of the rival banking clan. Many more members of both families were killed in the faction-fighting that ensued, but the Medici family managed to retain their power and influence.
See also: The Sicilian Mafia 138–45

KABUKIMONO GANGS
16th–17th centuries

The end of Japan's Sengoku period, marred by civil war and unrest, saw the marginalization of its great Samurai clans and left many well-armed warriors without an occupation. Some formed criminal gangs, as kabukimono ("strange ones") adopting flamboyant hair- and clothing-styles, and often carried elaborate, highly decorated or oversized weapons. The gangs were involved in crimes from major robberies to minor hooliganism. Many believe these gangs to be the precursor to the modern Yakuza.
See also: The Triads 146–49 ▪ The Yakuza 154–59

FRANÇOIS RAVAILLAC
May 4, 1610

A Catholic fanatic, Ravaillac made several attempts to meet and convert his country's Huguenot (French Protestant) king, Henri IV. Ravaillac tried to join a Jesuit group in 1606, but was rejected when he told them about his religious "visions," which the Jesuits considered to be the hallucinations of a madman. In one, Ravaillac believed God had told him that it was his duty to convert Henri IV. The king's moves against the Netherlands, a Catholic nation, angered Ravaillac. When his attempts to convert the king proved fruitless, Ravaillac waylaid the royal carriage in a Paris street, then climbed up and stabbed Henri to death. He was tortured, drawn, and quartered for his act of regicide, and his body was torn apart by angry mobs.

See also: Jean Calas 203 • The Assassination of Pertinax 304

CATHERINE MONVOISIN
1677–82

Fortune-teller Catherine Deshayes, Madame Monvoison—known as "La Voison"—was the head of a network of self-styled sorcerors and alchemists who sold their services to aristocratic French families in the so-called Poison Affair. Her followers sold poisons and amulets, and arranged "black masses" for aristocrats, which resulted in the death of over 1,000 people. Thirty-six of her followers were rounded up and executed in the "burning court," and La Voison herself was burned at the stake for witchcraft in February 1680. The affair later took on a political dimension, when La Voisin's daughter, Marie-Marguerite, named Madame de Montespan, King Louis XIV's mistress, as one of her mother's clients. Due to the resulting scandal, the burning court was abolished in 1682.

See also: Alice Kyteler 263 • Elizabeth Báthory 264–65

GREGOR MACGREGOR
1821–37

Scottish soldier MacGregor fought for the British in the Peninsula War before he joined Venezuela's fight for independence against Spain. During his career, MacGregor pretended to hold many different titles, but the most extravagant was his claim, upon returning to Britain in 1821, to have been made "Cazique of Poyais"—a fictional Prince of an imaginary Central American colony. MacGregor made a fortune selling shares and parcels of land in the colony, and even created a fake "Poyais" currency to convince buyers of its authenticity. Several hundred Scots went out to settle there, only to discover that their future homeland did not exist. MacGregor saw through several iterations of the scheme before he returned to Venezuela in 1838.

See also: The Crawford Inheritance 66–67 • The Black Friday Gold Scandal 101

TONG ORGANIZATIONS
1850s–

The name *Tong*—the Cantonese for "hall"—came from the meeting-places established by Chinese immigrants when they settled in North America. What began as societies for mutual support often became criminal organizations, associated most notoriously with the trafficking of women. Gang wars, called the Tong Wars, took place between 1880 and 1920 in San Francisco, as well as in New York and Chicago in the 1920s and 1930s. Many Tongs still exist today, purely as social clubs. They provide immigrant support services and act as meeting places for Chinese communities in major US cities.

See also: The Beer Wars 152–53 • The Yakuza 154–59

JOHN AND SARAH MAKIN
1892

When New South Wales brewery drayman John Makin was injured and unable to work, he and his wife became "baby farmers"—they took in illegitimate infants in exchange for payment. However, to cut costs, Makin and his wife murdered some of the babies, and periodically moved to new locations to make it hard for the infants' mothers to track them down. Their crime was discovered in October 1892, when the new owners of the Makin's house in Macdonaldtown tried to fix the plumbing and discovered the decaying bodies of two dead infants. Eventually, 12 bodies were found in three houses that the Makins had occupied. John Makin was hanged for his crimes in August 1893. Sarah was sentenced to life imprisonment, but was released on parole in 1911.

See also: The Lindbergh Baby Kidnapping 178–85 • Fred and Rosemary West 286–87

CASSIE L. CHADWICK
1897–1904

This Canadian-born swindler committed some minor forgeries and frauds before she moved on to her biggest con: fabricating an identity as the illegitimate daughter of Scottish–American steel tycoon Andrew Carnegie. On the basis of this pretend parentage, she secured loans of up to $20 million ($590 million today), and used them to

fund a lavish lifestyle. Banks were assured that she was due a large inheritance and would be able to pay the loans back. Her ruse was discovered, however, and when her scam fell apart in 1904, Carnegie denied all knowledge of her.
See also: The Crawford Inheritance 66–67 ▪ Harry Domela 70–73 ▪ The Tichborne Claimant 177

VINCENZO PERUGGIA
August 21, 1911

Both the poet Guillaume Apollinaire and the painter Pablo Picasso came under suspicion when da Vinci's great masterpiece, the *Mona Lisa*, disappeared from the Louvre, Paris. Two years later, Louvre employee Vincenzo Peruggia tried to sell the painting to galleries in Florence, in his native Italy. He was turned over to the police by gallery owner Alfredo Geri and Giovanni Poggi, the director of the Uffizi Gallery. Tried in Florence, Peruggia received a lenient jail sentence when he claimed that the theft had been motivated by patriotism. The painting was exhibited in Florence before it was returned to Paris.
See also: The Cellini Salt Cellar 56 ▪ Elmyr de Hory 70–73

HENRI DÉSIRÉ LANDRU
1915–19

Landru enticed wealthy widows to his home through lonely hearts ads in the Paris press. He is sometimes called the "Bluebeard of Paris" for the similarity between his actions and those of the folktale character. Landry seduced the women and secured their assets, then killed them, cut up their bodies, and

incinerated them to destroy the evidence. His crime was discovered when the sister of one of the victims tracked him down. The police found paperwork in his home that named his missing victims. Convicted of 11 murders, he was executed by guillotine in 1922.
See also: Harvey Glatman 274–75 ▪ John Edward Robinson 298–99

NATHAN LEOPOLD AND RICHARD LOEB
May 21, 1924

Friends since adolescence, Richard Loeb and Nathan Leopold came from wealthy Chicago families and graduated from prestigious colleges. Loeb had long toyed with the idea of the perfect crime as an intellectual game, and his obsession rubbed off on Leopold. In May 1924, the pair kidnapped 14-year-old Bobby Franks on his way home from school. Loeb bludgeoned him to death, and the pair disposed of the body in marshland, dousing it in acid to obscure Franks' identity. A pair of Leopold's spectacles found near the body led police to the killers. Their trial became a media circus, and culminated in a passionate plea against capital punishment by their defense lawyer, Clarence Darrow. The duo were sentenced instead to life imprisonment.
See also: The Murder of James Bulger 244–45 ▪ Ian Brady and Myra Hindley 284–85

GEORGE C. PARKER
1928

A succession of confidence-tricksters are said to have sold New York's Brooklyn Bridge (or,

more accurately, its toll-raising rights) since it opened in the 1880s. In 1928, George C. Parker was caught and sent to Sing Sing for life. He claimed to have conned naïve immigrants twice a week for 30 years. Considered by some to be the greatest conman in American history, Parker also notably "sold" famous New York landmarks, such as the Statue of Liberty and Madison Square Gardens.
See also: The Sale of the Eiffel Tower 68–69 ▪ Konrad Kujau 90–93

CHISSO CORPORATION
1932–68

Thousands died and many more became gravely ill after toxins containing mercury accumulated in the flesh of fish found in Japan's Minamata Bay, Kyushu. The toxins had come from the nearby Chisso Corporation's chemical plant, which had dumped the mercury into the water. Minamata Disease, as the illness was initially called, caused neurological and physical symptoms—including damage to the nervous system, visual impairment, and hearing loss. The corporation was ordered to clean up the bay, and was forced to pay millions in compensation to the victims and their families.
See also: The Bhopal Disaster 110–13 ▪ The Volkswagen Emissions Scandal 130–31

JOHN DILLINGER
July 22, 1934

One of a series of celebrity bank robbers to come to prominence during the Great Depression, Indianapolis-born John Dillinger pulled off over 20 successful bank

raids and escaped from prison twice before he was shot dead by FBI agents. The shooting of such a high-profile figure was an early triumph for J. Edgar Hoover's reformed investigative bureau.
See also: Bonnie and Clyde 26–29
■ Escape from Alcatraz 80–85

HAN VAN MEEGEREN
1937

A failed artist who became an extremely successful forger, van Meegeren specialized in the "Golden Age" art of his own native Netherlands. Forgeries of works by Franz Hals, Pieter de Hooch, and other greats were well-received, but his triumph was a "Vermeer," acclaimed as the 17th-century master's finest work. This painting proved to be van Meegeren's undoing, when it was discovered among the possessions of Nazi Hermann Göring. To avoid prosecution for selling Dutch property to the enemy, van Meegeren confessed to the lesser crime of forgery, but died of a heart attack about a month into his one-year prison sentence.
See also: The Cellini Salt Cellar 56
■ Elmyr de Hory 74–77

RUTH ELLIS
April 10, 1955

A 28-year-old former model and London nightclub hostess, Ellis achieved infamy when she shot and killed her lover, David Blakely. Her trial lasted for just 14 minutes and returned a guilty verdict. Ellis did not appeal the conviction, and she received the death penalty. Stories soon surfaced about Blakely's violent behavior towards Ellis, and

thousands called for her death penalty to be suspended. However, on July 13, 1955, as crowds lobbied for her life, Ellis became the last woman to be executed in Britain. Her case was a landmark in the movement to abolish capital punishment in the UK. In 2003, her family appealed to posthumously reduce her offense to manslaughter, due to the abuse Ellis had endured. The request was denied on the grounds that this distinction did not exist at the time Ellis committed the crime.
See also: Madame Caillaux 217
■ O.J. Simpson 246–51

CHARLES STARKWEATHER AND CARIL ANN FUGATE
December 1957–January 1958

After Starkweather, aged 18, killed 14-year-old Fugate's mother, stepfather, and half-sister, the couple ran off together. Over the next two months, they carried out another eight murders before they were captured. Starkweather was executed in the electric chair in 1959, furious that Fugate did not meet the same fate. The youngest person in the US to be tried for first-degree murder, Fugate served 17 years in jail. Doubt remains over whether Fugate was a willing participant in the killing spree, or a captive of her abusive boyfriend.
See also: Ian Brady and Myra Hindley 284–85

DICK HICKOCK AND PERRY SMITH
November 14, 1959

Convicts Dick Hickock and Perry Smith met in jail. After they were released, the pair decided to rob

the home of the Clutter family, in the rural city of Holcomb, Kansas. Smith and Hickock had been told by a fellow inmate that the Clutter home had a safe containing $10,000. When the pair discovered this was not true, they murdered Herbert and Bonnie Clutter, as well as their two youngest children. Smith and Hickock were captured after a six-week manhunt, and executed on April 14, 1965. Inspired by an article about the murders in *The New York Times*, fiction writer Truman Capote visited Holcomb with fellow writer Harper Lee. He amassed thousands of pages of notes on the victims, the suspects, and the community. His work was published in September 1965 as "non-fiction novel" *In Cold Blood*—the first and most celebrated work in the true crime genre.
See also: The Stratton Brothers 212–15

FRANK LUCAS
1960s–early 1970s

A native of North Carolina, Lucas came to New York City in the 1960s. His great innovation was to import drugs directly from the Golden Triangle (Myanmar, Laos, Thailand), rather than buying from Asian gangs. Lucas used military contacts to smuggle heroin from southeast Asia via military planes and bases. Legend has it that he even smuggled drugs in the coffins of dead servicemen. After a long investigation, Lucas was sentenced to 70 years in jail in 1976. His sentence was drastically reduced after he gave up the names of his accomplices—family members, the Mafia, and even corrupt members of New York's police department and Drug Enforcement Agency.

Released in 1981, Lucas went back to jail in 1984 to serve a seven-year sentence for drug offences. Since his release in 1991, Lucas has worked to repair the damage his drugs did to the New York neighborhood of Harlem.
See also: The Medellín Cartel 166–67 ▪ "Freeway" Rick Ross 168–171

MURDER OF KITTY GENOVESE
March 13, 1964

The stabbing of 28-year-old bar manager Catherine "Kitty" Genovese outside her apartment block in Queens, New York, is often cited as the classic case of the so-called "bystander effect." A report after her death claimed that more than 30 of her neighbors had witnessed the attack and failed to intervene. Recent researchers have cast doubt on how much "onlookers" actually saw or heard, and blamed *The New York Times* for misreporting the situation. Days after the attack, while under arrest for burglary, Winston Moseley confessed to stalking, raping, and murdering Genovese, as well as two other women.
See also: Craig Jacobsen 252–53

JACQUES RENÉ MESRINE
1965–79

Good at disguises, Mesrine became known as the "man of a thousand faces." He committed hundreds of crimes, in a repertoire ranging from robbery to burglary and kidnapping—not only in his native France, but also in Venezuela, the Canary Islands, and Canada. Mesrine gained a wide reputation

as a Robin Hood-like figure. Famed for his prison escapes, he was shot and killed in 1979 by a special task force dedicated to stopping him.
See also: Escape from Alcatraz 80–85 ▪ Ted Bundy 276–83

BANDIDOS MOTORCYCLE CLUB
1966–

Originally established in Texas by Vietnam War veteran Donald Chambers, this biker gang soon had affiliated chapters across the United States and Europe—and as far afield as Australia and southeast Asia. Club members across the world have been arrested for many crimes, notably drug-trafficking, assault, and murder. The bikers proudly identify themselves as "one percenters," a reference to the idea that 99 percent of bikers are law-abiding citizens, but the rest are "outlaws." The Bandidos are frequently involved in "biker wars" with rival gangs, such as the Cossacks and Hells Angels, for territorial control.
See also: The Wild Bunch 150–51 ▪ Hells Angels 160–163

ASSASSINATION OF MARTIN LUTHER KING JR.
April 4, 1968

The famous Civil Rights leader was shot on a Memphis motel balcony by white supremacist James Earl Ray. King's assassination led to one of the biggest FBI manhunts in history, and set off a spate of race riots across the country. Ray was caught in London, England, in July 1968, and extradited to the United States. Almost a decade later, on June 10, 1977, Ray was among half

a dozen inmates who escaped from Tennessee's Brushy Mountain State Penitentiary. The fugitives were quickly recaptured.
See also: Escape from Alcatraz 80–85 ▪ The Assassination of Abraham Lincoln 306–09

DONALD HARVEY
1970–82

This Ohio-born serial killer carried out his crimes in the course of his duties, first as a medical orderly and then as a nurse—during which time he is believed to have killed more than 50 patients. Eclectic in his methods, Harvey used everything from sophisticated poisons to crude suffocation to murder his victims.
See also: Dr. Crippen 216 ▪ Harold Shipman 290–91

EDWIN JOHN EASTWOOD AND ROBERT CLYDE BOLAND
October 6, 1972

Guns drawn, these two plasterers walked into the rural Faraday School, in Victoria, Australia. They ordered six girls and their teacher into a van. The men left a ransom note threatening to kill their captives if they did not receive AUD $1 million (about $7.4 million US today), but the plan did not work: 20-year-old teacher Mary Gibbs escaped with her charges, and their abductors were captured. Boland received a 17-year sentence, while Eastwood received 15 years. Eastwood later committed a second mass kidnapping in 1977.
See also: The Kidnapping of John Paul Getty III 186–187 ▪ The Chowchilla Kidnapping 190–195

PETER SUTCLIFFE
1975–80

Truck-driver Peter Sutcliffe prowled Bradford, Leeds and other towns in the north of England, attacking and killing women. His victims were often prostitutes, and in many cases the so-called "Yorkshire Ripper" also mutilated their dead bodies. West Yorkshire Police were criticized for attaching too much importance to a tape, purportedly recorded by the "Ripper," that was subsequently discovered to be a hoax. Nonetheless, Sutcliffe was apprehended in January 1981 and convicted on 20 counts of murder.
See also: Jack the Ripper 266–73 ▪ Andrei Chikatilo 292

PATRICK HENRY
1976–77

Seven-year-old Philippe Bertrand was snatched by Henry as he left school in Troyes, France, in January 1976. Henry called Philippe's mother to demand a ransom but garrotted the boy soon after, all the while continuing to seek money from his parents. Henry's trial made history in January 1977, when his lawyer, Robert Badinter, persuaded the court not to insist on the guillotine, which heralded the end of capital punishment in France.
See also: The Lindbergh Baby Kidnapping 178–85 ▪ The Abduction of Aldo Moro 322–23

SALLINS TRAIN ROBBERY
March 31, 1976

Members of the Irish Republican Socialist Party waylaid and robbed a Cork–Dublin mail train outside Sallins, County Kildare, and made off with around £200,000 ($1.6 million today). Although three men—Osgur Breatnach, Nicky Kelly, and Brian McNally—were found guilty, authorities relied too heavily on the men's confessions. Allegations of coercion saw their convictions overturned.
See also: The Great Train Robbery 31–35 ▪ The Wild Bunch 150–51

ALAIN LAMARE
1978–79

The case of the "Killer of l'Oise" rocked France—and not just because of his attacks on young women. He ran over several victims with his car, and also picked up and murdered several female hitchhikers. The killer, Alain Lamare, was discovered to be one of the very gendarmes involved in the investigation. Diagnosed as schizophrenic, he was declared unfit for trial, and now resides in a French mental hospital.
See also: John Leonard Orr 48–53 ▪ Daniel M'Naghten 204–05

JONESTOWN MASSACRE
November 18, 1978

More than 900 men, women, and children died after drinking a soft drink laced with cyanide. The massacre took place at a settlement established by cult leader Jim Jones in Guyana, South America. The leader of the "Peoples Temple" died along with his followers, having persuaded many to commit "revolutionary suicide." Others were forced to swallow the poison.
See also: Sadamichi Hirasawa 224–25 ▪ The Manson Family 230–37

DENNIS NILSEN
1978–93

Nilsen brought homeless young men and gay men that he picked up in bars back to his apartment in Muswell Hill, London, to murder them. He strangled his victims until they fell unconscious, then drowned them in his bathtub. The "Muswell Hill Murderer" engaged in necrophilia with his victims after ritualistically bathing and dressing them. He dissected and disposed of the bodies: some were burned; others hidden under the floorboards or in drainpipes. Nilsen's crimes were discovered when the remains blocked his building's drains.
See also: Andrei Chikatilo 292 ▪ Jeffrey Dahmer 293

ASSASSINATION OF GEORGI MARKOV
September 11, 1978

After his defection to the UK in 1969, Bulgarian writer Georgi Markov became a major irritant to his country's Communist regime. Markov was standing at a bus stop in London, England, when he felt a sharp jab in his leg; he died four days later. Forensic experiments determined the cause of death was a ricin pellet that had been shot into his thigh. Markov said he saw someone with an umbrella at the scene, which led investigators to theorize that a modified "umbrella gun" had been used to inject Markov with the pellet. Although the killer was never caught, many suspect he was a KGB member who worked with the Bulgarians.
See also: The Murder of Roberto Calvi 241 ▪ The Poisoning of Alexander Litvinenko 326–31

FRANCIS HEAULME
1979–97

"Criminal Backpacker" Francis Heaulme strangled and stabbed at least nine victims. He is suspected of killing a great many more across France. His nomadic lifestyle and random choice of victims made it difficult for regional police forces to pin Heaulme down. His police interviews were a mixture of truths and falsehoods, and Heaulme formed an adversarial relationship with investigator Jean-François Abgrall. Heaulme has Klinefelter's Syndrome, which means he has an additional X (female) chromosome, but Heaulme confounded investigators when he confessed to rapes—actually the work of his accomplice—that Heaulme was biologically incapable of committing. Heaulme received multiple life sentences during trials in 1997 and 2004.
See also: The Zodiac Killer 288-89 ▪ Colin Pitchfork 294–97

CHEUNG TZE-KEUNG
1980s–1998

This Guangxi-born gangleader carried out a series of high-profile robberies in Hong Kong before he turned to kidnapping for ransom. The abductions of Victor Li in 1996 and Walter Kwok in 1997 won him worldwide notoriety. Li was the son of Li Ka Shing, reputedly Asia's wealthiest man, and Kwok was the son of Kwok Tak-Seng, the founder of Hong Kong's biggest property development company. Both men were released after their families paid massive ransoms. Cheung was arrested in August 1998 and was found guilty of several crimes, including robbery, kidnapping, and smuggling firearms and explosives. Cheung was executed by firing squad in December 1998.
See also: The Kidnapping of John Paul Getty III 186–87 ▪ The Kidnapping of Patty Hearst 188–89

COR VAN HOUT AND WILLEM HOLLEEDER
November 9, 1983

Freddy Heineken, the 60-year-old CEO of an international brewing corporation, was snatched, along with his chauffeur, from outside the company's head office. They were held in Amsterdam in a hut with a secret double-wall. When the police failed to find them, Heineken's family paid the ransom. The police then received an anonymous tip giving Heineken's location—and the names of three of the kidnappers. The ringleaders, Cor van Hout and Willem Holleeder, fled to Paris, while their accomplices Martin Erkamps, Jan Boellaard, and Frans Meijer, were arrested. Van Hout and Holleeder were eventually arrested in France and sent back to the Netherlands, where they served 11 years in jail for the kidnapping.
See also: The Lindbergh Baby Kidnapping 178–85 ▪ The Kidnapping of John Paul Getty III 186–87

JOSEF FRITZL
1984–2004

Eighteen-year-old Elisabeth Fritzl's father Josef had been abusing her for seven years when he imprisoned her in the basement of their home in Austria. Elisabeth spent 24 years trapped underground. During this time, Josef abused and raped her, fathering several children. Some were taken upstairs to live with Josef and Elisabeth's mother, who had initially reported her daughter missing. Josef later told his wife that Elisabeth had joined a cult. Elisabeth and her children escaped in 2008 after one child had to be taken to the hospital. After Fritzl presented the medical staff with a suspicious note "from Elisabeth" about the girl's medical history, the staff contacted the police, who reopened Elisabeth's missing person's case. When Fritzl allowed Elisabeth to visit the child, staff alerted the police, who detained her and learned the full story of her father's abuse. In 2009, Josef Fritzl was sentenced to life in prison.
See also: The Kidnapping of Natascha Kampusch 196–97

THOMAS SWEATT
1985–2005

A young short-order cook, Sweatt set fire to houses, cars and property across Washington, D.C. and Maryland—often those belonging to attractive men he followed to their homes. When he was finally caught—thanks to DNA analysis and video footage that placed his car at the scene of a fire—Sweatt admitted to starting nearly 400 fires that caused several fatalities and injuries. He was active for longer than any arsonist in the US.
See also: John Leonard Orr 48–53 ▪ Jeffrey Dahmer 293

ADOLFO CONSTANZO
1986–89

Cuban-American Constanzo was drawn into drug-dealing in adolescence, but had a parallel interest in his culture's traditional witchcraft-cum-Catholicism cult of Santería. Beginning by boiling up bones from graveyards, he and his "narco-satanist" followers soon began to kill their own sacrificial victims at his desert compound in Rancho Santa Elena. More than 20 people were killed in the hope of imbuing Constanzo with dark magical powers. Constanzo and his followers fled to Mexico City after the bodies were discovered. When police visited his apartment for an unrelated investigation on May 6, 1989, Constanzo panicked and opened fire at the cops. Preferring not to be taken alive, Constanzo ordered follower Alvaro de Leon to shoot him. With Constanzo dead, his followers were arrested and prosecuted for the murders.

See also: The Manson Family 230–37 ▪ Elizabeth Báthory 264–65

AILEEN WUORNOS
1989–90

This Michigan-born serial killer began to work as a prostitute on the highways of Florida in her mid-teens. She appears to have met all seven of her victims in the line of work—the first, Richard Mallory, picked her up on Interstate 75. All were shot at close range and, when captured, Wuornos claimed that they had tried to rape her. Wuornos was caught when her victims' possessions began to show up in local pawn shops, and the police used her former lover, Tyria Moore, to extract a confession from her. Found guilty of seven murders, Wuornos was sentenced to death, and executed by lethal injection in October 2002.

See also: Phoolan Devi 46–47 ▪ Elizabeth Báthory 264–65

SINALOA CARTEL
1989–

Originally a marijuana-smuggling operation based in northwest Mexico's Sinaloa State, this gang was established by Pedro Avilés Pérez. Since 1989, under the leadership of Joaquín Guzmán Loera, "El Chapo," it has grown into one of the most powerful and wide-reaching crime syndicates in the world. In addition to marijuana, the Sinaloa cartel are allegedly responsible for much of the heroin, cocaine, methamphetamines, and MDMA smuggled into the United States. "El Chapo" has escaped from prison three times—first, in 2001, after being incarcerated in 1993. He was recaptured in 2014, but escaped in July 2015. Caught a third time in January 2016, he escaped once more that November, and yet again became one of the US and Mexico's most wanted men.

See also: Hells Angels 160–63 ▪ The Medellín Cartel 166–67

BEVERLEY ALLITT
February–April 1991

This child-killer was a nurse on the children's ward at Grantham and Kesteven Hospital, in Lincolnshire, UK. Allitt used her position to murder at least four children, and attempted to kill at least nine more over a 59-day period in 1991. On April 22, Allitt was tasked with watching over 15-month-old Claire Peck, who had been admitted for an asthma attack. Peck went into cardiac arrest and died on Allitt's watch. Doctors at the hospital were suspicious: they had noticed how often children left alone in Allitt's care experienced cardiac arrests.

Investigators later discovered that these were caused by insulin injections. In May 1993, Allitt was convicted and received 13 concurrent life sentences.

See also: Elizabeth Báthory 264–65 ▪ Harold Shipman 290–91

GUY GEORGES
1991–97

Dubbed "The Beast of the Bastille" by the Paris press because he operated in the vicinity of the historic prison, Guy Georges raped, tortured, and murdered seven women between the ages of 19 and 32. Since the 1970s, Georges had indulged his violent tendencies by strangling, raping, and stabbing young women. He was already serving a prison sentence—during which he was allowed out in the day for good behavior—when he began to commit murders in 1991. Arrested after a police manhunt in 1998, Georges readily confessed to his crimes and was diagnosed as a "narcissistic psychopath." He was, however, declared sane and fit to stand trial, and was sentenced to life imprisonment in April 2001.

See also: Jack the Ripper 266–73 ▪ Ted Bundy 276–83

NICK LEESON
1992–95

Whizz-kid Leeson was sent to Singapore in 1992 to run the derivatives trading desk for Barings Bank, one of Britain's oldest banking names. Lauded as the company's star trader, Leeson's reputation was left in tatters in 1995, when it was revealed that he had lost the company £832 million ($1.6 billion today). Leeson hid his

losses in a secret error account that was never checked or spotted by a senior compliance officer, and the numbers continued to build. Leeson suffered disastrous losses after the Kobe earthquake in Japan, and fled the country. He was arrested in Frankfurt later that year and sentenced to six and a half years in prison for fraud and forgery.
See also: Bernie Madoff 116–21
▪ Jérôme Kerviel 124–25

JEAN-CLAUDE ROMAND
January 10, 1993

French imposter Romand crashed out of his medical course after failing his exams, but spent 18 years pretending to be a qualified doctor and researcher, albeit without any actual position. He convinced his wife that he was an expert in arteriosclerosis, and was investing his earnings in hedge funds while he lived off her money. Believing that he was about to be exposed, Romand snapped in 1993, and murdered his wife, children, parents, and mistress to ensure that his secret was safe. He then attempted suicide, taking pills and setting his house alight—however, the pills were ineffective and the fire poorly timed. Romand was rescued but arrested when the bodies were discovered. He was sentenced to life in jail.
See also: The Crawford Inheritance 66–67 ▪ Harry Domela 70–73

PAUL BERNARDO AND KARLA HOMOLKA
1990–92

This Canadian couple raped and murdered teenage girls in Scarborough, Ontario—starting with Homolka's younger sister, Tammy, in 1990. Homolka had apparently promised Bernardo her sister's virginity as a Christmas present. Sedated, Tammy Homolka choked on her own vomit midway through the assault, and died. In 1991, the pair struck again, killing 14-year-old Leslie Mahaffy. In 1992, they raped and killed 15-year-old Kristen French. Their spree ended in 1993, when police investigated a series of rapes, and found that Bernardo's DNA matched the perpetrator's. Homolka, meanwhile, had moved in with her family after being severely beaten by Bernardo. She confessed to their crimes, and was sentenced to 12 years. Homolka was released in 2005, but Bernardo remains behind bars.
See also: Ian Brady and Myra Hindley 284–85

THE CARLTON HOTEL JEWELRY HEIST
August 11, 1994

The setting for the Cary Grant–Grace Kelly film *To Catch a Thief* (1955), the Intercontinental Carlton in Cannes, France, became the scene for possibly the most audacious real-life jewel heist of all time. Three gunmen burst into the hotel's jewelry store with machine guns blazing, and escaped with jewelry worth just shy of $60 million. Police later discovered that the guns were firing blanks. The robbers were never found. In 2013, the hotel was targeted once again, when an armed robber walked into a jewelry exhibition in a salon off the lobby, and stole items worth over $100 million.
See also: The Antwerp Diamond Heist 54–55 ▪ The Hatton Garden Heist 58–59

RAINER KÖRPPEN
October 1, 1996

With his son Sven acting as an accomplice, housepainter Rainer Körppen took millionaire German businessman Jakub Fiszman from his Eschborn office and held him for ransom. Nine days later, the demand was met, but when police entered the kidnappers' mountain hideout a few weeks later, they found Fiszman's body. He had been dead for some time. The Körppens had abducted Fiszman's six-year-old nephew six years earlier. Unlike his uncle, the boy was released once the ransom was paid.
See also: The Lindbergh Baby Kidnapping 178–85

THE WEST MESA MURDERS
2001–05

In 2009, the remains of 11 women and a fetus were found in open country west of Albuquerque. They had been buried in shallow graves a few years before. All of the victims were prostitutes and all had been reported missing. While forensic evidence offered little insight into how the victims were killed—or by whom—their similar ages, lifestyles, and burials have led investigators to think that a single serial killer killed them all.
See also: Craig Jacobsen 252–53
▪ Ted Bundy 276–83

THE MURDER OF MEREDITH KERCHER
November 1, 2007

The body of this British exchange student—who had been raped, stabbed, and suffocated—was

found locked inside her room in Perugia, Italy. Amanda Knox, her American roommate, called the police when she returned home and found the door locked. Knox was soon implicated in the murder—as was her Italian boyfriend, Raffaele Sollecito, and local criminal Rudy Guede, whose bloody handprint was discovered at the scene. All three were convicted, but there was little evidence linking Knox or Sollecito to the murder. Knox also claimed that she was manipulated and physically intimidated by the Italian police when they questioned her. Knox spent close to four years in an Italian jail. After a media circus that lasted several years, both Knox and Sollectio were cleared. Guede remains in prison.
See also: Kirk Bloodsworth 242–43 ▪ The Dreyfus Affair 310–11

DIANA, HUNTRESS OF BUS DRIVERS
August 2013

Clad in black, and wearing a blond wig, a middle-aged woman shot and killed two bus drivers on two consecutive days in Mexico's Ciudad Juàrez. An E-mail to a local news agency, purportedly from "Diana, Huntress of Bus Drivers," claimed responsibility for the attacks. More than 100 women had been raped, murdered, and left in parking lots or the desert after boarding the city's buses. "Diana", herself a victim, held the drivers responsible and saw the shootings as a way to bring the killers to justice. Despite searches, police in Juàrez were unable to discover the vigilante's true identity.
See also: Phoolan Devi 46–47 ▪ Lizzie Borden 208–11

OSCAR PISTORIUS
February 14, 2013

The South African paralympic sprinter fired four shots through a closed bathroom door at his house in Pretoria, and killed his girlfriend, Reeva Steenkamp. Pistorius claimed that he thought there was an intruder and acted to defend himself and Steenkamp. The prosecution appealed a conviction of "culpable homicide," and he was found guilty of murder in 2015. The brevity of Pistorius's six-year sentence shocked both prosecutors and women's rights activists—the minimum for murder is normally 15 years in South Africa. In August 2016, a plea to increase the length of the sentence was rejected.
See also: Dr. Crippen 216 ▪ O.J. Simpson 246–51

DEREK WHITE
2014–16

A Canadian driver on the NASCAR—National Association for Stock Car Auto Racing—circuit, White was part of a $500 million tobacco smuggling ring. White, of Mohawk descent, lived in Kahnawake, Montreal, and much of the tobacco brought from North Carolina was sold on this and other Indian Reserves, to avoid the high taxes that the Canadian government placed on tobacco sales. White was also involved in transporting tobacco over the border. Several other members of the smuggling ring were arrested, and White gave himself up in March 2016. He was suspended by NASCAR that April.
See also: The Theft of the World Cup 37 ▪ "Freeway" Rick Ross 168–71

BOKO HARAM
14 April, 2014

This militant Islamist group abducted 276 schoolgirls from a secondary school in the town of Chibok, northeast Nigeria. The girls were taken to insurgent territory farther north. Around 70 of the girls escaped or were released, but more than 200 remain captive as negotiations continue. Twenty-one girls were released in a deal brokered by the Red Cross and the Swiss government, but conflicting reports—all denied by officials—claim that girls were either exchanged for the release of Boko Haram commanders held by the government, or a large ransom.
See also: The Kidnapping of Patty Hearst 188–89 ▪ The Chowchilla Kidnapping 190–95

BANGLADESH CENTRAL BANK HEIST
January 5, 2016

Founded in 1973, SWIFT—the Society for Worldwide Interbank Financial Telecommunication—runs a closed computer network for many of the world's major banks to transfer funds. In 2016, a group of unknown hackers used the identities of employees from Bangladesh Central Bank (a SWIFT member) to send dozens of illegal transfer requests—totaling almost $850 million—to foreign banks. Many of the transfers were blocked or recovered, but $81 million vanished. Whether it was an inside job or the work of ingenious hackers remains unknown.
See also: The Société Générale Bank Heist 44 ▪ The Hatton Garden Heist 58–59

INDEX

Page references in **bold** are where the reader will find a specific criminal, criminal incident, or victim of crime discussed at length.

QUOTE ATTRIBUTIONS

ACKNOWLEDGMENTS

DK would like to thank Marek Walisiewicz of Cobalt id for editorial assistance in the early stages of this book.

PICTURE CREDITS

18 Getty Images: Culture Club (cr). **19 Getty Images:** Culture Club (bl). **21 Mary Evans Picture Library:** (cr). 22 Getty Images: Print Collector (bl, br). **23 Getty Images:** Time Life Pictures (tl). **24 Getty Images:** Bettmann (cr). **27 Getty Images:** Bettmann (tl). **28 Alamy Images:** John Frost Newspapers (tr). **29 Getty Images:** Bettmann (cr). **Alamy Images:** Granamour Weems Collection (bl). **32 Getty Images:** STF (bl). **33 Getty Images:** Keystone (tr). **35 Getty Images:** Popperfoto (tr). **Alamy Images:** Trinity Mirror/Mirrorpix (br). **37 Getty Images:** Rolls Press/Popperfoto (br). 40 John F. Ciesla: (tr). **41 Getty Images:** Time Life Pictures (bl). 43 FBI: (br). **45 Getty Images:** Acey Harper (cr). **46 Getty Images:** Jean-Luc Manaud (cr). **47 Getty Images:** Lange Jacques (tr). **Alamy Images:** IndiaPicture (bl). **51 Wikimedia Commons:** Gedstrom (tl). **53 Getty Images:** Wally Skalij (tr). **54 Alamy Images:** Philipp Hympendahl (cr). **55 Dorling Kindersley:** (br). **56 Getty Images:** Attila Kisbendek (br). **58 Getty Images:** Photo by Metropolitan Police via Getty Images (cr). **59 Press Association Images:** Elizabeth Cook (tl). **64 Mary Evans Picture Library:** Albert Harlingue/Roger-Viollet (cr). **65 Getty Images:** DEA Picture Library (tr). **Getty Images:** Photo 12 (bl). **66 REX Shutterstock:** Dagli Orti (tl). **69 Getty Images:** Bettmann (tl). **71 Getty Images:** ullstein bild (tl). Getty Images: Print Collector (tc). 72 Topfoto: ullstein bild (tl). **73 Alamy Images:** INTERFOTO (tl). **75 REX Shutterstock:** The Independent (tl). Getty Images: Carl Court (br). **78 Press Association Images:** (cr). **82 Getty Images:** Josh Edelson/AFP (tr). **83 Getty Images:** Bettmann (tr). **85 Getty Images:** Bettmann (tr). **87 Getty Images:** Janette Pellegrini (tl). **88 Alamy Images:** Moviestore Collection Ltd (cr). **89 Getty Images:** Susan Wood (cr). **Getty Images:** Bettmann (bl). **91 Getty Images:** ullstein bild (tl). Science Photo Library: James King-Holmes/Celltech R&D (tr). **92 Getty Images:** Michael Urban (tr). **93 Alamy Images:** INTERFOTO (br). **94 REX Shutterstock:** Newspix Ltd (bc). **95 REX Shutterstock:** Newspix Ltd (tl). **101 Getty Images:** Bettmann (bc). **104 Getty Images:** Pictorial Parade (tl). **105 Kat Ran Press:** (br). **107 Getty Images:** Bettmann (tr, bl). **109 Getty Images:** David Frent (tl). **111 Getty Images:** AFP (tl). **112 Getty Images:** Bettmann (bl). **113 Getty Images:** Indranil Mukerjee (tr). **Getty Images:** Justin Lambert (bl). **115 Alamy Images:** Anthony Palmer (tr). **Getty Images:** Fotos International (bl). **118 Getty Images:** Bloomberg (tr). **119 Getty Images:** Barton Gellman (bl). **121 Getty Images:** Mario Tama (tl). **122 Getty Images:** Stephen J. Boitano (bc). **123 Getty Images:** Dave Einsel (tl). **125 Getty Images:** Bloomberg (tr). **127 Alamy Images:** Reuters (tr). 129 123rf.com: Mikko Lemola (tl). **131 Getty Images:** Sean Gallup (tl). **137 Mary Evans Picture Library:** (tr). **140 Alamy Images:** Art Archive (tc). **141 Getty Images:** AFP (r). **143 Alamy Images:** Reuters (t). **145 Alamy Images:** Fabrizio Villa (tr). **Getty Images:** Franco Origlia (tr). **147 Alamy Images:** epa European pressphoto agency b.v. (tr). **149 Getty Images:** Philippe Lopez (cr). **Getty Images:** Laurent Fievet (bl). **151 Getty Images:** Jonathan Blair (t). **153 Getty Images:** Chicago History Museum (tr). **156 Getty Images:** The Asahi Shimbun (tr). **158 Getty Images:** The Asahi Shimbun (bl). **159 Getty Images:** Jiangang Wang (tr). **161 Getty Images:** Chuck Nackle (tl). **162 Getty Images:** Bill Owens/20th Century Fox/ Hulton Archive (t). **164 Getty Images:** William Lovelace (br). **167 Alamy Images:** Reuters (tl). **169 Getty Images:** Ray Tamarra (tl). **170 Alamy Images:** Wellaway (tl). **Getty Images:** Jean-Marc Giboux (bl). **171 Getty Images:** Barbara Davidson (t). **176 Getty Images:** Superstock (br). **177 Mary Evans Picture Library:** The National Archives, London, England (l). **Getty Images:** Rischgitz/ Stringer (r). **180 Getty Images:** Leemage (tr). **181 Getty Images:** Apic (tc). **182 Getty Images:** Bettmann (c). **183 Getty Images:** ullstein bild (tl). **Getty Images:** Bettmann (br). **184 Getty Images:** New York Daily News (bl). **185 Getty Images:** New York Daily News Archive (tr). **187 Getty Images:** Popperfoto (tc). **Getty Images:** MCT (bl). **189 Getty Images:** Bettmann (tr). **192 Getty Images:** Fresno Bee (tr). **194 Getty Images:** Fresno Bee (t). **195 Getty Images:** Fresno Bee (tr). **Getty Images:** Bettmann (bl). **197 REX Shutterstock:** Sipa Press (tr). **202 Alamy Images:** Sabena Jane Blackbird (cr). **204 Getty Images:** Illustrated London News/ Stringer (cr). **205 Mary Evans Picture Library:** (bl). **207 Wikimedia Commons:** The Illustrated Police News (tr). **209 Getty Images:** Chicago Tribune (tl). **211 Getty Images:** Bettmann (tr). Alamy Images: Granger Historical Picture Archive (bl). **214 Mary Evans Picture Library:** (br). **215 Alamy Images:** Chronicle (bl). **216 Library of Congress:** (br). **217 Getty Images:** Keystone-France (cr). **220 Getty Images:** Archive Photos/Stringer (bl). **221 Getty Images:** Archive Photos/Stringer (tl). **223 Getty Images:** Bettmann (tr). **225 Getty Images:** Bloomberg (tr). **Topfoto:** Topham/AP (bl). **227 Getty Images:** Bettmann (tr). **228 Getty Images:** Donald Uhrbrock (b). **229 Getty Images:** Shel Hershorn—HA/Inactive (tl). **Science Photo Library:** Sherbrooke Connectivity Imaging Lab (tr). **232 Alamy Images:** Courtesy: CSU Archives/Everett Collection (br). **234 Press Association Images:** AP Photo (t). **236 Alamy Images:** Pictorial Press Ltd. (tl). **237 Getty Images:** Bettmann (br). **238 Alamy Images:** Avalon/ World Pictures (bc). **239 Getty Images:** Fairfax Media (tl). **240 Getty Images:** Ron Galelia (cr). **242 Getty Images:** Mladen Antonov (cr). **244 Getty Images:** (cr). **248 Getty Images:** Archive Photos/Stringer (tc). **249 Getty Images:** Archive Photos/Stringer (tl). **Getty Images:** Mike Nelson (bl). **250 Alamy Images:** Reuters (tl). **252 Las Vegas Police Department:** (bc). **253 Alamy Images:** National Geographic Creative (tr). **Alamy Images:** The Science Picture Company (bl). **255 REX Shutterstock:** Film Four/ Lafayette Films (tl). **256 Getty Images:** Jon Levy (br). **263 Alamy Images:** imageBROKER (br). **265 Getty Images:** Ipsumpix (tr). **Alamy Images:** INTERFOTO (bl). **269 Bridgeman Art Library:** Jack the Ripper, illustration from "Le Petit Parisien", 1891 (engraving with later colouration), Dete, Beltrand and Clair-Guyot, E. (fl. 1884) / Private Collection / ©Bianchetti / Leemage / Bridgeman Images (tr). **271 The National Archives, London, England:** (tr). **273 REX Shutterstock:** The Art Archive (tl). **Alamy Images:** Chronicle (tc). **Getty Images:** Hulton Archive/Stringer (tr). **275 Getty Images:** Bettmann (tr). **278 Getty Images:** Bettmann (tr). **280 Press Association Images:** AP Photo/ Steve C. Wilson (t). **281 Press Association Images:** AP Photo (tc). **Getty Images:** Acey Harper (tr). **Getty Images:** Bettmann (bl). **283 Getty Images:** Bettmann (tl). **285 Getty Images:** Keystone (tc, tr). **287 Press Association Images:** PA Archive (tr). **289 Getty Images:** Bettmann (tl). **290 Alamy Images:** British News Service (bc). **292 Alamy Images:** Sputnik (cr). **295 Press Association Images:** Elizabeth Cook (tl). **Getty Images:** Bettmann (br). **296 Alamy Images:** TravelStockCollection— Homer Sykes (bl). **298 Getty Images:** AFP (cr). **305 Alamy Images:** Granger Historical Picture Archive (cr). **307 Alamy Images:** Glasshouse Images (tr). **308 Alamy Images:** The Protected Art Archive (bl). **309 Library of Congress:** (b). **311 Alamy Images:** North Wind Picture Archives (tr). **313 Getty Images:** Apic (tl). **314 Alamy Images:** Niday Picture Library (tl). **318 Getty Images:** Keystone-France (bl). **319 Getty Images:** Rolls Press/Popperfoto (t). **320 Getty Images:** New York Daily News (tl). **321 Getty Images:** Bettmann (tl). **323 Getty Images:** Bettmann (tl). **325 REX Shutterstock:** Sipa Press (tr). **328 Getty Images:** Bloomberg (tr). **330 Getty Images:** Natasja Weitsz (tl). **331 Getty Images:** Carl Court (bc).